BIG MONEY IN FRANCHISING

BIG MONEY

in Franchising

Scaling Your
Enterprise
in the Era of
PRIVATE EQUITY

ALICIA MILLER

Figure.1
Vancouver / Toronto / Berkeley

The material in this publication is current to the date of publication and is provided for informational purposes only. Names of entities and URLs may be subject to change post-publication.

Laws, regulations, and procedures are constantly changing. This book is sold with the understanding that neither the author nor the publisher is engaged in rendering professional advice. It is strongly recommended that legal, accounting, tax, financial, insurance, and other advice or assistance be obtained before acting on any of the information contained in this book. The personal services of a competent advisory professional should be sought.

This Content is for informational purposes only, you should not construe any such information or other material as legal, tax, investment, financial, or other advice. Nothing contained here constitutes a solicitation, recommendation, endorsement, or offer to buy or sell any franchises, securities, or other financial instruments. All Content in this book is of a general nature and does not address specific circumstances of any particular individual or entity. Nothing in this book constitutes professional and/or financial advice. You alone assume the sole responsibility of evaluating the merits and risks associated with the use of any information or other Content in this book or third party information sources provided herein before making any decisions based on such information or other Content.

The franchises mentioned in this book are not endorsements. No statement in this book is to be construed as a recommendation. Prospective franchise buyers are encouraged to perform extensive due diligence when considering a franchise opportunity.

Every effort has been made to ensure accuracy. Neither the author nor publisher assumes any responsibility or liability related to errors or omissions.

Trademark Notice
The PE Profit Ladder is trademarked by Alicia Miller SPE LLC.
Product, platform, or corporate names mentioned in this book may be trademarked or registered trademarks, and are used only for identification and explanation without intent to infringe.

United States Library of Congress Control Number: 2023915622

Cataloguing data is available from Library and Archives Canada
ISBN 978-1-77327-237-5 (hbk.)
ISBN 978-1-77327-238-2 (ebook)

Design by Jazmin Welch

Editing by Karen Milner and Don Loney
Copy editing by Melissa Churchill
Proofreading by Nancy Foran
Indexing by Stephen Ullstrom
Author photo by Robb McCormick Photography

Printed and bound in Canada by Friesens

Emergent Growth Advisors
Columbus Ohio
www.emergentgrowthadvisors.com

Figure 1 Publishing Inc.
Vancouver BC Canada
www.figure1publishing.com

Figure 1 Publishing works in the traditional, unceded territory of the xʷməθkʷəy̓əm (Musqueam), Sḵwx̱wú7mesh (Squamish), and səlilwətaɫ (Tsleil-Waututh) peoples.

Contents

13 Author's Note: What Is Business-Format Franchising?

15 **Introduction**

17 Understanding and Aligning with Private Equity Is Critical to Your
    Franchising Success
21 Is This a Positive or Negative Story? Well, It's Complicated
23 How This Book Is Organized
24 What I Want for You

PART ONE
HOW PRIVATE EQUITY CAME TO DOMINATE FRANCHISING

27 **Chapter 1**
    Understanding Franchising's Enduring Appeal

29 Franchising's Innovative Approach to New Business Creation
32 Why Do Entrepreneurs Like Franchising?
33 Why Does Private Equity Like Franchising?

37 **Chapter 2**
    The Private Capital Landscape—
    Part One: The Big Money Players

38 Private Equity Firms Aren't a Homogeneous Group
39 The Diverse Range of Private Equity Players
    40 Private Equity
    42 Institutional Investors Making Direct Investments
    44 Family Offices
    48 Wealthy Individuals
    48 Independent Sponsors
    49 Strategic Buyers
    50 Hybrid Investors

53 Chapter 3
The Private Capital Landscape—
Part Two: The Big Money Strategies

54 Three Primary Private Equity Franchise Investment Types:
Growth, Value, and Turnaround
55 Growth Investors in Franchising: *Incubate and Accelerate*
60 Value-Based Franchise Investing: *Extend and Expand*
64 Turnaround Investors in Franchising: *Reengage and Reinvent*
70 Disclosure Risk

73 Chapter 4
The Parallel Tracks of Private Equity and Franchising:
Where It All Began

74 Franchising Showed Tremendous Early Promise
75 Raising Capital: Private Equity's Early Days
77 Parallel Expansion Paths
80 Franchising: Not Just a US Phenomenon

83 Chapter 5
Family Pizza Night Looks Like a Pile of Cash:
Private Equity Discovers Franchising

87 Early and Dominant Private Equity Entrants into Franchising
88 Private Equity's Platform Strategy Is a Strong Fit for Franchising
90 The 2007–2009 Financial Crisis and Recovery
92 The Rise of the Private Equity Profit Ladder: The Secondary Trading Market

94 Chapter 6
Private Equity and Multi-unit Operators:
"Small" Business Consolidates

95 The Big Shift in Small Business
101 Power Dynamics in the Franchisor and Multi-unit Franchisee
Relationship
103 What Signal Does Private Equity Investing Activity at the Outlet Level Send?
104 International Private Equity–Backed Multi-unit Operators
105 It's Getting Warm in Here!

106 Chapter 7
A Frog, More Big Money, and the Final Missing Piece

106 Distraction and Perception
108 Big Money in Plain Sight

114   The Franchise Private Equity Investor Pool Continues to Grow

116   If You Don't Make New Friends, at Least Get Aligned

PART TWO
THE PRIVATE EQUITY PLAYBOOK IN FRANCHISING

121   **Chapter 8**
Private Equity's Playbook for Growing Franchise Businesses

122   The Due Diligence Playbook

124   The Private Equity Operations and Growth Playbook

     126   1 The Private Equity Playbook Implements Franchise Growth Accelerators

     128   2 The Private Equity Playbook Also Applies Other Proven Methods

     130   3 The Private Equity Playbook Is Hyper-focused on Generating Results

     133   Building a Value Creation Plan

135   **Chapter 9**
Private Equity's Franchise Platform Playbook

135   The Platform Strategy Has Proven High Returns

136   Operational Advantages of Platforms

139   Steps to Build a Platform

143   **Chapter 10**
Private Equity's Emerging Brand Playbook

144   Playbook Practicalities: Run Your Best Plays First

147   Typical Emerging Brand Challenges That Are *Not* Off-putting to Private Equity

150   Common Emerging Brand Challenges That *Don't* Interest Private Equity

153   **Chapter 11**
Private Equity Compensation: 2 and 20

153   Incentives and Private Equity Decision-Making

157   No Matter What Happens, Private Equity Is Set Up to Win

160   **Chapter 12**
When Everything Clicks: Positive Impacts on Franchising from Private Equity's Playbook

161   Private Equity's Top Contributions to Franchising

162   Further, Faster: Incubating, Elevating, and Accelerating Franchises

163 Stronger, Better: Infrastructure, Support, Scale, and Longevity
    164 Better Infrastructure
    165 Improved Financial Controls, Professionalism, and Franchisee Support
    166 Improved Stability
    167 Investments in the Brand's Future
168 Growth Focus: The Bright Side
170 Game On!: Private Equity Blocks Weak Entrants and Forces Aging Concepts to Up Their Game
    176 What This Means for Preparing for Launch: Most Emerging Brands Never Emerge
178 Unlocking New Wealth Opportunities: Creating a Robust Trading Market for Franchise Businesses

PART THREE
THE PRIVATE EQUITY PROFIT LADDER IN FRANCHISING

183 **Chapter 13**
Accelerating Organic Growth at Each Step Up the Private Equity Profit Ladder

184 Ladder Structure: The Secondary Buyout Market
190 Trading Up, Down, and Across the Ladder
    191 The Lower Rungs
    193 The Middle Rungs
    194 The Top Rungs
196 Planning Your Wealth Creation Strategy
203 Ladder Math from Private Equity's Perspective
210 Ladder Math from the Seller's Perspective

212 **Chapter 14**
Building Enterprise Value Through the Power of Platforming and Multiple Arbitrage

212 A Simple but Powerful Value Creation Model
220 Hard Work and a Predictable Playbook, Not Alchemy
223 Frogs and Old Warhorses
228 The Secondary Buyout Market Moving Forward

PART FOUR
DOWN THE LADDER: "SMART MONEY" BLOOPERS IN FRANCHISE INVESTING

233 **Chapter 15**
How to Destroy Franchise Value

234 Five Steps Down the Profit Ladder

237 **Chapter 16**
Overleverage: The Burden That Keeps on Taking

239 Franchising's Bankruptcy Track Record
    244 Key Elements Needed for Successful Turnarounds
    245 Continuously Building Insights and Market Expertise
247 The (Positive) Evolution of Private Equity's Franchise Debt Strategy
253 Whole Business Securitization
    256 Key Whole Business Securitization Takeaways
        260 Whole Business Securitization Implications for Franchisees
        263 Whole Business Securitization Implications for Franchisors
264 What to Do Next? Make Sure You Are Well Informed

265 **Chapter 17**
More Private Equity Head-Scratchers and Flameouts in Franchising

266 Short-Timers' Syndrome: Starving the Future to Profit in the Present
271 Not Protecting Unit-Level Profitability
277 Growth Focus: The Dark Side
    278 Is the Business Primarily Focused on Selling Franchises?
    279 Field-Stripping Enterprise Value: Sold-Not-Open Arbitrage
    281 Built to Flip
    283 Bastardization of EBITDA (Earnings Before Interest, Tax, Depreciation, and Amortization)
285 Destroying Franchisee Trust

PART FIVE
MOVING FORWARD WITH PRIVATE EQUITY

291 **Chapter 18**
Engaging with Private Equity

292 Founders and Franchisees Should Start with "Why"
294 "What" Matters Most to You?

297 "Who" Is Important to You?
    298 Networking with Other Founders and Franchisees Who Have Worked with Private Equity
    300 How Important Is It to You That Your Private Equity Partner Has Franchising Experience?
303 "Wait": Not Ready for a Private Equity Partner?
    305 Returning to Your Draft Value Creation Playbook

309 **Chapter 19**
What to Expect When You're Expecting . . .
to Be Acquired by Private Equity (or Already Have Been)

311 For Franchisees: What to Expect If Private Equity Buys Your Franchisor
    315 *Now* Is the Time to Establish an Independent Franchisee-Owner Association
    316 Maintain a Sale-Ready Stance
317 For Franchise Founders (and Management Teams): What to Expect Once Acquired by Private Equity

323 **Chapter 20**
The Future of Franchising and Private Equity

324 Evolving Market Forces
326 Franchise Generation 4.0 (a.k.a. the Post-pandemic Years)
    328 Near-Term Considerations
331 Franchising Has Changed in Four Critical Ways Thanks to Private Equity
332 While Powerful, Private Capital Must Still Reckon with Fundamental Franchising Truths
334 The Culture Question
    335 Chief Alignment Officers, a.k.a. Independent Franchisee-Owner Associations

340 **Ways to Connect**

341 **Appendix**
    341 Resources for Franchise Disclosure Documents
    342 Recommended Reading
    343 Educational Resources
    344 Online Resources

346 **Acknowledgments**

348 **Notes**

376 **Index**

List of Tables and Figures

171   **Table 1:** Second and Third Generations of Franchising (Before and After Private Equity Entry)

200   **Table 2:** Aggregate Future Principal Payments on Term Loans at December 26, 2021

251   **Table 3:** Leverage (Total Debt/Adjusted EBITDA) for Select Brands

186   **Figure 1:** The Private Equity Profit Ladder

214   **Figure 2:** 2019–2022 EBITDA Multiples by Deal Size

249   **Figure 3:** New Leveraged Loans and Debt Multiples, by Year

255   **Figure 4:** How Securitization Works

257   **Figure 5:** 17-Year Franchisor Trend—Switch to Securitization Financing

259   **Figure 6:** Leverage Levels of Large, Highly Franchised Brands

261   **Figure 7:** Securitization: Preferred Financing Vehicle for Franchised Restaurants and Growing Prominence in Non-restaurant Franchises

Case Studies

43   Public Pension Investments in Franchising

67   Carvel and Roark Capital Group

69   Arby's and Roark Capital Group

70   Checkers/Rally's

110   Roark Capital Group

130   Levine Leichtman's Playbook to Accelerate Franchise Brands

144   Emerging Brands and 10 Point Capital

145   Emerging Brands and MPK Equity Partners

175   Authority Brands and Franchise Development

198   Tropical Smoothie Cafe

205   Wetzel's Pretzels

216   The Dwyer Group/Neighborly

218   Building Platform Value: One Acquisition at a Time

220   JAN-PRO

226   Jenny Craig and SBO Trading

240   Friendly's and Sun Capital

242   Sbarro and MidOcean Partners

269   CKE Restaurants and Roark Capital Group

275   Massage Envy and Roark Capital Group

AUTHOR'S NOTE:
WHAT IS BUSINESS-FORMAT FRANCHISING?

THERE ARE TWO MAJOR types of franchising: traditional franchising and business-format franchising. Traditional franchising includes license agreements such as car dealerships and soda bottling. Professional sports teams and movie/character series are also referred to as franchises because the business arrangement is a license agreement.

But business-format franchising is what most people think of when they think of a "franchise." It allows individuals to open their own branch of a business within their local communities under a license agreement and also gives them an operating format, including the brand, methods, and systems to run a business. In turn, franchisees agree to operate the business under the prescribed operating standards and methods of that franchise. Franchising enables people to go into business without needing to invent a concept entirely from scratch.

Business-format franchises comprise a wide range of businesses (in over 300 categories), including quick service restaurants, home and personal services, retail, automotive, and many other categories. The vast range of available franchise options and price points often surprises and delights prospective business owners looking at franchising for the first time. This book focuses on business-format franchising only.

For entrepreneurs, inventors, and creators,
and for their capital partners.
Vision, combined with action and the right support,
can change the world.

Introduction

FRANCHISING IS THE EPITOME of "small business." Half of the more than 805,000 US franchise outlets are owned by single-unit franchisee entrepreneurs. But modern franchising can also be described as many small businesses rapidly consolidating into larger businesses at both the franchisor (brand) level and the franchisee (outlet) level. Franchise growth and consolidation are increasingly supported by private equity money and institutional capital. This investing activity is so expansive that private equity has become a preeminent force of change. Franchising, perhaps the greatest engine of small business creation ever invented, has thus undergone a transformation. It is now dominated by private equity.[1] But is this a good thing? And how does it impact entrepreneurial outcomes?

> **Private equity (PE) firms raise funds from outside investors, such as pension funds, wealthy families (including family offices), and university endowments, and they invest that money in equity in companies.**

Last spring I received a call from a franchise founder and consulting client who has become a good friend. He told me, "I get calls and emails every week from private equity firms and family offices. I will forward the emails to you. Can you please take a look? Do you know any of these firms? Are they worth talking to?"

If you're a successful franchise founder, you're probably inundated by similar "fishing" calls and emails from PE firms looking for acquisition opportunities. You started a business with a great concept you believed in, and you stayed focused on running and growing your business. It got early traction and attracted enthusiastic franchisees. Over time you built the brand and created a business model and culture you're proud of. Then the phone started to ring. Off. The. Hook!

On the other hand, if you're the owner of a franchisor brand that's stalling, your frustration with your lack of progress is heightened by the growth of competitors. You've noticed the influence of private equity, and press reports indicate new franchise agreements are getting signed. You're asking yourself, "Why isn't my brand growing faster? Can PE help get my company back on the growth path? Or is that my exit strategy? What is my business worth? Would partnering with a family office or a franchise platform be better? And why can't I just borrow PE's growth playbook to grow the business myself?"

> **A franchise platform is a collection of several different franchise brands all operating under a common holding company. A true platform follows a shared services model, where brands under the same corporate umbrella share common back-office functions, such as tax and accounting, and pool their spending to secure better pricing from suppliers. Ideally, platform participants also share cross-marketing and -selling benefits because they seek to serve the same customers and recruit similar franchisees. An example of a franchise platform is Neighborly, which owns more than 30 home services–focused concepts. Neighborly, and its predecessor the Dwyer Group, has been backed by several PE firms and is currently owned by KKR.**

If you are a franchisee, you see PE at work in franchising, and you may be concerned about what that means for your business. You're asking yourself, "What happens if my franchisor or the platform my franchise is part of is acquired by PE? Will my operating costs change?" And if you're a multi-unit franchisee, you may be receiving PE inquiries directly. In this case, you might be asking, "Can I partner with PE to help my business expand? Is PE a potential buyer when I'm ready to retire? How should I prepare?"

If you are a prospective franchisee, you're learning about the franchise model and exploring various options available to you. Private equity probably wasn't on your radar. But given PE's dominance, you'll need to expand your investigation aperture to at least consider PE's influence over your chosen franchise path.

I wrote this book primarily to help franchise founders and current franchisees understand the tremendous influence private equity now has across our sector so you can make smarter wealth-planning and partnership choices. This book squarely addresses how franchising has changed and accelerated thanks to PE. It also shares valuable inside information about PE's investing process, selection criteria, trading dynamics, and mindset, as well as things to watch for.

However, management teams, prospective franchisees, and other stakeholders will also benefit from this information. Where applicable, I have added specific advice for these other groups as well so you can plot successful career paths and make better strategic choices. I believe that prospective franchisees especially (and their advisers) need to know this information before investing in a franchise business. This book offers an important and impartial crib sheet that clearly explains how PE works and PE's typical franchise investing strategies.

> **If you are active in any aspect of franchising, or considering starting or expanding a franchise business, you need to understand the strategies, tactics, and thinking behind today's dominant force in franchising: private equity firms.** *You will never see franchising the same way again.*

UNDERSTANDING AND ALIGNING WITH PRIVATE EQUITY IS CRITICAL TO YOUR FRANCHISING SUCCESS

Private equity started making franchise investments substantial enough to get noticed in the late 1990s. Perhaps the flashiest early PE/franchise deal took place in December 1998, when Bain Capital caught the attention of Wall Street with its $1.1 billion buyout of American multinational franchise Domino's Pizza. That deal was a "classic" leveraged buyout in grand 1990s style. By investing a relatively meager $385 million and financing the rest of the purchase, the very definition of a "leveraged" deal, Bain reportedly made more than 500 percent on its original investment.[2] PE activity in franchising gradually picked up starting in the mid- to late 1990s through mid-2007, then significantly accelerated after the global financial crisis of 2007 to 2009. In other words, PE's franchise investing activities gathered momentum relatively recently.

The acquisition of high-profile, large brands and franchise platforms (in some cases with high leverage to match) creates big headlines. But consider PE's impact on small franchise businesses where there is little to no leverage involved. Investors (including PE-backed platforms) who specialize in acquiring emerging brands provide needed expansion capital and are staffed with experts dedicated to helping lift less mature concepts. The positive impact of PE on the franchising sector, especially working with emerging and fast-growth franchise businesses, has been nothing short of profound.

> **Private equity transforms every sector it infiltrates. To win in franchising today and be truly empowered, you must understand PE's pervasive influence and how their decisions impact you.**

Franchising was bound to attract private equity's attention eventually. It's just too good a moneymaker for PE to resist, with a compelling entrepreneurial narrative to boot. But what most people outside PE don't realize is that, just like franchising, PE investors also follow a highly systems-based approach. PE methods aren't mysterious or unknowable. Quite the opposite! Private equity investors are methodical and analytical, and they follow predictable investing habits. This is especially true when PE makes investments in franchise businesses that are themselves highly systematized, that follow predictable growth curves, and that have known best practices.

> **The investing mindset and profit-building strategies PE brings to franchising follow a predictable playbook. Understanding this playbook and aligning your own interests with PE's interests can help you create the outcomes you want for yourself and for your franchise business. And avoiding the downsides of private capital investing also requires keeping PE's methods in mind.**

Consider the following important trends and changes:

- Franchisors and multi-unit franchisees encompassing more than 700 brands in the US alone have partnered with private capital.[3] These brands represent over half of more than 805,000 US franchise outlets and 8.7 million jobs.[4] And that was before Subway (the largest franchisor in terms of number of outlets, 20,000+ US locations) agreed to be acquired by Roark Capital Group.

- At least 350 private equity firms have played a part in the expansion of franchising at the franchisor (brand) level, franchisee (operator) level, or both. This is almost surely an understatement (and still growing) because much private capital activity goes under- or unreported.

- The average leveraged buyout transaction multiple has nearly doubled in the last two decades.[5] We will discuss creating enterprise value, multiples paid, and multiple arbitrage extensively, but especially in Chapters 13 and 14.

- PE groups now also control nearly all the sizable multi-brand franchisor platforms that (as of this writing) are not yet publicly traded. Examples include Neighborly (owned by KKR), Full Speed Automotive (MidOcean Partners), Inspire Brands (Roark Capital Group), and Authority Brands (Apax Partners).

- A private equity transaction is increasingly perceived as an attractive alternative to going public given public company reporting demands and other considerations, as we recently saw when Subway opted for a PE transaction after long being privately held. If already public, there are numerous incentives for franchise businesses to go private again with PE's help.

- Although half of all franchise outlets are still operated by single-unit entrepreneurs, consolidation is also rapidly occurring at the unit level. Many multi-unit operators (MUOs) are themselves backed by private equity or have received direct institutional capital. This includes the largest franchise operator in the US, Flynn Group (2,600+ outlets, $4.5 billion+ in sales, 75,000 employees).[6] Private capital firms are now one of the biggest buyers of franchise *outlets*, not just franchisors—creating important new exit options for retiring franchisees. This also impacts franchisor-franchisee relationship dynamics.

- There are more than 9,200 traditional private equity firms worldwide,[7] approximately 5,000 of which are in the US.[8] These numbers ignore thousands of family offices and other private capital sources, such as wealthy individuals. This means a huge field of potential investors has yet to discover franchising.

▸ Globally, private capital is sitting on at least $2 trillion of "dry powder" (committed funds that haven't yet been deployed), a 21 percent increase year over year.[9] And PE's actual buying power is substantially greater with the use of debt.

▸ PE's use of debt in franchise investing has moderated considerably. There is more consistency of approach, and PE's use of debt isn't an outlier compared to publicly traded or other privately held franchisors. And in the case of smaller investments, debt isn't used at all.

▸ Franchising contributes 3 percent of US gross domestic product (GDP),[10] but private capital has allocated much less than 3 percent of their total available funds to the franchise sector. So we are far from saturated in terms of PE investments in franchising![11]

Although PE now dominates the franchise landscape, there is still tremendous runway for additional PE investments in franchising.

▸ Hundreds of new franchise brands launch each year. There are now two distinct camps of brand founders. First, there are those who created a concept and then decided to franchise. Many of these founders are still learning about franchising and aren't aware of how PE has changed the marketplace. This increases risk for them and their franchisees. Competing against PE-backed franchises and platforms is expensive and difficult, making it harder for emerging brands to break out. The second, newer group of brand founders create companies intentionally "built to flip" to PE. This recent, somewhat concerning, phenomenon will be discussed further in Chapter 17.

▸ PE market activity has also tightened competition for new franchise license sales within legacy concepts. Many of these franchisors already face pressure to reinvent products and services and even brand identities to keep up with competitors and changing customer preferences, as well as to appeal to new groups of customers. But legacy brands also face significant pressure to both recruit new operators and keep the outlet expansion engine humming. Expansion-minded franchisees have many choices, including a significant number of resales coming available over the next 10 to 15 years, thanks to retiring baby boomers.

> **PE-backed franchises and platforms have significantly altered the competitive landscape. Emerging brands in particular face a very different marketplace compared to even five years ago! And legacy brands (whether publicly traded, privately held, or backed by PE) face enormous new pressures also based on this new competitive dynamic.**

▶ Thanks to this hypercompetitive market created in part through PE's influence, once any brand stalls, more assertive turnaround efforts are often necessary. Stalled franchises face a steep climb to convince franchisees to "believe" again enough to add new units.

> **While PE has created a dominant position, franchisees still hold an important card. As a group, franchisees must largely buy in and support the direction of the business, or PE can't *fully* execute its growth and profit agenda. A good franchisor-franchisee relationship lifts investments, while a poor relationship can humble and frustrate PE intentions and create a brand stall-out. We will see that there are interesting power dynamics within what should be a naturally symbiotic franchisor-franchisee relationship.**

IS THIS A POSITIVE OR NEGATIVE STORY? WELL, IT'S COMPLICATED

Private equity's influence over franchising has been largely positive, especially for emerging and midstage growth brands. Modern franchising is a vital new business-creation and job-creation engine with tremendous positive impact for our economy. In 2023 alone, franchising created around 254,000 new jobs and 15,000 new businesses[12] and contributed $860.1 billion to the US economy, a 4.2 percent year-over-year output increase.[13] PE's focus on building portfolio company infrastructure, adding franchisee support, funding expansion initiatives, and improving unit-level economics is a positive force within franchising and thus also for our economy.

PE's financial backing and strategic assistance have become critical support mechanisms to incubate and grow emerging franchise brands. In addition, competitive pressure brought to bear by PE-backed brands on some legacy franchise brands (whether publicly or privately held) has in many cases pushed management of those legacy brands to reinvest in the business in ways franchisees have long been clamoring for, an indirect positive outcome. No matter the stage of a franchise business, PE investment can prompt a significant shift in operations and results.

> Gaining private capital support represents a key inflection point that has advanced many emerging franchises into *viable, valuable, and scalable* businesses. And for many larger, established brands, PE support similarly has taken brands to the next level, ensuring long-term *strength* and *sustainability*.

Partnering with private equity has put many brands on a high-octane growth path, enriching franchisees, investors, and founders along the way. We can also credit private equity with improving outcomes for franchisees and with helping to "professionalize" franchising in important ways that are healthy for franchising generally. But there has also been a learning curve. Private equity has made mistakes. And when PE comes in and pushes franchisor management to make changes, franchisees are not always happy with those changes.

> Despite PE's many positive contributions to franchising, PE has also presided over negative outcomes, value destruction, and stall-outs. This book provides a guide to avoid problems and conduct thorough due diligence on potential sponsors, management teams, and capital partners.

Key reasons for these difficulties include excessive leverage, missed opportunities to build better relationships with franchisees, not protecting unit profitability, overly aggressive growth, and underinvesting in innovation. These missteps represent poor franchise model execution and ineffective change management. But in some cases, typical PE tactics—especially the use of leverage—just went too far.

HOW THIS BOOK IS ORGANIZED

Part One outlines why the franchise model appeals both to franchisees and PE investors. The spectrum of investors is described by type and strategic approach. In addition to traditional private equity firms, we'll take a close look at family offices (FOS), a compelling private capital alternative for many founders and multi-unit franchisees. A brief history will be covered along with learnings and outcomes. PE came late to franchising, but they certainly made up for lost time!

Part Two walks through PE growth playbooks in detail with high-lighted case studies. We also look at PE's positive impact on franchising tied to those playbooks. We'll walk through private equity math and how PE maximizes its own compensation, with implications for the franchise ecosystem. This discussion is continued in Part Three, where we cover buy/sell activity in more detail.

Part Three covers what happens when companies engage in private equity transactions and thus step onto, or trade up or down, what I call the PE Profit Ladder. We'll also address what it means if the franchise you're involved with, or considering, is already climbing up the ladder. Risks facing both unaffiliated and emerging franchises will be discussed.

Although PE has been largely positive for franchising, on balance we must also reckon with and hold PE accountable for poor sponsorship. Part Four addresses the top value-destroying private equity moves in franchising—the disappointments, head-shaking mistakes, and lessons learned—illustrated with case studies and interviews. This section provides a road-map of things to avoid and a guide back to responsible brand stewardship.

Part Five tackles how to engage constructively with potential private capital partners and how to prepare for a due diligence process. Finally, we'll look at the future of PE and franchising. Significant external pressures loom, putting a strain especially on small businesses but also threatening the franchise model itself. However, this critically important engine of entrepreneurial business growth and job creation can be protected and strengthened by understanding the important role and strategies of PE and how to build productive relationships with private capital.

WHAT I WANT FOR YOU

I am passionate about small business, entrepreneurship, and franchising. Eventually, even the most independent-minded franchise founders and multi-unit franchisees can benefit from having a capital and strategic thought partner. Many find that partner within the private equity world. Sometimes it's simply time to retire and move on to other adventures, so creating the best exit possible is key. And of course PE activity impacts other stakeholders such as suppliers as well. I want to see as many positive franchising outcomes as possible. I am inspired every day by the brilliant founders, franchisees, advisers, executives, and investors I'm honored to work with.

As a former multi-unit franchisee within a PE-backed franchise system, I have firsthand operating experience with PE-related change and franchisee impact. In my professional consulting, the study of franchising best practices along with the intersection of private capital investing methods in franchising is my unique area of focus. I also invest at both the franchisor and outlet level alongside my PE partners and provide management and board-level advisory services to franchise businesses and private capital firms investing in the franchise sector. My perspective is shaped by this broad experience. My goal is to inform and empower you with the information you need to successfully navigate and achieve your personal goals.

If you believe this book will help others make good franchising decisions, please share it with your network and consider posting an online review! Extra resources and reader bonus materials are provided online at www.bigmoneyinfranchising.com. If you wish to provide feedback or get in touch, contact information is included in the closing section.

Best wishes for your franchising journey!

PART ONE

How Private Equity Came to Dominate Franchising

CHAPTER 1

Understanding Franchising's Enduring Appeal

In 1888 Martha Matilda Harper opened her first Harper Method hair salon. Her goal was to empower women via business ownership. There are now more than 120,000 personal services franchise outlets alone, employing more than 577,000 people.[1]

MY FRIEND NADEEM BAJWA started in franchising like I did—delivering pizzas. I drove for Domino's Pizza as a teenager growing up in Southern California and worked for a terrific husband-and-wife team who were so proud to own their first store. Nadeem drove for Papa Johns while a college student at the Indiana Institute of Technology. We both ended up becoming multi-unit franchise business owners.

Nadeem is a franchising success story. He originally came to the United States from Pakistan, hoping to one day work in a corporate job, but instead found success as a franchise entrepreneur. From his humble beginnings delivering pizzas starting in 1994, he progressed to managing one store, then multiple stores, and then whole regions. Eventually he decided to open his own business as a franchisee. He started with one Papa Johns location in East Liverpool, Ohio, in 2002. He found an inexpensive location and bought used equipment. It was a true bootstrap operation. The success of that first site blew the doors off his business plan—he booked four times more revenue than he expected! He added another location. And another.

As he continued to expand, he added new outlets and acquired some from retiring franchisees. There have been ups and downs along the way, to be sure, but he maintains a sense of humility and gratitude about his experiences. He says, "I'm not in the pizza business—I'm in the people business. Everything I do is focused on my team and how I can help them be successful." He is now on the other side of the table, in a position to help other people and provide employment. He provides the type of leadership and training opportunities for his own team that he himself received when he was starting out.

Nadeem is now one of the largest franchisees in the Papa Johns system, with nearly 200 locations across 11 states and counting. (Papa Johns itself has grown from its start in 1984 in Jeffersonville, Indiana, when the founder sold pizzas out of the back of his father's tavern, and is now publicly traded, NASDAQ: PZZA.) Nadeem has even related his story on Capitol Hill, meeting with lawmakers to help them understand the importance of franchise entrepreneurship and the challenges that business owners face. He points out, "No one would have been impressed if I had opened Nadeem's Pizza. I joined an established system with a strong brand so I could focus on growth and developing my team. It's been an incredible journey, and I'm not done adding stores yet!"[2]

Caitlin McTigue is another franchise success story. Every week I treat myself to a few of her Club Pilates classes to be transformed. For 50 magical minutes, I stretch, strain, and push myself in an effort to reverse time and regain some of the flexibility and strength of my youth. Every class is packed and has long waitlists because their teaching approach gets results!

Caitlin is also a franchise business inspiration. She owns five Club Pilates locations and is working on opening her sixth. She started as an analyst at J.P. Morgan, worked in key account management at several health care firms, and earned her MBA at the Ohio State University Fisher College of Business. Although she enjoyed her corporate work experiences, she longed to work for herself. She discovered Club Pilates while searching for a Pilates certification program. After a class, I asked her about her experiences as a franchisee. She said, "I fell in love with the brand. I also felt strongly that the concept would do well here."[3] She went on, "I don't think I could have been as successful, or moved as quickly to build up this business, without the help and support of the franchise behind me. The core team is amazing and gives me a lot of support. They helped me find the right locations and negotiate the site leases. They taught me how to market my business. Both my husband and sister now work with me, and I'm focused on opening my next location."

FRANCHISING'S INNOVATIVE APPROACH TO NEW BUSINESS CREATION

What is it about the franchise model that allowed both Nadeem and Caitlin to create these substantial enterprises for themselves and jobs for their employees, given that they have such different backgrounds? The International Franchise Association, franchising's main trade association, has called franchising "a catalyst for entrepreneurship" and "the most democratic wealth-creation tool in human history."[4] A proven franchise concept provides the operating system through which to establish and run a business rather than starting from scratch. This approach has been tremendously successful around the world, empowering hundreds of thousands of entrepreneurs as brand licensees, creating millions of jobs, and driving billions of dollars' worth of economic activity. Franchises also deliver important products and services to customers—one community and one neighborhood at a time. This "last three feet" of interaction with, and distribution directly to, end customers is what makes franchising both global in scale and hyperlocal in execution.

Like Nadeem's inspiring story, many multi-unit franchisee operators got their start as frontline workers in a franchise business, their first step onto the opportunity ladder. Franchising provides a growth path for those interested in taking on larger roles or becoming franchise owners them-selves, offering employees training and the chance to build their leadership and entrepreneurial skills. Some then go on to purchase their first location and gradually build their enterprise. A proven franchise model provides aspiring business owners an operating playbook, established brand, and support. At its core, that is why the franchise model as we know it has endured. It is why thousands of new units are opened and new jobs are created every year by franchise entrepreneurs, and it's why franchising is a global success story.

In a study conducted by Oxford Economics for the International Franchise Association, 32 percent of franchise business owners surveyed said they would not have been able to own a business if they were not franchisees. This proportion was higher among female franchisees (39 percent). People of color are more likely to be owners of a franchise business (26 percent) than a nonfranchise business (17 percent).[5] Similarly, although veterans make up 7 percent of the US population, they punch well above their weight in franchising, making up 14 percent of franchisees.[6]

> **Franchising provides a critical opportunity ladder and training ground, available nowhere else, for millions of would-be business owners and their employees. For more than a century, franchising has been an important economic engine of new business and new job creation.**

Franchise experiences are ingrained in our lives and routines. But how many people stop to think about the engine that drives a franchise? That the businesses they frequent are local outlets of a regional, national, or global franchise, and those local outlets are owned by people who often live in their own community? I have my own busy-working-mom routine that on many days includes picking up a morning smoothie at Tropical Smoothie Cafe, stopping at the UPS Store to ship a package, taking an afternoon class at Club Pilates, and later grabbing takeout at Dave's Hot Chicken. (Mom saves dinner!) Our youngest child learned to swim at our local Goldfish Swim School. We often stop at Rita's Italian Ice for a sweet treat. And so on. These outlets are owned by franchisees who live in my community. Franchisees are active participants in their communities in other ways, such as sponsoring local youth sports leagues and charity fundraising efforts. We all have similar rituals and relationships with franchise businesses that are integrated into our busy lives.

Franchise outlets have operations-focused entrepreneurs at the helm. These are not conglomerates making decisions from some faraway place. Franchise entrepreneurs empower their management teams and front-line staff to best serve customers. When I can't figure out how to get an ordering or scheduling app to work on my phone, my local franchise outlet gladly assists. If I have a billing issue, I just talk to the local outlet manager. If something is missing from my takeout food order, the local store team quickly makes it right.

Ever tried to get human assistance when your airline loses your luggage? Or tried to speak to an actual person at your insurance company to discuss billing or coverage? Or tried to get help when ordering hot concert tickets and the mobile app or website keeps crashing? Have you ever sat on hold for hours trying to interact with a government agency that has been given a big mandate and yet is chronically understaffed? Ever wandered through today's new ghost towns—big box retail—and noticed there are no employees visible *anywhere?* If you need help in these situations, you're usually stuck submitting help desk tickets to a faceless and what often feels like an immoveable corporate megalith. You hope to get a response, but you don't really expect one. Or you try to persuade an unforgiving internet chatbot to PLEASE *for the love of Mike let me speak to a human being!* In comparison, franchise outlets often run circles around big companies and government entities when it comes to customer service, because franchise outlets are hyperlocal in their execution format and directly connected to their customers.

Similarly, franchise employees have a direct relationship with the owner and management team of each outlet. Franchisees take pride in running good businesses and have local community standing as respected business owners and employers. Many franchisees, even MUOs with large holdings, will post their personal contact information online or in their outlets so customers and employees can reach them directly with questions or concerns. This is in sharp contrast to the layers of gatekeepers between traditional corporate management and the customers they serve.

> The franchise model isn't just an entrepreneurial system. It creates something that is often missing in our modern world—human connections.

WHY DO ENTREPRENEURS LIKE FRANCHISING?

Many people who want to run their own business are capable investors, leaders, and managers. But there are few true *inventors* in the world. And for inventors, building significant scale is traditionally very challenging and capital intensive. The franchise model was designed with this reality in mind. Non-inventors can adopt franchise processes to go into business. To succeed, they must be self-starters and sales- and operations-focused, but they need not start from scratch. Meanwhile, inventors can benefit from the scale that can be created using the franchise model to attract franchisees as expansion partners.

> A proven franchise system provides numerous benefits:
>
> ▶ operations manual, policies, and procedures
> ▶ replicable methods and processes
> ▶ business measurement tools (key performance indicators)
> ▶ standardized equipment, site design, and supplies
> ▶ field coaching
> ▶ start-up training and site selection assistance
> ▶ branding
> ▶ marketing support
> ▶ a community of other franchisees sharing best practices

The franchise community is an underappreciated aspect of franchising that outsiders don't see but that insiders know is a key benefit of the franchise model. Best practices are openly shared across system founders, managers, and franchisees. Think of it as a massive entrepreneurial network around the world, working every day to improve and grow their local businesses. Participants often feel they belong to something larger as a result. Again, those relationships and connections matter across the franchise model.

If you're a franchisee, you know that the most successful operators are the ones that have mastered the operating system of their particular brand and added innovative touches to incrementally improve their processes and execution. Your entrepreneurial drive has led to your personal success and success for your team. You know that any system, no matter how good, requires discipline, strong relationships, commitment, and effort.

So, your mindset is focused on improving and growing the business. You watch and listen to what is happening with your brand, but you're also connected to what's happening in your local market. You stay on top of trends that may one day require you to adjust your business approach in some way. You are receptive to new thinking and techniques to accelerate your business. Similarly, if you're a brand founder or franchise executive, you're constantly watching the market for trends, new entrants, and changes that may impact the franchise system. Something that has come to your attention is private equity activity in franchising.

WHY DOES PRIVATE EQUITY LIKE FRANCHISING?

Private equity investors understand that many enterprises, especially small businesses, suffer from lack of capital and direction, a.k.a. strategic support. As a result of PE's capital and strategic assistance, the business is put on an accelerated growth trajectory and key business processes are optimized. In exchange, the PE sponsor creates a return for their own investors. There are many inherent strengths of the franchise model that make it attractive to a range of private capital investors:

▶ There are high corporate margins.
▶ Franchisors have the potential to create tremendous scale with comparatively low capital expenditure.
▶ Brands can grow quickly with the right unit-level economics.
▶ Cash flow is predictable because the parent company is paid from top-line system revenue.

▶ The future (i.e., investment business case) can be validated numerically; activities such as opening the development funnel, expanding new markets, and ramping up units to maturity are all activities that can be modeled and tracked.

▶ Once core franchisee support is in place, adding more units doesn't require significant increases in support, driving high corporate cash flow.

▶ PE can apply well-established growth levers to significantly accelerate brands.

▶ Franchise regulations and case law in the US and elsewhere are established.[7]

▶ Diverse, long-term revenue stream may include royalties, fees, and rebates.

▶ There is low customer concentration, meaning business success doesn't depend on only a few customer relationships.

▶ Debt financing is available.

▶ Platforming (a common PE tactic) is highly effective in franchising. (Platforming will be discussed at length in Chapters 9 and 14.)

▶ A robust secondary transaction market for trading franchise businesses is now in place, giving investors more exit certainty and liquidity options. (What I call the PE Profit Ladder will be covered in Chapters 13 and 14.)

These system benefits of franchise brands lead to higher enterprise valuation (usually expressed as a multiple of EBITDA: earnings before interest, tax, depreciation, and amortization) than are experienced by many non-franchised companies.[8]

> **Franchising has many attractive qualities for private capital investors. There are opportunities for PE to leverage the inherent strengths and best practices of the franchise model itself, and then to apply operational and financial techniques to build the business and increase enterprise value. And to make money. A *lot* of money.**

This young marriage between PE and franchising benefits from sharing some similarities and common objectives. Like a proven franchise, private equity has its own well-honed, systems-based, and people-centric playbook to grow franchise businesses. The playbook is grounded in analytical rigor and data-based decision-making and sets specific goals for the assets it holds. Since franchise businesses share similarities, this playbook can be redeployed over and over.

> At the unit level, businesses are very different by sector; but at the corporate franchisor level, running a franchise system is very similar across industries. Once you become an expert in the franchise business model itself, your market opportunity is huge.
>
> At the system level, your risk is distributed across multiple operators. That distributed knowledge throughout the organization is powerful. Once you reach scale, the recurring revenue nature of the royalty revenue stream is almost like a software subscription model. The franchise agreement usually lasts 5 to 10 years and can be renewed, so you've essentially captured the royalty revenue from that unit in perpetuity. The revenue stream is relatively predictable so long as that unit remains open.
>
> —**CAROLINE STEVENS**, investor, MPK Equity Partners[9]

> The franchise model can be highly valuable. Once you get the flywheel spinning and franchisees are investing in your brand by building out stores, it's remarkably capital efficient at the corporate level. As long as you maintain the discipline in managing the brand and avoid overleverage, the potential is enormous.
>
> —**J. DAVID KARAM**, chief executive officer, Sbarro[10]

When it comes time to exit, PE again follows a predictable system to market and sell their portfolio companies. Strong unit-level results drive the best valuation and attract the next owner or enable taking the business public via a stock offering. Just as franchising has success levers and best practices, private equity has its own proven strategic and tactical playbook.

Another common trait is flexibility. The franchise model creates consistent quality and brand experiences, and yet it flexes to handle local market conditions and evolving customer preferences. Likewise, PE follows a systems approach but pivots as conditions require.

Private equity investors are more aligned with their franchise partners in terms of their entrepreneurial mindset than many people realize. PE has been called "capitalism's misunderstood entrepreneurs."[11] They're just a different kind of entrepreneur, focused on business acceleration, backing other entrepreneurs (in this case, franchise brand founders, established franchisors, and franchisees running their own businesses), and return on investment as their primary success metric. PE will either back or bring in managers who are adept at building out franchise systems. Growing the business to create investor returns can create a win-win for their aligned stakeholders. Employees of franchised outlets benefit from new job creation and growth opportunities, including the potential to become franchisees themselves.

> Most of the top brands now have, or used to have, PE backing. But franchising is unique in that even when private equity buys a franchisor, it is still essentially backing entrepreneurs—franchisees—who are personally very invested in their businesses. Franchisees have a high degree of engagement. PE loves that.
>
> —AZIZ HASHIM, managing partner, NRD Capital[12]

Founders, management, franchisees, and their private equity partners are most successful when dedicated to ensuring mutual success and stakeholder value. The more profitable, replicable, and resilient the operating system at the unit level, the faster and more sustainably franchise brands grow. And the more focus put on nurturing communication and the quality of the franchisor-franchisee relationship, the more engaged and productive franchisees are likely to be.

▼

What does the investor landscape look like? For founders and multi-unit franchisees looking for a private capital partner, there are many options. Let's turn next to examine the different types of private capital investors, categorized by structure and basic strategies. For franchisors and franchisees looking to be successful, it's critical to understand what PE options exist, how these investors function in the pursuit of profit, and how they make decisions.

CHAPTER 2

The Private Capital Landscape—Part One: The Big Money Players

As pointed out in a recent investing webinar, private equity looks for evidence an acquisition will ultimately create the required return. "We're looking for growth deals, cash flow deals... high-quality deals with good leadership teams and good cultures. This isn't venture investing."[1]

PRIVATE EQUITY AS AN investing category is a $10 trillion behemoth,[2] but not all PE investors are the same. They may operate from a similar playbook, but there is a wide spectrum of PE activity and a variety of players with differing strategies. This chapter describes the major types of private capital investors in franchising and identifies what sets them apart. It will help you determine the type of partner that could be a fit for your personal and business objectives, whether you are a franchisor or a franchisee looking for expansion capital, a strategic thought partner, or a lucrative exit. If you're an executive within a franchisor, your career depends on understanding private equity—whether as the owner of a company you work for, an investor backing franchisees in your system, or a competitive force in the marketplace.

Let's review the basic landscape.

PRIVATE EQUITY FIRMS AREN'T A HOMOGENEOUS GROUP

First, it is important to recognize the diversity of private capital active within franchising. Think of it as a spectrum across which private capital firms (and even different funds managed by each of those firms) will stretch based on their preferred investing style, sector expertise (e.g., emerging brands, restaurants), current strategies, market focus, average hold time, preferred investment amount (e.g., it is difficult for a large fund to write small checks), and other criteria.

Firms have different reputations, cultures, and track records. Some PE firms prefer to be the first institutional capital into a franchise system and to cut a deal directly with the founder (called a "proprietary deal"). Others prefer to work with more mature brands and to acquire portfolio companies via a formal "banked" process (auction run by an investment bank). Some specialize in operating unit consolidation at the franchisee (outlet) level. A few firms specialize in distressed situations, turnarounds, and workouts.

Some PE firms carefully avoid overpaying for companies as core to their investing strategy and are quite willing to lose deals if they believe the winning bidder is overpaying. Other firms are more aggressive on the front end in terms of willingness to pay or how they justify the acquisition price. Either way, once PE owns the asset, the pressure is on to deliver the business case—driving fairly predictable strategies and tactics.

PE firms may also be distinct based on their planned exit path. For some, selling to another PE firm in a secondary deal or to a strategic buyer is their preferred approach. Others are more focused on exiting via an initial public offering (IPO) or plan to hold the investment for a long time. And within the time span of a fund, PE manager choices shift as the need to deploy or return capital changes during the life of the fund.

> Most people outside private equity see PE as a homogeneous group. In reality, PE firms vary widely in focus, sector experience, approach to working with management, and franchising track records, as do their strategies across time and across the funds they manage.

Despite PE's diversity of investing approach and track record, many PE firms have the unfortunate tendency of "showing up" looking and talking the same. One franchise founder I spoke to sniffed derisively and told me, "Money is a commodity. These PE firms are all the same. I only care about getting the best price for my business." It was no surprise to me that he found out the hard way there are vast differences between firms! He ended up having to conduct more than 30 full-blown management presentations (after his arrogance had already turned off a number of qualified suitors) to finally find a match when he brought his company to market. Don't let PE's outward appearance of homogeneity fool you into thinking that firms and players within them are interchangeable. He wasn't willing to do smart prep work up front. You are smarter. You're taking the long-term view, you're open-minded, and your advance planning and networking will improve your outcomes.

THE DIVERSE RANGE OF PRIVATE EQUITY PLAYERS

Let's look at the range of players in the PE world in more detail. As a point of clarification, this section will emphasize the diversity of the PE landscape. But throughout the book, for our discussion purposes and ease of writing, when I refer to "private equity" or "PE," I will include all the following types together, with extra weight given to traditional private equity firms because they are so active in franchising. As we go along, I will identify significant differences in investing behavior between the groups, such as family office or hybrids compared to traditional PE, where applicable to the topic at hand.

Private Equity

Also called "financial buyers," traditional private equity firms raise money from institutions such as pension funds, university endowments, and sovereign wealth funds, as well as from wealthy individuals and families. Those investors are called "limited partners" (LPS). PE managers are called "general partners" (GPS). Funds are then invested via a "blind pool," meaning that LPS don't control what investments GPS make. GPS may co-invest using their own money, usually putting up only a small amount (typically only 1 to 5 percent) in the deals they put together, and then use a combination of investor funds and debt for the balance of the financing they need to acquire companies. The average PE fund length is 10 years across all industry sectors. PE holds on to portfolio companies an average of 5.4 years, up from 3.2 years in 2010.[3] Although PE has a "short-timer" reputation, there are many examples in franchising where PE owners hold portfolio companies longer to maximize investor returns. And while PE also has a reputation for investing little up front while loading acquisitions with debt, in fact the average PE equity contribution is now more than 50 percent.[4] And as previously mentioned, small franchise acquisitions by private capital firms tend to be all-cash transactions.

In cases where the PE firm wants to hold an investment longer than the fund will allow, it can raise what is called a "continuation fund" to allow early investors to exit and bring in new investors. Or it can sell an asset to another fund it also owns, called a "GP-led secondary" deal. More on that strategy in Chapters 13 and 14, when we discuss the PE Profit Ladder.

The use of leverage, active engagement with management, and different investment timelines distinguishes private equity from other investor types, such as venture capital and hedge funds. Traditional PE firms are not themselves operators—they run businesses through management teams governed by a board of directors. To protect their investors, most PE firms need to acquire majority stakes in businesses, but some will consider minority stakes, especially when riding alongside majority investors such as another PE firm. When investments are made in partnership with other

PE firms as co-investors, it is often referred to as a "club deal." Collaborative investments with groups of PE firms participating can include large acquisitions, such as the $1.5 billion acquisition of Burger King from Diageo PLC by the triumvirate of Bain Capital, Texas Pacific Group, and Goldman Sachs Private Capital in 2002.[5] PE may also make investments in partnership with management.

PE strives to return at least three to four times (3× to 4×) invested capital (known as MOIC, or multiple of invested capital) to their investors within an average of 5 years. For improved bragging rights, they hope to return much more. Research demonstrates that across PE for hold times of less than 2 years, a 2× MOIC gross of fees is the average return, stabilizing around 2.5× after 5 years or more.[6] Within franchising, PE has demonstrated even better returns.

> A well-run franchise business can deliver significantly higher-than-market returns on capital for a relatively low investment, one of the reasons PE is now so active in franchising.

At the end of the day, PE's entire purpose is to outperform public markets; otherwise, investors in PE funds would simply move their money to more liquid and less risky options. Franchising is not a capital-intensive business for the parent company (franchisor) once enough scale is achieved to support franchisees, and scale can be achieved quickly in a well-run system, driving strong corporate returns. Adding more franchisees doesn't mean adding a proportionately larger corporate support staff. Scalability makes franchising particularly attractive to PE investors.

PE is generally opaque about their investing activities. Occasionally some PE firms crow about their strong returns at the portfolio company level in press releases or on their websites—for example, Edison Partners' website announcement that it generated a 14× return exiting Liberty Tax.[7] More commonly, information is quietly leaked via a "source close to the company."

PE managers must be cautious and follow regulatory guidelines when reporting on *fund-level* performance.[8] But *portfolio company* results can be discussed more openly, and this is also more relevant to franchise stakeholders. For franchisees, the availability of public franchise disclosures provides a unique advantage compared to buying a nonfranchise, privately held business. Much of the deal trading information (such as price paid for the business and debt service) is disclosed in portfolio company financial statements. Company growth and key changes to the model can be tracked across ownership changes via information also contained in public disclosures as well as by speaking directly to franchisees.

> Traditional private equity firms' entire role is to deliver superior investing returns compared to public markets. To understand PE's mindset, you must first understand this clarity of purpose. PE's mandate also drives predictable choices in the selection and management of franchise businesses.

Institutional Investors Making Direct Investments

Increasingly, LPs such as pension funds want to make direct investments in companies, sometimes independently and sometimes as minority partners alongside private equity firms. Direct investments by this group experienced 16 percent compound annual growth from 2008 to 2017.[9] For example, the largest US pension fund, CalPERS (California Public Employees' Retirement System), recently announced plans to set up two direct investment buyout funds managing a total of $13 billion.[10] The Ontario Teachers' Pension Plan made a $300 million investment in The Flynn Group, the largest restaurant operating group in the US.[11] The British Columbia Investment Management Corporation made a significant minority investment in home services franchisor platform Authority Brands.[12]

> I expect to see more direct institutional investing activity in franchising, especially investments in large or mature franchise brands and platforms and multi-unit operating groups.

Selling off minority stakes in portfolio companies to direct institutional investors can repay initial investors early. LPs making direct investments can reduce management fees paid to PE, yet still benefit from riding alongside GPs who are actively engaged with their portfolio companies.

CASE STUDY: PUBLIC PENSION INVESTMENTS IN FRANCHISING

Through pension fund investments in private equity funds, many firefighters, public school teachers, police officers, and other city and state employees are also franchise investors. Thus millions of retirees indirectly benefit from and depend on the success of franchising via their pension investments. Pension plans may hold investments directly in publicly traded franchises or indirectly via PE funds.

Roark Capital Group provides a good example. In 2022, Roark (PE's most prolific franchise investor) completed its sixth flagship buyout fund, with at least 155 LPs committed. Disclosed investors include New York State Common Retirement Fund, Oregon State Treasury, and the Tennessee Consolidated Retirement System.[13] Investors In prior Roark funds include public pensions such as the New Jersey Division of Investments, State Universities Retirement System of Illinois, the Regents of the University of Michigan, and Washington State Investment Board,[14] to name only a few.

Another example is the Los Angeles City Employees' Retirement System (LACERS). Since the inception of the LACERS private equity program in 1995 through the end of calendar year 2022, LACERS has committed $7.6 billion to 353 private equity partnerships, of which 276 remain active.[15] LACERS has invested in PE firms active in franchising through different funds. Examples include Harvest Partners, the investor behind Encanto Restaurants (a YUM Brands franchisee), Hand & Stone Massage and Facial Spa, Driven Brands, and Neighborly; Incline Equity Partners, which had previously been invested in LYNX Franchising; and Roark Capital Group.[16]

CalPERS invests on behalf of more than 2 million retired and working members (38 percent of whom are school employees or retirees). In addition to investments in PE funds active in franchising, CalPERS also has direct investments in publicly traded franchise businesses. These currently include, or have previously included, McDonald's, Taco Bell, Domino's Pizza, KFC, Pizza Hut, Wingstop, Wendy's, Papa Johns, Carrols Restaurant Group (one of the largest Burger King and Popeyes franchisees), Aaron's, Bloomin' Brands, Choice Hotels, Claire's, Darden Restaurants, Dine Brands Global, Hilton Hotels, Marriott Hotels, Nathan's Famous, Planet Fitness, and others.[17] CalPERS has investments in large franchise suppliers as well, such as Kraft Heinz, real estate trusts with restaurant investments, and investments in franchise debt.

> Hundreds of thousands of small business owners become entrepreneurs through the franchise model. But it should be acknowledged that the story of franchising's critical importance to the us economy is deeply interconnected across multiple direct and indirect stakeholders. It is thus important to protect the franchise model and use caution when considering any changes to long-standing regulatory frameworks. Franchising is truly a full-circle—local community to Main Street to Wall Street—ecosystem.

Family Offices

Family offices (FOs) pool the wealth of one or more families and individuals and invest on their behalf. They don't need to sell assets or raise new funds within a certain amount of time like traditional PE firms. Keep in mind that some FOs like to make direct investments, others prefer to invest in traditional private equity funds, and still others may engage in both strategies. Each family office has a different investment approach. Some are responsible for allocating a pool of assets across multiple asset types, while others are responsible for one asset allocation strategy and a subset of the total available capital. According to a 2022 survey by Montana Capital Partners, 71 percent of family offices and foundations, compared to 49 percent in 2021, now allocate 15 percent or more of their portfolio to private equity.[18] Funds under management are substantial. The wealthiest FOs have assets in the billions of dollars. In a 2017 survey of 262 family offices, the average FO portfolio was $926 million.[19]

Just like traditional PE firms, FO investors making private direct investments in franchising typically like to back growth stories and strong management teams. Some FOs have sector expertise in franchising; others are content to be generalists. Like private equity firms, family offices do extensive analysis and improve financial reporting in firms they acquire with the objective of uncovering areas of opportunity. But they are also different from traditional PE firms in important ways:

They invest their own money. Family offices typically invest out of their own fund, or pool money from other family offices and wealthy individuals, rather than investing on behalf of pension funds and university endowments.

They may have longer investing timelines. FOs tend to be more "patient" capital because, unlike traditional PE firms, FOs aren't tied to "sell by" dates to return funds to institutional investors. FOs also aren't under pressure to raise their next fund (but they may still feel some pressure to deploy capital and put it to work). FOs may be content to hold an investment "forever"; this is a consideration for you if you are a founder or franchisee and rolling some equity forward. Depending on your personal and estate-planning objectives, FOs' longer horizon could be an ideal fit for you or not, depending on your own hold horizon. (Some FOs are willing to negotiate buyout options on any equity rolled forward to enable a seller to exit prior to the FO's intended hold period.) Given their longer time horizon, FOs can make major platform bets and then spend years patiently bolting new acquisitions into the platform without any pressure to quickly monetize that platform before maturity has been achieved.

> We are a family office. We're not investing out of a short-term fund, so there is no set time by which to return capital. That approach resonates with founders and operators who are also looking to stay involved in the business, grow their own capital, and, above all else, do the right thing for the business. We will hold a portfolio company for much longer than a private equity fund if we believe doing so will create more value for us and for founders in that second exit. However, we don't always hold our portfolio companies longer. We exited two investments most recently after four years. But we invest with a long-term partner-like mindset and then sell at the right time based on the market climate and business performance, no matter what.
>
> **—CAROLINE STEVENS**, investor, MPK Equity Partners[20]

They may use leverage differently. FOs may or may not use leverage in their transactions. While private equity has a reputation for using high leverage, in fact, GF Data found that for the first three quarters of 2022, family offices were actually investing in *less* equity (45.8 percent) in their platform transactions compared to their private equity peers (52.4 percent).[21] But FOs also may not use leverage at all. It depends on the FO. For this reason, if an FO tends to prefer more modest debt positions, it may not be as competitive in a banked auction process where higher bidding may be fed with higher debt. For the first three quarters of 2022, GF Data found this amounted to a half-turn difference in price between FO-backed deals (7.6× EBITDA) compared to their PE peers (8.2× EBITDA).[22] Thus, many FOs prefer either proprietary deals or partnering with founders who value the flexibility and longer time horizon an FO partnership offers.

They can often be more flexible. Depending on the FO, it may get very involved in coaching its management teams, it might be willing to sponsor emerging brands with longer growth runways... or it may prefer to be a passive investor. FOs may be more willing to be minority investors or to get creative negotiating certain deal terms. So while family office investors are generally following the PE growth playbook, they may also deviate from that playbook in ways that are relevant to your franchise business (could be positive, negative, or neutral depending on your objectives and the FO in question). This should be part of your consideration set if you are evaluating family office capital partners.

> Going after the highest price offer can be a mistake. That one may not have the highest certainty of closing. In my experience, family office close rates are often higher compared to private equity within my area of focus [multi-unit restaurants].
>
> —**RICK ORMSBY**, managing director, Unbridled Capital[23]

> Small brands don't have enough EBITDA to be interesting to most traditional private equity firms. For small deals it may be more expensive to do the due diligence and close the deal than the actual price of the business. Traditional PE firms have a shorter time frame. They need to meaningfully grow EBITDA, and for emerging brands it's just hard to do that within a short window. Because we're backed by a family office [JM Family], we have a long-term investment strategy. We are "buy and hold."
>
> —**JONATHAN THIESSEN**, chief development officer, Home Franchise Concepts[24]

Cultural fit may factor differently into the investment equation. Family offices may combine other mandates, such as support for local businesses or social causes, within their investing strategy. This may or may not be a fit for your objectives. In addition, since many family offices are investing proceeds earned from their own entrepreneurial family ventures, there is often strong cultural alignment with franchise founders and multi-unit franchisee entrepreneurs.

> Meeting with private equity, I could already feel the squeeze. I met with several firms, first in 2018 and then again in 2020. They seemed like nice people, and they had a good track record in franchising. But yet, I could still feel the coming squeeze! That may not always be the case, of course, but it's what I felt at the time. I felt my team would be at risk. I knew I needed help to get my business to the next level, but I didn't want to sacrifice my team and the culture we'd worked so hard to build over 35 years in the process.
>
> It's all about your goals. For me and my family's business, working with a family-managed platform like HFC [Home Franchise Concepts] was a much better fit to grow the business and preserve our culture.
>
> —HEIDI MORRISSEY, president, Kitchen Tune-Up and Bath Tune-Up, Home Franchise Concepts[25]

If you already suspect that PE isn't a fit for you currently but you need help taking your business to the next level, family offices can be a compelling alternative source of private capital. In that case, start networking with FOs active in franchising and with founders who have gone this route.

> Family offices are increasingly active franchise investors and are as unique as the wealthy families that fund them. If you are a founder or multi-unit franchisee looking for flexible expansion capital, and especially if you prefer a minority partner at this time, a family office partner may be a good option to consider.

Wealthy Individuals

Separate from family offices, which set aside funds and build out a dedicated investing team, "celebrity" investors (high-profile entrepreneurs, professional athletes, etc.) have been active franchise investors at both the brand and multi-unit operating level. Their participation is especially prized by brands seeking to sprinkle high-recognition fairy dust on their concept (i.e., public awareness and validation).

> **Wealthy individual investors making personal bets are becoming more influential especially within the emerging franchise brand ecosystem as angel or minority investors. Many have investing experience in other sectors or business ownership experience, including as franchisees.**

Examples of franchises that have employed this fundraising strategy include Wetzel's Pretzels, Blaze Pizza,[26] and Dave's Hot Chicken[27] (there are common founders and investors across all three brands).[28] Some of this investment happens organically: a celebrity may simply be a local customer and contacts that brand to see if there are opportunities to partner or invest. Other times the investments are found through wealth management specialists.

Independent Sponsors

Also called "fundless sponsors," this investor type looks for acquisition opportunities first and then raises needed acquisition funds.

> **Unlike traditional PE firms or FOs, independent sponsors don't have an existing dedicated vehicle or pool of money to invest out of.**

Many fundless sponsors are former operating executives and tend to be well connected among private equity firms, family offices, and individual wealthy investors. However, these independents risk missing opportunities when sellers lose patience and opt to talk to buyers with dedicated funds who can close deals much faster. (If you are a founder or multi-unit franchisee contacted by a potential PE buyer, before you spend too much time answering questions, ask what fund they are investing out of and the total size of the fund to understand whether there is actually a dedicated fund or not. We will cover engaging with PE in detail in Chapter 18.)

Strategic Buyers

Strategic buyers are distinct from financial buyers because, beyond seeking a financial return, they are motivated to make specific kinds of acquisitions to build their business (i.e., getting into a new market or product category). I'm including them in the list of investors because they should not be overlooked. Although they do not fall under the parameters of private equity, strategic buyers are influential players on the deal ladder. Strategics compete for deals with PE and sell companies to PE, and they carry some of the same mindset because their investing teams are often staffed with former PE or investment bankers. Examples of strategic acquisitions include Ace Hardware's 2019 acquisition of the Handyman Matters franchise[29] and VCA's (pet hospitals) 2014 acquisition of the Camp Bow Wow franchise system (dog boarding and daycare).[30] As a particular franchise business evolves, strategics may become more or less of a fit as a potential growth and capital partner.

> Maintain an awareness of strategics. Even if it's not a fit this time around, that could change at your company's next inflection point.

Peter Ross, CEO and co-founder of Senior Helpers, describes the evolution of changing needs and different inflection points in his own business:[31]

> We were owned by two private equity firms before we sold to a strategic buyer. The only strategic we met across all three processes was during our last sale, and it turned out to be the best fit at that point in time. There was lots of interest from PE firms during these three sales. Things changed, and there were many more firms looking at us the second and third time around. But we felt deep experience in post-acute health care was really important for the next phase of the company's growth. That's why in the most recent process we selected a strategic partner, Advocate Aurora Enterprises.

And when corporate priorities change (as can happen), strategics may return to PE to divest assets. This was the case when Pernod Ricard[32] (which had just taken control of Allied in July 2005) announced in December 2005 that it planned to sell Dunkin' Brands out of the Allied portfolio to Bain Capital, the Carlyle Group, and Thomas H. Lee.[33]

Hybrid Investors

Hybrid private capital investors blend two or more of the above characteristics. One example is a PE-backed strategic buyer, such as a franchise platform. This type of powerful hybrid acquires brands that are highly accretive to the platform, which means this buyer may be willing to work with emerging brands or may be able to justify higher acquisition prices. Because they are backed by PE, their intention is to grow the platform both organically and through acquisition until there is a strong opportunity to sell the platform up the PE Profit Ladder to a larger entity, or to take the platform public. Examples include restaurant platform Inspire Brands (Roark Capital Group) and home services platforms Threshold Brands (the Riverside Company) and Premium Service Brands (Susquehanna Private Capital). Inspire Brands targets well-established brands, while Threshold and Premium Service Brands have demonstrated a willingness to nurture emerging brands.

Another example of a hybrid buyer is a multi-unit operator investing its own funds or using, or co-investing with, outside funds but still running the show. Hybrid buyers may act more like patient capital in terms of their ability to hold investments longer, depending on their use of investment partners or lenders. These groups are often hands-on investors that get very involved in running their portfolio companies. This differentiates them from traditional PE firms, who, as mentioned earlier, run the business through managers. They may prefer lower leverage (or none) on their portfolio companies because they are investing their own capital. They have the flexibility to own whole brands, roll up operating units within multiple brands, take on growth companies, and turn strong corporate models into franchise models, and they even may be willing to take on turnarounds. This opportunistic flexibility, patience, and willingness to take on managerial roles themselves is something traditional PE firms can't duplicate because it falls outside PE's typical sponsor-grow-and-sell mandate.

A great example of a PE-operating hybrid is Gala Capital Partners, based in Los Angeles, California. Gala's founder is both an accomplished multi-unit, multi-brand franchisee and also the owner of, or co-investor in (as of this writing), franchisors Mooyah Burgers, Cici's Pizza, Dunn Brothers Coffee, Dillas Quesadillas, and Rusty Taco.[34] Gala rejects the use of debt in emerging brand acquisitions. As Anand Gala, founder and managing partner of Gala Capital Partners, explains, "We like to have the flexibility to get the business in the best shape it can be, and those early years are very critical. It's better not to have that outside pressure from lenders." For example, when Roark-backed Inspire Brands was ready to divest emerging brand Rusty Taco, Inspire felt Gala would be a strong fit. "They were considering what was the best home for Rusty, and it just so happened that our name popped up.... They wanted to find someone that specializes in smaller brands and who will really care."[35]

The week of the Rusty Taco acquisition, I had the opportunity to interview Gala Capital's founder, Anand Gala, for *Franchise Times*. He cited Gala's operating experience, tenacity, and ability to work hands-on with emerging brand managers to optimize supply chain, menu choices, and execution. Gala summarized, "Smaller brands often don't think about the business this way. We balance innovation with operating practicalities to create more unit profitability."[36]

For some investors, there are also key innovation advantages to working with emerging brands—for example, in the restaurant sector around menu and customer experience innovation. A hybrid investor that blends strong operational support with private capital backing can accelerate brands while exposing themselves to creative ideas that larger companies may never see. This is exactly the approach followed by the Savory Restaurant Fund, backed by Mercato Partners. Savory focuses on strategic investments in brands typically with 5 to 50 units and helps them to achieve greater scale.

> In response to increased competition for deals and given the steady stream of new brand entrants coming into franchising and attempting to get traction, I predict we will see continued growth in the participation and influence of hybrid investors and private capital–backed platforms and incubators. These investors bring needed strategic assistance to young brands otherwise unlikely to break out.

▼

So, the landscape of big money players is extremely diverse. But are the players' strategies to create return on investment equally diverse? Or are there common playbooks?

CHAPTER 3

The Private Capital Landscape—Part Two: The Big Money Strategies

"We've had 47 meetings with founders over the last two days. We'll have some good opportunities coming out of this conference."

—**PRIVATE EQUITY VICE PRESIDENT**, heard at the bar at the most recent International Franchise Association annual conference

NOW THAT YOU UNDERSTAND the diverse landscape of franchise investors, let's look more closely at the top strategies employed by the players to drive profit. Just how does each type of private capital partner carve out their own winning strategy, and what are the implications for franchising? What patterns are visible? Players fall along a broad spectrum based on their strategic approach, the types of franchise investments they target, and why. Understanding the PE spectrum and thinking ahead, it is easier to anticipate

- ▶ which PE strategic approach is most likely to bring solutions and experience that match a particular brand's current challenges and opportunities,
- ▶ how to build or improve a franchise business to appeal to different target buyers, and
- ▶ the likely playbook the current PE investor (or the next PE investor) will employ during their ownership to create and extract maximum value.

> There is logic to PE industry segmentation and stratification. There are also clear strategies informing PE's playbooks and franchise investing activities. Once these are apparent to you, potential matches, outcomes, and stakeholder impacts become more predictable.

THREE PRIMARY PRIVATE EQUITY FRANCHISE INVESTMENT TYPES: GROWTH, VALUE, AND TURNAROUND

Now that you have a sense of the PE landscape, we'll focus on the three major investment approaches in franchising: growth, value, and turnaround. It's useful to characterize deals this way no matter what financial strategies or mechanisms are used to accomplish the investment (e.g., mix of equity, debt, convertible, minority partners, family money, management buy-in, investor money). I am ignoring real estate–focused strategies, an entirely separate category with whole books devoted to the topic.

It has been said that private equity embraces complexity to create profit. In other words, PE firms are willing (sometimes the only ones willing) to invest in broken companies and overlooked sectors or to boldly make acquisitions even during down markets while betting on a comeback. This is a common misunderstanding about private equity. It is estimated that only 3 to 10 percent of all PE investing is focused on distressed investing, depending on market cycles.[1] This is mirrored in PE's involvement in franchising, where growth and value investments are far more common. This is the *opposite* of complexity. PE follows a clear playbook to succeed and prefers relatively safe bets.

PE firms active in franchising follow middle market trends and generally avoid turnarounds. Why? Because the franchise distribution model is executed by franchisees—*independent* business owners. Franchisee independence is core to the strength and resilience of the franchise model, but it also significantly complicates and lengthens turnaround projects. Franchise contracts ensure broad brand and operational compliance. But only franchisee engagement and excitement about the future of the brand cause franchisees to lean in and invest in opening new units, acquiring resales, adding marketing, and accelerating remodels.

> **To be blunt, it is extremely difficult and expensive to turn around a struggling franchise at the brand level within the typically short three- to eight-year PE hold period. This is why growth- and value-focused PE investing is much more common than turnaround investing within franchising.**

Heavy-lift projects add risk, cost, uncertainty, and time. PE generally prefers proven models, good fundamentals, and backable management teams. Any issues need to be fixable in the short term, such as renegotiating supply contracts, improving franchise license sales, or refreshing marketing to drive increased customer traffic.

Growth Investors in Franchising: *Incubate and Accelerate*

At its core, franchising is a *growth model*. A desire for growth provides the motivation to go through the complex franchise recruiting, registration, and process and training creation and codification, and to establish and maintain all the relationships that are key to franchising success. Franchisors and growth investors try to provide incentives, in turn, for franchisees to embrace expansion. For PE growth investors, the focus is on increasing top-line revenues, improving margins and profitability at both the corporate and franchisee level, getting new units open, expanding service and product lines, executing tuck-in acquisitions (add-ons), and improving key performance metrics. Growth initiatives are then accomplished through the managers that run the portfolio companies. As James J. Goodman, president of Gemini Investors,[2] remarked,

> We are active at the board level, but we're generally not involved at the operating level. If we're doing more than that, it suggests we were wrong about our initial thesis about the business. For example, when we invested in Buffalo Wild Wings back in 1999, the team had already taken it to a good level and had a good concept. They were looking for outside help and

guidance. They were talented. It was a great team, a fun team. We tried to be helpful at the margin where they needed it.

When we invested in Wingstop in 2002, the seller recognized he was more of a founder, more entrepreneurial than a manager. We partnered with the team and helped on operating decisions that would drive greater growth and scale. It was designed to be open from 4 PM to 11 PM. We expanded it to operate more like a mainstream restaurant concept. That's when it really took off.

> **Growth equity is the fastest-growing category of private equity investing. Together with late-stage venture capital, both are adding assets under management at twice the rate of standard buyout funds. According to Bain, by 2021, growth equity and venture assets under management reached 82 percent of the buyout total.[3] Growth-type investing drives tremendous activity in franchising.**

Remember also that PE investors are risk averse and want as much outcome certainty as possible. This is in dramatic contrast to venture capital investors, who experiment widely, fail fast, and are willing to spread their bets knowing some of those bets won't work out. In the venture capital world, for example, investors may spread their bets across 10 pre-money (not yet profitable) start-ups, hoping for a few break-out successes. It is difficult to know which new pharma or technology research and development (R&D) efforts will lead to a hit. But if only a few brands in a private equity portfolio created a positive return on investment, that outcome would be a failure! And PE doesn't usually invest in pre-money companies, another difference compared to the venture capital approach.

> **PE investors in franchising strive for a consistent hit rate and at least a 3× return on capital invested in each portfolio company within five years, based on conservative projections.**

This is a good place to comment on the difference between "small and unproven" versus "big growth potential." Forget marketing spin and think about this from PE's perspective. Every emerging franchise brand has "open space" for growth by virtue of being small. That's not the same thing as having significant growth potential!

It all comes down to whether the operating model is attractive and financially rewarding for franchisees. Generally, PE likes to see franchisees earn back their initial investment in less than 24 months (the faster the better, of course) and maintain strong cash flow (at least $100,000 to $250,000 owner's benefit per unit) thereafter for full-time concepts, especially if a fixed site is required. ("Owner's benefit" is the total dollars owners can pull out of the business in free cash flow generated, owner salary taken, or nonbusiness expenses that are written off to the business and therefore beneficial to the owner.) Another way to look at it is that the business should return annually to franchisees at least 15 to 20 percent of their original investment, because investing in a franchise (even in an absentee operating model) is not a passive investment.

The profit hurdle for a part-time concept with low start-up costs is different than for a restaurant or family entertainment concept with a much higher start-up cost. A part-time, low-cost-of-entry concept with an average annual owner's benefit of $50,000 per outlet might be perfectly acceptable to franchisees and PE investors because that concept was designed and marketed as a side hustle. A higher-cost concept such as a restaurant, early childhood education center, or family entertainment park, in contrast, would probably need to show a $500,000 annual owner benefit (or more) to provide an acceptable return on risk and investment for franchisees given the higher investment and liquidity requirements.

> Does your brand deliver category-leading return on investment potential for franchisees as well as available growth upside that is fundamentally attractive to PE? Building a highly valuable brand for franchisees is what drives greater PE interest—and thus, in the long run, even greater enterprise value.

Finally, even if PE growth investors intend a relatively short hold period, they still have to invest something into the future of the company to attract another buyer and facilitate a good exit. The next buyer needs to see positive momentum; a viable development funnel; positive feedback from franchisees; evidence of at least some supporting investments in technology, infrastructure, and talent to help carry the business forward; and ideally also see franchisees returning to buy additional territories. Only then will the next buyer be willing to lean into a better multiple than was paid for the business by the previous PE buyer. From this perspective, PE interests and those of franchisees in particular should be well aligned in a growth investing model.

Here are some of the franchise qualities that attract growth-focused PE:

- strong unit-level economics, same-store sales, and unit profitability
- category-leading cash-on-cash return for franchisees
- strong growth trends in a non-fad category
- solid proof of concept, ideally proven beyond home market
- highly replicable model, track record of operations
- significant available growth space for additional outlets
- healthy development funnel (i.e., conviction that 100 percent of units sold will open)
- successful and expansion-minded franchisees who provide positive validation about their franchise ownership experience
- founder who is willing to stay in the business, or at least roll significant (10 to 20 percent or more) equity forward in the deal
- backable management team with a strong track record
- differentiated customer offering and brand (note: branding is less important than a great operating system and growing outlet footprint in "fix my problem" categories discovered via Google search, e.g., "clean my gutters")
- proven ability to ramp franchisees to profitability
- subscription or recurring revenue models
- EBITDA margin at unit level >15 to 20 percent
- proven resiliency through up-and-down market cycles

Preferences vary among PE firms based on the following:

- corporate EBITDA size
- number of outlets
- level of infrastructure investment required to scale
- mix of franchise and corporate outlets
- entry price point (total investment required) for franchisees
- simplicity of unit operations
- whether that investor is the first institutional capital into a company, secondary buyout re-trade, take-private, or take-public
- industry or sector fit
- competition with other portfolio companies
- whether PE prefers to participate in a banked auction or find their own deals

Let's hear from a dedicated growth investor, Levine Leichtman Capital Partners. As managing partner Matthew Frankel puts it,[4]

We do a white space analysis for every investment. If the study says there is room for only 300 locations in the US and no international opportunity, that's probably not a franchise we would invest in. The reason is because we want to triple the store base, for example, but there still has to be significant growth potential available for the next owner as well. We aim to more than triple the cash flow of our portfolio companies. The right brands can grow quickly, but it must be compelling economically for the franchisee or it won't scale. We look for proof of concept, strong same-store sales, ability to dramatically scale the store base, and strong unit profitability.

The most successful PE investors in franchising acquire brands with good fundamentals, build solid relationships with franchisees to drive growth, and make at least some investment in the future of the company even if that future is outside the current owner's planned hold period. After all, the next buyer is buying the future, so that future must look bright to earn a premium price. *The better the economic model for franchisees, the more promising the future of the brand.*

Value-Based Franchise Investing: *Extend and Expand*

Once a franchise or platform has achieved significant scale, value-focused PE investors enter the picture. Value investors look for large, well-established franchise businesses with predictable cash flow that they can potentially hold for a longer period of time. Acquisition targets generally have a good track record of unit-level performance and a stable franchisee base. There is still evidence of growth and significant expansion potential, but the pace of growth may have slowed. Increased focus is often placed on new market entry (e.g., international), nontraditional site development or alternative distribution methods, product and service extensions, and keeping the existing base updated and relevant.

The biggest risks in this type of franchise investing are related to investor choices in how they manage a scale brand and keep franchisees engaged. Sometimes franchises in this category are starting to age and could do with a brand refresh, investments in marketing, technology, or other updates. PE missteps include overuse of debt, complacency (coasting too long on the cash flow), lack of attention to the quality of the franchisee-franchisor relationship, not protecting unit-level profitability, and underinvestment in the future. Investors need to keep an eye on trends and franchisee sentiment to avoid a stall-out.

> A value investor's ownership tenure is typically less transformational and more about driving efficiencies, refining the operating model, and maintaining predictability at scale. Owners may also *extract* significant value for themselves and their investors. Franchisees will continue to experience positive outcomes provided PE owners protect unit-level profitability and continue to invest in the future of the business.

In large systems some multi-unit operators may themselves start to look like value PE investors. They focus on driving operational efficiencies together with top-line revenue and often pivot toward consolidation versus aggressive new outlet growth. Since new territory development opportunities may be more limited in systems that already have a large footprint of outlets, MUO unit expansion in those systems is more likely to happen via acquiring existing units from retiring franchisees rather than engaging in heavy de novo (new) development efforts. Co-branding (two brands in the same location) is another option. This has the potential to drive higher sales per square foot and more brand outlets while avoiding new site building costs (only a retrofit/split-the-box remodel is required).

Like growth equity, value-focused PE investors also follow their own predictable playbook. In addition to benefiting from operational improvements and brand growth, return on investment can also be extracted through financial engineering. Common methods include charging management fees to portfolio companies, securitizing future royalty streams (converting this asset into a loan or marketable security), recapitalizing dividends, making loans to portfolio companies, collecting fees for arranging portfolio company financing, and other strategies. Consolidating purchasing under fewer suppliers and setting up rebate systems is a hybrid tactic combining operational and financial engineering; it is commonly applied by value investors to create new profit pools for the parent entity and often, but not always, to unlock cost savings for franchisees.

Before I receive an avalanche of email debating my definition of franchise "value investing," allow me to make an important clarification. "Value investors" in the public markets refers to a well-known investing strategy of buying stocks that appear to be underpriced relative to their intrinsic value.[5]

> *"Value investing" within the franchise and private equity context describes a completely different strategy compared to stock investing.* Financial buyers of a franchise business who are value investors are betting on the acquisition target's stability and strong cash flow. PE's strategy and tactics used to extract a return on investment depend on preserving and growing that income stream.

In fact, these acquisitions are often expensive because the business is kicking off so much cash! Since the brands have already achieved some scale, rapid growth in existing markets often isn't available, but instead a focused effort to open new markets may be undertaken. (Such as bringing in new master franchisees to open new countries for development.)

I thought quite a while about whether different terminology would be more useful here for readers, given the potential for confusion with value-based investing in stock markets. But since the strategy for this type of PE investor is focused on value preservation and especially on *value extraction based on that cash flow*, it felt right to name it "value investing." This will likely seem an even more fitting description when we get to discussions of how value investors often use leverage, related entities and rebate-paying suppliers, and other tactics and profit pools to pull cash out.

> While financial engineering tactics may be used in growth investing (depending on the size and cash flow of the portfolio company), growth investors primarily bet on operational improvements and aggressive expansion to drive a lift in enterprise value and thus create a strong return on investment. In contrast, value investors in franchising are much more likely to make financial engineering part of their core investment strategy in addition to operational improvements. They bet on cash flow preservation, stability, efficiencies, optimization, and gradual brand expansion, and steady rather than fast outlet growth.

A good example is Sycamore Partners' June 2022 acquisition of the Goddard School. Goddard's prior owner was Wind River Holdings LP, a family office. Over 20 years, Wind River carefully nurtured steady system growth, expanded the system footprint from 100 schools to nearly 600, and built one of the most respected brands in early childhood education.

Sycamore is a specialist in retail and consumer investments, including distressed brands purchased out of bankruptcy.[6] Sycamore is also known for its aggressive use of leverage.[7] For Sycamore, Goddard's continued promise provides diversity and stability within Sycamore's portfolio. The acquisition wasn't cheap, coming in (according to Goddard's 2023 franchise disclosure document, or FDD) at $1.092 billion. Sycamore's likely expectation is that Goddard will continue to grow incrementally, so Sycamore will benefit from holding a solid brand with dedicated customers, a stable franchisee base, and especially Goddard's *strong cash flow* to support leverage. Sure enough, shortly after Sycamore acquired Goddard, it put $427 million of debt on the business[8] and later that year paid out distributions of $403 million.[9] (Leverage will be discussed again in Chapter 16.)

Here are some qualities that attract franchise value investors:

- *big* cash flow
- proven operating model
- stable franchise system, low franchisee turnover
- significant scale or footprint
- excellent brand, well established
- differentiated customer value proposition, defensible market position
- continued growth prospects; doesn't need to be fast growing, but steady
- backable management team
- significant runway in the business without need for extensive capital investment to maintain strong operating cash flow
- opportunity to capture additional upside, such as through better supply chain management, launching new products or services, and so on

It should also be noted that by this stage in the franchise's life cycle, founding families have often exited if PE was involved earlier, during the faster growth phase, and especially if the business has traded several times. Daily management of the business transitions to a professional management team reporting to a PE-controlled board of directors. Franchisees may feel a shift in corporate culture as the founding family or team's influence dissipates across changes in ownership. This may be good, bad, or neutral depending on the system and individual franchisee opinions about these changes (some culture changes are positive).

The greatest risks of value investing in franchising come from taking PE's playbook itself too far. If owners focus too much on value extraction for themselves and not enough on protecting franchisee (outlet-level) profitability and the future of the brand via ongoing investments in keeping the brand relevant, a stall-out can occur. To the extent that publicly traded franchises start to act like value investors, the same disconnect can occur (e.g., using cash for stock buybacks to boost the stock price instead of brand longevity projects like R&D, product innovation, or brand-level marketing initiatives).

It is often at this stage (if it hasn't happened already) that modifications are rolled out via adjustments to the operating manual and/or as a condition of renewal, such as adding mandated new suppliers. Sometimes this is meant to take advantage of group purchasing discounts. In other cases the main purpose is to drive new profit pools for the corporate parent via rebates on total spend. Again, how this is perceived by franchisees depends on the circumstances and level of transparency the corporate parent undertakes to share the rationale for changes and what rebate money will be spent on, whether franchisees are included in decision-making, and whether pricing for new mandated suppliers is market-competitive. But it is clear that the gradual transition of brands into the hands of value-focused owners creates predictable tension points.

Now we'll turn to the bravest franchise investors of all—turnaround investors.

Turnaround Investors in Franchising: *Reengage and Reinvent*

Financial engineering can't fix fundamentally broken franchise models or troubled franchisor-franchisee relationships. Those situations may require rethinking the entire operating model, making sometimes significant investments in refreshing the customer value proposition, potentially educating an entirely new base of customers about the brand, making technology upgrades, and so on. On the franchisee side, there must also be acknowledgment that prior ways of doing business are no longer a fit and that unit-level investment in refreshes, remodeling, or technology may be needed as part of the reboot effort.

Typical private equity restructuring tactics (such as layoffs or moving production to low-cost markets) often aren't available in franchise businesses because franchising is an "asset light" model (unless there are corporate units or real estate). It takes time to build franchisee trust and buy-in for the turnaround plan, even longer for the fruits of that plan to show up at the unit level, and yet more time for franchisees' renewed faith to translate into positive validation and new commitments for expansion.

> Distressed franchises are incredibly difficult to turn around at the franchisor or brand level, even when liabilities have been shed via the bankruptcy process. Some turnaround projects have proven to be more than their PE investors bargained for, accounting for at least some of the missteps observed over PE's history of franchise investing.

You can't force existing franchisees to grow or to validate well to prospective franchisees. Franchisees decide whether, or how much, they will comply with new directives; whether they will agitate if they don't like change; or whether they will choose to add new units or even vote with their feet and leave the system. Even when franchisees have development agreements, they can slow-roll new site commitments, argue about site suitability, or otherwise delay new lease signings. If the brand takes those unfulfilled agreements back, and no one else is clamoring to buy them, the stall-out hasn't been fixed. The franchisor's development department can end up twisted into frustrated knots.

In addition to growth challenges, refreshes can be an especially fractious topic. Renewal and transfer approvals, especially in legacy systems, run into this remodeling and capex (capital expenditure) issue all the time. It's a top franchisee pain point, especially in systems with expensive real estate requirements, technology investments, or ongoing maintenance expenses, such as hotels and restaurants. Franchisors sometimes create friction by trying to implement new expenses or compliance requirements and by changing operating manuals without gathering franchisee feedback, considering feasibility, or protecting outlet profitability. Overly aggressive tactics by the franchisor when dealing with franchisees or tone-deaf communication strategies can lead to franchisee discontent and further turnaround delays.

This isn't just a PE issue. Independent and publicly traded franchises, especially large legacy brands, can find themselves facing the same difficulties. As Jonathan Maze, editor in chief of *Restaurant Business* puts it,[10]

> At least once every decade, some of these large brands decide to go after underperforming franchisees. They try to consolidate the system under better-performing operators and push their franchisees to reinvest in upgrades and refreshes. But the bad press and poor franchisee validation from these efforts make it harder to attract new franchisees into the system, so results often don't lift the overall business as much as hoped.

Whole-brand franchise transformations that rely only on replacing franchisees won't succeed. The reinvention must include significant changes and reinvestment at the corporate level. Franchisees must also be brought into decisions and their feedback gathered and acted on in a meaningful way. Successful franchise transformations thus depend as much on skillful change management as they do on specific reinvention, innovations around products and services, marketing, technology, and customer engagement.

Serious and widespread franchisee disagreement with management about the direction of the franchise, or concerns about unit profitability issues, can lock up a system of any size. Eroding franchisee trust makes even small attempts at change harder. Worse, if enough franchisees are frustrated and angry, or feel they don't have much to lose by speaking out, franchisees have proven that they can and will go nuclear with class-action lawsuits against the franchisor or leak their frustrations to the press. If investments in the future of the brand also lag thanks to short-term-minded ownership or too much debt, a stall-out could result.

But let's use caution here. Anecdotal franchisee discontent is not always a signal of widespread system weakness. Franchisees can have very different perspectives on the same issues. Some may be facing very different challenges than others. For example, the complaints of some disgruntled McDonald's (which is publicly traded) franchisees received press coverage in Q4 2022 and the first half of 2023 regarding proposed changes to renewal requirements and other issues. At the same time, system sales for Q4 2022 hit records and McDonald's stock by April 2023 was trading at record highs.[11]

Franchisee pushback isn't the issue in and of itself; sometimes you have to dig deeper to understand the real root of the problem. How widespread is the discontent? Is the independent franchisee association involved? Are franchisees returning to buy resales and expansion units, or are they closing and leaving the system? What are revenue and profitability trends? PE investors may not be discouraged if there are specific issues they can deal with to turn around lagging performance, but a true turnaround situation with widespread franchisee discontent and falling metrics across the board will usually turn PE buyers off. The majority will pass on turnaround projects unless that is their special area of expertise, with heavily discounted price expectations to match.

Unit turnarounds at the franchisee level *within otherwise strong systems* are much more common (with or without PE) and much less risky. You can replace an underperforming operator or move a location in an otherwise good concept and improve results. But whole-brand turnarounds in franchising are extremely difficult. Let's look at two short turnaround case studies, both Roark Capital Group–backed brands, by way of illustration.

CASE STUDY: CARVEL AND ROARK CAPITAL GROUP

Roark's first franchise investment was to acquire Carvel in 2001 for $26 million.[12] This represented a significant "down round" for Carvel, given that the prior owner had paid $80 million in 1989. The Carvel system faced known challenges. Store count had dropped from almost 800 in 1985 to around 400, but the company was distributing ice-cream cakes in more than 5,000 supermarkets. Franchisees were reportedly unhappy about the entrance into grocery and what they felt was a lack of innovation. Roark's founder Neal Aronson had big growth ambitions for the brand. When interviewed at the time of the acquisition, Mr. Aronson cited many expansion objectives and a plan to put significant resources into creating national scale.[13]

Roark stabilized Carvel and improved franchisee relationships. At the end of 2022, Carvel had 326 us franchised locations, 1 co-location, and 30 outlets outside the us. This is down 11 percent since the acquisition and down 56 percent from Carvel's peak. Carvel has instead expanded into more than 8,500 supermarkets (up 70 percent since the acquisition, ironic given original franchisee concerns).

Carvel showcases the risk (changing market and competition) and sometimes necessary recalibration (of distribution strategy) required for successful long-hold franchise investing. Franchising is at its core both a growth and *distribution* model. Sometimes changing market conditions require new channels and strategies. There are now more than 100 frozen treat, bakery, and similar franchise concepts in the us alone.[14] Many quick service restaurants, smoothie concepts, and others have added frozen treats. Consumers today have different dining and grocery shopping habits. Demographics have shifted.

Sometimes franchise units need to close in favor of other distribution outlets or move to different locations. Franchise critics may see unit closures as always "bad." But reality is often more nuanced, especially for legacy franchise brands. It is true that some franchisees just aren't a fit and need to exit or that some locations need to close based on changing market conditions. But Carvel provides an example of how optimizing outcomes at the brand level may also include expanding through nonfranchise distribution channels as competition, and especially customer buying habits, change.

It's also important to note that although the number of Carvel franchise units has declined, the investment appears to have returned very well for Roark through grocery expansion, operating cash flow, fees, and dividend recapitalizations or royalty-stream securitizations taken over the years. Carvel's financials are now consolidated under Focus Brands. Even during the pandemic year of 2020, Focus Brands kicked off $66 million in net cash from operating activities and had $852 million of long-term debt.[15] Net parent distributions in 2020 were $180 million. In the year ending December 25, 2022, total long-term debt was $1.175 billion, and the parent was paid a cash distribution of $541 million.[16] Management fees paid between 2020 and 2022 were $131 million.[17]

It is also worth mentioning that Focus Brands is currently pursuing a multiyear transformation effort that is already appearing to show results. Across the Focus Brands portfolio (Auntie Anne's, Carvel, Cinnabon, Jamba, McAlister's, Moe's, and Schlotzsky's), more than 650 license agreements were signed, and 400 new units were opened in 2022.[18] Carvel's 2023 FDD shows Carvel expects to open 14 units in 2023 and has a sold-not-open funnel of 88 units. This is up from a funnel of 76 units as of December 31, 2020.[19] At the end of the day, what franchisees want most from PE sponsors is proactive management of portfolio brands to ensure long-term stability and good earning potential for franchisees.

CASE STUDY: ARBY'S AND ROARK CAPITAL GROUP

Roark's experience trying to turn Arby's around is another good example of how difficult franchise turnarounds can be. By 2010 Arby's was in distress, and its poor performance was also noted by numerous restaurant analysts and journalists. One even called Arby's performance the worst in the history of the modern restaurant industry.[20] The brand was suffering from the poor economy and low customer ratings, was losing to stronger value-based competitors such as McDonald's, and was struggling under its then owner, Wendy's.[21] Some franchisees, including large MUOs, declared bankruptcy.

Roark acquired a majority share of Arby's when the system had 3,600 units[22] and brought in a well-respected CEO, Paul Brown. Arby's concept development added new menu items that reinforced Arby's meat specialty to give customers a new reason to engage with the brand. Brown refocused the company on this unique appeal (roast beef) and launched a catchy new national ad campaign ("We Have the Meats") to succinctly capture that differentiation and drive customer traffic. Store designs were refreshed. Brown spent time in front of workers and franchisees to rebuild relationships and improve communications.[23]

Arby's unit-level profitability has improved under Roark. Average unit volumes grew from $868,000 in 2011 to $1.308 million in 2021. Franchisee EBITDAR (cash flow prior to interest, taxes, depreciation, amortization and before paying rent) grew from $161,000 to $294,000 per unit.[24] Yet despite repositioning the brand and improving unit profitability, the number of outlets has declined. From 3,600 units in 2011, in 2023 Arby's had more than 3,500 locations in nine countries.[25] Unless a market is completely saturated, the best signal of turnaround success is when existing and new franchisees start adding new units again. At least for now, it appears the turnaround hasn't resulted in franchisees choosing to invest more to add new outlets.

It is also worth pointing out that some franchise turnaround and failure situations that make headlines today are in fact a hangover from bad decisions by prior owners. These were attempted turnaround projects that never actually turned or brands that *became* turnaround projects under former owners. PE sponsors of known turnarounds who are not aggressive enough with their revitalization agenda, especially if coupled with heavy debt put on the business, are often doomed to fail from the start. Frankly, it seems Big Money should know better. Checkers/Rally's is a good example of a brand that has, unfortunately, landed here.

CASE STUDY: CHECKERS/RALLY'S

After about 15 years as a publicly traded company, Checkers was taken private by Wellspring Capital Management LLC in 2006 in a $188 million deal.[26] Wellspring held Checkers/Rally's for many years and tried to sell it in 2012.[27] Ultimately, the company was sold to Sentinel Capital Partners in 2014. Sentinel then sold Checkers/Rally's to Oak Hill Capital Partners IV LP in 2017 for $525 million when it had 840 locations. Interestingly, the company only added 68 locations under Sentinel's ownership. And the sale transaction added $280 million of debt, according to Checkers's FDD.[28] Sales fell after the acquisition, and ratings agencies downgraded the company. By mid-2023, Oak Hill ceded control to its lenders, Arbour Lane Capital Management, Garnett Station Partners, and Guggenheim Investments, in order to avoid bankruptcy.[29]

DISCLOSURE RISK

One final note on franchise turnarounds. Franchisors and their private equity owners have been sued for not disclosing the full extent of a turnaround situation to prospective and current franchisees. This disclosure risk creates another barrier blocking greater PE interest to take on franchise turnarounds. This is yet another reason you don't want your brand to land here. It's much harder to attract outside capital to help dig you out of whatever hole you're in!

For example, in 2015, when North Castle was looking for a path forward for its struggling Curves franchise, it did what PE often does—it paid a consultant (in this case Parthenon EY, a subsidiary of Ernst & Young) to conduct a study. The consultant's report indicated that Curves had a so-called negative halo and estimated that 15 percent of locations would close each year if no action was taken.[30] This seems like a due diligence miss as North Castle surely would have benefited from knowing this information *before* investing. And it got worse. A group of franchisees later sued. According to the lawsuit, the company did not disclose the dire situation as outlined in the report to existing franchisees or disclose the information to prospective franchisees in the franchise disclosure document while continuing to market and sell franchise license agreements.

Failed turnarounds, owner missteps, and lack of communication with franchisees can create bad optics that go far beyond a single troubled brand. For example, US senator Catherine Cortez Masto (Nevada) cited the Curves lawsuit in an April 2021 report urging stricter franchise regulation, enforcement, and penalties.[31] The legitimacy of the entire franchise model can be questioned when brands stall or turnarounds fail, in what amounts to whole-sector gaslighting. This ignores all the other brands running strong systems. Similarly, PE mistakes and failed turnarounds create negative optics for PE generally as effective franchise brand stewards, even when the majority have moved their portfolio companies forward. Either way, the risks and extended timeline involved ensure most PE firms won't consider franchise turnarounds.

> Once a franchise system is in distress, only the hard work of investing back into the brand, rebuilding or reinventing both the customer and franchisee value propositions, consolidating what's left of the system under the best possible operators, and rebuilding franchisee trust will turn the brand around. That's a massive, expensive, multiyear undertaking with one big unknown—whether franchisees will ever get on board.

▼

What does private equity's franchising investment history reveal? What was the key tipping point that encouraged PE to enter franchising in the first place? It's an American business story that is fascinating, layered, and at times sensational.

CHAPTER 4

The Parallel Tracks of Private Equity and Franchising: Where It All Began

"We didn't start out to create an industry, we just wanted to buy companies and make them better."

—**HENRY KRAVIS**, co-founder and co-executive chairman of KKR[1]

DESPITE THE NATURAL SYNERGIES between private equity and franchising, it is still a fairly new relationship. Business-format franchising as we know it has been around for more than 100 years, but PE only came on the franchise scene starting around the 1990s with accelerating activity relatively recently.

> Franchising achieved tremendous success and scale decades before private equity itself became an industry.

What happened to galvanize PE activity in franchising in the first place? To understand the initial spark of PE's attraction to the franchising model and how the relationship evolved over time, I find it useful to break down the history of modern franchising into distinct "generations":

- ▶ Franchise Generation 1.0: 1920 to 1960—early years
- ▶ Franchise Generation 2.0: 1961 to 1990—pre-PE
- ▶ Franchise Generation 3.0: 1991 to 2019—post-PE
- ▶ Franchise Generation 4.0: 2020 forward—post-pandemic

FRANCHISING SHOWED TREMENDOUS EARLY PROMISE

Where did franchising begin? There have been land-usage "franchise-style" agreements going back hundreds of years. Benjamin Franklin offered what was technically a "co-partnership" agreement in 1731 to establish printing houses, and in the 1860s, Albert Singer used a "franchise-type" contract to expand the sale of his sewing machines. The first true business-format franchise was a network of beauty shops, created in 1888 by Martha Matilda Harper. She provided training and branded products and grew her salon network to 500 shops by the mid-1920s.[2]

But the origins of modern business-format franchise brands, some of which are still around today, began with a few concepts in the 1920s and blossomed from there. Early visionary companies that started franchising their operating concepts between the 1920s and the 1960s created the first sustained wave of franchise adoption.[3] I think of this as "Franchise Generation 1.0," a.k.a. "the early years." The idea of using a consistent business format and brand to open multiple outlets via a network of individual license partners was both appealing and practical. The model then enjoyed decades of favorable tailwinds thanks to several waves of economic expansion, a post–World War II population boom, growth of the suburbs, more dual-income households and America's increasingly car-centric society, as well as ongoing demand for entrepreneurial opportunities.

The number of franchise concepts grew as companies realized the power of the franchise distribution model to build scale. Following are just a few examples of recognized brands today that started to franchise their business concepts between 1920 and 1960, organized by when those brands first began to franchise (according to the company websites):[4]

A&W (1926)	Dairy Queen (1943)
Maid-Rite (1927)	Duraclean (1945)
Howard Johnson (1935)	Carvel (1947)
Arthur Murray Dance Studios (1939)	Baskin-Robbins (1948)

Martinizing (1949)	H&R Block (1956)
Kentucky Fried Chicken (1952)	MIDAS (Muffler Installation Dealers
Holiday Inn (1954)	Association) (1956)
Burger King (1954)	Spherion Staffing (1956)
Avis (1955)	Terminix Termite and Pest Control (1957)
Dunkin' Donuts (1955)	International House of Pancakes (1960)
McDonald's (1955)	

Franchising demonstrated its suitability as an effective growth and distribution model for many different types of businesses. Entrepreneurial brand founders partnered with individual franchisee entrepreneurs to expand.

> From the very beginning, a *mutually beneficial franchisor-franchisee relationship* was the core success component underpinning the entire franchise model.

Many concept founders and franchisees alike self-funded, got help from friends and family, or relied on their own local banking relationships to start or expand their franchise businesses. This "bootstrap" entrepreneurial image of franchising persists today, and in many cases it is still representative of franchise businesses. It remains difficult for many independent small businesses to find adequate start-up and expansion capital.

RAISING CAPITAL: PRIVATE EQUITY'S EARLY DAYS

Private investments in business ventures are "as old as capitalism."[5] In the early 20th century, wealthy individuals and merchant bankers sometimes stepped into distressed businesses or good buyout opportunities. For example, J. P. Morgan (the man, not the bank) bought out Carnegie Steel in 1901.[6] One of the buyout recipients used the proceeds to start an early family office, Bessemer Trust, which is still investing today.[7] Henry Ford completed a shareholder buyout to gain control of Ford Motor in 1919.[8] During this period, ongoing consolidation created a high volume of mergers and acquisitions (M&A) activity, rather than private investments. From 1895 to 1920, an average of 186 US companies each year were absorbed via mergers.[9]

Two companies founded in 1946, American Research and Development and J.H. Whitney & Company, were among the first US private equity firms to raise outside capital to make investments. Another early entrant was Industrial and Commercial Finance Corporation in the UK, founded in 1945 by the Bank of England and others to provide funds for small and medium-size businesses. Shareholder banks let the corporation raise external funds starting in 1959.[10] These and other early participants completed a few buyouts in the 1950s and 1960s.

But the private equity industry we know today was strongly influenced by a small group of visionary financiers such as Jerome Kohlberg, Jr., Henry Kravis, and George Roberts. These PE trailblazers saw acquisition opportunities in successful businesses whose founders were set to retire. This key insight was combined with a differentiated acquisition approach—namely, a more aggressive use of debt than had been common up to that time.[11] Kohlberg, Kravis, and Roberts together completed a series of buyouts from 1965 to 1975 while at Bear Stearns. In 1976, the trio left to form their own buyout firm (Kohlberg Kravis Roberts & Co., later known as KKR) with $120,000 of start-up capital.[12]

Another early visionary who started in this period was Thomas H. Lee, who founded Thomas H. Lee Partners LP in 1974 and became a prolific restaurant investor. Other financiers began raising their own funds and acquiring companies. Examples of other early PE firms include Deutsche Beteiligungsgesellschaft mbH (Germany, 1965),[13] Warburg Pincus (1966),[14] TA Associates (1968),[15] Quilvest Capital Partners (PE investor since 1972, family investor since 1888, starting in Paris),[16] Cinven (European buyout fund, 1977, raised first independent fund in 1996),[17] Forstmann Little & Company (1978),[18] Clayton, Dubilier & Rice (1978),[19] and Candover (European buyout fund, 1980).[20]

PARALLEL EXPANSION PATHS

While the PE industry was in its embryonic phase, franchising continued its rapid expansion from the seeds planted by the early visionaries.

> In 1950, there were fewer than 100 business-format franchises. By 1960, more than 900 companies had operations involving 200,000 franchised outlets.[21]

The list of now-familiar franchise names continued to grow, including Pizza Hut, Marriott, Roto-Rooter, 7-Eleven/Southland, Dunhill Personnel, Wendy's, Pearle Vision, Orange Julius, Tastee Freeze, and Sheraton, just to name a few.[22]

This is the start of "Franchise Generation 2.0," a.k.a. "pre-private equity," the period in which private equity firms themselves got off the ground but hadn't yet discovered franchising. This period stretched from 1961 to around 1990. The second generation was marked by franchising's rapid growth, international expansion, clarification around certain franchise rules, and a significant number of franchise public offerings. This period also saw the first big wave of intergenerational transfers of franchise businesses from parents to adult children, demonstrating franchising's resilience and long-term potential. The influence of "founding families" and "early adopters" on the cultures within some franchise systems solidified as the second generation of franchisee operators took over. This "values ballast" provided an important common reference point as franchise systems navigated changing times, evolving customer habits and preferences, and continued growth across decades. These relationships, voices, brand values, and associated institutional memories would become a factor once PE entered these brand systems—but that was still years away.

As the sector matured, franchisors began taking their companies public to raise capital for further expansion. Examples of early franchise public offerings include Holiday Inn (1957), International House of Pancakes (1961 offering, IPO on NASDAQ 1991), H&R Block (1962), ServiceMaster

(1962), McDonald's (1965, NYSE 1978), Kentucky Fried Chicken (1966), Dunkin' Donuts (1968), Denny's (1968), Taco Bell (1970), FotoMat (1971),[23] Southland (renamed 7-Eleven [public offering 1968, NYSE 1972]),[24] Pizza Hut (1972), Wendy's (1976), and Century 21 Real Estate (1977).

> Before the first private equity firms even emerged, US franchising already had created dozens of familiar household names with large footprints. Many franchise systems had also by then raised expansion capital by going public, creating a new cohort of franchise millionaires.

To be successful, franchise businesses must protect brand consistency and quality for the good of the entire system. As franchising continued to grow, questions about how various regulations applied or did not apply to franchising needed to be addressed—for example, whether franchising mechanisms, such as controlling brand standards or requiring franchisees to make certain purchases, violated antitrust laws. Several legal challenges to the franchise business model during Franchise Generation 2.0, including a landmark case involving Carvel ice cream franchisees in 1964, confirmed the basic structure of the franchise model, acknowledging that these types of brand controls and operating standards are both legitimate and necessary to a business model like franchising. Later, in 1980, the courts rejected an antitrust challenge related to franchise controls in the McDonald's system.[25] These decisions set the stage for even further franchise expansion.

Despite these legal clarifications about the legitimacy of the franchise model itself, by the 1960s and 1970s, franchising's growth also attracted some bad actors under the pretext of franchising. To an unsuspecting potential buyer, there were on offer nonfranchises pretending to be franchises, unproven franchise models, and unsubstantiated earnings claims. Bad actors eventually generated enough franchisee complaints that the Federal Trade Commission responded with the Franchise Act of 1979. Also known within franchising as *The Franchise Rule*, it required certain presale disclosures by franchisors and clarified what representations about earnings potential franchisors could and could not make.

Some states created their own franchise rules. In 1970, California was the first state to regulate the sale of franchises.[26] State-level regulations continue to be revised today, with additional stipulations around presale disclosures, terminations, transfers, and other matters. While at times complex to navigate, these rules of engagement ultimately solidified the franchise model, contributing to franchising's continued growth and importance as an engine of new business and job creation.

Just as key regulatory decisions supported and legitimized franchising, private equity also got a boost around this same time. Changes to the tax code made leveraged acquisitions more attractive thanks to interest write-offs to reduce taxes.[27] Junk bonds came into use during this period as well, helping to facilitate larger buyouts.

Private equity then received extra gas in its engine, thanks to changing rules related to pension fund investments. In 1974, the Employee Retirement Income Security Act was adopted. This act prohibited corporate pension funds from holding certain types of investments in their portfolio, including private equity. Not surprisingly, PE fundraising fell in 1975 to $10 million. It wasn't until the rules were later relaxed in 1978 that pension funds started pouring money into private equity.[28] *Time* magazine reported that PE raised $39 million in 1977, but only a year later, in 1978, that figure increased to $570 million.[29] Today, nearly 88 percent of public pensions in the US (representing more than 34 million Americans) have some exposure to private equity,[30] and PE investments make up 13 percent of public pension portfolios. Total US pension assets invested in PE funds reached a high of $500 billion for fiscal 2021, according to the Boston College Center for Retirement Research,[31] up from $300 billion in 2018.[32]

As the money rolled into PE funds and junk bonds enabled the use of more debt in transactions, leveraged buyouts took off. More than $1.3 trillion of assets traded hands, and 28 percent of the largest 500 companies (Fortune 500) in the US were acquired between 1980 and 1989.[33] More than 2,000 leveraged buyout transactions took place.[34] Yet most leveraged buyouts and PE investing activity still remained outside franchising.

Market turbulence in the late 1980s and early 1990s as well as some bank-ruptcies (in some cases related to below investment grade bonds, a.k.a. "junk bonds") then temporarily chilled most M&A dealmaking. Public-to-private deals also dried up in the early 1990s.[35]

FRANCHISING: NOT JUST A US PHENOMENON

All the while, franchising continued to grow—one entrepreneur, one out-let, and one community at a time. Brands like McDonald's became ubiq-uitous. In 1980, there were 5,000 McDonald's outlets. Only seven years later, there were 10,000.[36] US franchising also proved it could take brands into international markets.* And this international expansion wasn't just a US phenomenon. Homegrown franchise concepts were launched in other countries and started their own global expansion. For example, Kumon (Japan) started franchising education centers in 1958 and added its first overseas expansion unit (in New York) in 1974.[37] Jollibee (Philippines) was founded in 1975, started franchising its restaurants in 1979, and began expanding outside the Philippines in the mid-1980s.[38] Tim Hortons (Canada) started franchising its coffeehouses in 1964 and began expand-ing internationally in 1984, first to the US.[39]

New franchise brand entrants continued to emerge and expand as part of Franchise Generation 2.0, thanks in part to the previously mentioned changes to franchise disclosure rules. These rules leveled the playing field and encouraged new entrants who could now launch and market their novel franchise concepts just as the larger, more established brands had decades earlier.

---

* Examples of US franchise brands expanding into other markets during this period include Kentucky Fried Chicken (Britain, Jamaica, and Mexico, mid-1960s), McDonald's (Canada and Puerto Rico, 1967), Holiday Inn (Netherlands, 1967), Pizza Hut (Canada, 1967; Australia and Europe, 1971; Hong Kong, 1981), Wendy's (Canada, 1975), and Domino's (Canada and Australia, 1983). See company websites for more history.

An eager crowd of displaced workers was looking for fresh opportunities at just this juncture. Due to a wave of corporate and manufacturing layoffs between 1979 and 1995, 43 million jobs were lost[40] (ironically, some via PE-led leveraged buyouts in other sectors). Many of these would-be entrepreneurs began to consider franchise business ownership as their next move. Each success got noticed and in turn encouraged other would-be entrepreneurs to look at franchising as a wealth creation opportunity. This growing awareness often happened at the grassroots level, as people noticed neighbors, colleagues, and family members getting into franchising.

> Recall that Franchise Generation 1.0 ended in 1960 with 900 franchises in the US and around 200,000 outlets. By the end of Franchise Generation 2.0 in 1990, there were more than 3,000 franchises representing more than 450,000 franchised outlets across a range of investment levels and sectors.[41] Franchising got off the ground without private equity's help in Generation 1.0. Likewise, Generation 2.0, characterized by explosive growth, also expanded without PE assistance.

Franchise M&A popped up intermittently during the late 1980s and mid-1990s. For example, Sonic's management completed a $10 million buyout in 1986.[42] Bahraini investment bank Investcorp purchased Carvel in 1989 for $80 million.[43] There were also acquisitions by strategic buyers to augment their product and service portfolio. For example, PepsiCo purchased Pizza Hut (1977), Taco Bell (1978), and KFC (1986).[44]

Perhaps the best signal of what was to come was found in the hotel sector. For example, Neal Aronson founded US Franchise Systems in 1995 and built the company over five years to become the 10th-largest multi-brand hotel company in the US, with 1,100 hotels open or under development across all 50 states and five countries.[45] Reportedly, when US Franchise Systems was sold to the Pritzker family in 2000,[46] it delivered a return of 5.5 times (also expressed as 5.5×) the original investment.[47] Aronson would go on to found Roark Capital Group in 2001. Roark would later become one of the most prolific and influential PE investors in franchising.

▼

Despite franchising's fast expansion, increasing visibility, success raising funds in public markets, and steady royalty cash flow that would eventually attract PE's attention, at this stage franchising still wasn't broadly on private equity's radar.

Until suddenly it was.

CHAPTER 5

Family Pizza Night Looks Like a Pile of Cash: Private Equity Discovers Franchising

Was there a dramatic moment that caused a change in franchising? As Malcom Gladwell points out in *The Tipping Point: How Little Things Can Make a Big Difference*,[1] big changes in our modern world can follow from small events. Suddenly all those small changes add up.

SUCCESS OFTEN BREEDS IMITATORS and fast followers. PE firms have the capital and investment mandate that drives them to pile into entire sectors seemingly overnight—especially after early investors demonstrate success. That's exactly what happened in franchising.

> At this stage "Franchise Generation 3.0," a.k.a. "post-PE," began, and it stretched from around 1991 to 2019. This era was marked by dramatic changes in technology, franchising's proven resilience through several recessions,[2] another wave of intergenerational business transfers, and most importantly, the entrance of private equity investors into franchising. PE's learnings during its earliest days entering franchising continue to impact PE investing strategies today.

What tipped franchising into PE's sights? The first major wave of PE investment in franchising was marked by the following activity:

Early entrants arrived and placed some bets. In retrospect, you can imagine a few prescient heads turning nearly in unison, as if on a giant swivel, to suddenly "see" franchising. But at the time, the participants likely didn't view themselves at the crest of the coming wave. The franchise sector was largely out of the trading frenzy throughout the 1980s.[3] Starting in the mid-1990s, a few PE firms, especially those with visibility to retail businesses and shopping malls, started to dip their toes into franchising. For example, Catterton Partners along with a consortium of others invested in Baja Fresh (1998),[4] Argosy Private Equity invested in American Huts, a 95-unit Pizza Hut operator (1998),[5] American Securities Capital Partners bought the struggling El Pollo Loco from Advantica Restaurant Group (1999),[6] and Gemini Investors bought Buffalo Wild Wings (1999).[7]

Three mega-deals created significant visibility. At the end of the heady leveraged buyout era, three mega-acquisition deals led by Bain Capital—Domino's Pizza (1998), Burger King (2002), and Dunkin' Brands (2006)—elevated the entire franchise category's attractiveness and visibility to other PE firms. There was nothing subtle about these three deals. Bain's $1.1 billion buyout of Domino's Pizza created significant market attention in December 1998. Then Bain Capital, Goldman Sachs Private Capital, and Texas Pacific Group teamed up to purchase Burger King for $1.5 billion in 2002,[8] putting down only 14 percent of the purchase price, or $210 million.[9] But the dealmaking community was even more inspired by Bain's reported 500 percent payback on its modest $385 million initial investment when it took Domino's public in 2004. Bain would take out other distributions from the Domino's business in various chunks, including a 2003 refinancing, proceeds from the 2004 IPO, and what the press dubbed a "monster" dividend of $897 million in 2007.[10] (The use of debt will be discussed in Chapter 16.)

Bain, Goldman Sachs Private Capital, and Texas Pacific Group then successfully pulled off a reinvigoration at Burger King that enabled a public offering in 2006. After initially paying only five times EBITDA in 2002 for the troubled company,[11] the IPO raised $425 million.* But that was after the PE investors had taken out more than $800 million in dividends and fees, including a $367 million dividend paid right before the IPO, funded with $350 million in new debt. The investors retained a stake in the company and sold their shares over time, netting an *additional* estimated $900 million.[12] Also in 2006, Dunkin' Brands was acquired by Bain, the Carlyle Group, and Thomas H. Lee Partners for $2.425 billion in another high-profile deal.[13] Debt from the acquisition was refinanced in 2010 and total debt climbed to $1.87 billion,[14] while the PE owners soon took out an attention-grabbing $500 million dividend.[15]

The tech bubble and junk bond markets burst. Keep in mind that many investors of all types took a real shellacking when (1) the technology and telecom bubble burst from 2000 to 2002, and (2) bankruptcies related to junk bonds created a wrenching downstream impact in other sectors, such as retail. So, high-profile paydays like the three previously mentioned Bain deals got attention in part due to their sharp contrast with more negative market stories.

Going private had new appeal. PE also benefited from reforms put in place after scandals in publicly traded firms such as Worldcom and Enron. The Public Company Accounting Reform and Investor Protection Act of 2002 (known as "Sarbanes-Oxley") put stringent new regulations and reporting requirements on publicly traded companies. This had the effect of driving some public companies to consider going private with PE's help. As Dina Dwyer-Owens, at the time chair of the Dwyer Group, explained in a 2003 interview about the decision to take the Dwyer Group private with the help of PE firm the Riverside Company.[16]

---

* This represented quite a turnaround in circumstances for the company. When Burger King was acquired from Diageo in 2002 for $1.5 billion, Diageo itself had to guarantee $850 million of debt because Burger King had been struggling. (See Rachel Stevenson, "Diageo Guarantees $850M Loan to Secure Burger King Sale," *The Independent* [UK], December 14, 2002, https://www.independent.co.uk/news/business/news/diageo-guarantees-850m-loan-to-secure-burger-king-sale-135997.html.) The investors put significant effort into turning around the business and as a result were able to bring Burger King to the public market only four years later.

It's become harder and harder to be a publicly traded company. We're fairly small in the scheme of public companies, so going public just didn't afford us the opportunities we were hoping for. We were producing the earnings results that the market kept telling us to produce, yet the stock wasn't getting the value we would have hoped for. And it's difficult to raise money when your stock's not performing at the level you'd like it to. We decided to simplify and focus on growing the business.

Remember that many franchise systems had long since gone public, creating an ample field of go-private opportunities for PE dealmakers to pursue. And for those companies no longer planning to go public, PE was well positioned to provide exits for early investors. Creative debt instruments encouraged deal activity and provided additional support for the PE investing model, at least in large companies where leverage could be applied.

Impressive multi-unit empires continued to be steadily built by expansion-minded franchisees. These were high-cash-flow businesses with strong growth prospects and lots of open space for further development. The operating models were easy to understand.

Two more high-profile PE moves received market attention. Two visionary PE firms, Levine Leichtman Capital Partners (LLCP) and Roark Capital Group, came on the franchise scene at this time. LLCP took Quiznos private in 2000 in a transaction that received significant press coverage.[17] Neal Aronson, coming off recent success exiting the US Franchise Systems Inc. hotel platform he built from 1995 to 2000, founded Roark Capital Group in 2001; that same year, Roark made its first franchise investment—Carvel. Roark was founded specifically to invest in franchise and multi-unit businesses, providing additional validation. Money continued pouring into PE. All that capital had to be deployed.

Meanwhile, franchising continued its steady global expansion. We can imagine that after the tech bubble burst, some previously favored companies suddenly looked like highly speculative investments compared to more straightforward franchise businesses like selling pizzas, cleaning carpets, or running fleets of pest control vans!

Thus, a confluence of factors conspired to make franchising suddenly both attractive and visible to PE dealmakers looking for new ideas. Together, these factors were the tipping point that changed franchising when private equity entered en masse.

> Private equity suddenly got it and realized that franchising was resilient, had many attractive attributes, and was largely untapped in terms of PE infiltration. PE was also in a critical position to provide capital and strategic support to help founders and multi-unit franchisees take their businesses to the next level.

EARLY AND DOMINANT PRIVATE EQUITY ENTRANTS INTO FRANCHISING

While Bain established an early high profile in the sector, some of the most active PE firms in franchising today made their first franchise investments early on during this Generation 3.0 period. The Riverside Company, Levine Leichtman Capital Partners, and Roark Capital Group created early and sustained leadership positions in franchise investing, albeit pursuing completely different franchise investing strategies at the bottom, middle, and top of the PE Profit Ladder respectively. (The deal ladder will be discussed in detail in Chapters 13 and 14. For now, recall our prior discussion about how PE firms exist along a spectrum of investing sizes and strategies.) Just these three firms now represent a quarter of known PE franchise investments at the franchisor level as of this writing: 186 of 700+ brands and counting.

More PE firms piled into franchising after the 2001 recession. A sample of this acquisition activity includes the following:

- ► Apollo Management: Sylvan Learning Systems Inc. (2003)
- ► Argosy Private Equity: AmBath / Re-Bath (2002)

► Argonne Capital Group: acquired 31 development rights and 35 existing units of IHOP's largest individual franchisee (2004)[18]

► Bain: Dunkin' Brands (2006)

► Banc Boston Capital[19] and Goldner Hawn Johnson & Morrison Inc.: took VICORP Restaurants private (franchisor of Baker's Square and Village Inn) in a $174 million deal (2001)[20]

► Brazos Private Equity Partners: Cheddar's (2003)[21]

► Brockway Moran & Partners: acquired units of Golds Gym (2003)

► Charlesbank Partners: Papa Murphy's (2004)

► Core Value Partners: Burger King, acquired 127 operating units out of bankruptcy from one of Burger King's then largest franchisees, AmeriKing (2003)

► Gemini Investors: Wingstop (2002)[22]

► Levine Leichtman Capital Partners: Cici's Pizza (2003)[23]

► The Riverside Company: The Dwyer Group (2003)

► Roark Capital Group: Carvel (2001), Money Mailer and FASTSIGNS (2003)

Next, private capital realized that a favorite PE strategy—platforming—worked well in franchising and had megawatt profit potential. PE would ultimately double down on establishing, and trading, franchise platforms. The significant growth of platforms and the consolidation of fragmented sectors has itself changed franchise competition.

PRIVATE EQUITY'S PLATFORM STRATEGY IS A STRONG FIT FOR FRANCHISING

Creating platforms and adding to them via tuck-in acquisitions are core PE investing strategies across industries. Early franchise platforms such as ServiceMaster and the Dwyer Group in the 1980s and 1990s proved that acquiring an anchor business and then adding highly accretive similar businesses (called "tuck-ins") to create a multi-brand platform serving a common customer base (a favorite PE strategy) worked well in a franchise business. This was another attractive attribute that encouraged more PE investments.

For example, one of the earliest thematic franchise platforms outside of restaurants was ServiceMaster. Founded in 1929, ServiceMaster started acquiring other home service brands in the 1980s, including Merry Maids (acquired in 1988 for $25 million),[24] Terminix (acquired in 1986 for $165 million),[25] TruGreen (acquired in 1999 for $250 million, spun out again in 2011),[26,27] and American Home Shield (acquired in 1989, later spun off).[28] ServiceMaster also acquired nonfranchise units (e.g., in the pest control sector), sometimes converting them to franchise operations. In 2007, PE firm Clayton, Dubilier & Rice acquired the entire ServiceMaster platform for $5.5 billion,[29] and later raised $610 million on the public market in 2014.[30] After spinning off some assets and acquiring additional brands, ServiceMaster (and several sub-brands) was itself then split off from the Terminix holdings[31] and sold to Roark Capital Group in 2020 for $1.5 billion.[32] ServiceMaster and the Dwyer Group helped inspire the creation of nearly two dozen other home services franchise platforms.

YUM Brands, which was created in a 1997 spin-off of restaurant assets from PepsiCo (after Pepsi got out of the restaurant business), was an early non-PE-backed multi-brand platform, demonstrating that PE weren't the only players riding this consolidation wave.[33] I will go through the math of "multiple arbitrage" in Chapter 14 so you can see the financial benefits of platforming from PE's perspective (and for any seller rolling equity forward). There are also back-office and supply chain synergies, as well as cross-marketing and sales opportunities at both the customer and franchise license sales levels. Multi-brand franchise platform creation and investing are broadly appealing to both financial and strategic investors.[34]

> To summarize, the period from the 1990s until around 2010 (roughly the first two-thirds of Franchise Generation 3.0) saw the first major wave of private equity investments in franchising, including large buyouts, public-to-private deals, consolidation of franchisee operating units, and the first big push into multi-brand platforming.

As PE investments in franchising became more numerous, so did their portfolio companies' focus on marketing and franchise sales. This touched off a mini-boom among franchise brokers, outsourced franchise sales organizations, lead generation, public relations, and marketing firms supporting both customer-facing and franchise sales marketing efforts. Emerging brands especially began experiencing higher franchise recruiting and start-up costs due to this consolidation around efficient platforms and PE-backed investments to push growth.

THE 2007-2009 FINANCIAL CRISIS AND RECOVERY

Market dislocations create acquisition and consolidation opportunities and that held true during the financial crisis, with a few private equity franchise acquisitions being completed. For example, in 2008, Sentinel Capital purchased 123 corporate-owned Pizza Hut restaurants,[35] and Roark acquired Primrose Schools.[36] But most PE interest in franchising temporarily cooled in that period, along with the market. Lender support was much harder to find. Pitchbook noted 50 franchise-related PE deals in 2007, but only 24 in 2008 and 11 in 2009. (Combined, these 85 deals represented $12.5 billion of transactions.)[37]

Eventually, the dealmaking hiatus was partially broken by the undeniable lure of franchising as an investing opportunity and also by a group of publicly traded franchise businesses going private. In 2010, 3G Capital took Burger King private for $3.3 billion in another high-profile transaction.[38] (Recall that Bain, Texas Pacific Group, and Goldman Sachs Private Capital had taken the company public just four years prior in 2006.)[39] Initial public offerings during this period were scarce. In 2008, there were only 29 total IPOS (none was a franchise business), a 49 percent volume drop from 2007.[40] However, starting in 2009, a wave of franchise IPOS caught the market's attention and signaled improving market optimism.

> As markets gradually recovered after the financial crisis, franchising was back on PE's radar, thanks in part to a fresh wave of franchise IPOs demonstrating ongoing market support for franchise businesses.

Several large franchise systems and even some large franchisee operators went public during this period and raised impressive amounts of
money despite the recent collapse of the housing and financial markets.
Here are a few examples:[41]

▶ Hyatt Hotels, 2009 IPO—raised $950 million (second-largest New York
  Stock Exchange IPO that year)[42]

▶ GNC Holdings LLC, 2011 IPO—raised $360 million in its third attempt at
  an IPO[43]

▶ Dunkin' Brands, 2011 IPO—raised $423 million[44]

▶ Arcos Dorados, 2012 IPO (large McDonald's franchisee; 1,970 units in 20 countries and territories)—raised $1.25 billion, 43 percent more than expected[45]

▶ Burger King returned to the New York Stock Exchange in 2012 via a reverse
  merger just two years after going private (as previously mentioned) via
  3G Capital[46]

▶ Potbelly, 2013 IPO—raised $105 million, shares rose 141 percent the first day[47]

▶ RE/MAX, 2013 IPO—raised $220 million, priced above target[48]

▶ Hilton Worldwide, 2013 public offering—raised $2.34 billion, the largest
  share sale by a hotel company up to that time;[49] this was even more than the
  $1.8 billion Twitter raised in its own November 2013 public offering[50]

The Hilton transaction was notable for its size and for the company's
growth under its new PE owner prior to going public. The positive press
attention for this and the above public offerings helped renew broader PE
interest in franchising.

Blackstone Group LP acquired Hilton in a 2007 leveraged buyout
and took it private for $26 billion. Of that, reportedly only $5.6 billion
was equity; the rest (78 percent) was debt.[51] Blackstone hired a new CEO,
Christopher Nassetta, invested in various successful growth initiatives, and
retired some debt. As Nassetta told a hospitality reporter about the management team's efforts together with PE owner Blackstone, the focus was
on transforming the business. It was a solid brand with global presence but
needed new energy and to refocus. The team relied on the brand's strong

culture and were able to get aligned around a purpose to accomplish great things as a team.[52]

This successful reinvigoration of the company allowed Hilton to go public again in 2013. Between 2015 and 2018, the stock price rose. Blackstone gradually sold its shares for a total profit of $14 billion, almost three times its original equity investment.[53]

Not all franchise IPOs during this period were acclaimed. In 2012, Bloomin' Brands (Outback Steakhouse, Carrabba's Italian Grill, and Bonefish Grill) had to cut both its offering price and number of shares offered in its IPO. After being acquired by Bain and Catterton Partners in 2007, by the time Bloomin' filed for its IPO, the company had $2.1 billion in debt. It hoped to raise $300 million to pay off $248 million in senior notes but raised only $161 million.[54] We will return to the use of debt in PE transactions in Chapter 16.

THE RISE OF THE PRIVATE EQUITY PROFIT LADDER: THE SECONDARY TRADING MARKET

Recovering franchise M&A activity after the financial crisis was enabled by gradually improving lender support and market optimism, successful franchise IPOs despite headwinds, low interest rates, and the fast-growing pool of private capital looking for a home. Franchise founders who wanted to exit were again courted by suitors eager to inject institutional capital into growth brands. But renewed market optimism also facilitated exits for PE investors who had bought in during the prior wave and now were ready to monetize those investments. The franchise secondary trading market gradually came together.

> Starting around 2010 as the deal market gradually improved, a wave of secondary trades of franchise businesses *between PE firms* was a critical new development. The prior major wave of PE investors needed an exit, while other firms were looking for companies to buy. The PE Profit Ladder was coming together with key players staking out their preferred rungs.

The rise of the secondary buyout (SBO), or secondary trading, market is critically important for PE investors. Greater exit certainty and more exit options reduces risk, supports higher acquisition prices, and provides a mechanism to return investor capital. It is much easier for PE to lean in a bit, if necessary, to get a deal done if an expanding list of "up-ladder" firms are looking for good buying opportunities. Brands can be grown and then traded to other firms who continue to grow these brands before they trade yet again.

Key roles along the ladder solidified as PE firms positioned their franchise portfolio companies for secondary deal exits to other PE firms, not just IPOs. For example, Gemini Investors' 2002 acquisition of Wingstop achieved a high-profile secondary transaction when it sold up-ladder to Roark in 2010. (Roark later took Wingstop public in 2015.) FASTSIGNS traded between Roark (2003), Levine Leichtman and LightBay Capital (2014), and Freeman & Spogli & Co. (2019). The SBO mechanism and related opportunities for sellers is covered in detail in Chapters 13 and 14.

▼

Along with the beginnings of the SBO market, outlet consolidation is another important development to discuss, a trend that picked up steam during Franchise Generation 3.0. Private equity has made an impact here too.

CHAPTER 6

Private Equity and Multi-unit Operators: "Small" Business Consolidates

"The baby boomer generation owns more businesses than any other generation ever in history...
and are selling off their established, successful small businesses at record rates. These businesses provide an unprecedented opportunity for acquisition entrepreneurs to focus on running, growing, and innovating a business immediately, all while enjoying a stability not found in startups."

—**WALKER DEIBEL**, *Buy Then Build: How Acquisition Entrepreneurs Outsmart the Startup Game*[1]

WE WILL RETURN SHORTLY to our timeline. It is worth pausing here to recognize that PE activity during Franchise Generation 3.0, from 1990 to 2019, also included significant investments at the *operator* (franchisee) *level*, not just at the brand (franchisor) level. This investing activity has significant implications for franchisees, and also for how franchising is generally perceived by the public and by lawmakers and regulators. Franchisees in particular need to understand and track PE investing activities within systems they are a part of (or are considering becoming a part of).

THE BIG SHIFT IN SMALL BUSINESS

Access to capital has always been critically important to franchising, which at its core is a growth and distribution model. Traditionally, multi-unit franchisees often expanded using cash flow from existing units to add more outlets, via either new site development or acquisitions from retiring franchisees. Local banking relationships also have been important enablers, although banking consolidation made getting access to expansion financing more challenging for many franchisees. But now PE is a major enabler of outlet consolidation. Remember that PE investors are not operators. PE backs or brings in proven management teams and then either finances the acquisition of existing units in the franchise system or pursues de novo (new) builds—or both.

> Private capital are active investors within some franchise systems at the outlet level. The secondary trading mechanism (trading assets between PE firms) also includes trading outlets in many of those same systems, partly contributing to consolidation under larger operators. This represents another significant shift in franchising.

Outlet consolidation often makes both financial and practical sense. There are scale efficiencies and better opportunities to retain key talent in larger organizations. While it is true that many franchise systems traditionally started as a collection of individual owner-operator outlets, the evolution is clearly in favor of multi-unit ownership and consolidation within systems over time, provided unit-level economics are attractive, of course. Large franchisee operators drive scale through operational excellence. Every task must be replicable, teachable, and delegated to frontline staff. This is exactly how the franchise model is supposed to be executed.

There are more multi-unit operators (MUOs) than ever before, and those operators are rapidly getting larger. This is evident today in franchise market data, according to FRANdata's 2022 *Multi-Unit Franchisee Buyer's Guide:*[2]

► Approximately 44,000 MUOs control more than half (54 percent) of all franchise units in the US and drive $200 billion in sales.

► Some sectors skew much higher. MUOs control 82 percent of all quick service restaurants, 78 percent of beauty-related franchise outlets, 70 percent of sit-down restaurants, and 53 percent of automotive franchise units in the US.

► While the average MUO owns 5.2 franchise locations, up from 4.8 in 2011, MUOs with more than 50 units jumped 114 percent from 2010 to 2020, making it the fastest-growing category of multi-unit franchisees.

► Eleven percent of MUOs diversify and become multi-*brand* operators.[*] Growth-minded franchisees are increasingly looking beyond their own system, and they have many options. Competition to attract and retain strong MUOs is fierce.

It is true that half of franchise outlets are still owned by "mom-and-pop" single-unit operators. Franchising provides business ownership opportunities otherwise unavailable to many first-time entrepreneurs. But franchise outlets are rapidly consolidating under operators who themselves are getting larger and larger and are often backed by private equity.

This consolidation trend was under way before PE came along, and it has only accelerated as PE investing activity in franchising has increased. Restaurants are an often-cited example, but this pattern is repeating in other sectors and within brands possessing strong unit-level economics and operating models suitable for consolidation with the help of a capital partner.

---

[*] The US is highly consolidated in terms of multi-unit franchisee ownership. This is partly due to PE's influence. To compare, after the US, India is the largest franchise market with 4,600 active franchisors. But India's 200,000 franchise outlets are owned by 170,000 franchisees, so most are single-unit owners. In New Zealand and Australia, two markets with the highest per capita number of franchise outlets, only approximately 15 percent of Australian franchise units are owned by multi-unit franchisees. New Zealand is more consolidated with MUOs reported in 70 percent of New Zealand franchise systems. But of those systems, half report that MUOs have five or fewer units. (Sources: Global Franchise, Franchising.com, Franchise Council of Australia, and Franchise New Zealand.)

This activity demonstrates two important points:

1   Private capital has become an important strategic option supporting growth at the franchisee level as well as at the brand level.
2   The unit-level value proposition in a growing number of franchises is strong enough to attract sophisticated PE investors—a positive trend.

PE's activity within the Planet Fitness franchise system provides a good non-restaurant example of consolidation happening at the franchisee level in high-quality systems with good unit-level economics. PE firm TSG Consumer Partners acquired the Planet Fitness system[3] for $505 million[4] at the end of 2012, when it had 618 locations.[5,6] Around the same time, other PE firms started gobbling up Planet Fitness operating units and then later began trading those consolidated holdings to other PE firms. Exaltare Capital Partners with support from Brightwood Capital Advisors LLC started by acquiring 15 clubs in 2012 and gradually added to their portfolio through both acquisitions and new club development.[7] The footprint grew to include more than 100 clubs before the outlets were sold in 2021[8] to Towerbrook Financial Partners.[9] JLM Financial Partners acquired 59 Planet Fitness locations in 2016 and grew the footprint to 160 locations before selling to American Securities in 2020.[10] Taymax (franchisee of 52 clubs) was acquired in 2013 by Clearlight Partners and Riveria Investment Group (a family office)[11] and was sold again in 2018 to Trilantic North America.[12] Trilantic continues to acquire and consolidate outlets within the Planet Fitness footprint.[13] This type of PE activity is now mirrored in many other franchise systems and verticals when strong unit-level economics combine with a certain amount of system maturity and proven ability to drive both growth and scale efficiencies.

Over the last 10 years, we have completed about 20 platform and add-on transactions and invested at the outlet level in more than 250 franchised locations. Our entire approach is focused on building the business. For us that means investing in our management teams and really partnering with them. For them to be successful, they need to feel supported and have development opportunities. Our relationship is built on candor, trust, and alignment around common goals. We're proud not just of our business results but of the positive impact on our entire team as well.

—**OMAR SIMMONS**, managing partner, Exaltare Capital Management[14]

Planet Fitness is now publicly traded (NYSE: PLNT) and at the end of 2022 had more than 2,300 locations. In the approximately 10 years since private capital entered at the unit level, around half of Planet Fitness US outlets have been acquired by private equity, and the total number of outlets also grew to be nearly four times larger in that same period.

There are numerous examples of multi-unit franchisees who have created large and sophisticated enterprises that themselves are backed by private equity or family offices. As mentioned, the largest MUO, Flynn Group, has nearly 2,600+ units and is backed by private equity. Flynn has his own team of data scientists studying opportunities to raise prices without losing customers.* One of the largest non-restaurant franchisees is Team Car Care; the owner of nearly 500 Jiffy Lube locations is also backed by private equity (Wynnchurch Capital).[15] When franchisees with large holdings retire, so long as a strong management team is in place, those businesses can be very attractive to PE buyers. For example, Dunkin's largest Florida franchisee sold all 100 of his units to Exeter Capital in 2022.[16] Even large corporate acquirers are active investors in operating units. In May 2023, petroleum giant BP completed its $1.3 billion acquisition of TravelCenters of America, which has an operating agreement for more than 600 restaurants, including KFC, Taco Bell, Dunkin', Burger King, Pizza Hut, Arby's, IHOP, and Dairy Queen.[17]

It is worth noting that just as PE firms are not all the same, MUOs are also not a homogeneous group, meaning MUOs have different needs, experience levels, capital structures, communication styles, and support

---

* Flynn Group announced plans in May 2023 to acquire the Pizza Hut Australia license from PE firm Allegro Funds, which will add 260 restaurants to its footprint, its first international expansion. In August 2023, Wendy's announced a new master agreement with Flynn to develop 200 new units in Australia. (Sources: News.Com.Au, Allegro company website: www.allegrofunds.com.au and Wendy's August 9, 2023, press release, https://www .prnewswire.com/news-releases/the-wendys-company-and-flynn-restaurant-group-announce-new-master-franchise -agreement-for-australia-301896583.html). In 2023, Flynn added its first non-restaurant brand, Planet Fitness.

requirements. Treating all MUOs the same is a common oversight, especially when management teams attempt to communicate or craft programs for franchisees. A 50-unit owner is different from a 2-unit owner. An owner of 20 units across four brands is very different from an owner of 20 units in the same brand. A PE-backed operator employing a professional management team to run the business is different from an MUO run by the founding franchisee's family. And so on.

Investing in multi-unit operators isn't a fit for every PE investor active in franchising. For example, all of Levine Leichtman's 28 franchise investments to date have been at the franchisor level. James J. Goodman, president of Gemini Investors (an investor at the franchisor level in Buffalo Wild Wings, Wingstop, Garbanzo Mediterranean Grill, and Premier Garage,[18] but with no multi-unit operator deals), put it this way:[19]

> We've been very active investing in franchisors; it has been one of our most successful industry segments. With regard to multi-unit franchisees, however, we've looked at a number of opportunities to invest at the outlet level, specifically in restaurants, but haven't been able to invest there. We felt the valuations were a little inflated. For an MUO franchisee opportunity in a strong restaurant concept as an example, we feel five to six times EBITDA is reasonable. The challenge is that franchisees don't control their territories and have limited growth prospects in the respect that they have to max out their four walls and then add units to grow further. There are limitations on what the franchisor allows. Compared to the franchisor, there is also a sensitivity to downturns because royalties are paid out of top-line revenue. So, the multiples have to be reasonable.

Adviser Rick Ormsby, managing director of Unbridled Capital, who has sold more than 2,000 restaurants since 2018, concurs:[20]

> If you remove outliers at the high end, and distressed unit sales at the low end, 90 percent of healthy franchise restaurant units will sell between 4.5 to 7 times EBITDA. Then you factor in whether remodels are needed, geography, size of the overall deal, average unit volumes, and the lease

situation. Those top five factors typically impact the value by 1 to 1.5 turns [multiple of EBITDA] in either direction.

Family offices are also active in backing multi-unit operators, but because FOs often don't publicize their activities (there is little need since they are not raising institutional capital), this area of franchise investing is undercounted and underappreciated.

> There is an opportunity for mutual relationship building between the franchise and family office communities, with many more productive partnerships still to be found there. I predict we will see more of this activity as both founders and franchisees look for expansion capital and exit alternatives and family offices continue to discover the power of the franchise model.

Sometimes PE will come in wanting to invest at the operator level, but if they haven't thought it all the way through, it can end up problematic. The capex requirements require digging to understand, to know what will be approved by the franchisor in terms of remodels. In a typical franchised restaurant, you need to invest $200,000 to $700,000 in refreshes every 10 to 20 years. That's a big nut if you buy 100 restaurants! Second, PE's required high returns often are highly dependent on new unit development. Many systems either aren't large enough to have large multi-unit groups for PE to acquire, or the bigger systems have the opposite problem: there isn't enough greenfield potential. The third issue is the restrictive franchise agreement. I've seen agreements where if the PE firm exits early, they owe money to the franchisor. So that may not align to PE's hold period. From that perspective, family offices are often a better fit. They are long-hold investors.

—RICK ORMSBY, managing director, Unbridled Capital[21]

POWER DYNAMICS IN THE FRANCHISOR
AND MULTI-UNIT FRANCHISEE RELATIONSHIP

It is a much different commitment for private capital to come in and invest on the franchisee side of the business. Franchise contracts are designed to defend brand standards and thus are one-sided by design. When disagreements arise between franchisees and the franchisor, it may be prohibitively expensive, especially for small franchisees, to pursue remedies via the court system if a solution cannot be hammered out privately. Given the deep PE pockets now backing many franchise systems, theoretically this power imbalance is even more in favor of franchisors compared to franchisees. MUOs of any type can sometimes negotiate favorable terms often captured in a side letter to the franchise agreement, a privilege not available to all franchisees. This can cut both ways, since franchisors sometimes want something different from PE-backed MUOs, such as guaranteed payments if PE wants to exit the system early. But franchisee agreements remain one-sided in favor of the franchisor by design. Since the power imbalance is skewed to benefit franchisors, why would PE and sophisticated multi-unit operating groups themselves choose to sign up on the *other* side of the relationship as franchisees?

Because multi-unit franchisees, their capital partners, and their franchisors are united under a common profit motive to run good franchise businesses. Furthermore, the MUO's success, confidence in the model, and positive validation are all important to the brand and franchise system. PE-backed MUOs invest carefully in models and management teams they believe in. They understand periodic changes need to be made to keep the model relevant. All parties are deeply committed to executing under the franchise model, and each has a distinct role to play. As Greg Flynn, founder of MUO Flynn Group, said, "I've always been committed not to have disputes with our franchisors. We're tied at the hip. For us to fight is just mutually destructive. In nearly 25 years of doing this, I've never had a fight with a franchisor, and I don't think I will."[22] The profit motive and commitment to the franchise model successfully align these groups for mutual gain, on both sides of the aisle as it were.

> **Large operators have influence with their franchisor. It is a compelling counterweight to franchisor contractual power. Successful MUOs use that voice constructively. Aligned PE-MUO blocks can be especially formidable.**

There are incentives for franchisors to allow consolidation, especially when weaker operators are bought out by better operators. But it also prompts franchisor soul-searching about how much consolidation is too much, especially when funded by debt (with or without PE involvement). While large operators have influence and a voice, it is also true that no operator (so far) has been viewed by their franchisor as "too big to fail" in terms of granting concessions to the operator to keep them in business. Overleverage (whether backed by PE or not) is a common MUO issue since debt is often used to pay for outlet remodels and acquisitions. In most large systems, the franchisor collects and studies outlet financial information and thus the franchisor is well aware of which of its operators are at risk. One of the largest MUO bankruptcies to date was restaurant operator NPC International in 2020 (1,225 Pizza Hut and 385 Wendy's locations), which had been backed by a string of PE firms over the years (Merrill Lynch Private Equity in 2006, Olympus in 2011, and Eldridge in 2018). In its bankruptcy filing, NPC cited pandemic costs, a high debt load of $900 million, and "unsustainable" capital expenditure demands under Pizza Hut's franchise agreement.[23]

Pizza Hut, in the midst of its own turnaround, declined to offer NPC relief on its contractual obligations. Remodels remain important to the brand's revitalization. Instead, NPC's assets were sold for $801 million to other operating groups.[24] Exits and resales can recalibrate remaining units under new ownership possessing healthier balance sheets. From that standpoint, the franchise contract works as intended to manage long-term system stability, whether a franchisee is a single- or multi-unit operator, and even if that operator is backed by private equity or a family office.

What Signal Does Private Equity Investing Activity at the Outlet Level Send?

It is important for prospective franchisees to consider whether private equity is involved at the franchisor (brand) level. But the presence of PE backing the franchisor shouldn't be treated as an automatic validation of that model's viability or, of course, its suitability for specific franchisees, because that is very case specific. Likewise, PE activity, or lack thereof, at the franchisee (outlet) level is another important signal especially for prospective franchisees to consider, but you will need more information.

If PE is *not* investing at the outlet level, it may be that the franchisor does not allow institutional capital in the system as franchisees. This is often true when management especially sees value in an owner-operator model. Or the brand may be too small or immature to attract private equity. Since PE likes to build scale quickly, they prefer to do roll-up acquisitions of outlets in systems where there are a lot of good outlets available to buy as well as greenspace for new builds. Smaller companies just don't have the footprint to give PE the scale they want within a five- to six-year time frame.

But it may also be true that *private equity may simply not find the operating model and unit-level economics attractive!* This is the big "gotcha" that you want to avoid, so understanding *why* PE is not active rolling up units within a system is worth a little time to explore and think about. If PE firms are *not* investing at the unit level, this also impacts competition for resales and valuations.

Too many new franchisees start businesses without considering their exit strategy. This is always a mistake! Validate whether your desired exit is realistic and evaluate resale signals within a system you're considering joining as a franchisee. Together with information about whether franchisees are returning to buy expansion units, private equity consolidation and new development activity within franchise systems provides another important signal about unit-level profitability and the franchise value proposition.

Money finds its way to where it is treated best.

—**CHRIS DULL**, chief executive officer, Freddy's Frozen Custard & Steakburgers[25]

Private capital is not an active outlet consolidator in every franchise system. This is an important signal for franchisees to consider in two respects:

1 If PE is an active buyer of outlets within a franchise system, it tends to lift valuations and provide more exit options for franchisees as well as competition for resales. And the *absence* of PE activity at the outlet level means the opposite is also true.

2 If PE is not active at the outlet level, there is a gating issue somewhere preventing or providing a disincentive for PE to come in. As a franchisee, it is important for you to understand whether PE is an active investor at the unit level, and if not—why not?

INTERNATIONAL PRIVATE EQUITY-BACKED MULTI-UNIT OPERATORS

While this book is primarily focused on private capital's impact on US franchising, it should be noted here that PE is very active at both the brand and multi-unit level outside the US as well. While PE isn't quite as dominant in other franchise markets compared to the US, the activity and trends are clear.

Going back to the Papa Johns example that opened this book, PE has invested both in large US MUOs such as PJU Holdings Inc./PJ United (backed by The Halifax Group)[26] and in international expansion. Here are two recent examples:

1 An agreement was expanded to develop 650 new restaurants across India with PJP Investments Group (backed by Dubai-based PE firm Levant Capital), already a Papa Johns franchise partner in the UAE, Saudi Arabia, and Jordan.[27]

2 An agreement was signed with Hong Kong–based PE firm FountainVest Partners to open 1,350 Papa Johns stores across China by 2040. This represents 25 percent projected growth in the Papa Johns global footprint. FountainVest also owns a majority stake in CFB Group, which owns 160 Papa Johns restaurants across Shanghai and southern China.[28]

> Private capital is especially active outside the US market backing MUO operators, acquiring large territory development rights, and trading blocks of existing units.

IT'S GETTING WARM IN HERE!

Up next is the story of an awakening, as the franchise community gradually recognized in the middle of Franchise Generation 3.0 (after PE activity was already well under way) that "something was happening" with private equity in franchising. Initially, PE was seen as just another capital source, not the dominant change agent it was rapidly becoming.

▼

The humble frog has much to teach us about change awareness. In the next chapter, we will walk through the chain of events.

CHAPTER 7

A Frog, More Big Money, and the Final Missing Piece

Franchising has demonstrated more than a century of resilience. Now that PE is a dominant factor, new adaptations are required to win.

LIKE THE PROVERBIAL FROG immersed in a pot of water on a stovetop, when did the franchise sector itself realize things had profoundly changed thanks to private equity? Did the franchise community feel the heat increasing, or was everyone too distracted by dealmaking to notice? And why does this matter now?

DISTRACTION AND PERCEPTION

It turns out that private equity's interest in franchising and all the deal-making was very distracting (and in many ways still is), especially for a community wired to celebrate entrepreneurship and business success. A comprehensive review of industry conference agendas, presentations, legal symposium white papers, franchise sector reports, and articles going back over the entire period starting with PE's entrance into franchising until today, as well as interviews with key leaders, is revealing for the absence of deep discussions about trends and meaning. Instead, when the subject of PE made the agenda, typical discussion topics were tactical, such as how to make your business attractive to a private equity buyer, how to craft a good deal, how the sale process works, contractual considerations, risk management, seller earnouts, and similar topics.

In other words, the focus was on transaction mechanics, legal considerations, and deal case studies, seemingly ignoring the bigger picture and the massive shift in the franchise power structure that was already under way. These unperturbed franchise community discussions about PE, buried among many other discussion items on busy agendas, are very telling. They reveal just how fast PE swept in and caught the broader franchise community off-guard. Largely absent was any talk of the wider implications of PE involvement in franchising or PE's growing *influence*. It's fair to say awareness of PE activity in franchising didn't hit the franchise community's broader consciousness until after the financial crisis, when PE franchise activity resumed and accelerated. Before that, only those with direct exposure to PE activity had a significant head start and preview of what was to come.

> In 2006, the Dunkin' deal got headlines, but then the financial crisis took our attention away from PE for a while.
>
> **—CHARLIE CHASE**, chief executive officer, FirstService Brands and former International Franchise Association chairman[1]

> Prior to about 2010, the IFA [International Franchise Association] didn't talk much about private equity. Then, suddenly, we saw a bunch of PE transactions happen. As more private equity firms entered and realized the value of the franchise model, the IFA became more aware.
>
> **—STEVE SIEGEL**, senior adviser to the Riverside Company and former International Franchise Association chairman[2]

Siegel credits Bob Rosenberg, former president of Dunkin' Donuts and also a former International Franchise Association chairman, with being one of the early voices that helped make the IFA aware at the leadership level of PE's growing interest in franchising and PE's potential as growth partners.

> I became aware of private equity in the mid-'80s when a New York bank approached me with a way their private equity arm could take us private.

We demurred at that point and remained publicly owned. The benefits and potential private equity offered were further explored when Dunkin' had to put itself up for sale when facing a hostile takeover attack in 1989. Ultimately, to avoid purchase by what we considered an unqualified financial buyer, we sold the company in 1990 to an English strategic buyer, Allied-Lyons PLC, for $325 million.

When I retired in 1998, I was recruited by the private equity concern, Bain Capital, to be a director of Domino's. That acquisition was the first that Bain had made into food service. I introduced Bain Capital to the successor management for Dunkin' in the hopes that if Dunkin' was put up for sale that Bain would be considered a likely buyout partner. I had gotten to know and admire Bain and their managing partners through the board membership at Domino's. I felt the Dunkin' brand and business would thrive under Bain's ownership.

Sure enough, in 2006, Allied-Lyons (now called Allied Domecq) was sold to Pernod Ricard. Pernod, in turn, was only interested in the spirits part of Allied's business and put Dunkin' Brands, which had by then been merged with Baskin-Robbins, up for sale. Bain Capital, along with Carlyle and Thomas Lee Private Equity, bought Dunkin' Brands for $2.4 billion.

—**BOB ROSENBERG**, former president, Dunkin' Donuts, and former chairman, International Franchise Association[3]

Around 2010, I noticed a change. We turned the corner and suddenly you looked up and there were a bunch of new private equity faces and names you'd never heard of before. Suddenly there was awareness and you could feel the page turning. PE is now part of the very fiber of franchising. Institutional capital is everywhere.

—**SCOTT FRITH**, chairman and chief executive officer, Happinest Brands[4]

BIG MONEY IN PLAIN SIGHT

Private equity's entrance into franchising was, and remains, a fundamentally disruptive force in franchising because PE firms are not passive investors; in fact, it's quite the reverse! PE's fingerprints—mostly for better, but yes, sometimes for worse—are all over modern franchising. However, the magnitude of PE's influence across franchising and PE's breadth of involvement remain largely unacknowledged to this day. Even many people with franchise experience do not fully register the scope or importance of private capital to modern franchising or think through the implications to their own franchising outcomes. And, of course, when selecting franchise opportunities, prospective franchisees likely don't have PE on their radar at all.

> The elephant in the room that wasn't being discussed then (and largely still isn't, even today) was "What is all this private equity activity going to *mean* for franchising? *Where is this headed?*" PE was seen as a capital partner enabling faster growth and unit consolidation within systems, not as a market disruptor. But PE isn't just a source of capital. It shapes markets and outcomes for all sector participants, not only the ones directly transacting with PE.

Many PE franchise investors appear to prefer this "all around us" approach to working within the franchise sector, and yet in some ways they are also oddly at a distance from the franchise community. For example, despite the expanse of PE's franchise activities and influence, fewer than a dozen private equity firms are themselves members of the International Franchise Association. Portfolio companies may be members, but given that PE controls the boards of their portfolio companies and therefore decision-making, maintaining a direct line of communication on key issues impacting the entire franchise sector would be beneficial.

> How should private equity participate in the conversation about the importance of the franchise model to our economy? They need to be in the room, not in the lobby at franchise events cherry-picking founders they want to talk to about possible partnerships. We have seen that the most effective PE-backed brands are committed to making sure their management teams are following franchise best practices, including going through the CFE

program. [The Certified Franchise Executive is a rigorous and comprehensive professional development program for franchising.[5]] They build good relationships with their franchisees. They are strong sponsors and supporters of everything the IFA does on behalf of franchising. They are real supporters of the franchise business model.

—**MATT HALLER**, president and chief executive officer, International Franchise Association[6]

In terms of learning about industries and making their mark, PE teams are very, very good at researching entire sectors, moving in, building influence and relationships, and ultimately creating a dominant position while at the same time being a bit enigmatic in their dealings. To their credit, when change is needed, PE can be extremely nimble. They look at every deal and constantly hone their selection criteria. PE investors move fast, often do not declare their intentions, and work both through and around existing influencers to ultimately replace that knowledge with their own expertise and perspective. The frog is left in water that's now boiling, wondering how the water got so hot, so fast!

Do the activities of private capital investors influence each other? Yes, of course! PE firms watch each other not just to keep tabs on market valuations but also to understand what's working and what isn't. Perhaps no other PE firm active in franchising has been as influential as Roark Capital Group. As the saying goes, "The man on the top of the mountain didn't fall there."[7]

CASE STUDY: ROARK CAPITAL GROUP

Founded in 2001 by Neal Aronson, Roark's presence and playbook exert a heavy influence boiled down to a few big themes:

Vision and leadership: Roark was one of the early PE firms that saw the potential of franchising and committed to investing in the sector. Roark has been active in the International Franchise Association since 2002 and has made good use of this early access to learn about various brands and operating models while in turn sharing some of its thinking about franchise investing. Those who were listening got a head start on PE activity in franchising. Founder Neal Aronson received the International Franchise Association's Hall of Fame recognition (the association's highest recognition) in 2023 for his "demonstrated commitment to excellence in franchising."[8]

New PE entrants and franchise investing activity: Roark provides an undeniably compelling example that has inspired others to follow, including the establishment of funds and whole firms devoted to franchise investing.

Platforms: Roark didn't invent platforming. But Roark's scale and successful platforming activity increased awareness and validated the approach within a franchise context.

More aggressive "down-ladder" dealmaking activity: Roark's presence as a well-capitalized and aggressive investor increases competition and prices for deals just *below* where Roark typically likes to play, because Roark is viewed as a later potential buyer. Deals of all sizes fall along a spectrum based on the size and type of private capital sponsor most likely to be a fit. Roark is at the top of the deal ladder. We will discuss the PE Profit Ladder in Chapters 13 and 14.

Seller price aspirations and price inflation: Roark's visibility, and at times aggressiveness, when bidding also affects seller price expectations even for brands that are much less mature as well as general market expectations. (It is very important for sellers to understand the market and tap expert guidance to understand appropriate sale comparatives.)

Reminding us that franchise turnarounds are challenging, even for seasoned investors: Roark has attempted brand turnarounds (e.g., Carvel and Arby's), but it's not Roark's core investing strategy. That said, Roark is also persistent and has proven that diligent efforts to transform brands can pay off. This is recently evident in the Focus Brands portfolio (Auntie Anne's, Carvel, Cinnabon, Jamba, McAlister's, Moe's, and Schlotzsky's), which is starting to see the benefits of a three-year transformation effort. Focus signed more than 650 license agreements and opened 400 new units in 2022.[9]

Importance of sticking to your strengths: Roark acquired Rusty Taco (then called R Taco) along with Buffalo Wild Wings when it purchased publicly traded Buffalo Wild Wings for $2.9 billion (including debt) in 2017.[10] Rusty Taco is a compelling emerging brand, but Roark is a scale player. This thematic clarity eventually caused it to divest Rusty Taco from its Inspire Brands portfolio in 2022 to Gala

Capital Partners, as previously discussed. Inspire Brands' chief growth officer, Christian Charnaux, told *Restaurant Business* that Inspire's integrated shared services model was better optimized for scale brands and that Rusty Taco would be better off partnering with an emerging brand specialist. [11]

Value of a longer-term hold: With $35 billion in assets already under management,[12] Roark has proven it is adept at pulling cash out of scale franchise businesses and is transparent about its intention to hold brands longer than is typical of other PE firms. That said, Roark has also demonstrated that it is willing to do shorter holds or sell some portion of its equity interest when it makes sense to do so—for example, when taking portfolio companies public (e.g., Wingstop, acquired in 2010, IPO 2015; and Driven Brands, acquired in 2015, IPO 2021) or when divesting assets in the interest of sticking to its core strengths (e.g., divesting emerging brands Rusty Taco, held 2017–2022, and Roark's minority stake in Naf Naf Grill, held 2015–2021).[13]

Roark has had an immense impact on both franchising itself and the investing behavior of other PE firms. But what about Roark's impact on its own franchisees?

Roark's experience also demonstrates that even large PE firms have limits on their power within the franchise model. Franchisors can enforce the franchise agreement, but they can't compel franchisees to grow. Even when there are development agreements, there are a number of ways franchisees can delay or decline to follow-through. (Penalties notwithstanding.) One of the easiest ways to assess franchisee satisfaction and profitability is to track license agreements and unit growth. Are growth-minded franchisees returning to open new outlets? Is the system growing overall? Are new franchisees eager to join the brand? Do existing franchisees provide validation to potential franchisees that the business is run well and provides a good return on investment? If a brand has saturated a market, are franchisees clamoring for resale opportunities?

This reality is nuanced in brands that have already achieved significant scale (key markets may be saturated, prompting development of nontraditional sites). But the same force of gravity (i.e., the pull of franchisee opinion expressed in their willingness to expand) applies to Roark as it does every other PE sponsor. You can see this dynamic playing out in Roark brands, which have an interesting mix of net unit growth trends:

▶ Some Roark brands see strong outlet expansion—for example, the recent Focus Brands expansion. Nothing Bundt Cakes grew 110 units in just the first two years after being acquired by Roark.[14] Orangetheory had 360 studios when Roark's acquisition was announced in early 2016,[15] and the franchise celebrated its 1,500th milestone location opening in mid-2022.[16]

- ▶ A few brands are adding units, but more slowly:
  - ▷ Jimmy John's had 2,500 locations when acquired by Roark in 2016 for $2.3 billion and by mid-2023 had 2,800 locations.[17] CKE brands Carl's Jr. and Hardee's have grown from 3,413 units to 3,800 units in Roark's decade of ownership.
  - ▷ In now-divested FASTSIGNS, unit growth grew from 440 franchised stores[18] to 550 during Roark's decade-long hold period from late 2003 to 2014.[19]
- ▶ Some have seen net unit growth over Roark's total hold period but recently are trending down. For example, Massage Envy had 800 locations when acquired by Roark in 2012[20] and ended 2022 with 1,083 locations. But from 2017 to 2022, net units actually declined by 90 locations, ending each year during that period with fewer units.[21]
- ▶ Some brands are essentially flat. For example, Sonic had 3,600 units when Roark took it private in 2018; Sonic ended 2022 with 3,546 units. Inspire Brands (six brands, including Sonic and Arby's) announced 800 new outlet openings in 2021 in part due to an impressive international expansion push. However, with hundreds of units in other locations also closing, total units across the entire Inspire portfolio only grew by 64 outlets that year. Only 30 percent of owners are returning to acquire more units or add new brands, according to coverage by restaurant industry publication QSR.[22]
- ▶ Some brands have declining unit count or have adjusted their distribution focus—for example, in our Carvel case study, although there are some encouraging signs if development units open as part of the larger Focus Brands reinvigoration currently under way.

Fundamentally, franchisee interest in expansion is a critical barometer of enterprise value, quality of the franchisee-franchisor relationship, and franchisees' belief in their own long-term earning potential.

Expansion-minded multi-unit operators can and do vote with their money and their feet in a sort of entrepreneurial emigration, if you will. The question is, is that emigration an "emigration of enthusiasm" deeper into the brand or other brands held by that PE sponsor, or an "emigration of disappointment" toward outside options? Top operators are highly sought after by franchisors, for both de novo agreements (to grow the system) and for resales (to manage retirements and improve unit-level performance). Franchisees must be generally happy with the system, their relationship with management, and their own profitability and they must believe in the brand's future... or these independent business owners won't *choose* to grow and will also drag their feet on fulfilling prior development agreements. There are many brands competing for MUO attention and investment.

> The competitive marketplace for franchisee talent, which Roark did its part to excite, now exerts pressure back onto Roark brands just like all others. Multi-unit operators are a tough crowd to win over, especially in sectors that have been consolidating for years or where MUOs are themselves backed by PE and thus face pressure to make a return for their own investors.

THE FRANCHISE PRIVATE EQUITY INVESTOR POOL CONTINUES TO GROW

Returning to the timeline and chronology of PE investments in franchising, activity once again accelerated after the 2007–2009 financial crisis. New private equity firms continued to proliferate and enter franchising, creating a seemingly bottomless pool of investment capital to feed franchise deal activity. Prequin, a company that provides research and data on the alternative assets industry, including private equity, counted only 24 traditional PE firms in 1980.[23] By 2013, there were 2,797 private equity firms headquartered in the US alone, with investments in 17,744 companies.[24] Today, there are more than 9,200 PE firms globally, 5,000 in the US, and both pools continue to grow.[25] The water was already hot, but now it is also crowded like a water park in the middle of summer!

Many active PE investors in franchising today were themselves founded as recently as 2010 or later. Some are formal spinouts of other firms or are new firms launched by partners with prior franchise investing experience.

For example, 10 Point Capital (the first on this list) was founded by part-ners with prior franchise investing experience at BIP Capital, Roark, and US Franchise Systems. This newer cohort (by no means a complete list) of more recent entrants include the following:

- 10 Point Capital
- Butterfly Equity
- CenterOak Partners
- Exeter Capital
- Garnett Station Partners
- Incline Equity Partners[26]
- LightBay Capital
- Main Post Partners
- MPK Equity Partners (a family office)
- Princeton Equity Group[27]

Another large cadre of PE franchise investors was founded between 2000 and 2010 (not a complete list and also recent compared to franchis-ing's overall timeline), with many partners on this list also having prior PE experience with other firms:

- Argonne Capital Group
- Eagle Merchant Partners
- Golden Gate Capital
- KSL Capital Partners
- MidOcean Partners[28]
- Roark Capital Group
- Thompson Street Capital Partners
- Trilantic Capital Partners
- TZP Group

It is mind-boggling to think about the impact on franchising from the activities of so many recently founded private capital firms!

This means investors with longer franchise experience and a history of many successful franchise exits (sometimes across multiple firms) have something that differentiates them—a track record. But it also speaks to the vibrancy of this intersection of franchising and private capital—new opportunities continue to be created and new teams form or enter, all looking for solid franchise investments.

IF YOU DON'T MAKE NEW FRIENDS, AT LEAST GET ALIGNED

No franchisee can be successful without alignment with their franchisor, and vice versa. Now that PE is a dominant force within franchising, they are yet another group for stakeholders to align with. PE is single-minded in the pursuit of profit to create return on investment for their LPs. The key tension points are the intersections between PE goals and tactics (as temporary owners of franchise brands and largely using other people's money to invest) and the goals and tactics available to other stakeholders, especially franchisees, who are investing a relatively greater percentage of their own money and tend to be more focused on the long term. These groups are linked by binding one-sided contracts in favor of their franchisor and what is supposed to be a deeply interdependent relationship.

As a franchise founder or franchisee, if you can closely align your own interests with those of private equity, you can ride along and create a win-win. But the onus is on *you* to make sure this happens. If you are a corporate employee of a PE-backed franchisor, your performance lens must now include how you serve the interests of both franchisees and PE ownership. If you are a supplier, your value proposition to portfolio companies is under more scrutiny.

Franchisees do not control brand-level decisions no matter what the ownership structure. But what's different in a PE-backed company is that management decisions and chosen initiatives are *predictable* even when PE ownership changes. Franchisees are not powerless, but their power lies in their relationship with management and in their value as a demonstrated strong operator of that brand. Franchisees' ultimate success thus requires alignment with ownership and PE's playbook in the pursuit of profit, which is where we turn next.

▼

We've looked at the past, and we will return to the future and Franchise Generation 4.0 at the end of the book in Chapter 20. It's time now to explore in detail how PE functions and makes decisions, and what that means for you as a founder, franchisor, or franchisee. Now, it's all about the present moment and about scaling your business or planning a successful exit.

PART TWO

The Private Equity Playbook in Franchising

CHAPTER 8

Private Equity's Playbook for Growing Franchise Businesses

"We are a repository of lessons learned. When we sit down with a management team, we draw upon that experience as well as on hundreds more businesses that we evaluated and passed on. We challenge management to think about the business in new ways."

—**MATTHEW FRANKEL**, managing partner, Levine Leichtman Capital Partners[1]

PRIVATE EQUITY HAS A business case for every investment and comes into every acquisition with a draft game plan. Early meetings with management help to shape and crystallize that plan to focus on the highest value creation operational initiatives. However, PE firms are not operators. Initiatives undertaken must be executed by the franchisor's management team. Once a franchise has a private equity partner, typically there are improvements in long-term sustainability, the core customer value proposition, and unit-level economics. The entire value creation model in franchising depends on unit operating performance and especially franchisees' commitment to the brand. PE acts as a strategic thought partner to their portfolio company management teams. Sometimes PE is the first outsider to challenge management decision-making and to really drill into the business data to uncover new opportunities for improvement and growth. As a result, this partnership typically moves brands forward.

I say "typically" because there are exceptions. Not every PE franchise investment has been successful. A learning curve is visible through PE's history of investing in franchise businesses, and, as we have seen, PE has learned the hard way at times that franchise turnarounds are very challenging. But based on industry data, most private equity investments in franchising have driven positive outcomes for those systems. This is especially visible when the first institutional capital comes in, and across the early PE partnerships as the business continues to grow.

> There is now significant overlap between the top 400 brands in the US ranked by system revenue[2] and the list of 700+ brands with a history of PE sponsorship at the franchisor level, franchisee level, or both. And for many emerging brands launched after PE entered franchising, attracting PE support or joining a PE-backed platform stabilized and accelerated those young brands, putting them on a stronger path.

THE DUE DILIGENCE PLAYBOOK

The private capital playbook begins before a company is acquired, with the due diligence process. Because it is important for sellers to be well prepared for buyer due diligence, a more detailed guide as well as some tools and checklists to help you and your team prepare are available as reader downloads at www.bigmoneyinfranchising.com. We will also cover how to maintain a "sale-ready" stance in Chapter 18.

A summary from PE's perspective is useful here. One of the ways private capital ensures good outcomes for themselves and their investors is to conduct careful due diligence up front. Now that PE has become more knowledgeable about and comfortable with the franchise model, this due diligence can move fast. There is a list of common data points PE will focus on to gain an understanding of the business:

- ▶ speed of new unit ramp-up and cash-on-cash return for franchisees
- ▶ overall franchisee value proposition and return on investment
- ▶ deep analysis of unit-level economics and system performance; differences among regions, time in business / start date ("vintage"), markets, and so on

- understanding key performance indicators, including trends and areas for improvement
- primary growth drivers and model accelerators
- assessing sold-not-open backlog
  - How likely are those outlets to open and when?
  - Is there any potential to accelerate those openings so outlets can start producing royalty income faster?
- best, worst, and middle business case scenarios and key contingencies
- analysis to determine growth potential (territory availability with the right characteristics)
- corporate unit performance compared to franchise units
- corporate site leases, if applicable
- competitive landscape and financial comparatives
- customer value proposition, trends, and surveys—confirming whether customers see the offering is unique, valuable, and that demand is sustainable
- pricing and trends
- quality of franchisee-franchisor relationship
- interviews of franchisees; franchisee surveys and key franchisee pain points/dissatisfiers
- mix of single/multi-unit owners, regions/markets
- marketing effectiveness, both corporate and unit level
  - spend, tracking, fund collection, comparatives
  - link to key performance indicators and growth
  - areas of opportunity
- management team assessment, talent bench and gaps
- review of all franchise and development agreements and receipts
- intellectual property, trademark review, and so on
- technology stack and gaps and opportunities to improve the franchisee and customer experience; loyalty programs
- regulatory/compliance due diligence
- legal due diligence
- assessment of comparative deals (e.g., multiple paid)

Does all of this require substantial effort? Yes, of course. But PE teams are adept at evaluating this type and amount of data quickly and thoroughly, especially if they have experience in franchising. From this due diligence effort, PE will construct their business case for investment.

> **Remember, PE's goal is to return at least three times (3×) invested capital and ideally much more during their planned hold period, based on conservative projections.**

PE meets with management during due diligence, developing a relationship early in the process. In the words of Phil Loughlin, a partner at Bain Capital,[3]

> We are long-term investors in how we think about growing businesses. We're one of the only large private investment firms whose founders didn't primarily come out of the investment banking world; our roots are management consulting, strategy, and operations. That culture informs everything… starting with our due diligence. It continues on to how we support management teams as they seek to refine their long-term vision and to inflect or transform the businesses they run.

THE PRIVATE EQUITY OPERATIONS AND GROWTH PLAYBOOK

During due diligence, PE discusses with management a preliminary list of potential initiatives or additional areas to investigate post-close. Priorities are set, goals are established, and accountability is assigned to appropriate leaders and teams. Team compensation is tied to achieving those goals. If any talent or process gaps were identified during due diligence, those gaps will be among the first issues addressed. If the acquired company is joining a platform, there is another layer of introductions and integration to fulfill that part of the business case. The management team will also be introduced to the PE firm's support network, including lending sources for franchisees, marketing and public relations firms, real estate and construction resources, franchise sales, technology and back-office solutions, and so on. A cadence is also established for reporting and updating the PE partner to address any issues that come up, and a calendar of board meetings is established to cover the PE firm's fiduciary duty to monitor and manage the investment for their investors.

So the basic scaffolding and prioritization of the operations and growth playbook is created during due diligence. Many founders and management teams lose the opportunity to make business improvements far ahead of a transaction. They gather data but don't analyze what it's telling them or fail to act on it. PE is very good at bridging that gap, which is one reason they are effective investors.

> The playbooks we will go through in detail over the next few chapters can help you and your leadership team create a value creation plan. Looking at your own business, there are often clear opportunities to improve before you ever engage with private capital. Or you can use this information as a jumping-off point for discussions about where PE could come in and help accelerate your business and what type of partnerships you should be exploring. For additional help in this effort or for a referral, see "Ways to Connect" in the resources section.

To see an implementation of the PE playbook in action post-acquisition, let's look at the example of Freddy's Frozen Custard & Steakburgers to walk through common growth playbook elements, and augment it with perspectives from other PE firms to build out the full picture.

Freddy's was acquired by Thompson Street Capital Partners in 2021. At the time, the nearly 400-unit restaurant brand had a strong regional reputation, excellent food quality, passionate brand fans (called "FredHeads"), and a significant pipeline of units under development. It was a solid business, with sales up 13 percent in 2019.[4]

How did working with private equity accelerate an already strong brand that had achieved some scale? As Thompson Street's lead director on the investment, Joe St. Geme, outlined in an interview when the acquisition was announced, the team's focus was clear: "We ultimately want to spend our time and money where we know there will be an immediate impact to driving sales and franchisee profitability."[5] In other words, Thompson Street planned to implement the PE franchise growth playbook.

1. The Private Equity Playbook Implements Franchise Growth Accelerators

When PE investors come into a franchise business, they tend to invest in predictable growth accelerators. In the case of Freddy's, Thompson Street brought in an experienced and franchise-savvy CEO, Chris Dull, and partnered with management to execute on that growth playbook. Dull also had prior experience working with three different PE sponsors. Thompson Street further set up the team for success in terms of how they structured the deal. As Dull explains, "Our PE sponsor created a straightforward single-debt facility, and the PE firm itself provided no debt and isn't charging management fees. This approach drives tremendous cash flow to help drive growth initiatives."[6]

Dull outlined the post-acquisition growth priorities as follows:

Focus the entire organization on improving unit-level profitability. The management team made four-wall unit profitability their primary focus and made adjustments to franchisee support to follow through on that commitment.

> The franchise business coaches [FBCS] used to be focused on upholding Freddy's standards and compliance. We shifted the FBCS' focus to profit and loss [P&L] analysis and profitability coaching. We used to collect franchisee P&LS annually—we started collecting them quarterly. This was a cultural shift in the organization. We told franchisees, "We want to see your numbers because your numbers matter to us." Then we provided dashboards with KPI [key performance indicator] benchmarks to help franchisees see their profitability in more detail that could then drive specific improvement actions.

For our FBCS, looking closely at P&Ls and doing profitability coaching was also an evolution. We made additions to the team, made sure we had the right people in the right roles, added training specific to profitability coaching, and built out the finance function to support our efforts. This area of coaching is something we continuously strive to improve.

—**CHRIS DULL**, chief executive officer, Freddy's Frozen Custard & Steakburgers[7]

Expand and improve the franchise development function. This included building out the team and streamlining management reporting lines. The company put together a more focused outbound sales effort and more clearly articulated the benefits of Freddy's business model for franchisees. For example, Freddy's charges lower royalties (4.5 percent) and marketing fees (1.5 percent) compared to competitors. The company also created incentives for high-performing franchisees to add expansion units. Nontraditional sites were added in high-traffic locations to increase market saturation and awareness (different sizes, venues, etc.). For example, Freddy's opened its first airport location in 2021, casino locations in 2022, and its first baseball stadium location in 2023.[8] As a result, Freddy's added 300 new commitments to their development backlog and accelerated opening timelines. They expect to open more than 50 restaurants every year for the foreseeable future.

Focus on real estate and construction processes and support. As part of the reinvigorated development function, real estate and construction processes, tools, and support received heavy focus. This also helped to manage new-build costs. The company had a large backlog of development units but needed an improved support function to accelerate openings.

Make improvements to marketing. Freddy's built a more meaningful marketing budget (by improving consistency of collecting on existing agreements) and with that budget created campaigns to drive customer traffic and engage more with customers. Gradually, more traditional and social media were added, and the company made investments in a loyalty platform. With this infrastructure in place, the company plans to focus more on menu innovation to drive customer options and higher visit frequency.

Tie operational improvements to increasing customer satisfaction and engagement. Since food quality and value were already excellent, the team focused on improving drive-through delivery speed. Freddy's also invested in a mobile app, workforce management software, point of sale software to better integrate with pickup and delivery, online ordering, and other improvements.

Renegotiate supplier agreements to lower franchisee costs. Freddy's put out a request for proposal: "something Freddy's has never done, to ensure franchisees get their products in the most cost-effective manner."[9]

Since the acquisition, Freddy's has opened more than 100 restaurants and recently celebrated the opening of its 500th location.

2. The Private Equity Playbook Also Applies Other Proven Methods

Freddy's management utilized a number of initiatives in the PE franchise growth playbook to transform the brand. But in terms of resources and operational support to scale businesses in its portfolio, private equity has other significant resources and strategies that are brand agnostic and may not even be specific to a franchise business. This is akin to a professional athlete who has a specific game-day playbook, but also the benefit of broad experience and instincts gained by doing something many times. In the PE world, this "muscle memory" includes the following actions:

- following a disciplined due diligence and acquisition process
- buying at a reasonable multiple (based on a conservative business case)
- considering terminal value in the initial business case
- using leverage to improve deal returns
- closely studying every angle of the business and key performance indicators to uncover new areas for improvement or growth opportunities

- implementing business intelligence, improving data gathering and reporting (e.g., analyzing opportunities to make price increases, monitoring competitors)
- earning rebates and fees from the supply chain where practical
- renegotiating supply chain contracts to reduce costs
- structuring deals to improve returns and trying to cap downside risk
- recapitalizing portfolio companies when market conditions are favorable
- taking advantage of multiple arbitrage opportunities (via platforms and tuck-in acquisitions, where applicable)
- keeping management focused on both unit- and corporate-level operating performance and cash flow
- growing the business through investments in marketing, sales, new products/services, or new market entry
- improving set-up costs, analyzing site requirements to find cost efficiencies (e.g., optimizing outlet size and per square foot earning potential)
- making product/service improvements
- refining the model to reduce labor, operating, and launch costs
- reducing the number of corporate initiatives to only those with the most impact
- cutting funding for unproductive activities and management's pet projects
- maintaining excellent financial controls and closely monitoring portfolio companies
- swapping in better talent where needed and filling gaps
- bringing in third-party tools or assistance where needed (e.g., call center support, marketing, real estate and construction, public relations)
- encouraging exits for low-performing franchisees and consolidating under higher-performing operators (i.e., enforcing brand standards, providing resale incentives)
- implementing new license agreements in cases where new fee structures or licensing language improves overall system viability
- driving scale and cross-brand efficiencies (where applicable, e.g., platforms)
- building and maintaining relationships with other PE firms that are potential exit landing zones for portfolio companies
- maintaining a sale-ready stance

3. The Private Equity Playbook Is Hyper-focused on Generating Results

PE-backed management teams choose a few high-value initiatives and operational levers to make a sizable impact on portfolio company performance as quickly as possible. They don't try to tackle the entire playbook list, or at least not all at once!

> While playbook strategies and tactics are predictable, each plan is bespoke, uniquely crafted for the brand and situation. Knowing the situation of a brand you are associated with, you can start to make educated assumptions about what tactics will be prioritized by incoming PE owners, or the next owners when the business trades again.

When management teams first start working with private equity, often PE's biggest value add is taking a fresh look at the business and empowering management through investments in specific growth initiatives.

CASE STUDY: LEVINE LEICHTMAN'S PLAYBOOK TO ACCELERATE FRANCHISE BRANDS

Levine Leichtman Capital Partners follows a field-tested approach to drive franchise brand growth in larger brands that have already achieved some scale. Like most PE investors, LLCP only invests based on a solid business case and comes in with a draft plan. Meetings with management further refine the strategic and tactical plans. As managing partner Matthew Frankel explains,[10]

> When we evaluate a franchisor opportunity... our value creation plan starts well before we make an investment... during due diligence. We're building a business case. We listen to the management team and their ideas for growth and improvement. Together we create the value creation plan, which is bespoke for every business we invest in.
>
> For example, in our first meeting with Homevestors we challenged management with new ideas, and in some cases the team said, "We haven't thought about that." We came out of that meeting with a long list

of value creation initiatives that ended up generating material benefits for both the franchisor and the franchisees.

According to Frankel, LLCP's typical franchise acceleration playbook has eight elements:[11]

1 **Improve unit-level economics for franchisees.**
   We are nimble and always looking for ways to improve ULES [unit-level economics], especially now that so much activity has shifted from in-store to digital. For example, we consider, "Can we shrink the box?" [Make the unit smaller.] Can we make the build less expensive for the franchisee in light of this big shift to digital?"

2 **Improve and build out the franchise development function.**
   Sometimes we get into a brand and franchise development is already very effective, such as when we acquired Tropical Smoothie, which allowed us to focus on other initiatives. But in the cases of Mountain Mikes Pizza, Lawn Doctor, and Senior Helpers, as examples, all had outsourced franchise development. That's more typical for small brands, but once you reach a certain scale the strategy needs to evolve. Together with management, we built out internal franchise development teams and helped drive accelerated franchise sales. For Nothing Bundt Cakes, we upgraded the franchise development team and targeted specific markets to build scale in new geographies.

3 **Drive increased same-store sales.**
   We look for product and service expansion options. We work with the team to approach pricing decisions in an analytical way. There are often marketing opportunities. For Nothing Bundt Cakes, their franchisees were not consistent with their local marketing spend or effectiveness, so we consolidated everything and brought in a top-tier marketing firm to roll out a custom and targeted marketing campaign for each region for the franchisee's local advertising co-op. We did something similar for Homevestors.

4 **Use acquisitions as a lever (platform).**
   If you have a really strong management team, you can add complementary brands. We did that for Global Franchise Group. That's what we ultimately did when we created Happinest Brands, although that's not the reason we originally invested in Lawn Doctor. We loved

that business. As time progressed it made sense to create a multi-brand home services franchisor platform. Scott Frith is an incredible CEO and a partner that we had real confidence could successfully build out a multi-brand franchisor platform. We partnered over the last 12 years from the time they were a single brand, and we actually reinvested in order to build out the platform.

For Senior Helpers, because franchisees are not operating a four-wall store, we offered franchisees incentives to go buy a book of business from local independents and tuck it under their existing Senior Helpers businesses. This initiative helped franchisees grow faster and provide real scale to their businesses. This program was a win-win for the franchisor and the franchisee. It was such a successful initiative that we rolled it out to other portfolio companies, including FASTSIGNS and Interim Healthcare.

5   Prepare for and facilitate resales.

To the extent that you have wrong fit between the brand and a franchisee, we evaluate ways to sunset that situation and find a franchisee who is a better match for the brand and/or geography. It's a symbiotic relationship. If franchisees aren't happy, the brand will suffer. It's better to sit down with underperforming franchisees and have a candid conversation about their objectives. Sometimes they want to move on and do other things but don't know how. We can help them find a buyer. Franchise development isn't just about selling new locations; a good franchisor will help facilitate resales too. During the tenure of our investment in Senior Helpers, we were able to execute more than 50 resales, and average sales growth for those territories was approximately 40 percent the year after a resale was completed.

6   Improve supply chain efficiency and cost.

Many franchisors aren't professionally managing or coordinating the supply chain for their franchisees. In these cases, there are opportunities to drive more efficient supply chains for the franchisees, which in turn helps the brand, the franchisees, and the franchisor. In the case of Homevestors, we found opportunities to partner with key vendors (e.g., lenders, title insurance, building supplies) to benefit the system and drive higher profit margins.

7   **Evaluate, prepare for, and pursue attractive opportunities to expand internationally.**

Most of the franchise brands that LLCP purchases have the majority of their stores in the United States. One value creation lever that we evaluate is whether the franchise is well positioned for international expansion. In some cases, international expansion will be a key focus for future growth. Sometimes international expansion is not necessary to build and scale the business to meet our growth objectives. Every investment is different.

8   **Invest in technology.**

This ties back to growing same-store sales, improving franchisee support, and driving better unit-level economics. The right tech stack and enabling apps can make a big difference in the customer experience as well as make things more efficient for franchisees.

Building a Value Creation Plan

PE's basic value creation playbook for a franchise business contains many elements that are proven to increase enterprise value. The plan is customized for each portfolio company and situation. It is further adjusted as the business evolves and as PE's hold period weighs on decision-making. You and your team can borrow from the PE playbook to construct your own value creation plan. But you must be committed to putting data behind these decisions and priorities if you truly want to follow the PE way.

Value Creation Plan—Framework for Assessment

▶ Current state assessment—corporate and unit-level profitability
▶ Current business trends
▶ Goals and objectives—financial and operational targets (1-, 3-, 5-, and 10-year)
▶ Gaps and opportunities
  ▷ Break financials into five-year plan view, highlight key gaps and opportunities along with required investments

> ▷ Processes, talent and organization structure, key initiatives
> ▷ Franchisee validation and feedback
> ▷ Key opportunities to improve unit-level operating model and speed of financial return for franchisees
> ▷ Third-party enablers/dependencies; desired future state
> ▷ Risk mitigation
> ► Priorities, timing, and cost

Focus for now on framing out your observations and comparing your findings to the playbook described in this chapter. We will return to this when we talk about how to engage with potential PE partners.

▼

Next, we will examine the playbook for one of PE's favorite value creation strategies: platforming.

CHAPTER 9

Private Equity's Franchise Platform Playbook

"The landscape has changed dramatically. Our ability to support our operating partners very well right from the beginning with the benefit of our platform resources just out-strips what a bootstrapped competing brand can provide."

—**PAUL FLICK**, chief executive office, Premium Service Brands[1]

CONSOLIDATING SECTORS AND CREATING value-add platforms are two common PE strategies that are particularly well suited to franchising because the franchise sector is fragmented and thus ripe for consolidation. Creating a well-integrated shared services model adds value and reduces costs, especially considering franchise businesses have similar back-office functions.

THE PLATFORM STRATEGY HAS PROVEN HIGH RETURNS

To create a multi-brand franchise "platform," the PE sponsor typically will first buy an "anchor" company with a good management team. Other companies highly accretive to enterprise value will then be added (called, literally, "add-ons" or also "tuck-in" acquisitions) to build on that foundation.

The buy-and-build platforming approach is a preferred value creation strategy (in or out of franchising) for one simple reason: high returns.

In a 2016 study by Boston Consulting Group and the HHL Leipzig Graduate School of Management of more than 2,370 merger and acquisition transactions, buy-and-build deals generated an average internal rate of return of 31.6 percent from entry to exit, compared with 23.1 percent for standalone deals.[2] It's perhaps no surprise that add-ons represented 60 percent of North American deals in 2012 but grew to nearly 80 percent of total buyouts in 2022.[3] The beneficial "multiple arbitrage" math of platforms will be detailed in Chapter 14.

OPERATIONAL ADVANTAGES OF PLATFORMS

There are clear advantages to a well-developed platform. Top platforms that have successfully created tangible value for both customers and franchisees stand out.

Standardization and replicable processes improve return on investment. Boston Consulting Group points out that regardless of the sector, increased standardization of operational improvement initiatives and replicable processes are key success factors driving higher enterprise value.[4] Franchising is already a system-oriented business model that strives to be highly replicable. PE works with management teams to energetically execute franchise best practices and systematize everywhere possible.

Improving operational and supply chain efficiencies lowers costs and provides career development opportunities. Franchises have common and largely undifferentiated back-office functions, so clear efficiencies are gained by combining brands onto a single platform and sharing services. Then new services can be added and shared across platform brands to improve both the customer and franchisee experience—for example, a shared call center, customer care team, centralized appointment setting, and mobile phone scheduling app. Pooled buying can lower supply chain costs. In addition, a larger organization is more attractive to top talent and gives existing employees more career development opportunities, both of which improve corporate employee retention and the level of support provided to franchisees.

Making sales and marketing processes more efficient and effective at both the customer and franchise development level to help drive growth. The more units a multi-brand platform has, the more able the corporate team is to negotiate beneficial national customer contracts, creating new revenue opportunities for franchisees. Larger scale can improve marketing efficiency. Once there are enough outlets across brands in the same geography, there are natural cross-selling opportunities to share customer lists and provide different services (e.g., one franchisee delivers mosquito spraying and landscaping services, another cleans gutters and hangs holiday lights). Better customer message targeting and improved marketing fund effectiveness drive higher same-store sales. And being part of a platform improves franchise sales efficiency as well while providing franchisees with built-in territory, product, and service expansion options.

> Our franchise development team alone has 25 people, whereas many emerging brands don't have that many people on their entire corporate team. They may have only one person in franchise development and outsource the rest. All of our brands benefit from the additional exposure as well. It's tough for an independent small brand to compete with our visibility. We also have shared services, national accounts, buying power across all our brands, which includes things like insurance, vehicles, computers, iPads, and financing. We have an entire team working to source better deals for our franchisees.
>
> **—JONATHAN THIESSEN**, chief development officer, Home Franchise Concepts[5]

We focus on marketing immediately. We have playbooks in place and we're targeting the same end customer across all of our brands. We can be very cost-effective through our national accounts and cross-marketing. For example, if we acquire a brand with $12 million in system revenue and

our entire platform has $300 to $400 million of system revenue, that's a
much larger base of marketing spend to leverage. We can immediately get
the phone to ring for franchisees of new brands we acquire at no additional cost to them. Their existing marketing fund contribution just goes
so much farther being part of our platform. And there are other scale
benefits such as training and tools, like our best-in-class relationship management application.

—PAUL FLICK, chief executive officer, Premium Service Brands[6]

Sector experience tends to drive better results. Finally, research has
shown that buy-and-build investments outperform when they increase
the platform company's presence in a particular industry, as opposed to
diversifying its business lines.[7] As any good athletic coach will say, "practice makes you better" and "you need to invest 10,000 hours to really learn
a skill." Most people in franchising would agree it takes time to learn the
franchise model itself and nail implementation. In addition, there are
benefits to knowing a particular sector well, including unique sales, service,
marketing, licensing, and regulatory nuances of that category, especially in
the case of specialized or more regulated sectors (e.g., elder or child care,
health services, disaster remediation).

I think we're still early in the story for home services platforms. It's a
$600 billion sector. So even the largest franchise platforms are small
compared to the overall market opportunity. It's a very fragmented sector.
Really good platforms can play a significant role in delivering a better customer experience, better opportunities for franchisees, and more resources
thanks to a shared service environment. Success begets more success with
franchisees.

Consumer needs are changing faster than the market can respond.
That's where a well-run platform can come in and deliver extra value to
serve customers better. Fragmented industries have trouble meeting customers where they are, but we can drive extra customer value and a higher

level of service across our brands. Now we're in a longer-term fund that will give us time to pursue our growth thesis, partnering with emerging brands and bringing them into our platform. It's working.... You put more fuel on what's working.

—SCOTT FRITH, chairman and chief executive officer, Happinest Brands[8]

STEPS TO BUILD A PLATFORM

The process for creating and building out a platform is straightforward and predictable:

Develop conviction around a theme or sector. First, PE studies the market and selects a subsector or theme (e.g., home services, wellness) for investment based on growth potential, business model attractiveness, and potential for platform synergies. For example, multiple businesses can serve the same set of customers and value can be created by integrating that customer experience.

Develop a target list for exploration and possible outreach. Highly fragmented sectors offer abundant acquisition options (including non-franchise businesses that could be converted to franchises or held as corporate stores to boost parent EBITDA). PE investors move quickly and won't waste time negotiating with intractable sellers in fragmented sectors—PE just moves on.

Create a strong "anchor" with the first brand acquired. This is especially important with regard to C-suite talent. For example, recall LLCP's comments about the strong CEO, Scott Frith, who was part of the Lawn Doctor acquisition that several years later became the anchor brand and team that created the foundation for the Happinest Brands home services platform.

Focus on acquiring highly accretive brands. Acquisitions should improve company financials and also bring talent, products and services, footprint, or other value to the business. Platforms may have more willingness to bring in subscale brands providing they are accretive to the platform in other ways (e.g., key talent, compelling unit-level model). To the extent a target has significant strategic value, platforms can also lean into a more aggressive valuation.

Create an integrated approach to customer engagement. There is value in giving customers coordinated communication or service experiences or anticipating life cycle needs. For example, a single mobile app could be used by customers to order all home services: seeding in the spring, landscaping/mowing and mosquito prevention in the summer, gutter cleaning in the fall, and putting up holiday lights in the winter. This can be accomplished through shared service models, purchasing, technology tools, customer care services, operational support, cross-marketing, and sales training. For example, consider the "continuum of care" provided by franchise businesses in the Best Life Brands portfolio—backed by the Riverside Company. The Best Life platform is a span of brands and service offerings providing comprehensive "senior care advising" via elder care, estate sales, placements, at-home nursing, and in-home recovery.[9]

Add operating partners and fractional executive support as needed. It helps to maintain dedicated assets or a pool of fractional executives to help squire the growth of each acquisition. In the case of platforms, integration often takes greater management skill and technology investment than start-ups can usually access. It is useful to have executives on standby to assist, especially those with experience integrating acquisitions into a cohesive platform.

Create a governance board with additional layers of support. Building platforms requires constant integration and refinement as new offerings and teams are added and synergies are pursued, then realized. A well-functioning board addresses the PE firm's fiduciary duty to its LPs and also can provide an additional backstop of expertise to help the company through integration challenges, if the right talent is on the board. It is easy for the management team to get mired in the moving pieces of the integration and lose sight of the overall business case. Remember that PE owners are not operators (unless they are one of the hybrid investor types we discussed). Regardless, strong boards for portfolio companies, and especially for platforms, tend to include senior executives with significant operating experience to provide additional eyes on the business, perspective, industry connections, and support. This usually starts during the due diligence phase. Expert operating executives brought under PE's due diligence veil can weigh in on the acquisition business case and help write the value creation plan before the business is even acquired. (This is a significant portion of my own professional consulting practice.) This is recognition of the fact that in franchising, financial engineering strategies aren't enough—there is a heavy operational component to success. Post-acquisition, external operating executives brought in as board directors can be a useful bridge, translator, and facilitator between PE and management and sometimes also franchisees.

Remember, not all platforms are created equal! If you are a founder, franchisor, or franchisee, do your due diligence on what benefits are actually being experienced by participants. Promises of supply chain cost savings must be fact-checked. Keep size and scope in mind too. A "platform" of only five brands with a handful of outlets is more "village" than "platform" in my view, although they probably don't market themselves that way when selling franchises! A mature operation with a dozen or more brands, each with significant scale, just offers more.

Creating platforms is a common private equity technique with a clear playbook to drive value creation. Well-integrated franchise platforms that achieve scale provide

- proven high parent returns,
- operating efficiencies and competitive advantages,

- ▶ improved sales and marketing results,
- ▶ differentiated, sustained value for both customers and franchisees, and
- ▶ expansion options and economies of scale.

Once the mechanics of franchise platform creation and expansion are well understood, the playbook can be replicated across multiple service verticals. Some of the most active PE franchise investors are now serial platform creators and/or buyers. They see value in taking this approach to building franchise businesses and have become adept at managing platform creation and growth.

▼

Now that we've looked at PE's franchise playbook and modifications of that playbook specific to platforms, let's turn to the emerging brand playbook.

CHAPTER 10

Private Equity's Emerging Brand Playbook

Every large franchise system in existence today started by recruiting that first, brave franchisee entrepreneur. Today's big business was yesterday's small business.

PRIVATE CAPITAL ALSO HAS a specific playbook to lift emerging franchise brands.[1] Remember that growth investors active in franchising are split into two distinct groups: those willing to incubate emerging brands (e.g., Riverside, 10 Point Capital) and others who, unless adding to a platform, prefer to wait for brands to graduate from the emerging brand stage and demonstrate proof of concept and scale before PE comes in to drive acceleration (e.g., LLCP, Harvest Partners). The first type of PE investor has modeled their investing approach to manage the predictable lack of infrastructure common among emerging brands. They will invest if the concept itself is solid and if there is significant potential for growth and return on investment that compensates for the lift and time required to build the brand. "Emerging," for our purposes, generally means brands with 30 or fewer open franchise units, but frequently fewer than 10. How many active franchise brands fall into this group? *Thousands.* Most never break out. This is something private capital investors new to franchising and prospective franchisees often don't realize.

PLAYBOOK PRACTICALITIES: RUN YOUR BEST PLAYS FIRST

Emerging brands usually depend on franchise fees to fund support and get units open. There are benefits to having a well-capitalized group backing you during this critical *build* stage!

> **Private capital can accelerate and increase emerging brands' chances of reaching maturity in part because PE investors don't rely on franchise fees to fund growth initiatives such as building out the support team, opening new corporate stores, and so on. Having that backing gives emerging brands more time and assistance to fine-tune their model before they get larger.**

Following are two snapshot examples demonstrating the type of attention PE brings specifically to emerging brands. Notice both the laser focus and careful choice of initiatives appropriate to where emerging brands are in their life cycle.

CASE STUDY: EMERGING BRANDS AND 10 POINT CAPITAL

Emerging brands need special attention to develop into a mature franchise system that can achieve significant scale. To avoid becoming a future turnaround candidate, it is critical to build the correct infrastructure, carefully plan territory and sales execution, create a strong unit-level economic model, and recruit the right-match franchisees who can be successful in your concept. Knowing this, 10 Point Capital (a specialist in emerging brand development, especially restaurant brands) only backs brands it views as having a strong operating model and the potential for significant growth. Then, it focuses on three primary areas:

▶ **Market planning:** We develop a multiyear, comprehensive unit-growth strategy based on franchisee success drivers, geographical priorities, competitive trends, and real estate considerations.

▶ **Sales execution:** We employ enhanced franchise sales and marketing tactics to generate more, and better, qualified leads, using data, accountability, and compensation to ensure superior results.

> ▶ **Pipeline activation:** We are focused on optimizing every step along the pipeline to scale, from sales to opening, to ensure quality new locations get up and running as quickly as possible. By investing heavily into analytics and support, we set franchisees up to win from day one.[2]

PE tactics and strategies to build enterprises are quite logical. The "magic" lies in the deeply analytical approach PE takes to identifying the most impactful improvement opportunities, taking a strategic view of the business, and especially driving team follow-through.

PE emerging brand specialists are focused on refining the operating model aligned to franchise best practices before pushing aggressive expansion. As we have discussed, later reinvention in a franchise context is hard work. Building right in the first place is smarter.

CASE STUDY: EMERGING BRANDS AND MPK EQUITY PARTNERS

MPK Equity Partners invests in promising emerging franchises. Young concepts have unique needs and benefit from a strategic thought partner early in their life cycle to grow smarter from the beginning. As MPK Equity Partners investor Caroline Stevens explains,[3]

> We are a small team, too small to run the business ourselves. Our role is to provide coaching, analytical rigor, franchise-specific vendor relationships, and franchising best practices. Often emerging brands need to revise their franchise disclosure document and better articulate unit-level performance to make the opportunity really clear to candidates. The franchisor's reporting capabilities may be limited. We'll go in and increase visibility to data that probably already exists but maybe isn't being collected and analyzed to help drive and improve that business. We help them put together a reporting package and hire a controller or CFO. We help the team focus on key performance metrics and compare

those to budget, year to date, cash flow forecasts, units sold, lead conversions, and so on.

We also help the management team think through their one-, three-, and five-year plans. How can they achieve their objectives? How are things being done today, and how is that working out for the franchisor and franchisees? We look closely at franchisee P&Ls, system sales by unit type, and the fee structure. The franchisor needs to cover its overhead so they can provide support to franchisees.

Each brand has unique needs. We act as a strategic thought partner to empower a bigger vision of the business and then to put the pieces in place to execute on that vision. We invest in franchise development, marketing, support, and adding talent. If there is an acquisition management wants to pursue, we can help them figure out if it's a good investment, and we're a source of capital to fund the acquisition.

Building back-office infrastructure to support franchisees is an expensive, and somewhat thankless, task prior to royalty breakeven. Although 60 to 80 percent of back-office functions are the same across franchise businesses, each brand has to make significant investments to build up its own training, franchisee support, accounting and finance function, marketing team, and so on. PE investors willing to bet on good brands early can get in at a relatively low price and multiple, but company cash flow is going toward building up the support infrastructure and that keeps EBITDA at a modest level. Sponsors need to see significant growth potential to drive cash flow and recapture the benefits of their efforts via a good exit.

The Riverside Company is another firm that has successfully elevated many smaller franchise concepts. Riverside's work with Neighborly is perhaps the most well known, but the company has made more than 50 franchise investments as of this writing.

One of our goals to help entrepreneurs transform their franchise business is to promote a change in mindset. When you're an entrepreneur, you may be wearing 15 hats all at once. It can be uncomfortable or maybe not even feasible for that entrepreneur to invest in the staff they really need. They end up trying to do too much.

We come in as a capital partner with conviction in the long-term value of the business. We have seen the j-curve lift created with the right investments in people, processes, and best practices made early on. So now the entrepreneur can hire those additional people. You can invest in the technology and building out the training function. It's that scalability mindset. We think of adding those key hires, infrastructure, and support as *investments*, not expenses.

—**JEREMY HOLLAND**, managing partner—origination, the Riverside Company[4]

TYPICAL EMERGING BRAND CHALLENGES THAT ARE *NOT* OFF-PUTTING TO PRIVATE EQUITY

It's worth noting that the time frame for fully monetizing emerging brand investments is usually longer, and investors understand that.[5] There are other challenges to investing in these kinds of companies, but not every potential PE partner is put off by them. The following list is applicable only to those PE growth investors willing to invest in sub-scale brands:

The business is undercapitalized. This is music to PE's ears! Many emerging brands are launched without sufficient capital, but access to enormous capital is exactly what PE brings to the table. The budget minimum to reach enterprise breakeven based on royalties collected—not franchise fees—should be at least $2 million to $3 million. Why? Because depending on the concept, brands don't usually reach royalty self-sufficiency (the point where royalties cover corporate costs) until the brand has grown to 50 to 75 open units. Some brands using high-cost sales channels or with lower average revenue per unit must grow even larger to achieve royalty self-sufficiency.

Franchise founders who don't understand this market dynamic can launch and realize too late that they are undercapitalized. For emerging brand specialist investors, if the concept demonstrates solid unit-level economics, PE can step in and immediately help those brands.

The unit operating model is compelling but requires optimization. Often emerging brands launch franchising on the basis of strong unit performance in one or a handful of corporate units. Then the first franchise units launch, and their performance doesn't always align to corporate store performance. Capital partners can drill into the model to help improve operating performance and efficiency—to a point. Streamlining services and improving training to lift franchise units close to corporate-level performance is one thing. That is vastly different from reinventing the entire model because it's not strong or replicable in the first place. The more the model needs a rethink, the less valuable and the fewer PE suitors the emerging franchise will have.

The business has immature operations and support infrastructure or management team gaps in coverage or experience. This is usually due to being undercapitalized but also can result from founders who don't understand what it takes to build a sustainable franchise business. This type of gap doesn't put off PE buyers so long as talent and process upgrades aren't too expensive and so long as their investing model (and especially the acquisition price) compensates them for building out this needed infrastructure. If the buyer is a platform, the acquisition can be tucked in and benefit from platform synergies, talent, and shared services. Several PE-backed platforms have built out special teams specifically to help guide and support new brand integration into the platform so franchisees especially can feel the benefits right away. Examples include Threshold and Best Life Brands (Riverside), Five Star Franchising (Princeton Equity Group), and Premium Service Brands (Susquehanna). However, if the management team isn't "backable," this adds time, cost, and risk for the PE sponsor, which lowers the price or kicks traditional PE investors out of the mix altogether. Family offices and hybrid investors may be willing to take on the CEO role themselves, but traditional PE will not be interested because it's not their model.

Many of the larger PE firms have a stable of operating partners. They bring that expertise. These are talented former executives who are attracted to partnering with private equity. Smaller franchises couldn't have attracted that person. But the PE firm can attract them. Then the operating partner can come in on an interim basis or permanently to help get the company to the next level.

—**JAMES J. GOODMAN**, president, Gemini Partners[6]

The business has low corporate EBITDA combined with a large sold-not-open funnel, specifically due to use of high-cost sales channels. A big sold-not-open funnel is attractive to PE only if it's real! But emerging brands can get themselves into trouble when they don't have adequate resources to support all those openings. A large sold-not-open funnel can thus transfer enterprise value to a PE buyer—and not in a good way from the perspective of the seller! We'll talk about this again in Chapter 17.

The brand is not yet franchised, but it shows great promise. PE is comfortable buying corporate-only models that have the potential to be successfully franchised or with units that can be reflagged. This approach is especially true of platform buyers with existing infrastructure in place to smooth the transition. Some keep those corporate units because they lift EBITDA, build the corporate talent bench, and drive cash flow. For example, Full Speed Automotive (currently backed by MidOcean Partners), one of the largest franchisors and operators of automotive aftermarket repair facilities with more than 900 units, works with independent providers to reflag those units to one of its franchise brands, in addition to pursuing new store development.

> Keep in mind that sector fragmentation provides many opportunities for PE to acquire either franchised or nonfranchised businesses and reflag or convert them.

For example, there are more than 293,000 US and Canadian commercial and residential services companies, of which 94 percent are small and medium-sized businesses. In this group, there are more than 14,000 HVAC (heating, ventilation, and air conditioning) companies alone.[7] Imagine if you are the owner of an emerging HVAC franchise concept with 10 open units that isn't already part of a platform. Potential PE and platform partners have many options. Emerging brands can struggle to break out and also struggle to command any sort of premium in a sale transaction. They must bring something truly differentiated that is also validated within unit-level P&Ls.

COMMON EMERGING BRAND CHALLENGES THAT *DON'T* INTEREST PRIVATE EQUITY

These issues fall outside the playbook. Even emerging brand PE specialists usually won't bother and certainly won't pay a premium to acquire and fix these problems:

You recruited the wrong early franchisees. The wrong operators don't validate well to others, may not follow the system, and won't help build your brand. This is a "back to the drawing board" problem and one of the most common issues observed with emerging brands. PE doesn't have the time or inclination to unwind your false start. Refocus on your ideal operator and recruit only that type of franchisee going forward. A corollary to this is the question, "What is the criticality of the operator to the success of the unit?" If you design a model that is highly dependent on the skills of the operator, that creates risk and prevents a robust MUO recruiting effort later.

Your operating model is immature and has poor unit-level economics. If your model hasn't yet gelled, "there is no there, there." It's only an idea, not a battle-tested model that can be replicated. If that model also hasn't been proven across enough markets and types of real estate, its scalability will be questioned. PE wants to light a fire under undercapitalized brands *with a compelling franchisee value proposition* to accelerate growth. Focus on systematizing everything so franchisees can successfully ramp up and achieve strong profitability.

The business has unproven customer appeal and has been unable to drive customer traffic. Do customers want your brand's products and services at prices that allow franchisees to be profitable? Is there enough customer demand for your offering? How resilient are your products or services to recessions? How did the business manage through the pandemic? Weak answers to these questions drive predictably weak PE interest in unproven brand concepts.

The management team is dysfunctional or the corporate culture is toxic. Have you ever been to a dinner party with a couple having an argument? You can't wait for that meal to end! Similarly, PE doesn't have the inclination to sort out dysfunction on your management team, particularly if they are all partial owners in the business (messy capitalization table). PE also doesn't want to fix a toxic relationship between you and your franchisees; PE wants to back a strong, well-oiled team with engaged franchisees.

The business has significant legal problems. PE will usually pass until after you sort things out.

The business has a risky-looking sold-not-open development funnel. Some franchisors now attempt to sell their way to a PE deal by quickly selling hundreds of license agreements despite having only a small base of open outlets. But the larger the unsold/open ratio, the more suspect that funnel appears.

> Remember that PE is in the business of making risk-adjusted investment decisions to deliver returns for their investors. That big sold-not-open funnel represents risk to the extent that PE can't create confidence as a buyer around what that funnel represents. The more proof points the better.
>
> **—JEREMY HIRSCH**, senior vice president, Houlihan Lokey[8]

I believe some emerging brands are going about growth in the wrong way. They believe they should be selling licenses and don't think carefully about the franchisees they're recruiting into their system. I think that's a big mistake. They believe they need to sell to aspiring entrepreneurs, but that's the wrong profile. You want someone who will follow the system if you have a really good system.

There are many new PE firms coming into franchising now. For those who already have experience in franchising, a huge sold-not-open funnel is a big red flag. Often when you dig in there, you find they've sold licenses to anyone with little regard to whether they will be good operators. Also, those multi-unit agreements can tie up future growth. If you sell six territories but only one opens, if the agreement isn't written correctly it is difficult to get those five other territories back. The franchisee opened one unit and also now has a nice moat around their outlet where no one else can operate. This locks away growth potential. Sophisticated capital partners want to see the quality of franchisees and how well they ramp up performance. Existing agreements are carefully reviewed to ensure enough greenspace is available.

—JEREMY HOLLAND, managing partner—origination, the Riverside Company[9]

The business relies on fads and low-differentiation models. If your concept is a blatant copycat, only a platform buyer missing your version of a painting or pest control concept, or whatever, is likely to be interested. If your concept looks faddish, PE will wait to see if it has legs before buying.

▼

Now that you know PE's playbook and its variations to increase the value of their portfolio companies and extract return on investment, how does PE's own compensation weigh on decision-making and prioritization? What should franchise stakeholders know?

CHAPTER 11

Private Equity Compensation: 2 and 20

Financial incentives can drive behavior.
But so can intrinsic motivations and incentives,
such as an entrepreneur's need to create. Private
equity and franchising intersect in that hot zone.

NOW THAT WE'VE REVIEWED PE's franchise playbook, let's look at how PE expects to be rewarded for their efforts and how compensation structure impacts PE decisions. As a franchisor or multi-unit operator whose business is on PE's radar or already has been acquired, or if you sold your business and have rolled equity forward with your PE partner, how PE is compensated might be the least of your concerns. But it is also true that compensation drives behavior. PE's behavior and strategies to achieve their own objectives are now tied to you and your franchise business. Or, more accurately, you are tied to them.

INCENTIVES AND PRIVATE EQUITY DECISION-MAKING

Remember that a traditional private equity firm's entire mandate is to deliver better returns than public markets, using funds raised to invest in equity in businesses. So, successful fundraising fundamentally validates PE's existence. It's the foundation from which they can do their work. But PE is also paid fees from that base of assets, typically 2 percent of assets under management, meaning that PE also cares very much about each successive fundraise because it's a lucrative source of income. When assets under management commitments increase over time (especially recommitments from prior investors), it signals that the firm's LPs believe in the investment approach. Increasing the firm's assets under management over time is what creates steady, huge earning potential for PE managers, especially senior executives in PE firms.

PE also is paid out of profits created, usually 20 percent of profits achieved after hitting a set hurdle profit rate (often 6 to 8 percent). Sometimes larger LPs will demand fee recapture as well, as part of the hurdle before profit sharing is paid to the PE firm.

Salaries in PE are generous. According to a 2019 survey by Heidrick and Struggles, a global executive search and management consulting firm, the *lowest*-paid investment professionals at North American PE firms (associates and senior associates) earned on average between $234,000 and $420,000 annually, including bonuses.[1]

Building a successful PE career where you climb the ladder of seniority into even richer pay grades and perhaps even launch a spinout fund of your own is a compelling path. It should thus come as no surprise that PE professionals take their work very seriously and are focused on driving the best results possible for their investors. They want to build a good reputation for their firm and also a solid personal reputation.

Profits earned from good portfolio company stewardship, and whatever financial engineering tactics are used to extract additional profit, create an attractive bonus opportunity and ensure the ability to raise more funds based on that investing success, which will then earn 2 percent in fees. This "2 and 20" fee approach is industry standard. New funds and competition sometimes force PE to adjust, such as reducing their fees, to win investor commitments. (If LPs demand fee recapture, those management fees can sometimes be offset by portfolio company management fees, so at least some portion of management fees still get paid, it's just buried on portfolio company P&Ls rather than being billed directly to LPs.) Fees can be clawed back or recaptured based on negotiated terms.

There are other financial benefits for PE managers: profits taken from investing activities are called "carried interest," which in the US is taxed at the current capital gains rate of 20 percent (lower than on other kinds of income). And interest on debt can be written off against taxes at the portfolio company level. But the 2-and-20 standard, based on assets under management and profit bonuses, respectively, is basically how the PE compensation model works. Why does this matter within a franchising context?

> Private equity generally avoids excessive risk. PE is always mindful of their reputation for success and want to protect their path to future fundraises. They are aware of their fiduciary duty to their LPs and their mandate to drive a good return on investment. Consistently good performance across portfolio holdings and funds, not wild performance swings via riskier bets, is what enables ongoing successful, and larger, fundraising. And PE must demonstrate successful portfolio company exits (or at least returning funds to investors through recapitalizations or selling minority interests) to raise their next fund.

Why risk a turnaround when more predictable franchise investing opportunities are available? PE would rather deliver consistent performance. For traditional private equity firms (separate from family offices, strategics, sovereign wealth funds, direct LPs, and individual investors), *it's all about raising the next fund.* PE firms are then under pressure to deploy funds as soon as practical. Once funds are deployed and are at work as investments in portfolio companies, they can get on with raising their next fund. And on it goes. New PE may experience delays in new fundraising if forced to buy smaller companies that take longer to drive to a profitable exit, or if market cycles otherwise delay good exits. But once the ball gets rolling and a newer PE firm demonstrates good exits, there is plenty of capital out there looking for a home.

> Private equity can improve returns in a number of other ways (not used in every case, but there are many options):

- ▸ buying companies using other people's money and debt but little of their own capital (GPs usually invest only 1 to 5 percent)
- ▸ monitoring fees charged to portfolio companies (these may or may not be shared with LPs)
- ▸ charging fees to arrange financing for portfolio companies
- ▸ taking tax benefits of carried interest (taxed at the capital gains rate in the US) compared to higher earned-income rates
- ▸ taking tax benefits of writing off interest at the portfolio company level
- ▸ capturing rebates and fees from captive supply chains and entities
- ▸ selling corporate assets (e.g., real estate) and leasing them back
- ▸ using dividend recapitalizations and securitization to fund distribution payments
- ▸ lending to their own portfolio companies (earning interest on that debt while portfolio companies write off loan interest to reduce taxes)

In addition to company-specific tactics to improve results and thus PE's earning power, private capital habits and tactics honed over many years of investing also ensure that PE is well compensated for their efforts.

PE tactics to improve fund investment returns include the following:

- ▸ buying and selling smart
- ▸ creating a more valuable company—EBITDA growth
- ▸ creating a more valuable company via acquisition—multiple arbitrage *plus* EBITDA growth (we will cover multiple arbitrage in Chapter 14)
- ▸ using leverage or adding more leverage (recapitalization of debt)
- ▸ using lines of credit to buy companies (an increasingly common strategy because it can boost returns)
- ▸ timing cash flows in and out of the fund
- ▸ selling (securitizing) recurring-fee revenue streams (e.g., royalty streams in a franchise context)
- ▸ selling minority positions to other PE firms or LPs midway through the hold period, to repay investors early and de-risk the investment

NO MATTER WHAT HAPPENS, PRIVATE EQUITY IS SET UP TO WIN

Private equity investors are effective at molding circumstances to their benefit. This is core to their DNA and the supporting business processes PE has created to achieve required returns for their investors, such as retiree pension funds. While PE investment in a franchise business is a good signal of potential, PE watchers should use caution to avoid taking assumptions too far. Private equity has multiple ways to take money out of portfolio companies and hedge risk that aren't available to franchisees and founders.

Multiple ways to take money out: Private equity can often make money for themselves and generate respectable investor returns, even when their portfolio companies fail or stall out. PE investors use favorable lending structures and operating agreements to ensure their invested capital comes out first. PE has demonstrated they can pull significant money out even from portfolio companies heading into bankruptcy.

Low litigation payout risk: Even when PE-backed companies face litigation or judgments, those costs are generally borne by the portfolio company (usually via additional debt), not the management team or PE backers. For example, El Pollo Loco paid $36 million in late 2019 to settle several lawsuits, including some brought by franchisees,[2] the cost of which was simply added to the company's existing $150 million debt revolver. At the time, the company was publicly traded, but PE firms Trimaran Partners and Freeman Spogli & Co. were major shareholders, owning 46 percent of the company and having three affiliated directors out of nine serving on the board.[3]

Low GP skin in the game: As mentioned, in traditional PE firms, GPS personally invest only 1 to 5 percent. Debt and LP investor funds and co-investor funds make up the balance in acquisitions. GPS don't sign personal guarantees for loans on the business. This is in contrast to franchisees and founders, who may have a lot of their own money at stake in their business and may have made personal guarantees to landlords and lenders; PE managers avoid the same level of personal financial risk.

Advantageous banking relationships: PE's relationships with financial institutions make loan restructuring more accessible, and the objective is for PE to avoid triggering loan covenants. PE may also be both equity holders and lenders to the same portfolio companies. In contrast, founders and individual franchisees often use their personal savings, retirement nest egg, home equity, or credit cards to finance their businesses.

Experience: Private equity investors have experience acquiring and building companies. They have clear sale objectives, market knowledge, and extensive connections to plug any information gaps. PE owners are also highly knowledgeable about selling businesses. Exiting franchisees or founders often have never sold a business before. They need a successful sale outcome because a significant portion of their net worth is tied up in the business. They are often far more dependent on third-party advisers than an experienced PE deal team is.

Investing with the end in mind: PE considers terminal value up front in their business case. First-time franchisees and founders often do not do this work or may not have accurate exit data. Serial entrepreneurs who have sold other businesses, and experienced multi-unit operators who have bought and sold units, have been through an acquisition process. They are much better prepared than first-time franchisees and first-time founders. PE owners try to keep portfolio companies "sale ready," while founders and franchisees who haven't already been through a sale process often don't know what or how to prepare in advance.

Access to information: Private equity firms (and their bankers and various advisers) have inside information about deal multiples paid, deal structures, and, critically important, what deals are *not* getting closed *and why!* PE investors also learn over time other players' bidding and management track records. PE possesses (or can get access to) information and experience the majority of founders and franchisees just don't have, unless they are very well connected with M&A insiders. If your brother-in-law is a pharma venture capitalist or you had one passing conversation with a PE investor at a conference, these do not count as being well connected. (An emerging brand founder actually gave me these two examples to demonstrate how wired into PE he thought he was!) *You will be your own worst enemy if you think you know more than you do in this high-stakes game.* (In Chapter 18 we will talk about productive ways to engage with PE and advisers.)

Flexible hold periods: Private equity investors can take longer hold positions if needed, depending on the fund. They can be opportunistic and responsive when markets shift, to take advantage of an exit opportunity that presents itself earlier than planned, or to hold longer if need be. Founders and franchisees may feel outsized pressure to try to "time the market" to create a perfect exit scenario. This is difficult from a practical standpoint. PE's investment case doesn't depend on perfect market timing; PE ensures their portfolio companies maintain a sale-ready stance at all times, just in case.

▼

Understanding PE's strategies and tactics and aligning your own objectives to PE's playbook as much as possible allows you to draft alongside their efforts. You now know where and why PE is likely to invest in the business, their value creation plan post-close, and how PE will try to create a good exit. You can use this information to make better choices and build your own wealth. Let's turn now to top positive outcomes for franchising resulting from PE's playbook and from strong alignment with management teams and franchisees.

CHAPTER 12

When Everything Clicks: Positive Impacts on Franchising from Private Equity's Playbook

Surround yourself with the right people. Those who help you build, who lift you up, celebrate your success, have your back, and are wired for growth.

PRIVATE EQUITY'S IMPACT ON franchising has been largely positive. Many PE-supported brands have experienced more growth, market brand awareness, and stability, and provided better support and value for franchisees, than they would have been able to create on their own. While turnaround private capital investors are a rarer breed in franchising, there are also examples where PE partnerships put struggling brands on a healthier path. Multi-unit franchisees have also benefited from partnering with private equity to fulfill their growth vision. The rest of the franchising sector has been forced to up its game to compete against PE-backed brands and platforms or risk losing top franchisee talent and customers.

PE has a history of using aggressive financial engineering tactics to drive higher return on investment. When PE initially came into franchising, many followed this familiar playbook. But as PE investors have gained experience within franchising, increasingly PE has opted for a more operational approach to franchise value creation.

Private equity has undergone an evolution in their franchise investing approach, partly forced on PE by middle market conditions and franchise necessity, and partly as a choice by smart profit-seeking PE firms to improve their returns. Underlying reasons include the following:

▸ Smaller franchise brands naturally invite an operational improvement approach to value creation rather than only financial engineering, because small brands can carry only low (or no) debt.

▸ As the secondary buyout market has matured (PE firms buying and selling companies to each other), each new PE owner is forced to do something "different" to achieve acceptable returns. (Secondary buyouts will be covered in detail in Chapters 13 and 14.) Financial engineering cannot be the sole source of investing returns in such a scenario.

▸ Competition for the best franchisee talent in a crowded but rapidly consolidating market with plenty of available resales puts pressure back on PE ownership and portfolio company management teams. It is the franchisor's responsibility to protect unit-level profitability and maintain good relationships with franchisees to give them reasons to *want* to grow—in other words, to keep the new outlet growth spigot turned on while also motivating franchisees to keep up with required refreshes and updates.

PRIVATE EQUITY'S TOP CONTRIBUTIONS TO FRANCHISING

On its own, franchising achieved scale and opened hundreds of thousands of outlets *without* PE's help. So what has PE brought to the table that franchising couldn't accomplish on its own or that accelerated franchising beyond its existing upward path? What are the primary positive impacts of PE's entrance into (and now dominance of) franchising? What are the outcomes of following the PE playbooks described in previous chapters? The addition of a strong-fit private capital partner has proven to elevate and significantly accelerate franchise businesses.

Private equity's top positive contributions to franchising include the following:

▶ further, faster: incubating, elevating, and accelerating franchise brands
▶ stronger, better: infrastructure, support, scale, and longevity
▶ growth focus: the bright side
▶ game on: private equity blocks weak entrants and forces aging concepts to up their game
▶ unlocking new wealth opportunities: creating a robust trading market for franchise businesses

We'll look at each of these in turn, including case studies and the voices of founders and franchisees.

FURTHER, FASTER: INCUBATING, ELEVATING, AND ACCELERATING FRANCHISES

The first two positive outcomes—taking franchise businesses further, faster—are almost two sides of the same coin, both direct outcomes of PE following its growth playbook. The transformation agenda for a brand may be as broad as creating an entirely new platform or as narrow as swapping out a particular marketing vendor to improve customer traffic. Founders with a big vision sometimes can struggle to get the right pieces and investments in place to make their vision a reality, but that is exactly where PE excels in helping to accelerate their portfolio companies. Because PE isn't running the business day to day, they can drill into the model and think carefully about key inflection points and what investments are needed to accelerate growth. PE also has the benefit of working across many portfolio companies and thus has seen which efforts and investments tend to pay off and which don't. They start with objectives (they know exactly what they hope to sell the brand for). Then, PE works backward to align key initiatives and performance indicators. Finally, PE ties in specific management team accountability and puts incentives in place to ensure execution on their value creation plan. The vision becomes a reality.

> We always had a growth mindset. But partnering with HFC [Home Franchise Concepts] enabled us to take the business to the next level. In the first two years with HFC, we grew top-line revenue 148 percent, added 78 new locations for Kitchen Tune-Up and 40 new locations for Bath Tune-Up. For the first time, we exceeded $100 million in system revenue. We would never have been able to do that on our own that fast! One of my franchisees who has been with us 17 years validated to me that I did the right thing. That franchisee told me that I made sure our brand had a future, and that partnering with HFC was one of the smartest things I'd ever done for our franchisees.

—**HEIDI MORRISSEY**, president, Kitchen Tune-Up and Bath Tune-Up[1]

> Would I bring in PE if I had it to do over? It was absolutely the right thing. It was the best and right choice to satisfy the partners exiting, to help me deliver on my big vision, and to get the company to the next level. I had an amazing relationship with LLCP. They were supportive. I felt they had confidence in me and my abilities. There wasn't debate. They mostly stayed out of my hair. We agreed on how to build the business and everything happened as we had planned. What I appreciated most about them was their willingness to be open-minded. I felt from the very beginning during the interview process that we were always on the same page. We communicated on a weekly basis, and that really helped keep things on track. I just felt supported and confident working with them. It was a great experience.

—**DENA TRIPP**, co-founder, Nothing Bundt Cakes[2]

STRONGER, BETTER: INFRASTRUCTURE, SUPPORT, SCALE, AND LONGEVITY

To accomplish PE's vision of a franchise's future, the next step is to move from the big picture to a focus on specific tactics and operational improvements to enhance performance and returns, including the following three elements:

1 Franchisor support infrastructure often lags, especially in emerging and fast-growing brands. When PE enters, investments here make a material improvement in the lives of franchisees and their ability to ramp faster to profitability.

2 Improved financial controls and system monitoring provide long-term benefits to the franchise. This is especially true when management and PE sponsors are committed not just to tracking but also to continuously improving unit-level profitability.

3 Investments in the brand's future. To fulfill PE's growth and/or longevity agenda and with deep capital assets available, PE can invest in key differentiation and long-term value creation initiatives that brands may otherwise struggle to fund and execute.

We'll briefly address each item and hear feedback from those who have been through it and have seen the type of improvements that can be made.

Better Infrastructure

PE partners can bring in the right infrastructure and vetted partners to support the business case. They drill in to learn where franchisee expansion pain points exist and try to get in front of those issues. Ideally, the right partner should bring a suite of relationships and other partners and advisers who can help build the business—for example, lending partners, vehicle leasing, insurance, suppliers, construction and real estate selection support, and data analytics tools and analysts on the team who can take a mountain of raw data and quickly turn it into insights and prioritized improvement plans.

> What stands out to me is the level of support we can provide and our greater access to resources. The entire JM Family organization has more than 5,000 employees across various businesses, so we can tap into that expertise in human resources, legal, operations, and supply chain as

examples. They have an interest in using capital and all that extra assistance operationally to help us where needed.

As an example, right now everyone in service industries is having trouble getting vehicles. There are long wait lists. Amazon seems to have bought out the entire inventory of Ford Transit vehicles! But through our connection to JM Family, which owns one of the largest vehicle sales and distribution companies in the US, we were able to help our Aussie Pet Mobile brand get their hands on needed vehicles. We bet on growth and acquired those vehicles in advance. We have those connections and resources in house. So now our franchisees can come to training and drive away in their new vehicle if they want to do that.

—**JONATHAN THIESSEN**, chief development officer, Home Franchise Concepts[3]

Improved Financial Controls, Professionalism, and Franchisee Support

Private equity brings significant expertise preparing and analyzing financial statements, addressing working capital requirements, assessing unit-level health, and looking closely at the operating model to find opportunities to improve. Key activities include the following:

- ▶ PE tracks metrics and keeps management focused on continuous improvement.
- ▶ PE ties management accountability and controls back to the business case and identifies and closes gaps and risks to the plan.
- ▶ PE invests to make the model more appealing, scalable, and portable. This may also include product innovation and marketing.
- ▶ PE adds incentives to increase market penetration and boost franchisee adoption of core growth initiatives.
- ▶ Since PE wants to open 100 percent of units sold, PE owners may implement higher financial entry requirements for franchisees, add training, real estate and construction support (if a brick-and-mortar service delivery model), and tighten enforcement of development agreements (or sell smaller development agreements with fewer units) to create more certainty that franchisees will open and ramp up successfully.

▶ In larger PE-backed systems with a significant number of resales, franchisors want to see strong qualifications and financials from incoming franchisees, especially in the top 50 to 100 systems. Resales offer a significant opportunity to improve unit-level performance, but only if the franchisor follows a good process to ensure that new owners are a strong fit and have a capital plan to do needed remodels or investments to bring the outlets up to better-than-average performance. PE-backed brands usually tighten these requirements.

▶ PE eliminates redundancies, busywork, and dead ends that annoy franchisees and don't help the system make money.

▶ PE fills key talent gaps and puts a board of directors in place both to challenge management's thinking and to collaborate with the team on expansion plans.

▶ PE focuses on profitability. For example, they might tweak menus, add customer loyalty programs to increase visit frequency, or keep stores open for longer hours (e.g., Wingstop used to be open only in the evening, Gemini added new dayparts [new segments of the day where customers think of your offerings, e.g., adding breakfast items]; Bain pushed Dunkin' to diversify their beverage selection, giving customers new reasons to make Dunkin' part of their routine throughout the day).

Improved Stability

Along with better financial controls, PE can help portfolio companies become more stable with better capital planning and infusions if needed to improve the balance sheet. Studies show that PE ownership reduces the risk of portfolio company financial distress. For example, a study by Stanford, Harvard, and Northwestern universities about PE-backed firms during the 2007–2009 financial crisis concluded that PE-backed companies experienced smaller decreases in their investments than non-PE-backed peers, drove higher asset growth, and increased their market share during the crisis.[4]

Investments in the Brand's Future

While PE is mindful not to overspend on initiatives that cannot be monetized during their own hold period, there has to be some investment in the future for another buyer to be interested. PE tends to focus on building out infrastructure and functions that can create value that can be monetized at time of sale. For example, building out the franchise development team is a common choice. By bringing in strong franchisees and refilling the development funnel with units that are highly likely to open, a lift in enterprise value is created. Other investments may include building out the franchise business consultant team to coach franchisees and adding technology and customer engagement tools, brand marketing, product and service innovation, and so on.

Outside of the benefits of PE executing the growth playbook, systems tend to see general improvement in the day-to-day management of the business. Two major areas of improvement deserve additional discussion:

1 **Reinforce core operating standards and improve compliance.** Let's look at an operating example critically important to the restaurant industry: health inspections. A 2013 study by researchers from Stanford University and Harvard University focused on the operations of US restaurants acquired by private equity between 2002 and 2012. They documented significant operational changes in 103 restaurant chains and looked at health inspection records for 50,000 locations in the state of Florida. Their study found that operational practices improved after a PE buyout. Restaurants were cleaner, safer, and better maintained. The average reduction in health violations reached 25 percent in four years.[5] In fact, the study found that improvements in franchise units somewhat lagged corporate units because franchisees run independent businesses and because while franchisors can enforce contracts and standards, they can't control franchisee decision-making.[6] Change takes time, especially in a franchise system! But private equity ownership of restaurants was a key factor in accelerating improvements in operational practices.

2 **Improve cadence of unit-level refreshes.** New owners usually try to win franchisee support by making early high-profile investments to improve marketing and execution or offering incentives to encourage franchise expansion and site refreshes. But past a certain point, PE won't hesitate to push out underperforming operators or franchisees unwilling to make needed changes. PE moves quickly in alignment with their defined hold period and mandate. Reselling territories or consolidating them under better (or more cooperative) operators improves PE's chances to later sell the business for a profit. They need to move fairly quickly so the results are visible in time to recapture that value in the next transaction.

GROWTH FOCUS: THE BRIGHT SIDE

PE growth investments in franchising lead to innovation and a better long-term value proposition for customers and franchisees. For example, PE may invest to build out a customer loyalty mobile app, tied to improved mapping of the customer journey, and key marketing outreach or offers to improve that journey or create new reasons to engage with the brand. PE may invest in menu innovation to increase customer frequency or put marketing funds behind the launch of offerings in a new daypart to give customers reasons to engage with the brand at different times of day than they might traditionally have thought to do (e.g., Bain's changes to Dunkin' in the previously mentioned example).

> If you starve a business for capital and don't invest, it will show in the trends. In the long run you lose. But if you help the business grow in the right way, you will get a giant multiple when you bring it to the market because you did all the right things.
>
> **—MATTHEW FRANKEL**, managing partner, Levine Leichtman Capital Partners[7]

Private equity has refocused franchising's attention on unit-level profitability, especially when courting experienced multi-unit franchisees. In addition to launching new products and marketing efforts, PE often comes in with a desire to fundamentally rethink how every square foot of the outlet performs, the profitability of every product and how it can be enhanced, and all core supporting processes. Multi-unit franchisees speak this language. Focused PE efforts to prove out how certain initiatives and investments can lift the business thus tend to result in enhanced MUO confidence in the model and more franchisees willing to sign expansion agreements.

> I believe in the work we do. We make businesses operate with more accountability. We help build more sustainable performance and better investment for franchisees who are ultimately looking to do this as their source of livelihood.

—CAROLINE STEVENS, investor, MPK Equity Partners[8]

> When franchisors are focused on franchisee profitability, you see the result. Franchisees return to develop more locations, and you don't hear about misalignment.

—MATT HALLER, president and chief executive officer, International Franchise Association[9]

Technology is an obvious area of innovation. But what's unique about PE's approach is that they are laser-focused on the end result. They have zero vanity around the need to create something "proprietary" unless it can be proven this approach will lead to a superior return and a leading customer experience (but ideally that value needs to be at least partially realized during their own hold period). There are many cost-effective, ready-made technology solutions that with only slight customizations can provide a superior experience for customers or better efficiencies for franchisees. Developing proprietary systems also means you need to maintain and support them, something most franchisors are not staffed to accomplish. PE tends to prefer using off-the-shelf technologies and best-in-class third-party enabling solutions, again because of the time element. PE owners are quite happy to turn to existing solutions for call center support, expert advice on menu innovation, local digital advertising contracts between franchisees and marketing agencies, or common bookkeeping software that all franchisees are required to adopt, for example. The value is created by driving replicable systems and scale and then executing, and often not from developing new technology from scratch. In addition, PE is often more able to recruit strong technology expertise to the business and tap outside experts for additional advice and support.

> You must always innovate to keep up. We focused on adding more value for franchisees. We hired more support, upgraded the tech stack, and added some of the most innovative marketing platforms and resources to drive more customer demand. The technology also helped improve the customer journey. We're delivering more now than what a franchisee would have gotten without our PE partner. If the relationship with PE is well done, it should add a lot of value to the business.
>
> —SCOTT FRITH, chairman and chief executive officer, Happinest Brands[10]

Often the most visible and appreciated changes brought by PE franchise investors combine the growth mindset with investments in supporting initiatives, technology, and staff to execute on that growth agenda. But another of PE's positive impacts on franchising is a bit underappreciated: quality control.

GAME ON!: PRIVATE EQUITY BLOCKS WEAK ENTRANTS AND FORCES AGING CONCEPTS TO UP THEIR GAME

PE provides oxygen for a few brands but effectively raises competitive barriers and costs for others. And a more competitive environment also impacts legacy brands in particular, especially with regard to the war to recruit great franchisee talent. This means PE activity is forcing both PE-backed and non-PE-backed legacy brands to up their game to attract franchisees and keep brands relevant to customers.

Recall the timeline of modern franchising, which I have divided into four distinct, multidecade "generations":

► Franchise Generation 1.0: 1920 to 1960—early years

► Franchise Generation 2.0: 1961 to 1990—pre-PE

► Franchise Generation 3.0: 1991 to 2019—post-PE

► Franchise Generation 4.0: 2020 forward—post-pandemic (we will discuss 4.0 in Chapter 20)

While outlet expansion ebbs and flows along with market conditions, recessions, and so on, it's interesting to examine the differences between Franchise Generations 2.0 and 3.0, immediately before and after PE entered the equation in a meaningful way.

The difference between these two generations is stark (see Table 1, below). In Franchise Generation 2.0, the number of active brands grew 233 percent. But in the next generation, growth in the number of active brands was only 27 percent, a whopping 88 percent decline from generation to generation. In terms of the number of outlets, unit growth went from 125 percent in Franchise Generation 2.0 to 72 percent in Franchise Generation 3.0, a 42 percent decline. We can assume that outlet saturation is at least part of the reason for the slower pace of outlet-level growth. Certain categories (such as restaurants, which are over-stored in some categories and markets) would account for that. But we're growing (or *retaining* is perhaps a more relevant way to look at it) at the *brand* level much less now compared to the rate during the 30 years prior to 1990.

TABLE 1: Second and Third Generations of Franchising (Before and After Private Equity Entry)

FRANCHISE GENERATION	NUMBER OF ACTIVE FRANCHISE BRANDS	PERCENTAGE GROWTH IN NUMBER OF BRANDS	NUMBER OF FRANCHISED OUTLETS	PERCENTAGE GROWTH OF FRANCHISE OUTLETS
Franchise Generation 2.0: 1960 to 1990 (pre-PE entry)	Increased from 900 to 3,000	233%	Increased from 200,000 to 450,000	125%
Franchise Generation 3.0: 1991 to 2019 (post-PE entry)	Increased from 3,000 to 3,800	27% (88% decline from prior period)	Increased from 450,000 to 773,600	72% (42% decline from prior period)

US market only. Core market data from FRANdata.[11] Author analysis.

The 1960s, 1970s, and 1980s were boom years for franchising, and brands benefited from the rush of people looking for business ownership opportunities. It wasn't uncommon for franchises to achieve 100 to 125 or more operating franchise units *before* stalling out. And this happened even *with* the additional franchise regulations implemented during this generation! Brands listed as having 100 to 125 units during that era were often missing from franchise lists altogether only a few years later. Remember D'Lites? Founded in 1978, the company grew to more than 100 units, stopped franchising, and declared bankruptcy in 1987; what units remained were sold to Hardee's and rebranded. Remember Minnie Pearl's Chicken?[12] It went public but through a series of missteps didn't last. Several enterprising T-shirt companies today sell "Minnie Pearl's Chicken" shirts as a tongue-in-cheek tribute.

So what's changed? Many things are different now from what they were in 1990: technology, consumer preferences and habits, demographics, regulation, inflation, and so on. *But it's hard to ignore the entrance of private equity.* Private equity only backs some companies, and not others. New entrants now either need to arrive with an offering that's strong enough to break out under their own power or strong enough to attract the interest of PE firms and platforms willing to work with emerging brands. All others are essentially blocked from ever becoming relevant.

> PE-backed brands and especially PE-backed platforms have drastically raised the bar for franchisee recruiting and ramp-up costs.

Where else does PE's influence appear in the data? Net outlet growth has become highly concentrated. In 2019, Franchise Grade looked at 2,489 brands and the outlet growth of those brands from 2010 to 2018 using information contained in franchise disclosure documents. The top 654 brands (26 percent of the total) had net outlet growth of 80 percent or better (they were opening and sustaining far more outlets than closed). At the second tier, 38 percent were growing their outlet count, but slower than the top group. In the third tier, 217 brands (9 percent of the total) had flat outlet growth (either they were not adding new units, or they were adding and closing units at roughly the same rate, leading to flat outlet growth). And for the fourth tier, 665 brands (27 percent of the total) had shrinking outlet count.[13] More recent Vetted Biz data mirrors this deal concentration.

This is more evidence that something has materially changed *between the generations.* Franchisee talent recruiting has gotten extremely competitive. In Generation 2.0, 3,000 brands that survived and remained active eventually shared 250,000 in net unit growth, or 83 units per brand just running the averages. (This isn't to say that all brands added 83 units, just that this was the growth potential available to them on average.) Generation 3.0 saw 323,600 net unit growth. But now we know that after 2010, the top 26 percent of brands were seeing 80 percent or better net unit growth, leaving everyone else to fight over what was left. I believe this is one reason why the pace of growth in the number of active brands has slowed considerably.

As mentioned, there is meaningful overlap between the top 400 brands by system revenue and the 700+ brands with a history of PE activity at the franchisor level, franchisee level, or both. Emerging brands that are acquired by PE or PE-backed platforms are more likely to continue actively franchising. In 2023, FRANdata tracked 9,000 franchises, but only 5,000+ are "active" (still franchising). *Thousands* of franchise concepts launch but decide to stop franchising at some point because they just can't get any traction. It doesn't mean the business failed (although some do), but that many simply stop actively offering franchises. This also means that for the thousands of tiny franchise concepts that can't break out, there is little to no exit value at either the brand or outlet level. The cottage industry enabling new franchise launches doesn't talk about that. PE's dominance and influence has fundamentally changed the new franchisor start-up equation. The deck is stacked against a true bootstrap operation unprepared for the competition they will encounter.

> It's so much harder for small brands to get noticed now. Franchise sales organizations, brokers, and platforms get all the visibility. Within the broker networks and FSOs [franchise sales organizations], a lot of expertise, money, and attention gets put on the larger franchisor groups. It's hard

for emerging brands to play in that arms race. Smaller brands are realizing much earlier that they can't play the game. I've been in franchising more than 20 years. Whereas before brands could reach 125 units or more under their own power, now they stall out at 25. They can't keep up.

—JONATHAN THIESSEN, chief development officer, Home Franchise Concepts[14]

The franchise landscape has changed dramatically since I started in 2006. It's becoming more difficult all the time for emerging brands. In the home services space, it used to take $2 million to get a new brand up and running. I would estimate that cost has gone up at least 50 percent; it's closer to $3 million now. A platform just has so much more value and efficiency to offer franchisees compared to a homegrown operation. And everything is more expensive for start-ups. The barrier to entry, even just to get attention from the broker networks, is also higher. The cost per lead is higher. We generate significant organic leads in our territories because our brands are out there. We've also launched three new brands. Our ability to support our operating partners very well right from the beginning with the benefit of our platform resources just outstrips what a bootstrapped independent brand can provide.

—PAUL FLICK, chief executive office, Premium Service Brands[15]

We grew same-store sales 20 percent year over year and found significant cost savings for our franchisees by looking at every element of the supply chain and then issuing requests for proposals from new suppliers to drive franchisee expenses down. But even with all of our successes and positive franchisee validation that we're doing all the right things, we're only going to grow by 8 or 10 new franchisees this year! It's just so hard to get any attention in this market no matter how well franchisees are doing. I pretty much flushed $100,000 down the toilet this year on SEO [search engine optimization] to recruit more new franchisees and got nothing from it.

—FRUSTRATED EMERGING FRANCHISE CHIEF EXECUTIVE OFFICER (and friend of the author) who would like to remain anonymous because of his $100,000 SEO budget face-plant

CASE STUDY: AUTHORITY BRANDS AND FRANCHISE DEVELOPMENT

Authority Brands is a home services platform (as of this writing) backed by Apax Partners. Apax initially invested in 2018. The British Columbia Investment Management Corporation later invested as a minority partner in 2022.[16] (This is an example of direct LP investing, discussed in Chapter 2.) Prior to Apax, Authority Brands was backed by PNC Riverarch Capital, which invested from 2014 to 2018. PNC Riverarch led the company's first acquisitions and helped to establish the Authority Brands platform.[17] Under Apax, there are now 12 brands in the platform with the expectation that additional brands will be added.

Authority Brands provides a relevant example of the dynamic we're seeing related to the success of larger platforms recruiting franchisees. In just the second quarter of 2023, Authority Brands added 44 new franchisees, who together purchased 77 new license agreements.[18] That type of visibility and success signing new agreements is tough noise to rise above if you're a new brand in home services attempting to get attention from prospective franchisees.

Modern franchise market conditions are very tough for new brand start-ups, especially in sectors that have heavily consolidated around platforms, such as home services. But I believe this tougher start-up environment is ultimately positive for franchising. PE plays an important quality-control role by rewarding strong franchise performance with (1) attractive market valuations and buyout proposals, and (2) invitations to join growing platforms. Acquired firms receive help and capital investments in target growth initiatives. Meanwhile, PE generally ignores low-differentiation brands and those with poor unit-level performance and unhappy franchisees—especially at the lowest rungs of the ladder—while simultaneously raising the cost to compete against their own portfolio companies. PE firms are all actively looking for acquisition opportunities. Therefore, when brands aren't growing and aren't picked up by PE investors, it signals to the market that PE is thinking, "We don't see compelling growth potential here, even *with* our help." A stalled-out, unaffiliated franchise eventually can go from looking stale to looking troubled.

It turns out that Adam Smith's concept of the "invisible hand," which you learned about in Economics 101, describes the relationship between private equity and modern franchising very well, except that PE isn't invisible. Academics have long noted the power of invisible hand mechanisms or various forms of private governance to organize and bring order to markets and coordinate behavior. In this role, private equity investors are widely underappreciated, but in the case of franchising their impact has been profound. Said another way, in today's high-cost and challenging business environment, it helps to have Big Money backing your franchise business.

Some franchise critics would like to see more regulation of franchising to prevent unproven concepts from selling franchises. But whatever regulatory changes may occur, the market appears to already be solving that particular problem, thanks to PE's influence. Occasionally there are unworthy break-outs, but these are increasingly rare now compared to prior generations.

What This Means for Preparing for Launch: Most Emerging Brands Never Emerge

Competition now forces new concepts that want to break out to arrive with a pretty strong offering. After franchising efforts have begun, there isn't much time for "experimentation" with the hope that a concept will stick and resonate with the market. The smartest concepts launch well capitalized with strong corporate unit-level performance and a well-honed operating model already under their belt. They don't attempt to start selling franchises until they have perfected the model. For example, FRANdata's Q1 2022 *New Concept Report* identified 86 new franchise brands. Of these, 16 were affiliated with existing franchise brands through their parent company. Forty-seven percent of new brands reported annual average unit revenues (gross sales) of $1,299,297. Compared with the previous quarter, brands reporting more than $1 million in annual sales doubled from 11 to 22 in Q1 2022. Two brands were associated with platform companies. Two others had PE connections. The market has changed. At least some new concepts are launching at a more sophisticated level to compete. This is good for their franchisees and for franchising.

> PE involvement in franchising sets up weaker concepts to fail faster. A weak or ill-positioned brand that years ago might have achieved some scale is now much more likely to stall out while it's still small. Their wake is limited because only friends and family are likely to get pulled in. The rest of the market never even sees them.

When launching a new brand into this environment,

- be prepared for a longer ramp to royalty breakeven;
- design your concept with strong unit-level economics in mind;
- consider opening more corporate units to demonstrate concept viability and drive more corporate cash flow to support a longer ramp;
- show the concept translates to franchised units (e.g., if your corporate stores far exceed the performance of your early franchise locations, that issue needs to be addressed);
- demonstrate the brand's ability to drive unit-level traffic or customer count (without big advertising funds or a platform of shared leads behind you, your concept has to be hot enough to drive customer traffic—you can't depend on bridging that particular gap solely by leaning on franchisees' local marketing efforts);
- think about potential capital partners early and start networking and educating yourself about firms and platforms that work with emerging brands;
- think through where and how you plan to reach prospective franchisees (How will you rise above the crowd and get their attention? What is their awareness journey?);
- choose your early franchisees very carefully; and
- be thoughtful when filling key roles on your management team. One common reason otherwise promising smaller brands aren't acquired is that PE doesn't view management as "backable" and feels the effort to replace key players is too risky or costly within the PE's planned hold period. Specialist family offices, hybrid firms, and independent sponsors who raise capital and buy

companies to run themselves may be interested in that type of engagement. But traditional PE usually passes.

> Private equity wants to see proof of both concept viability and unit-level profitability—*even in emerging brands* (for those willing to work with emerging brands). Prospective franchisees should think about that example when considering joining an emerging concept.

UNLOCKING NEW WEALTH OPPORTUNITIES: CREATING A ROBUST TRADING MARKET FOR FRANCHISE BUSINESSES

PE activity in franchising has made some franchise businesses (at both the corporate and unit level) much more valuable. It used to be that retiring brand founders could pass their business on to the next generation, sell to business partners, or (for larger enterprises) go public. PE acquisitions of franchisors get attention, and this has been a wealth creation engine for founders of solid concepts.

But another, perhaps less appreciated, change is at the franchisee level. Traditionally, retiring franchisees would sell to corporate, to a new franchisee, or to their neighboring franchisee.

> Now franchisees who build good outlets within admired franchise systems can potentially look forward to one day selling to a PE buyer.

The better the operating model and the more cash the business throws off, the more likely the system will attract consolidators, including PE-backed consolidators. This drives prices up for good businesses and provides more exit options. This is a very positive development for franchisees, especially in legacy systems where retirements loom (if those systems have kept up with the times). You don't need to build an empire of 200 units to benefit. But you do need to perform at or above system averages and also be part of a good brand that is attracting PE activity at the outlet level.

PE has created a huge market for franchisees and increased valuations. Now [retiring franchisees] have options to sell their outlets to PE as well as to other franchisees. If that PE acquirer is going for scale, they may be willing to pay more.

—JEREMY HIRSCH, senior vice president, Houlihan Lokey[19]

Private equity has piled into franchising. There are astute fast followers who see the value of the franchise model. This has created extraordinary liquidation opportunities for entrepreneurs, both at the franchisor and franchisee level.

—JEREMY HOLLAND, managing partner—origination, the Riverside Company[20]

The timing is excellent, since we still have a huge number of baby boomer retirements looming. Without private capital funds in the market, this wave of units coming available could have depressed resales. Instead, there is plenty of money sloshing around ready to back strong operators and management teams who want to acquire units and build a larger enterprise.

> **PE activity opens many new exit options as well as raising valuations across the board for high-quality franchise businesses at both the brand and outlet level. Even those who choose not to interact directly with PE are beneficiaries of PE's market activity. The wealth creation opportunities for franchisees in particular have been significantly democratized.**

The onus is on individual founders, franchisors, and franchisees to choose carefully, execute well, and stay aligned with PE's momentum and direction even if they're not personally working with private capital partners. Benefits accrue to those *aligned* to the most powerful players in the franchise market, even if they aren't direct business partners—yet.

> **Summarizing private equity's positive impact on franchising, PE has proven their ability to**

> ▶ **accelerate brands and grow them to the next level;**
> ▶ **block unworthy concepts;**

- ▶ force laggards to get their act together or fall further behind, especially in the turf battle to attract top multi-unit operators;
- ▶ improve unit-level profitability as well as management's *focus* on unit-level profitability;
- ▶ invest in innovation and franchisee support;
- ▶ unlock new product and service opportunities to drive revenue;
- ▶ drive scale and operational efficiencies;
- ▶ attract strong management talent to the corporate team;
- ▶ stabilize and scale supporting infrastructure;
- ▶ improve franchisee access to financing;
- ▶ improve and streamline back-office processes;
- ▶ improve technology tools and organizational technology sophistication;
- ▶ add key performance indicator tracking and financial planning discipline;
- ▶ increase unit resale value; and
- ▶ create wealth and more exit options for aligned stakeholders.

▼

Let's now look more closely at the secondary buyout market as demonstrated by the PE Profit Ladder. Private equity uses this profit ladder to generate big returns for their investors and wealth for themselves. As a founder, franchisor, or franchisee, you can also use the same ladder to create wealth, but only so long as you stay aligned with private equity. And even if your brand isn't yet on the ladder, it is important to have a sense of what may come and what types of partners will be business accelerators.

PART THREE

The Private Equity Profit Ladder in Franchising

CHAPTER 13

Accelerating Organic Growth at Each Step Up the Private Equity Profit Ladder

The climb is everything.

THE PE PROFIT LADDER builds significant enterprise value through the expansion of trading multiples (the increase in the multiple of EBITDA the market is willing to pay) in two fundamental ways: first, by accelerating organic growth; and second, through multiple arbitrage. (We'll cover the latter concept in Chapter 14.) These are very different wealth creation strategies (and they can be combined!), but both take advantage of the PE Profit Ladder mechanism to help execute and monetize the strategy.

The process is straightforward and predictable. Yet many stakeholders leave money on the table when dealing with PE. Are you? Let's look at some common scenarios.

Missteps along the way or a lack of preparation erode value when it comes time to sell. PE buyers love to find undercapitalized businesses with "good bones." They will invest in processes and infrastructure that lift the business and consequently shift value to their firm and their own LPs. If this sounds familiar, what can you do to avoid being bought for less than your business should be worth?

If you work on the corporate team and the company is backed by PE, there are significant earning opportunities. PE moves fast to replace nonproductive cogs in the machine. Stay aligned and deliver. Knowing PE's value creation plan and objectives should help you focus on what matters most.

Some are too focused on hitting a magic EBITDA number before talking to PE. You're missing the much larger opportunity to roll equity forward with the right PE partner while reducing risk.

Some of you, I'm sorry to say, are beyond mere value leakage. You are literally shoveling money into the arms of people who understand the PE Profit Ladder better than you do. I'm here to help!

LADDER STRUCTURE: THE SECONDARY BUYOUT MARKET

The PE Profit Ladder is now well established in franchising. Picture a ladder with many rungs and several PE firms sitting on each rung. As PE investing activity within a sector matures, PE firms logically organize themselves in this way and eventually settle into their respective roles. Up and down the ladder, franchise systems and whole franchisee operating groups are traded. It's a hive of activity, with hundreds of firms participating. Re-trading between PE firms and platforms creates the outward appearance of a tangled web of relationships and deals. The same is true in the "take public, take private, take public again" loop enabled by PE. But a ladder is closer to how the mechanics work and is much easier to visualize. Technically, the trading of companies between PE firms is called a "secondary buyout" or SBO. (It's still called an SBO whether it's the second time a company has traded or the eighth.) At each major step up the ladder, and with each change in ownership, there are opportunities to grow the business and make improvements so both the PE owner and aligned stakeholders can take out more in profits. When PE is active in a sector as it is within US franchising, secondary buyout deals gradually become more common.

On the following spread is a simple graphic that lays out the PE Profit Ladder dynamic, various players, and key metrics to watch.

The Y axis shows the pace of openings, and the X axis the total number of units open. It is possible for brands to open units but not maintain them. Both are necessary to build a high-quality brand.

The three main types of investors are also shown: growth investors, value investors, and turnaround investors.

Growth investors are banking on aggressive growth by employing "build" and "accelerate" operational strategies.

Under the X axis, units sold but not open accumulate. Having some units in the development funnel is normal and potentially attractive to PE. But as sold-not-open (SNO) approaches 3x more than units opening, it starts to look like "SNO Theatre." Beyond this, selling >4x more units than are opening is a huge red flag for PE investors with franchise experience. It indicates an organization potentially more focused on selling than brand-building with a viable operating model.

There are two "no PE zones." The first is where brands are too small, weak, unproven, and under-capitalized. FRANdata tracks 9,000 franchises, but only 5,000 active brands.

The other includes brands that grew to some small scale then stalled. These are budding turnarounds. Given the effort required for a turnaround and the small scale of these brands, they are unlikely to attract private capital interest.

At the top of the ladder, "extend and expand" requires a commitment to investing in the future of the franchise. This rung of the ladder reminds us that today's value investor can actually push the brand into turnaround territory via poor stewardship, inertia, or overleverage. Underinvestment, negative franchisee turnover, and eroding differentiation can accelerate a downward slide. The biggest risk with franchise value investing is when owners milk that cash cow too long while the brand, offerings, and outlets age within the system. Later reboots can be expensive and risky.

It is critical for management, founders, and especially franchisees to think about where their brand is on the PE Profit Ladder and within their own brand lifecycle.

FIGURE 1: The Private Equity Profit Ladder

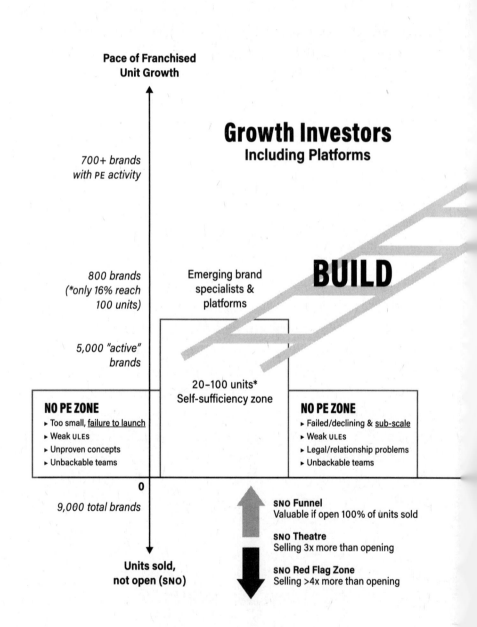

EXTEND & EXPAND

ACCELERATE

Value Investors
Including Platforms

Turnaround Investors

Sustained growth
& new market entry

Slowing growth, but
med/large scale

Flat, but med/large
scale

Declining units, but
med/large scale

Total
Franchised
Units
Open

Big Money in Franchising©

▼

The SBO trading mechanism provides an often necessary "changing of the guard," bringing new skills, fresh capital, and different perspectives at various inflection points in a company's life cycle. It also provides important exit options for founders and early investors, as well as for current PE owners who need to show a return. All of this has settled into a now predictable pattern. Financiers try to maintain their relative positions of advantage. Brands fight to compete in this altered landscape. Knowing the ladder is in place and understanding how the various participants act allows you to plan your own success and wealth strategy.

> In franchising, the PE trading ladder has become a significant competitive force unto itself. It has redefined and accelerated the typical franchise growth path and has also rewired participants' tactics and expectations.

PE may sometimes get into competitive bidding situations (auctions for truly special businesses can get sporty), but generally PE tries to carve out and defend a particular position on the ladder. It is to PE's advantage to organize the entire franchise landscape itself so that it is aligned to how PE wants to acquire companies and later position those companies for sale. This enables PE to build value, defend their own hunting ground, take advantage of multiple arbitrage opportunities, and anoint winners and losers.

PE firms sort themselves onto their preferred rungs on the proverbial deal ladder based on whether each wants to be the first institutional capital in a brand or wait until the target is larger and more proven, whether they prefer certain verticals (health care, home services, etc.), whether they prefer majority ownership or collaborative "club deals" in partnership with other firms, and other considerations. To avoid competing only on price, most PE firms and family offices try to add a little something special when competing for a franchise acquisition, such as building founder relationships well ahead of time, a deep knowledge of emerging brands or a particular sector, a compelling platform, and so on.

PE constantly looks for an inside track to increase their certainty of closing deals and avoid the hassle and expense of participating in an auction process they aren't certain to win. As one PE executive told me, "It's tough to stand out among 15 management presentations. I'm sure we all look the same to the sellers." And a few will use a reputation for aggressive bidding to discourage auction participants.

You can reasonably predict the methods PE will employ to achieve their target return on investment. If you are thinking about bringing on a capital partner, you can see the logical inflection points in your own business (or of a brand you're a part of). You can see what will attract PE and cause them to pay more for your business and what will diminish attractiveness and enterprise value in PE's eyes. You can also start to see where value is leaking out (or spewing out) along the way so you can create a plan and hold yourself accountable to reclaim that lost value. By understanding the private capital spectrum and stratification among the players, you can anticipate which firms (or at least which type) might come calling or might be a fit. You can do this by noting which PE firms choose to invest at which rungs on the ladder and which firms are logical potential buyers at various stages in any franchise company's life cycle.

Or not. Perhaps you're a founder and you've decided partnering with PE isn't a fit for you or your company. Perhaps you simply want to delay looking for outside capital. Maybe you're a prospective franchisee who loves a particular concept and you're tempted to ignore whether the brand is PE owned or not. After all, ownership may change anyway, right?

But what you must keep in mind is this: The entire franchise marketplace is now jumping on and off the PE deal ladder at various points, including franchisors, multi-unit franchisees, and whole platforms. Your competitor today may soon enjoy private equity backing or may join a PE-backed platform. PE-backed franchises typically get a big slug of investment dollars and strategic assistance, especially in the early years, to boost growth. If that happens, your competitor becomes more threatening. PE engagement changes the businesses they get involved with, but the entire marketplace also changes once PE firms start trading with each other. That trading mechanism helps companies grow because sponsors are working hard to achieve a good exit. Also, bringing in new perspectives and different skills at key inflection points tends to move brands forward. That is exactly the pattern that unfolded in franchising.

> Even if you choose not to step on the ladder yourself or put your business on the ladder, you still can't ignore the PE Profit Ladder.

TRADING UP, DOWN, AND ACROSS THE LADDER

Rungs on the ladder roughly equate to different levels of investment, company size, and business maturity. This includes add-on acquisitions, such as joining a platform that's already on the ladder. As acquired companies get larger, it's more tempting for PE to put higher leverage onto the business. (At the bottom of the ladder, leverage often isn't used at all because the acquisitions are too small.) Once a franchise steps onto the PE Profit Ladder, it will gradually continue to move up (or out, via sale to a non-PE-backed corporate strategic or hybrid with specific expertise) based on the unique dynamics of that franchise, market conditions, competitive forces, and the objectives of the PE owner. At the top of the ladder, the company will likely land in the bosom of a long-hold buyer or go public. (It can always go private again.)

In general, the larger the PE fund, the larger the check size (minimum equity investment) must be. It's inefficient and difficult to buy and monitor lots of little companies out of a large fund. Private equity firms generally want to raise another fund down the road (we discussed that dynamic in Chapter 11). Subsequent capital raises tend to increase with each new fund, which pushes PE to buy larger companies as well. Exceptions are made for highly accretive tuck-in acquisitions. Thus PE firms tend to move up the ladder over time as fundraising increases with each round, provided those firms can demonstrate a track record of successful exits and returning funds to investors. A steadfast commitment to emerging brands (e.g., investing out a dedicated microcap fund) is usually needed for PE to avoid "falling up the ladder," being pushed into buying bigger companies with every new fund.

It is now common to see franchise brands and multi-unit holdings trade up (or down or across) the PE ladder several times. Let's break down the process and provide some examples.

The Lower Rungs

With every trade on the ladder, a new private equity team takes command. Each firm will have different perspectives and skills than the previous team. Some PE firms (including PE-backed platforms and hybrids) are experts in working with early-stage franchises, typically those with fewer than 30 outlets, and are willing to do smaller deals or invest earlier in a brand's life cycle. Examples include the Riverside Company, 10 Point Capital, and Savory Restaurant Fund. Family offices, wealthy individuals, hybrids, independent sponsors, and platforms all play here. Fund-to-fund transfers (transferring portfolio companies between two different funds owned by the same sponsor) also happen if more time is required.

Successful private capital players have a robust network of operating executives and advisers they can tap to carefully craft and/or vet detailed value creation plans, as well as oversight by PE executives dedicated to successful execution of the strategy. These executives coach the team and provide a level of senior support and insight that small brands just don't typically have access to. The combined assistance package is a game changer for small companies and can drive significant lift in enterprise value. This is also why the majority of PE investments are now made in smaller companies across all industries, something often missed in discussions about private equity.

The most profoundly positive transformations happen with PE's assistance within the lower and middle rungs of the PE Profit Ladder. With these investments, PE investors are most challenged to think like operators (though they are not operators), which is why many will partner with proven operating executives, build out special support teams, and lean on advisers to ensure strong outcomes. Financial engineering strategies generally aren't available for smaller brands. The first few PE owners appear to contribute to the greatest absolute business lift (seen in trackable metrics), putting the business on a better trajectory.

The Riverside Company (founded 1988): Riverside's first franchise acquisition, in 2003, was the Dwyer Group. Riverside would ultimately buy and sell equity interests in Dwyer (later called Neighborly) three separate times. Dwyer was one of the early multi-brand platforms that helped touch off a boom both in new home services franchises and home services–focused platforms. (There are now at least 20 different home services multi-brand platforms in the US.) Riverside has partnered with over 50 franchise brands and recently completed their eighth platform investment, this time in the IT services space.[1] The company has intentionally occupied the lower rungs of the PE Profit Ladder and has methodically made itself one of the most successful and influential capital partners in franchising. Riverside believes its disciplined approach to investing, fund structure permitting smaller investments and longer hold periods, success building platforms, collaborative reputation, and focus on elevating emerging brands differentiates them in the industry.

Founders talking to private equity for the first time can understandably get frustrated with some of the feedback they get. Those entrepreneurs may think to themselves, "Here's another Harvard MBA with no experience running any business telling me how to run *my* business."

Our approach to the entire relationship starting with the initial conversation is very different. We say, "Tell us about your experiences. Tell us what you have discovered along the way." We come in with a desire to learn.

We have humility when working with founders. We don't tell them what to do. Maybe it's our Midwestern roots. We are students more than teachers. We recognize that founders are domain experts.

It also impacts governance. Many PE firms stack the board with their own people. We prefer to put experienced operators on the board—which we believe adds far more value. Our focus is on best practices and deeply understanding how the business performs optimally. Then we look at ways to extend that with the right investments in the business and especially people.

—JEREMY HOLLAND, managing partner—origination, the Riverside Company[2]

The Middle Rungs

Other PE firms are known as accelerators of larger but still growth-focused franchises. For example, Levine Leichtman Capital Partners and Harvest Partners work with larger brands (typically those already with 100–200 outlets or more) and try to keep those brands on an aggressive growth path. Family offices, platforms, hybrids, and some strategics play here. Institutional LPs may come in to make a direct investment with PE as the majority partner. The middle of the investing ladder is very crowded! Within the middle ladder rungs, keeping management focused on the operational playbook to accelerate growth remains key. But as greater scale is achieved, financial engineering strategies start to come into play. These drive incremental financial returns for the PE sponsor and their LPs.

PE activity within the middle of the profit ladder has also been largely positive for franchising because of the alignment of interests between growth-focused PE sponsors and franchisees.

Levine Leichtman Capital Partners (founded 1984): LLCP is notable for being an early mover franchise investor starting in 2000 and has remained consistently active in franchise investing since then. With over 28 franchisor investments, LLCP has demonstrated the ability to take established franchise brands and platforms to the next level. LLCP is a good example of a PE firm executing the franchise growth playbook in the middle of the deal ladder. Some of the most successful and iconic franchise brands and platforms (such as Tropical Smoothie Cafe, Lawn Doctor, Nothing Bundt Cakes, and Caring Brands International) were nurtured earlier in their growth trajectories and propelled forward by LLCP.

The Top Rungs

Finally, higher up on the ladder are the largest PE firms who may pursue public offerings for portfolio companies, keep portfolio companies long term, sell to a strategic buyer, or sell to another large PE firm. Bain Capital, KKR, and Roark Capital Group are examples of this type of franchise investor, although, of course, if market conditions don't permit going public or they receive a compelling acquisition offer, PE can always divest portfolio companies to alternatives such as strategics, family offices, fund-to-fund transfers, or another PE group, or allow LPs to make direct investments in portfolio companies. When franchise businesses land here, they may have already traded between PE firms multiple times. Or, they could be publicly traded and now going private. Sometimes a refresh of the value proposition or branding may be needed to get the franchise back on a growth path. If the franchise hasn't started international expansion or hasn't yet added new products, often these larger players have the relationships and experience to pursue these opportunities. But this is also rare air. Remember that only 4 percent of active franchise brands exceed 500 units. That's only 200 brands for the largest and best-capitalized PE firms to compete over... and most are already public or backed by PE. So it's a tight market.

Mega PE firms buying large franchise businesses may pursue a growth, value, or turnaround agenda. But whatever the strategy, it is executed at scale. The pursuit of various operational and cost efficiencies is also core to the playbook in the top rungs. More focus shifts toward growing and defending same-store sales. The pace of outlet expansion often slows within existing markets as available franchise territories sell out. Nontraditional sites may be added and international expansion strategies launched. Resales and unit-level consolidation are a factor within these systems.

And financial engineering strategies are absolutely a part of the playbook for large PE firms investing in franchises at the top of the PE Profit Ladder.

Roark Capital Group (founded 2001): Roark has acquired 108+ franchise/ multi-unit brands across a diverse set of industries, including restaurants, food, health and wellness, automotive, children's services, and business services. Roark has also established or purchased several prominent multi-brand franchise platforms, including Driven Brands, Focus Brands, Inspire Brands, Self Esteem Brands, ServiceMaster Brands, and Youth Enrichment Brands. Combined, these companies generate more than $77 billion in system revenue across 69,000 locations in 50 states and 89 countries around the world (pre-Subway acquisition).[3]

▼

PE thinks about this sequencing or threading of deals up and across the profit ladder from the outset and positions their portfolio holdings accordingly. PE plans their exit from the beginning and already has a business case with working assumptions about company valuation and potential buyers at exit. While working with their portfolio companies, PE keeps communication channels open between themselves and potential buyers. M&A insiders including bankers, intermediaries, and advisers stay plugged in to this information network.

If brands somehow falter on their way up the ladder due to changing market conditions or failure to correctly implement the franchise model, another transaction can bring in new eyes and fresh capital to try to turn the situation around, although, as discussed, slipping down the ladder in this way should be avoided. There are few investors interested in this type of work compared with the more certain path of accelerating and extending existing good franchise businesses.

> I also want to introduce here the concept of having a "good PE lineage" once a franchise brand steps onto the ladder. Your brand's success story and results can be enhanced if it is associated with one or more well-respected PE firms that themselves have a solid track record of driving growth and positive franchisee outcomes. Of course, for sponsors with a less positive reputation and outcomes, the opposite is also true.

PLANNING YOUR WEALTH CREATION STRATEGY

Many franchisees and brand founders have only vague ideas or have done little real planning regarding the terminal value of their company and what type of exit will maximize their long-term earnings. How long should you remain independent? What about rolling some equity forward with your new private equity partner? What could that be worth to you? How do you figure it out? As a brand founder or franchisee, you must ask, "How can I plan from the beginning to build an operation that has value and creates the option to attract a consolidator or PE firm?" Knowing how the profit ladder works will help you to be proactive about your own wealth planning.

> We sold to LLCP in 2012 and rolled 30 percent of equity forward. We made four times our money on that roll. When the business sold to Altares in 2016, they also let us invest, so we rolled some forward again. It just sold again in 2021 to a strategic acquirer.
>
> **—PETER ROSS**, chief executive officer and co-founder, Senior Helpers[4]

In the first deal, I rolled all my equity forward with LLCP. I had tremendous confidence in the brand and the partnership with LLCP. I didn't take any money off the table. But by the time the second deal happened,

I had already made significantly more on that first equity roll than I ever dreamed of. I was ready for a change at that point. I kept my own four bakeries, but I was ready to exit otherwise and retire.

—DENA TRIPP, co-founder, Nothing Bundt Cakes[5]

The secondary buyout market is where many franchise sellers ultimately make their greatest return, and yet information about it is missing from most everything written about franchise investing. If you choose to remain independent but aren't taking steps to move the business forward, your momentum may be decelerating compared to the rest of the market. Either way, be proactive. Outline your objectives and the best path forward, keeping the ladder options and your competitors in mind.

> Acknowledging and planning around the PE Profit Ladder is the critical missing piece in most of what is written about wealth creation in franchising. Awareness of private equity activity is critically important, whether you are a founder, franchisee, or other stakeholder.

Remember that once a franchise brand starts marching up the private equity ladder, there are only a few routes forward:

► Sell up the ladder in a few years to a larger private equity firm (or down the ladder if the business is mismanaged).
► Sell to a strategic or PE-backed hybrid, such as a platform.
► Execute a management buyout (often backed by PE, so it's a lateral move across the PE ladder).
► Execute an employee buyout via an employee stock ownership plan.
► Sell to a family office or other long-hold acquirer.
► Go public (there are several methods to accomplish this: IPO, direct offering, or alternative via reverse merger with a public shell company).
► Once public, you can go private again via PE.

At each step PE tries to grow the business and create a few turns' worth of incremental value (added multiple of EBITDA of value) to repay their own investors. But, ideally, they also create some upside opportunity for the next buyer, so that buyer is willing to lean into a higher valuation. A little meat should be left on the bone, as it were, so the next investor up the ladder can also make a good return. Low interest rates tend to drive deal prices up, creating long-term growth pressure to live up to the business case. This is one of the chief concerns as the business continues to trade up the secondary deal ladder. Does the music ever stop? Over several flips, if PE overpays to get deals done, it erodes value for owners at the top of the ladder if those acquisitions don't grow into those more aggressive valuations. Alternatively, longer hold periods may be required to fulfill the business case.

And at some point in large brands, growth will slow. No one in franchising likes to talk about this. But every brand in every market has a ceiling above which incremental outlet growth in saturated markets becomes difficult. To keep the growth spigot turned on, new markets must be entered. Underperforming operators must be pushed out. New products, services, or dayparts must be added or new marketing investments made to lift same-store sales. New distribution channels (e.g., licensing or selling directly to customers) must be added. The company may also consider adding smaller-format or nontraditional sites to fill in smaller tier 2 and tier 3 markets or reach new customers when primary markets are sold out.

When a franchise business successfully climbs up the PE Profit Ladder, secondary transactions and ownership changes become an integral part of a brand's growth story. Let's look at an organic growth example cultivated across multiple PE sponsors: Tropical Smoothie Cafe.

CASE STUDY: TROPICAL SMOOTHIE CAFE

Franchise businesses can successfully climb the PE Profit Ladder and thrive across multiple changes in ownership.

Positive brand outcomes across multiple PE owners are created through (1) following franchise best practices, (2) maintaining focus on unit profitability, (3) driving organic growth, and (4) attending to the franchisee

| relationship and satisfaction. As the saying goes, "franchising is simple as long as franchisees are happy and making money."

The history of Tropical Smoothie Cafe's (TSC) involvement with private equity owners serves as an example of this success formula. TSC was founded (under a different name) in 1997, and the first franchisee location opened in 1998. The business was rebranded to the now well-known name in 1999. By 2006, TSC had 200 cafés open, and by mid-2012, the system grew to 315 units. Average unit volumes at the time were $526,000, up 5 percent from the prior year.[6] As a consultant, I would summarize their history to this point by saying TSC had impressive unit growth as an independent brand, but with average unit revenues of only $526,000 in a concept that also requires the fixed expenses of brick-and-mortar locations, there was likely profitability pressure on franchisees, especially underperformers.

In August 2012, BIP Opportunities Fund LP invested $10 million to acquire a controlling interest in the company, and 10 Point Capital joined as a minority partner.[7] With this new capital and strategic expertise, TSC invested in menu innovations and marketing to grow both units and same-store sales. For example, the company added vegetables to its smoothies, a pioneering move according to Business Wire coverage at the time. (Now I know the origins of my own favorite TSC smoothie with spinach and kale.) The company also expanded its menu, doubled its marketing fund, and launched its first national television advertising campaign in March 2014.[8] TSC continued to grow under private equity ownership. It had 400+ cafés open by the end of 2014, 500+ by 2016, 600+ by 2017, 700+ by 2018, and 800+ by 2019.

In September 2020, Levine Leichtman Capital Partners, in partnership with management, bought the company when TSC had 870 units open and 500 more in development.[9] As previously mentioned, LLCP has deep expertise in acquiring larger franchise brands with still significant growth potential and scaling those businesses. The firm saw substantial room for TSC's growth, both domestically and overseas. In press coverage at the time of the acquisition, LLCP said, "The firm [LLCP] offers a structured equity approach in which the company invests a combination of equity and debt and doesn't over leverage the business... to ensure that Tropical Smoothie has the capital it needs to continue to expand."[10] Details of the deal were not disclosed at the time, but according to TSC's 2022 franchise disclosure document,[11] TSC was acquired by LLCP for $623.9 million, of which $242.3 million was debt. At 38 percent, this is indeed a modest amount of leverage by private equity standards.[12]

It should be pointed out that through these rounds of PE ownership, TSC average unit volumes continued to increase, and franchisees appeared to do well overall. Average unit volumes grew from $526,000 in 2012 when BIP and 10 Point acquired the company to $836,218 at the time LLCP acquired the company in 2020. Average unit volumes are over $1 million today. There have been terminations, closure of units for other reasons, and transfers across these different PE owners as well. (Between 2012 and 2021, TSC's FDDS show a total of 69 terminations and 80 "ceased other," including 18 during the pandemic.) However, there has also been a robust interest in TSC transfer units, including 44 transfers that changed hands in 2021. (Transfers are the sale of units by owners retiring and selling to other franchisees, both existing and new franchisees.) In addition, during the first three quarters of 2022, 70 percent of new units that were opened were expansions by existing franchisees,[13] a strong indication that franchisees are happy with unit-level profitability. If it were otherwise, they would not continue to add new units. The company had more than 1,300 locations open by the end of 2023.[14]

What is the end game for this particular LLCP investment? Analysts believe TSC could be worth at least $1 billion in a public offering.[15] But given that LLCP's investment in the business in 2020 is relatively recent, an IPO could be years away if it happens at all.* Long-term debt payments are structured to avoid overburdening the company in the near term. A balloon principal payment of $179.4 million isn't due until 2026.

TABLE 2: Aggregate Future Principal Payments on Term Loans at December 26, 2021

Fiscal year	(in thousands)
2022	$ 595
2023	744
2024	446
2025	595
2026	179,420
Total	$ 181,800

Source: Tropical Smoothie Cafe 2022 Franchise Disclosure Document. (Issued April 15, 2022.) Notes to Financial Statements. "8. Debt." p. F-19.

Presumably, the company could go public or trade again by that time and the balloon payment would be partially or fully retired out of the IPO or sale proceeds (or refinanced if a longer hold is needed). LLCP could sell the company to another

---

*   In 2021, the company spent $299,000 in advisory fees related to preparing for an IPO. (Source: 2022 FDD.)

large PE firm or large restaurant platform, such as YUM Brands ($33 billion market cap, publicly traded) or Inspire Brands ($30 billion system sales, held by Roark). LLCP took this exact route when it sold Nothing Bundt Cakes to Roark in May 2021.

TSC provides an example of the PE Profit Ladder when it works well. Each step up the ladder can build wealth and enterprise value. Specialist firms adept at working with emerging brands usually enter first. The focus at this stage is on growth initiatives, improving underlying unit-level economics, and systematizing core business processes. As the company scales up, larger PE firms that are also growth-minded eventually take over and continue to invest in initiatives focused on substantially scaling the business. Some of the larger firms have experience taking brands public, so when the timing is right those partners can be a good fit. Along the way, franchisees tend to see improvements in the core business model, support, technology stack, and especially marketing. This often translates into improved unit profitability, which encourages franchisees to expand. Those operators who are no longer a fit are proactively moved out of the business.

Franchisees benefit from robust interest in resales of good locations. If the net openings continue to rise and existing franchisees continue to buy expansion units, then retirements and ownership consolidation will naturally start to happen as the system matures. Under a proactive and well-managed franchise development program, management incentives are aligned with PE growth objectives, and a formal resale process delivers value to those franchisees who are ready to move on and need assistance to do so. In theory, this puts both PE and management on the same side as franchisees. All boats float higher as the tide rises on a wave of better franchisee and corporate-level profitability and improved franchisee confidence in the business.

Could Tropical Smoothie Cafe have achieved this scale and such strong unit-level results as quickly without private equity's help? Perhaps. It's difficult to know what *could* have been. But recall that, back in 2012, Tropical Smoothie Cafe had around 315 units with volumes of only $526,000. For a retail concept (i.e., there are site costs such as rent), this means the model was ripe for a rethink and some reinvention to drive higher sales and franchisee profitability. Improvements made to the business model and investments in marketing grew the brand to 1,330+ units by 2023, which is 322 percent unit growth. As an independent prior to PE involvement, it took TSC six years to add 115 units from 2006 to 2012. But a succession of experienced PE partners, working closely with an incentive-aligned and energetic management team that itself was highly engaged with franchisees, helped TSC add more than 1,000 units over the 11 years from 2012 to 2023. The company has seen 12 consecutive years of same-store growth and opened 170 new cafés in 2023, the highest number for the brand in a single year.[16]

This impressive growth was achieved in tandem with doubling average unit volumes and maintaining strong franchise satisfaction scores. TSC has made *Franchise Business Review*'s awards list every year since TSC started conducting the surveys going back to 2015, based on positive franchisee survey results.[17] TSC also received strong third-party validation from FRANdata, which awarded TSC with a top FUND score rating in 2023 for the third year in a row, based on unit success rate, unit-level profitability, and franchisee support.[18]

For Tropical Smoothie Cafe, partnering with a succession of strong private equity partners elevated the brand and took it *further, faster* than it probably could have achieved on its own in the same amount of time.

> What is the experience like for franchisees through these changes in ownership over the years? When a brand is well managed, the signals are clear: *top operators continue to expand and also validate well.* This is especially true in growth brands with PE backing. PE sponsors and management are focused on improving both customer and franchisee value propositions *as a core component of the growth agenda.*

Let's hear from the co-CEOs of DYNE Hospitality Group.[19] Currently the largest franchisees of the TSC brand, they recently opened their 100th location, in Little Rock, Arkansas.

I've worked in restaurants since I was 15 years old. I started washing dishes. I grew up in this industry. I love to serve my team, partners, and guests. I've been at it for 22 years now and I've probably worked in every position. There is no fancy story here, just a lot of hard work and grit. We're humble and grateful and have had great mentors along the way. It's clear to me that successful people find something they love and have a true passion for, and then figure out how to multiply it. That's the pattern and is also Franchising 101… it's a systematic approach.

When private equity came into TSC, each of the changes felt evolutionary. Leadership changed, standards improved, processes got tighter, menu items changed, and AUVs [average unit volumes] increased. But as a franchisee, it felt like a progression of the business. It wasn't disruptive. The brand has grown every year and continues to head in a good direction.

—NICK CROUCH, co-chief executive officer and co-founder, DYNE Hospitality Group[20]

There's a lot to learn as the business grows, so you need to be completely open to that. When you have 10 cafés it's a different business than when you have 25. It changes again when you have 50 cafés and then 100. For us, people, processes, and culture are all critical elements. We're always recruiting and developing our team from within.

At the brand level, as TSC grew and PE sponsors came in, there have been differences in leadership style. The biggest change I noticed was when we went from being founder-led to bringing in our first PE partner, BIP. They cleaned house, hired some new team members, moved the headquarters to Atlanta to have better access to resources and talent. All of that was very positive. They increased the national ad fund from 2 percent to 3 percent and told us it was to get a national ad program to help lift AUVs [average unit volumes]. It worked exactly like they said it would, and we had five years in a row of double-digit same-store sales growth under BIP.

—GLEN JOHNSON, co-chief executive officer and co-founder, DYNE Hospitality Group[21]

LADDER MATH FROM PRIVATE EQUITY'S PERSPECTIVE

How do private equity investors make money climbing the PE Profit Ladder? Ideally, they buy smart in the first place (avoid overpaying—said another way, PE needs to ensure they deliver on their business case). Then, of course, the goal is to sell the company up the ladder for more than they paid or to go public. Long-hold investors can pull significant cash out of the business each year after covering operating expenses. There are many ways for PE to take money out along the way as well, as has been discussed in detail (e.g., charge management fees at both the fund and portfolio company levels, take out debt to pay dividends, provide both debt and equity to the business).

> But in terms of selling the business for more than the PE firm originally paid, the more top-line system growth and bottom-line unit-level profitability PE can nurture within their franchise companies, the more valuable the business becomes.

You are also now well versed in PE's playbook to drive organic growth (as opposed to growth via acquisition, which we will cover next in Chapter 14 in the section about multiple arbitrage). The market, of course, pays a premium for larger, more profitable businesses. According to GF Data, for the 15-year period from 2003 to 2017, M&A transactions for businesses with a total enterprise value (TEV) of $10–25 million traded for an average 5.7 times adjusted EBITDA, while those with a TEV of $50–100 million traded on average for 7.3 times adjusted EBITDA. By 2022, this had risen to 6.3 times and 9.2 times, respectively. The 2021 range of TEV of $10 million to $250 million to trailing 12-month adjusted EBITDA was 3× to 18×, with an average purchase price multiple of 7.4 in 2021, and 7.5 by third quarter 2022.[22] In franchising, the multiples paid for large growth-oriented franchisors and platforms in recent years hit the teens and even above 20 times adjusted EBITDA for some deals. There is a clear size premium as well as higher market value for quality franchisor businesses with strong performance metrics. (The market in the second half of 2022 and 2023 cooled a bit as interest rates rose.)

> But PE can't fully capture the lift in enterprise value without creating a good exit of some kind. This is where the growth playbook and the PE Profit Ladder collide.

Let's look at another example.

CASE STUDY: WETZEL'S PRETZELS

Wetzel's Pretzels provides a good example of ladder math from PE's perspective, including the fees and other benefits PE may collect along the way. PE owners want to drive meaningful return on investor funds at each step while growing the portfolio company's business organically, which means driving system revenue and improved unit-level profitability to encourage franchisee expansion.

INITIAL INVESTORS

Wetzel's was founded in 1994 and expansion capital was provided by angel investors in 1997. That investor group reportedly included film producer John Davis, Hollywood lawyer Jake Bloom, and Northwest Airlines chairman Gary Wilson.[23]

PE PROFIT LADDER—STEP 1: FIRST INSTITUTIONAL CAPITAL

By 2007, Wetzel's had grown to $60 million in sales[24] across 190 locations.[25] According to Davis at the time, prior investors were looking to move on, but the company still had significant growth potential.[26]

Wetzel's jumped up on the profit ladder when Levine Leichtman Capital Partners announced they had acquired the company in early 2007. According to Pitchbook, LLCP paid $22.7 million for Wetzel's. Reports at the time indicated initial investors made 11 times their initial investment.[27] Early investor (and billionaire) John Davis quipped that Wetzel's made him a millionaire.[28] Wetzel's was LLCP's third franchise investment.

LLCP held Wetzel's for nine years. But the long hold made sense. LLCP at the time noted Wetzel's strong financial performance and history of EBITDA growth.[29] Under LLCP's guidance, Wetzel's reached 305 locations and $165 million in system revenue (2015),[30] representing 61 percent unit count growth, 175 percent system revenue growth, and 72 percent average unit revenue growth. (The unit growth is higher looking only at units open at least one year. According to Wetzel's 2016 FDD, the 2015 average unit volume was $596,000, which would represent 89 percent growth since 2006.)[31] Wetzel's balance sheet included debt of $14.8 million.[32] This was a loan from LLCP (LLCP Amicus Fund LP) and Wetzel's co-founder and CEO Bill Phelps. Interest accumulated and no payments were made due to extension agreements each year. The loan was repaid on step 2 of the ladder out of the 2016 sale proceeds. Presumably, LLCP put down $8.2 million for the company and had a separate debt instrument it owned for $14.3 million when it acquired the company. (As previously mentioned, LLCP invests in both debt and equity.)

PE PROFIT LADDER—STEP 2: CENTEROAK ACQUIRES WETZEL'S FROM LLCP

In September 2016, a PE consortium led by CenterOak acquired Wetzel's from LLCP for an undisclosed sum. A Golub Capital press release indicated the purchase was financed with $66.5 million in debt,[33] and according to Wetzel's 2017 FDD, $100.2 million of goodwill was sitting on its balance sheet (up from $28.8 million prior to the acquisition). Goodwill is the difference between the market price paid for a company and the fair value of the company's assets. According to Wetzel's 2017 FDD, fair market value of the company minus working capital at close was $45,956,000. So, this suggests the purchase price was around $145 million. (Wetzel's 2018 FDD later confirmed the 2016 purchase details and adjustments for working capital.)[34]

Wetzel's income from operations (no taxes or interest payments) in 2015, the year prior to the acquisition, was $9.2 million. Let's say there were $2 million of add-backs to get a very rough calculation of $11 million adjusted EBITDA. That suggests CenterOak paid a multiple of 13× EBITDA, which represents an attractive sale result for LLCP's investors. According to GF Data, middle market acquisitions in 2018 with total enterprise value of $100 to $250 million were 8.8 adjusted EBITDA. This is an example of both the "size premium" and the higher value the market can place on quality franchise businesses relative to market averages.

According to announcements at the time, LLCP achieved a return of 7× its initial investment.[35] Why did LLCP sell at that point? Levine Leichtman held onto Wetzel's longer than is typical for PE, something Wetzel's founder Bill Phelps noted in interviews at the time.[36] As I mentioned earlier, if you are a franchisee of a PE-backed brand, you can make some reasonable assumptions about that firm's planned hold time by looking at company press releases to determine what fund they are making investments from and when that fund was first launched, as well as their hold time for other similar brands in their portfolio.

CenterOak took some clear financial benefits out during its ownership tenure:

▶ Only two months after the acquisition in November 2016, CenterOak repaid itself $20 million by having Wetzel's take out a payment-in-kind loan.[37]

▶ Wetzel's paid its owners a $1.25 million distribution in 2019.

▶ Wetzel's wrote off $6.96 million in interest in 2019.

▶ Wetzel's received a Paycheck Protection Program loan via the Small Business Administration in April 2020 for $1.689 million. On January 11, 2021, the loan plus interest in the amount of $1.701 million was forgiven by the Small Business Administration.

▶ In July 2020, Wetzel's took a note payable from its owner, CenterOak Fund I LP, in the amount of $3 million, at 20 percent annual interest,[38] with a maturity date of December 1, 2021.

▶ Wetzel's wrote off $7.6 million in interest in 2020.

▶ At the end of 2021, total debt on the business was $87 million, with a large balloon payment of $85 million due in 2023. (The debt was renegotiated several times to increase debt while pushing out the maturity date.)

So, it appears that a dividend recap combined with other notes payable and other debt was completed along the way to push total debt up from the original $66.5 million to $87 million. This put Wetzel's "on the clock," so to speak. It signaled a pending sale by 2023 or the need to renegotiate loan repayment timing.

Let's revisit PE's growth playbook again. Even when brands are accelerated under proven brand stewards such as LLCP, the next PE owner looks with fresh eyes for new operational initiatives to further grow the business. Financial engineering alone won't accomplish that. Wetzel's unit growth under CenterOak was initially slow (inclusive of pandemic challenges), reaching only 318 franchised units by 2021.[39] A refocus on organic growth meant following a predictable playbook. CenterOak's playbook for Wetzel's included the following:

▶ Expanding into new geographies and venue types
▶ Making back-office enhancements and hiring additional staff, especially to support development, finance, and operations
▶ Adding new food and beverage options[40]

Under CenterOak's direction, Wetzel's management executed the growth playbook and saw improved business metrics. From 2020 to 2021, units grew 16 percent as the company added 45 new locations. Sales during that same period grew 19 percent.[41] System revenues hit $245 million. Adjusted average unit volumes in 2021 across all format types was $851,699,[42] up from $596,000 in 2015, a 42 percent improvement from the year prior to the CenterOak acquisition.[43]

PE PROFIT LADDER—STEP 3: STRATEGIC BUYER MTY FOOD GROUP ACQUIRES WETZEL'S

Wetzel's renewed momentum and demonstrated resilience even during the COVID-19 pandemic made the company attractive to potential suitors. In late 2022 (after a six-year hold), platform owner MTY Food Group acquired Wetzel's for $207 million.[44] CenterOak reportedly achieved a 12.2× EBITDA valuation multiple for Wetzel's.[45]

In just three jumps up the PE Profit Ladder starting with the first institutional capital in 2007, Wetzel's grew from 190 locations to 350 locations (84 percent growth) and from $60 million in sales to $245 million* in sales (308 percent growth). Enterprise value grew from $22.7 million to $207 million (812 percent growth). With each transaction investors at each step appeared to do well in terms of their return on invested capital. And PE owners also took tax benefits, dividends, distributions, loan proceeds, and various fees. For good stewards of franchise brands, the payoff for steady brand growth is monetized via the SBO trading mechanism as well as numerous PE techniques to extract value within the confines of the deals, refinancing, and fees charged along the way.

But most importantly, franchisees as a group also benefited during these jumps up the ladder. Benefits included more franchisee support, streamlining the menu and operating model, increased brand marketing, product expansion, steady system revenue growth, and outlet expansion (greater market awareness and a larger media budget). Average unit volumes grew a whopping 170 percent from 2006 to 2021. This amounts to a compound annual growth of 6.8 percent, which also outpaced inflation. (Inflation grew during the same period at a compound annual growth of 1.99 percent.)[46] The company ranked 249th in *Franchise Times'* 2022 annual survey based on system revenue and 231st in 2023.[47] Wetzel's received high marks in franchisee satisfaction surveys, including special mentions in 2021 and 2022 for franchisee profitability, culture, and innovation.[48] The International Franchise Association even honored one of Wetzel's longtime multi-unit franchisees, Steve Liebsohn, as 2022's Franchisee of the Year.[49]

Is there room for still more brand innovation and momentum after the most recent ownership change? Yes! In 2023, the company rolled out a new program, "Access to Equity," to make franchise ownership more accessible for women and ethnic minorities, offering support through financial discounts, education,

---

*   Trailing 12 months system sales at time of MTY acquisition.

and mentoring.[50] In 2023, the company had the largest development pipeline in its history (nearly 60 units), celebrated its 400th store opening, and expanded into new venues and formats.[51]

Because PE involvement at the franchisor level can be a big determinant of the overall value equation, as a franchisee or prospective franchisee, it's worth the effort to discover the answers to the following questions:

- Is the franchise backed by PE? How long ago was it acquired?
- What is that PE firm's franchise track record and trading history?
- How much debt is on the company's books, and when is it due?
- What investments are being made in the future of the business? What gaps exist?
- What are net growth and unit churn trends?
- Are unit-level economics improving?
- Are tier 1 markets still available, or has the franchise moved on to focus on selling tier 2 and fill-in markets in an effort to grow? Has the model been adjusted to account for the differences in these markets?
- Does this business provide a strong return on investment for franchisees? What is the cash-on-cash return?
- How does all of this compare to market trends and competitors?
- Has PE/FO/strategic sponsorship moved this brand forward?
- What is the likely next step on the PE Profit Ladder? Is the brand likely to trade again during your license agreement?
- Do current franchisees validate well? Would they enter the business again knowing what they know now? Are franchisee satisfaction surveys positive? Are existing franchisees adding new units? Are they buying resales that become available?

LADDER MATH FROM THE SELLER'S PERSPECTIVE

Let's take that same Wetzel's example from the perspective of a seller rolling a portion of their equity forward. Angel investors reportedly made 11× their investment when LLCP paid $22.5 million for the company. Wetzel's was sold in 2016 to CenterOak for around $145 million. What if those original angel investors had rolled some equity forward? They did well in their initial sale to LLCP, but the opportunity would have been even greater if they had rolled a small portion forward. Let's assume a very basic model with no contingencies or dilution. If only 10 percent of the $22.5 million purchase price had been rolled forward ($2.25 million), that 10 percent of equity would have been worth $14.5 million in the next sale in 2016, or another 5.4× return on their money. So instead of a gross of $22.5 million, the total would have been $37 million, or 64 percent more!

Too many sellers are focused only on short-term gain and don't consider the long-term equity roll value. Pay close attention to deal structure and don't lose sight of other details. There is a balance between capturing upside opportunity and capping your downside risk. Look carefully at all deal terms and get help thinking through what those terms could mean to you under a variety of scenarios. (Legal counsel and tax, wealth, and professional M&A advisers are a must.) And check references! For example, if there is an earnout (purchase price contingency, paid in the future based, for example, on the business achieving certain performance milestones), check with references to see if earnouts were paid in other deals, and if not, what were the circumstances. A large topline purchase price might look good on paper but depending on terms and contingencies could in reality be unattainable. Also, understand the investor's timeline and get clear on what the next three, five, or seven years look like to them. Ask, "What is your ability to make follow-on investments in the business (such as infrastructure, key hires, tuck-in acquisitions), and what is your plan to do so?"

▼

Now that we've looked at value creation based on organic growth at each step up the PE Profit Ladder, let's turn to examine PE's second critical value creation strategy relevant to the SBO deal ladder: multiple arbitrage.

CHAPTER 14

Building Enterprise Value Through the Power of Platforming and Multiple Arbitrage

Private equity loves add-ons. As Stewart Kohl, CO-CEO of the Riverside Company, once said in an interview, "We are doing around 75 add-on deals every year. We are an add-on machine!"[1]

THE CONCEPT BEHIND VALUE creation through multiple arbitrage within the franchising context is simple. By rolling up (acquiring) a number of small companies (valued at a single-digit or low double-digit multiple of EBITDA) into a platform, you can create a much bigger entity that is worth much more than simply the sum of all those smaller enterprises.

A SIMPLE BUT POWERFUL VALUE CREATION MODEL

Franchising is especially well suited for a value creation plan that depends at least partly on multiple arbitrage and rolling up units or entire brands to create a larger entity. The strategy works at both the outlet and multi-brand level but is especially potent for the latter. Smaller companies can benefit from being part of a larger entity with more staff, resources, and buying power. As a combined company, EBITDA will be higher, and the market will pay a higher multiple for that EBITDA. Add operational improvements, the PE growth playbook, and platform synergies to unlock cost savings and expansion opportunities, and over time the platform's value can dramatically expand when well executed.

> **For founders and early investors, it's also why careful consideration of how much equity you plan to roll forward and the track record of your acquirer are just as important as your first sale price and deal terms. Don't get so caught up in trying to land a "perfect" first deal that you lose sight of a potentially more lucrative second transaction, especially if you're joining a platform.**

As previously discussed, platforming is a common PE strategy well suited to franchising. Since much of the franchise back office (as much as 60 to 80 percent) is duplicative, significant enterprise savings and value can be created via shared services. There are also significant supply chain, cross-marketing, and franchise development advantages to being part of a collective. Platforming works at both the operator level (franchisee) and the brand level (franchisor).

The two simple figures on the following page help illustrate these points. Don't get hung up on the multiples because these are middle market averages. We've seen more aggressive multiples in the franchise sector for high-quality businesses. Just focus on the scale difference between small and large deals. The following figures show EBITDA multiples by deal size, by year (so you can see the range), and the average by deal size. The first figure shows EBITDA multiples by deal size and the differences over a span of four years. The other shows just the average by deal size.

FIGURE 2: 2019-2022 EBITDA Multiples by Deal Size

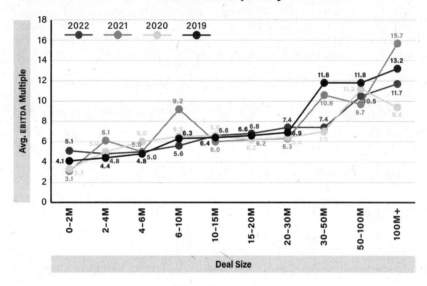

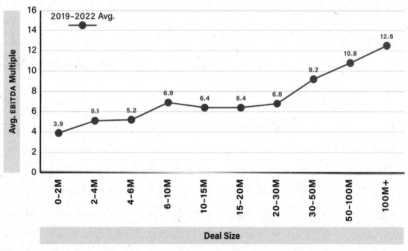

Source: Alliance of Merger & Acquisition Advisors Winter Conference 2022, and Dealware. Used with permission.

▼

Using these figures as our example, it's easy to see how acquiring several smaller companies with lower EBITDA multiples added together creates a more valuable entity even before synergies and growth initiatives take hold. Using these figures for a fictional example, let's say you acquire five companies, each with an enterprise value of $6 million, for around 5.2× EBITDA each. Even if you don't grow the companies at all, when combined, the total enterprise value is now $30 million, which could trade at between 6.8× and 9.2× EBITBA. So you've added between 1.2× and 4× extra value turns (turn: multiple of EBITDA) doing nothing more than pooling the EBITDA of six companies into one larger company. Said another way, the portion of EBITDA added with each acquisition is ultimately valued higher once part of a larger company. Of course, with platform synergies, time, and effort, you are likely to grow both top-line revenue and EBITDA. Let's say you grew the platform over several years from $30 million to $100 million in enterprise value. If you then sold the business, it would trade for at least 10.8× to 12.5× EBITDA, using the figure's averages as our example. In concept, this is how multiple arbitrage works, and it is the primary reason why PE loves creating and adding on to platforms. The combination of growth, cross-brand synergies, and platform cost savings can create a significantly more valuable business. Franchising has seen better than market EBITDA trading multiples, so the lift generated from tuck-in acquisitions and well-executed platform growth has been more dramatic.

Once combined into a larger entity, additional acquisitions can be financed with debt. ServiceMaster (Roark) used this approach to acquire Two Men and a Truck (see Chapter 16). The use of leverage can generate higher multiples on invested capital.

All of these benefits are why platforms (and even pseudo-platforms, umbrella holding companies, or conglomerates that aren't integrated as true platforms) have exploded across franchising. This brings us to one of the most influential franchise platforms: Neighborly.

CASE STUDY: THE DWYER GROUP/NEIGHBORLY

Neighborly started as the Dwyer Group in 1981. The company's history provides some good observations about the success of platforming and multiple arbitrage, as well as the value of being very focused and purposeful across several PE owners to drive maximum enterprise value and system growth. Dwyer/Neighborly's success helped inspire the proliferation of both new home services franchises and platforms, as well as the creation of platforms in other categories, such as family entertainment, eldercare services, business services, and others.

Let's look at the big jumps between each trade in the context of platforming:

▶ **1981:** The Dwyer Group is founded.

▶ **1993:** The Dwyer Group goes public.

▶ **2003:** The Riverside Company takes Dwyer private for $54.5 million.[2] At the time, Dwyer had created an already impressive multi-brand enterprise with 800 franchisees in the US and Canada and 275 franchisees in 15 other countries via master licensees. With Riverside's backing, the company continued to grow and acquire brands, building on the legacy and vision of its founder, Don Dwyer, Sr., who unexpectedly passed away in 1994.

▶ **2010:** The Dwyer Group is acquired by TZP Partners I, LP for $150 million.[3] At the time, Dwyer owned seven consumer and commercial services brands as well as full-service glass stores in a few markets. Franchise service brands included Aire Serv, Glass Doctor, the Grounds Guys, Mr. Appliance, Mr. Electric, Mr. Rooter, and Rainbow International.[4] At the time, the company had 1,500 locations and system sales of almost $800 million.

▶ **2014:** Riverside reacquires majority interest in the Dwyer Group for $164 million (including assumption of debt). Riverside's playbook included acquiring more brands to the portfolio, expanding the management team, building a new headquarters, and upgrading technology systems. By 2017, the company did a study to understand whether it was benefiting from cross-selling. The study revealed that only 2 percent of its 2 million customers had used more than one of the services offered across multiple brands owned.[5] As a result, the company launched a focused effort to improve cross-marketing and build out supporting technology. For Riverside's efforts over its 3.5 years of ownership the second time around, EBITDA grew 125 percent.[6]

▶ **2018:** Dwyer is acquired by Harvest Partners, VII LP for $918 million.[7] This would have represented approximately 15× adjusted EBITDA, based on disclosed financials and back-of-the-napkin assumptions about add-backs. The rebranding of the Dwyer Group to Neighborly was already in the works and was announced after the acquisition. Another Riverside fund reinvested in the transaction along with Harvest, marking Riverside's third investment in Dwyer/Neighborly.[8] So Riverside took some chips off the table but also bet that the platform would continue to grow, especially now that the company was more focused on cross-selling services and had rebranded. Riverside had good instincts. The change from Neighborly being a brand aggregator to delivering a more integrated customer experience would unlock significant new enterprise growth. The company continued to make acquisitions.

▶ **March 2021:** Neighborly completes $800 million whole business securitization (WBS).[9] Harvest Partners and Barclay's completed Neighborly's first ever WBS transaction in March 2021. (WBS will be discussed in Chapter 16.) The proceeds were used to partly repay Harvest's investment via a distribution of $163 million.[10]

▶ **September 2021:** KKR acquired Neighborly. At the time of the acquisition, the company had 4,500 franchises and had grown to 10 million customers, up 400 percent since 2017. It was at this point that Riverside finally exited. Riverside's total investment time would ultimately be 15 years. PE has a reputation for being focused on short-term gains. But Riverside's involvement in building the Dwyer Group/Neighborly demonstrates that some firms do stay involved for longer periods and can add tremendous value and strategic assistance to elevate and build substantial franchise brands and platforms over time. Terms were not disclosed at the time. However, financial statements in the 2022 Mr. Rooter FDD (a Neighborly brand) spell out the chain of events and valuation. According to those statements, it was a $2.14 billion transaction. (Cash paid to sellers was $1.9 billion, plus an equity roll-over value of $228 million.)[11] Assuming adjustments, this represents an EBITDA multiple in the low 20s. KKR has come back to the market for additional WBS transactions since the acquisition, including $410 million in 2022[12] and $408 million in 2023.[13]

Now that you have the platform-level picture and see the power of the multiple arbitrage strategy combined with organic growth, let's highlight some of the brand acquisitions along the way and think through the multiple arbitrage potential.

CASE STUDY: BUILDING PLATFORM VALUE: ONE ACQUISITION AT A TIME

The value created for roll-forward equity in a strong and growing platform can accelerate equity value faster, even without accounting for growth and benefits from being part of a platform, thanks to multiple arbitrage. Let's look at a few examples:

► Dwyer acquired Five Star Painting in January 2015 for $11.8 million (cash of $6.9 million, ownership interest of $4.8 million).[14]

► Dwyer acquired Service Brands International in June 2015 for consideration of $105.3 million. (Cash paid $102.3 million and ownership interest of $3 million.) This included Molly Maid, Protect Painters, Mr. Handyman International, and Frantech.[15]

► Dwyer acquired Drain Doctor in October 2015 for $5 million consideration. No ownership interest is listed in the FDD.[16]

► Window Genie was acquired in November 2016 for $8 million ($4.6 million cash, $900,000 earnout, and $2.5 million ownership consideration.)[17]

But at the next trade, in 2018, Dwyer was acquired by Harvest Partners for $918 million, approximately a 15× adjusted EBITDA valuation. Any equity interests from these smaller acquisitions, if rolled forward, would have benefited from the scale of the much larger transaction at the platform level.

This was repeated again in the next round of trading. For example, Mosquito Joe was acquired by Neighborly in 2018. In that year's FDD, financial statements were consolidated with the rest of what would become Neighborly, making it a bit more challenging to trace the chain of events. In addition, the Mosquito Joe and Real Property Management acquisitions were combined in the FDD and the acquisition value was consolidated to be $132 million together. However, we can go back and review Real Property Management's prior FDD. The Real Property Management 2018 FDD (issued prior to the Mosquito Joe acquisition) mentions that the February 2018 Real Property acquisition of $27.345 million was funded by an amendment adding $30 million to the platform's existing debt revolver.[18] Real Property Management cash flow from operations in 2017 isn't visible because of the consolidated statement, but the company had $2.3 million cash flow from operations in 2016, $1.9 million in 2015, and $1.7 million in 2014.[19] So let's assume with add-backs adjusted EBITDA was around $3 to 4 million. If the business traded at $27.345 million, that's a ballpark multiple of 6.8× to 9× adjusted EBITDA.

So now we know Mosquito Joe's trade value was $104.6 million ($132 million minus $27.345 million). This is impressive! Looking at Mosquito Joe's financial disclosures and making an educated guess about adjustments to EBITDA, we can assume a range of adjusted EBITDA of $5 million to $7.5 million or so. That would make the valuation 13.8× to 18–20× adjusted EBITDA.

Speaking of the power of organic growth combined with multiple arbitrage, Buzz Franchise Brands originally acquired Mosquito Joe in August 2012 with a $1.5 million capital contribution and the intent to develop the concept into a franchise. The founder of Buzz, Kevin Wilson, has a private equity background and also experience in four other franchise investments prior to Mosquito Joe. The team focused on building out a solid operating model, strong brand, and required infrastructure to support growth. Mosquito Joe began franchising in 2013 and grew to 288 units and $60 million in revenue before being acquired by Neighborly in 2018.[20] It is not clear from Neighborly's consolidated financial statements how much of the Mosquito Joe acquisition was rolled forward in equity, but when Neighborly traded to KKR there was another opportunity to build value if any equity was rolled forward from the already lucrative 2018 transaction. How has the brand done since? Mosquito Joe ended 2022 with 394 units, up 37 percent since the Neighborly acquisition.[21]

Keeping in mind my TEV/EBITDA estimates may be a bit off, the important takeaways are (1) where to look in disclosed financial statements for information, (2) the scale difference between smaller deals and larger deals, and (3) opportunities created from a combination of good brand stewardship, brand growth, and platform growth to drive multiple arbitrage upside. It is difficult for most emerging brands to duplicate on their own the multiple arbitrage mechanics gained from working with the right PE sponsors and/or platforms. And if founders roll equity forward in a platform strategy, the potential upside on that rolled equity can be significant.

HARD WORK AND A PREDICTABLE PLAYBOOK, NOT ALCHEMY

The multiple arbitrage realized through platforming is not investment magic. Critics of private equity, and of this commonly used PE strategy, gloss over the hard work done at each step on the PE ladder to evolve and transform brands when that work is done well—when something is created that is bigger and better than just the sum of its parts.

> There is clear evidence that for franchise brands moving successfully up the PE Profit Ladder, both operating processes and franchisee support tend to mature, even more so for those brands that join a strong and growing platform.

Let's consider another case study. JAN-PRO provides a singular example of many of the trends noted in this book all wrapped up into one brand story: the importance of platforms, deal re-trading, and successful growth while moving up the PE Profit Ladder.

CASE STUDY: JAN-PRO

JAN-PRO is an interesting PE Profit Ladder example for several reasons. First, it is a textbook example of how a franchise, when placed on the private equity ladder, is often bought and sold in a fairly predictable cadence of SBO re-trading to larger and larger private equity partners as the company continues to grow. At each stage in the company's life cycle, it has different needs and thus naturally aligns with the skills and objectives of different types of private partners along the way.

Second, the JAN-PRO example also demonstrates how moving up the PE ladder can promote long-term franchise growth. Since new JAN-PRO franchisees joined and existing franchisees added to their franchise count while the brand was on the ladder, it would be fair to assert that franchisees were largely satisfied under various private equity owners. Otherwise, the company could not have sustained its fast and consistent pace of growth over a number of years. None of the firms that owned JAN-PRO are turnaround investors. All are known as growth investors. This further signals franchisee feedback was largely positive during this period, or these particular investors would not have been involved with the company.

That isn't to say that challenges were absent across these transactions and ownership periods. Notably, the company was involved in a significant joint employer case that wound its way through the US courts for 10 years.[22] (There have been periodic challenges to the franchise model in recent years to try to redefine franchisors as "joint employers" of the employees of independently owned franchisee outlets. This effort has primarily been led by labor unions who see the more than 8.5 million people employed by franchise outlets as an attractive hunting ground to refill union ranks, which have dropped dramatically since the early 1980s. The US unionization rate is now the lowest on record.)[23] Despite the legal and labor controversies, multiple PE firms and franchisees saw value in the business and chose to invest in JAN-PRO. They drove steady growth of the business during this same period. Furthermore, JAN-PRO ultimately became part of a larger business services platform, and some of its multi-unit franchisees have themselves been private equity acquisition targets. All this growth and dealmaking reflects the overall resilience of the franchise model and franchising's enduring appeal, even where there are headwinds.

Let's look at the company's history to understand the impact of PE on its evolution. Commercial cleaning company JAN-PRO was founded in 1991 by Jacques Lapointe. He and his team grew the business over 15 years until JAN-PRO had 75 master franchisees and 4,500 unit franchisees. (Master franchisees act as the franchisor of record and provide in-market services and support in exchange for retaining a portion of royalties. This structure is often used outside the franchisor's home country, where localization and in-market support are critical to franchisee success.) The company exhibited solid and consistent growth. However, by 2006, Lapointe was ready to take the company to the next level, especially regarding strategic growth initiatives. In interviews at the time, Lapointe indicated that bringing in PE was partly a life choice and partly to help the company grow and evolve.[24] He chose Greentree Capital, an affiliate of J.H. Whitney (JHW Greentree Capital LP) and Starboard Capital Partners. J.H. Whitney was one of the first US PE firms, established in 1946.[25]

In September 2008, a recapitalization led by Webster Capital Management, Gemini Investors, and Midwest Mezzanine Funds was completed. According to Starboard Capital, the recapitalization returned in excess of 9x the original equity invested by Starboard and its partners and a company value 4.5x greater.[26] Starboard and its partners remained partially invested, but Webster became the principal equity investor. Gemini would have other successful franchise investments, including Wingstop, Buffalo Wild Wings, and Premier Garage, while Webster invested in Re-Bath. JAN-PRO was eventually organized under a parent company called Premium Franchise Brands, which in 2013 launched Maid Right.[27]

In October 2016, Incline Equity Partners acquired Premium Franchise Brands. In February 2019, the company announced the add-on acquisition of Intelligent Office. Premium Franchise Brands was renamed LYNX Franchising in April 2019.[28] The company continued to make acquisitions, including FRSTeam in June 2020.

In April 2018, LYNX sold Maid Right to Premium Service Brands. (Note the similar name to the original platform of Premium Franchise Brands, but this sale was to a completely different entity. I feel your pain. Stay with me.) Premium Service Brands itself is also actively pursuing a platform strategy. As of this writing, Premium Service Brands has acquired nine home services franchise concepts and is currently backed by private equity firm Susquehanna Private Capital LLC.[29]

In December 2020, private equity firm MidOcean Partners acquired LYNX Franchising, which by that time was a multi-brand platform with a collection of business services, including Intelligent Office, FRSTeam, and JAN-PRO Systems International.[30] JAN-PRO Systems International then had $600 million in system-wide sales across 7,500 franchisees.[31] Later, in 2021, the largest franchisee operator in the JAN-PRO system, RBJK Marketing, itself attracted private equity investment from Boathouse Capital to fund organic and inorganic growth initiatives, including expansion within the JAN-PRO system.[32] By the end of 2022, JAN-PRO added another 500 franchise units to reach 8,000 franchise units around the world and 125 regional developers in nine countries. As of this writing, JAN-PRO has been ranked the number one commercial cleaning franchise by *Entrepreneur* for 15 straight years and as a top franchise by *Franchise Business Review* for the last 9 years.[33] (The *Franchise Business Review* ranking is based on franchisee satisfaction surveys.) The LYNX platform was renamed again to Empower Brands.[34] Empower continues to acquire brands to expand the platform (e.g., April 2023: Koala Insulation and Wallaby Windows, and May 2023: Bumble Roofing.)

Once a franchise starts up the private equity ladder, it may be re-traded several times, as in the JAN-PRO example. If franchisees as a group are largely happy, they will continue to add units and will validate well enough to continue to attract new franchisees into the system. Franchisee satisfaction is the root of any strong and growing franchise system over the long term. JAN-PRO exemplifies the growing importance of franchise platforms and the complexity of often interwoven secondary deals in franchising.

> Successful relationships between a franchisor and private capital partners can help systems grow across ownership changes over many years, so long as each owner is dedicated to building value for all stakeholders and a sustainable brand.

FROGS AND OLD WARHORSES

Back to our proverbial frog in the pot of hot water. Leaving multiple arbitrage aside for a minute and going back to secondary buyouts in general, has the franchise community at large recognized the impact on franchising of SBO trading in general and of multiple arbitrage in particular? Yes, for big names like Neighborly and the largest platforms. But in my view, otherwise no. Outside of M&A insiders, investment bankers, and PE firms most active in this area, there appears to be little awareness in the franchise community of how SBO trading has blanketed the entire sector and changed outcomes for everyone. This is a situation I hope this book and my related published articles will rectify.

Even experts on franchising with exposure to PE clients, such as research firm FRANdata, haven't acknowledged that the *re-trading mechanism has itself become an influential force in franchising outcomes.* Two recent FRANdata articles exemplify this: "Old Is Gold" (November 2019)[35] and "From Unicorns to Warhorses" (March 2020).[36] In these articles, FRANdata noticed that more legacy brands ("old warhorses") were being purchased by private equity firms.

To FRANdata, this seemed to signal a shift away from smaller brands, stating, "Until early 2018, many PE firms targeted smaller, non-franchised 'unicorn' chains with an eye toward consolidating them into their existing portfolio and franchising the concept at a later stage."[37] This statement is curious both because it doesn't align to PE's extensive franchise deal history going back to the 1990s and because it also overlooks the major trends of SBOs and platform development. In reality, the uptick in deals specifically involving legacy brands ("old warhorses") is partly due to secondary buyouts, the proliferation of franchisor platforms, and the pressure for PE to find and close deals in a sector that is starting to look a bit picked over. (There are fewer unaffiliated scale franchise opportunities available.)

> A robust and mature secondary buyout market for franchise businesses at the brand level, and in some systems at the unit level as well, is now in place.

Much of the noted "old warhorse" M&A activity was simply the natural next step for brands that had been traded to PE years before. It was time to trade again.

FRANdata highlighted eight 2019 brand acquisitions (Servpro, Intelligent Office, Hooters, Budget Blinds, ABRA Auto Body & Glass, Perkins, Jimmy John's, and Jenny Craig). These eight turn out to exemplify the whirlwind of fast-shifting sands. The first two were traditional founder deals with private equity:

1 Servpro was closely held by its founding family before being acquired in 2019 for $1 billion, including debt.[38] Founded in 1967, the brand created significant scale long before PE became a factor in franchising.

2 Intelligent Office (founded in 1995, franchising since 1999) was also a founder deal, but it was acquired by a PE-backed platform (Premium Franchise Brands, later renamed LYNX and then renamed again to Empower Brands) that was itself already marching up the ladder and continuing to add more brands, as previously mentioned in the JAN-PRO case study.[39]

But secondary buyouts were behind the remaining six of the eight highlighted 2019 deals, and five (Servpro, Intelligent Office, Budget Blinds, ABRA, and Jimmy John's) were also part of broader platform activity. Regarding the secondary buyouts:

3 Hooters was acquired by H.I.G. Capital, Chanticleer Holdings, and other investors from the Brooks family in 2011 after 30 years of ownership.[40] Then the company was sold again to Nord Bay Capital and TriArtisan Capital Advisors in 2019.

4 Budget Blinds was acquired by JM Family Enterprises Inc. in 2019 within the Home Franchise Concepts platform acquisition (also included Tailored Living, Concrete Craft, and AdvantaClean brands).[41] Home Franchise Concepts was previously purchased by Trilantic North America in 2015 and had just announced it was adding AdvantaClean to its stable in early 2019 before the entire platform was acquired.

5 ABRA Auto Body & Glass was acquired by Palladium Equity Partners in 2011 and sold majority ownership to Hellman & Friedman in 2014, generating a 6.7× cash on cash return.[42] Then ABRA merged in early 2019 with Caliber Collison (backed by OMERS Private Equity and Leonard Green & Partners).[43] Caliber also had prior PE owners.[44] In 2019, the merged companies were then sold to auto platform Driven Brands (Roark).[45]

6 Perkins (founded in 1958) was acquired in 2019 out of bankruptcy by Huddle House for $51.5 million[46] after a loooooooooong history of re-trades. Perkins has been owned by strategics such as Holiday Inn and Marie Calendar's and PE firms such as Castle Harlan. It had a public offering (1987), was taken private again, and has been through more than one bankruptcy. It's more "project" or "fallen angel" than "old warhorse." Huddle House itself was recently traded, acquired by Elysium Management in 2018 from Sentinel Capital,[47] which had owned the brand since 2012.[48] Elysium is not a traditional PE firm but instead is the family office of Leon Black (co-founder of Apollo Global Management, a prolific restaurant investor). As previously mentioned, many family offices have the patience and flexibility to take on projects like Perkins.

7 Jimmy John's sold a minority stake (30 percent) to PE firm Weston Presidio in 2006[49] before agreeing to be acquired by Roark in 2016. Roark affiliate Inspire Brands then acquired Jimmy John's in 2019.

8 Jenny Craig was the eighth brand mentioned, case study to follow.

It is important to recognize that growing private capital interest and trading activity in franchising are partly due to secondary buyouts. It's like PE created its own weather system! So many brands and platforms are already on the ladder that SBOs fuel significant franchise M&A activity. The now

fully developed SBO market was the missing piece, the invisible hand driving direct dealmaking and indirect preparation activities as brands ready
themselves for later transactions.

Fund timing is not the only reason for PE exits. It's much too easy to
say, "Well, it's been six years, so that PE-backed franchise business will
likely trade again soon," even if it's historically likely for that PE firm. You
need more information. Validation with franchisees and a little research
will reveal important nuances. Is the brand headed in the right direction,
and is this a brand I want to be part of? What are other reasons that suggest a business will trade again soon? Have sponsors been effective brand
stewards, and are they a firm I'd like to know more about? Is this brand
trading because it's incredibly valuable and headed in the right direction,
and the sponsor wanted to monetize that? Or is this brand trading because
the current sponsor wasn't effective or new eyes and strategies are needed?
Has the market shifted faster than a short-term PE owner can realistically
address, and now the business needs a new home? Is this a positive inflection point, an attempt at redirection, or a bail-out by owners cutting their
losses? For prospective franchisees thinking of investing in a brand that has
traded at least once, it is worth the effort to gain a deeper understanding of
what's going on behind the scenes. For example, one of the "old warhorses"
(Jenny Craig) was being traded on the ladder, but the ladder first pointed
up and later down.

CASE STUDY: JENNY CRAIG AND SBO TRADING

Jenny Craig went private in 2002 with the help of ACI Capital Corp. and Deutsche
Bank AG's DB Capital Partners in a $115 million transaction.[50] (DB then spun out
its own deal team and 80-company portfolio, including Jenny Craig, newly creating MidOcean Partners.)[51] At the time, Jenny Craig was already experiencing
a multiyear decline in both revenue and units and was in need of turnaround
guidance. Jenny Craig's PE sponsor DB/MidOcean and management worked
to increase marketing and grow sales. Business improvement put Jenny Craig
on a path to be acquired by Nestlé (a strategic buyer that was pushing into the

nutrition segment) in 2006 for $600 million. This represented a 5× return on the original investment.[52]

When the market cooled and Nestlé later rationalized its holdings, it opted to sell the North American and Oceania portion of the Jenny Craig business to North Castle Partners in November 2013.[53] Although at the time of the deal the terms were not disclosed, the Jenny Craig 2016 FDD mentions that "total contingent consideration" for this 2013 deal was actually $112 million including $2 cash.[54] (That's not a typo.) North Castle was struggling with its Curves acquisition and was hoping the addition of Jenny Craig would drive beneficial cross-marketing and shared programs, creating a "one-of-a-kind wellness company."[55] When that didn't work out, North Castle sold Jenny Craig to H.I.G. Capital, the 2019 deal noted in the "warhorse" article.[56] Terms were not disclosed at the time, but according to Jenny Craig's 2021 FDD, $258 million cash consideration was paid, financed with $170 million of long-term debt and a $15 million revolver.[57] However, years of declining brand relevance, high debt on the business, and new weight-loss marketplace headwinds, such as the availability of weight-loss medications like Ozempic, ultimately finished off Jenny Craig, which went out of business in 2023.

The secondary trading cadence is fairly predictable once a brand is on the ladder. Sales to strategics (like the Nestlé example) often tumble back (also in a fairly predictable way) into PE arms once corporate objectives or market conditions change. But you still have to dig to get the full picture before you judge either a brand or the sponsor's track record. The reasons behind resales are as unique and nuanced as the brands, players, and situations involved. Trades may be "up," "down," "across," or even "out" if a brand flips to a corporate model and stops actively franchising. Trades happen for various reasons.

Of course, when one company is sold, the PE firm needs to redeploy capital, so it's also no surprise that after selling Jenny Craig and transferring ownership of Curves to the president of Curves in 2019, North Castle was ready to invest again. North Castle invested in European Wax Center at the franchisee level (EWC Growth Partners LLC), growing to 45 locations as of this writing.[58] Following this thread, other PE activity in EWC includes

MKH Capital Partners LP, a family office, which is building out a platform of European Wax Center locations.[59] At the franchisor level, EWC had a minority (30 percent) investment from Brazos Private Equity Partners and Princeton Ventures in 2013.[60] When EWC's founders later looked for new partnership options, General Atlantic made a strategic investment in 2018[61] and took the company public in 2021, raising $180 million.[62]

> This deal re-trading and the unfolding of franchise brand stories is happening all around us as portfolio companies trade between private capital owners. Remember, I said you'll never see franchising the same way again. Has your perspective changed?

THE SECONDARY BUYOUT MARKET MOVING FORWARD

The secondary buyout market[63] (also known as SBOs, "sponsor-to-sponsor," and what I refer to as the PE Profit Ladder) has taken time to develop but is now well established across private equity investing generally, and certainly within the franchise sector.

> In 2008, 40 percent of all PE exits were to another PE firm. (This is inclusive of all PE exits, not only franchise exits.)[64] During the very active first half of 2022, more than 60 percent of PE exits were to other PE firms.[65] The trend has since normalized to around 30 percent of deal volume.[66]

What does academic research say on the topic of secondary buyouts? A 2015 study on SBOs conducted by a team from the Swiss Finance Institute, the University of Amsterdam, the University of Oxford/Said Business School, and the Oxford-Man Institute studying 5,849 buyouts found the following:

▸ An important source of SBO value creation was the presence of what the research team called "complementary skill sets" between buyers and sellers. They found net present value, even net of fees, was large and positive. Deals completed between firms with complementary skill sets were associated with higher performance and more value creation for investors.

▶ SBOs were more likely to be exited via another SBO compared to exit via a strategic or IPO (43 percent compared to 20 percent). The study also found that once a company enters the SBO ladder, it is likely to stay there and avoid public markets in particular.[67]

This last point doesn't mean a franchise business will never go public, but rather that once on the SBO ladder, companies are more likely to re-trade (perhaps multiple times) before going public.

These findings are consistent with how secondary PE trades have organized themselves within franchising. At each step, expensive due diligence is undertaken to create a defensible business case. Trades between firms with complementary skill sets help push firms up the ladder at various inflection points in each franchise brand's growth cycle. When PE firms are effective stewards of their portfolio companies, there is tremendous potential to move brands materially forward. Driving both organic growth and growth via platforming can accelerate enterprise and stakeholder value. The sense of urgency is palpable. Brand lift can be significant.

The fully formed SBO market with many participants provides viable exit options to sell franchise investments "up the ladder" at key inflection points in a franchise's growth curve. More exit certainty and available exit options create more PE buyer demand for, and confidence to acquire, promising smaller brands down the ladder, and on it goes. The SBO ladder is now something of a self-feeding mechanism. As risk is lowered for PE, this facilitates further bets and ultimately more deal flow. This was the final piece missing in the franchising story, and it has now fallen into place. It is one reason why so many brands and multi-unit operators in the US now have PE backing.

But trading again and again *without* proactively adding value at each step puts strain on management and franchisees. When the business has already traded several times and isn't moving forward, putting the team through a sale process every four to five years is distracting. At some point you need a clean runway when everyone is focused on growth. It can be a lot of starts and stops if not well managed. Also, it gets harder to find different things to do. Along the way, PE owners try to keep the business on a growth path to maximize investor returns and avoid the dreaded "down round" risk, where the business is worth less than originally paid. But longer-hold investors often become a more logical choice after several trades. Unless a new sponsor comes along and will take a dramatically different approach to running the business, the stability of a longer-hold approach often makes more sense, provided that long-hold sponsor is committed to promoting long-term brand health and sustainability.

There is a clear playbook to create franchise value, both for growing the business and for monetizing that work via both financial engineering strategies and ultimately a successful exit. Yet for all of PE's many successes in franchising, Big Money's learning curve is equal parts fascinating and frustrating. Private equity sponsors have presided over a few head-shakingly-bad franchise outcomes.

▼

PE's various franchising missteps essentially create a guide of what *not* to do. For founders and franchisees looking for a PE partner, for franchisees considering brands to join or expand within, and for company managers trying to carve out a successful career track record of their own, this roadmap will help you avoid sinkholes. The previous two chapters were intentionally very "mechanical" and hopefully straightforward. Now, we're heading into a systems breakdown, where things get messy as we address investing mistakes and key learnings. And I also haven't forgotten about the power of relationships in franchising. In fact, relationship issues are at the heart of the many ways things can go wrong when PE fails as effective franchise sponsors.

PART FOUR

Down the Ladder: "Smart Money" Bloopers in Franchise Investing

CHAPTER 15

How to Destroy Franchise Value

"In my four decades of experience in franchising, the answer hasn't really changed. People get upset when they're not making money. That's at the root of it. The underlying financials have to work at the unit level and get above a certain threshold of success before you encourage people to open more."

—**AZIZ HASHIM**, managing partner, NRD Capital[1]

THE NEXT TWO CHAPTERS could also rightly be called "Private equity has been good for franchising, except when…" While PE's impact on franchising has been largely positive, PE isn't infallible. The question is, with private equity's access to information, analytical mindset, due diligence process, investing experience, and rich financial incentives to get things right, why do PE investors sometimes still fail as franchise brand stewards? What can go wrong when there is such a rigorous, disciplined playbook to follow? How can stakeholders, especially franchisees, avoid getting caught under PE's wheels when things aren't working? And moreover, beyond PE's fiduciary duty to their own LPs, what are PE's responsibilities to consider the impact of their profit-seeking decisions and protect stakeholders of the companies they own?

PE's occasional franchise failures and missteps (1) prove that while the franchise model is resilient, poor decisions at the managerial level—no matter what the ownership structure—can sink brands, (2) serve as a cautionary note for franchisees (just because a brand has attracted PE investment, that brand's future success is neither guaranteed nor always fulfilled), and (3) demonstrate that ignoring franchise best practices can ensnare and humble even the highest-profile private capital sponsors or management teams.

As these chapters unfold, you will see examples illustrating these points.

While some of the problems PE has presided over within their franchise portfolio companies are specifically linked to PE playbook tactics (e.g., the use of aggressive leverage), other problems are more the result of poor execution of the franchise model itself. As Jonathan Maze, editor in chief of *Restaurant Business*, succinctly puts it, "Concerns about private equity in franchising are overblown in the sense that some mistakes PE has made in franchising are actually mistakes of franchise model execution, not PE issues specifically."[2]

When private equity investments in the franchise sector go wrong, you don't have to squint too hard to see common themes. We'll go through each of these in turn with some notable case study examples and hear from stakeholders and experts. As a founder considering partnering with PE or as a prospective or current franchisee considering your options, the information presented here is critically important to you. In addition to looking for evidence of good outcomes as discussed throughout the book, you must also be on the lookout for trouble.

FIVE STEPS DOWN THE PROFIT LADDER

These issues are not exclusive to PE, but there are clear themes observed across the history of PE's franchise investments because PE tactics can themselves amplify some of these value destruction techniques as if on steroids by virtue of the speed and scale at which PE operates. Not surprisingly, these factors are the exact opposite of what it takes to build and sustain a franchise business that is valuable for all stakeholders.

Franchise Value Destruction: Things for *All* Players, Not Just Big Money, to Avoid

- ▶ Overleverage
- ▶ Short-timers' syndrome
- ▶ Not protecting unit-level profitability
- ▶ Growth focus: the dark side
- ▶ Destroying franchisee trust

I know it's tempting to sit back now and enjoy feasting on a few pages of schadenfreude at private equity's expense. However, when PE sponsors of a franchise fail, the damage is often magnified due to the use of leverage and what that failure signals to the market about the brand's trajectory. Both negatively impact stakeholders, especially franchisees.

Franchise missteps or failures under PE ownership are usually high profile. Bad optics combined with poor validation from existing franchisees make it harder to attract new operators and thus depress unit resale values. This can leave franchisees upset and financially compromised with fewer attractive exit options. Franchisees are contractually, financially, and personally tied to their outlets in ways that make it difficult for them to simply walk away. Frustrated franchisees may then aggravate matters by complaining to the press, which can further hurt brand value. Due to the unique nature of franchising, once franchisees lose confidence in management or ownership, it can be a long, painful process to rebuild franchisee trust and buy-in. And once a brand starts to lose ground, it is also expensive and difficult to rebuild customer awareness and loyalty. This slippery downward-facing ladder greased with leverage, missteps, bad publicity, and unhappy franchisees can derail entire franchise systems and impair franchisee investments for years—sometimes permanently.

It's also worth pointing out that when private equity franchise sponsors fail, they may have professional egg on their face, but they usually make money for themselves and their investors.

▼

As we have previously discussed, general partners typically invest comparatively small amounts of their own personal funds as an overall percentage of deals. PE can find many ways to take money out, even from troubled businesses. PE is mindful of their fiduciary duty to their own investors and, of course, want to win new commitments for their next fundraise. Because PE's risk is spread across their portfolio, they can also endure a few hits and mistakes. The same cannot be said for franchisees stuck in a system that's crashed or stalled out under PE.

In the next two chapters, we'll review in detail the top causes of franchise value destruction and discuss the path back to achieving better outcomes for all franchise stakeholders.

CHAPTER 16

Overleverage: The Burden That Keeps on Taking

It has been said that leverage is a force multiplier of your choices.

THE USE OF DEBT in and of itself is neither good nor bad in an M&A context; it's a business tool used primarily to improve financial returns. But overleverage combined with flawed execution of the franchise model is where some PE sponsors have gotten themselves into trouble. Overleverage is a critically important topic in franchising and thus deserves thorough discussion in its very own chapter. I suggest taking a brief stretch and grabbing the beverage of your choice. Then let's dive in.

> Since leverage is core to the private equity investing model, the problem of overleverage boils down to the PE practitioner. Responsible PE investors use debt thoughtfully. Others are too aggressive. And anywhere in the middle, franchise businesses can be impacted by execution mistakes, errors of judgment, overconfidence, and unanticipated market changes that make debt positions untenable while under the stewardship of genuinely well-meaning people.

Once a franchise is overleveraged, debt is a burden that keeps on taking. The resulting cash crunch can create a smothering downward spiral of cost-cutting and underinvestment in order to afford debt payments, which undermines the long-term strength of the business and ironically makes it that much harder to afford debt service. It's like a computer do-loop where you constantly cycle through "false" choices and can't move forward. In my experience, franchise founders most frequently say they don't want to work with private equity because they don't want to give up control. But their second most cited reason is often their fear that PE will put heavy debt on their business.

As a point of order, family offices, independent sponsors, individual wealthy investors, strategics, and hybrids may put different levels of debt, or none at all, on their portfolio companies compared to traditional private equity firms. Also, remember that in emerging brands debt is seldom a problem since PE firms usually pay cash and the business is too small to carry much (or any) leverage. This aligns to PE's lower and middle market investing patterns generally: the smaller the firm, the more likely an operational approach will be employed by PE to create (and extract) value, rather than a financial engineering approach.

PE sponsor philosophies about the use of debt can vary. Let's ask a dedicated growth investor, Levine Leichtman Capital Partners, about their philosophy on the use of leverage. As explained by LLCP managing director Matthew Frankel,[1]

> LLCP is atypical. We are focused on growth investing. It is core to our strategy to use less third-party debt, typically three to four turns only, compared to the market, which may use double that. Instead, we invest in both junior debt and equity to pay dividends to our investors.
>
> We see two negatives for too much debt. First, if the company hits a speed bump, the equity investors could lose their investment if lenders foreclose on the equity. Second, if interest rates go up, management now isn't focused on making decisions in the best interests for the brand versus what they pay their lenders. Money that was set aside for a new app or new point of sale system or whatever now must go toward paying interest. That's why we don't like it. It diverts cash flow that can help franchisees or grow the business, and growth is why we're investing in the first place.
>
> Other firms may like franchising because it supports high levels of leverage. We would rather have consistent returns where our investors can sleep at night. We'd rather take that tradeoff. We want no zeros, no

strikeouts at all, so our total portfolio produces a strong return compared to other firms using more leverage that have a few big hits but also some zeros.

FRANCHISING'S BANKRUPTCY TRACK RECORD

A 2017 study by the American Marketing Association, together with the Ivey Business School at Western University and several others, is revealing on the topic of franchise bankruptcies.[2] The study looked at 13 years of US bankruptcy filings involving both franchisors and franchisees between 1997 and 2009. This study's time span is important because it includes the first big wave of PE investing activity in franchising as well as several recessions.[3] Across the 1,115 franchise systems examined, the researchers could confirm only 41 cases of franchisor-level bankruptcies. Moreover, 354 systems (32 percent of those examined) had no bankruptcies at either the franchisor or franchisee level. There were more franchisee bankruptcies: the team counted 7,242 across 761 systems over the 13-year period. But accounting for hundreds of thousands of units and franchisees and the 13-year time span, even this seems a relatively low number.

> While there have been examples of franchise bankruptcies where over-leverage on PE's watch was a contributing factor, *overall there have been relatively few franchisor bankruptcies.*

In comparison, one in five US businesses of all types fails within the first year and fully half within five years, according to the US Bureau of Labor Statistics.[4] Franchising's resilience compared to other business types has long been noted.

But let's look briefly now at two cases where overleverage under PE ownership clearly contributed to the fall of well-known franchises, which filed for bankruptcy: Friendly's and Sbarro. These cases are also notable for the contrasting paths of the private equity firms involved. The first, Sun Capital, has now fully exited the franchise sector, whereas the other,

MidOcean, has become a prolific and highly visible franchise investor. For one of these brands, we'll end on a positive note. Sbarro has a compelling turnaround story.

CASE STUDY: FRIENDLY'S AND SUN CAPITAL

Sun Capital Partners Inc. (founded in 1995) used to be one of the most active PE firms investing in the restaurant sector, holding 13 brands over 15 years. The company had notable franchising successes. In the case of Bruegger's Bagels, Sun bought 100 percent of the debt and, according to the company, did a friendly conversion to equity, taking the company from over-leverage (10x) to no leverage. Sun improved Bruegger's operations, cut costs, remodeled outlets, and expanded.[5] Over an eight-year hold (2003 to 2011), Sun earned 13x on its original investment and an internal rate of return of over 30 percent.[6] EBITDA grew 76 percent during Sun's ownership.[7]

Sun Capital also managed to turn around struggling Captain D's Seafood. Captain D's was sold to Centre Partners in 2013.[8] Sun explained at the time that its success at Captain D's was related to taking an operational approach. Investments were made to expand and strengthen the corporate team, improve model efficiencies, update the menu and outlet design, improve food quality, and deliver more value to customers. As a result, same-store sales grew consistently.[9]

While Sun Capital had notable successes with some of its restaurant investments such as Bruegger's and Captain D's, Sun-owned restaurants (both franchise and nonfranchise format) have also landed in bankruptcy seven times according to the *Wall Street Journal*.[10]

The Friendly's case study shows what happens when too much debt collides with changing market conditions, recessionary pressure, lack of innovation, increased sector costs, and changing customer preferences. Operational improvement plans must show results fast enough to service debt, which is a tall order in heavily leveraged brands. Friendly's was already struggling before Sun Capital purchased it. But Sun's overreliance on financial engineering hastened Friendly's demise. This is ironic given that Sun itself credits its successes at Bruegger's and Captain D's to taking an operational approach.

Friendly's was founded in 1934 (then called Friendly; the name was changed to Friendly's in 1989). It was publicly traded between 1968 and 1979, until it was sold to Hershey Foods. Then Tennessee Restaurants (which also owned Perkins) bought the restaurant portion of the business (separate from manufacturing and retail distribution) from Hershey's in 1988.[11]

Sun Capital took Friendly's private in 2007 for nearly $340 million.[12] Four years later, in November 2011, Friendly's filed for bankruptcy. At the time, Friendly's had more than 420 restaurants and primary debt obligations of $297 million as well as various unsecured supplier and other debts, including $6.25 million in prepaid gift card obligations. Prior to the filing, Friendly's total adjusted EBITDA among all affiliates during the first eight months of 2011 was $17.8 million (for a ratio of 16.7x debt/EBITDA). At one point, the bankruptcy court reportedly had to get involved to convince the power company to keep the electricity turned on to the production facility so that 17 million gallons of ice cream wouldn't melt.[13]

Sun Capital was on both sides of the deal, with Sun affiliates providing operating loans to keep the business afloat. When no bidders came forward at auction, Sun was able to buy Friendly's in a "credit bid" sale by wiping out one of its own affiliate's $75 million loan to the company and assuming some of Friendly's debt. The restructuring plan also allowed Sun to shift responsibility for 6,000 Friendly's employee and retiree pensions to the government's Pension Benefit Guarantee Corporation.[14] This caused negative press coverage and prompted Pension Benefit Guarantee Corporation to accuse Sun Capital Partners of fraud. A settlement was ultimately reached.[15]

With a still heavy debt load, aging concept, and dated outlets in need of a refresh, Friendly's couldn't reboot. Friendly's closed 70 percent of its remaining locations from 2011 to 2020, down to 130.[16] In 2020, it filed for bankruptcy again and was sold for less than $2 million to Brix Holdings backed by Amici Partners Group.[17] Today, Sun Capital has exited restaurants and franchising. It sold its remaining holding, Smokey Bones, for $30 million in September 2023 to FAT Brands.[18] It originally purchased Smokey Bones in 2007 from Darden Restaurants for $80 million.

CASE STUDY: SBARRO AND MIDOCEAN PARTNERS

Fifty-year-old franchise brand Sbarro was acquired by MidOcean Partners* and Ares Management in January 2007 for $450 million[19] ($208 million was debt, according to BUYOUTS).[20] At the time, there were 1,000 Sbarro locations in 34 countries and 11,000 employees.[21] Sbarro reported EBITDA of $49 million in 2005 prior to jumping on the PE deal ladder.[22] But did the ladder lead up or down?

The acquisition timing turned out to be terrible. Changing consumer tastes, higher ingredient prices, and growing competition in both the pizza and quick service restaurant categories put enormous pressure on the company. Planned expansions in Brazil and Japan fell flat. The recession of 2007–2009 hit Sbarro shopping mall locations hard. Other companies acquired via MidOcean's Fund III reportedly also struggled during this same period, partially due to the financial crisis and the related drag on consumer spending.[23]

But carrying heavy debt also reduced optionality. Sbarro started missing interest payments. In August 2008, S&P lowered the company's ratings on its loan and $25 million credit facility. An S&P credit analyst attributed the downgrade to the possibility that Sbarro would breach financial covenants due to eroding operating performance and EBITDA.[24]

In January 2011, S&P downgraded Sbarro to "cc," a low "junk" status. The company notified lenders and the Securities and Exchange Commission about the potential of default.[25] Despite the company's eroding position, in June 2011, the company closed on a $325 million recapitalization.[26] Total debt climbed to $404.3 million by November 2011. With more debt loaded onto a declining business, what could possibly go wrong?

Sbarro declared Chapter 11 bankruptcy. After wiping out 70 percent of the existing debt, Sbarro's remaining debt (held by Guggenheim and Apollo) was still high. MidOcean's and Ares's equity stakes were reportedly wiped out.[27]

Sbarro continued to struggle. EBITDA continued to decline, to $21 million in 2011 and $15 million in 2012.[28] What the brand really needed was a proven operational leader at the helm with a well-conceived turnaround plan and partners patient enough to give management time to execute on that plan. As previously discussed, turning around a struggling franchise is one of the toughest assignments in business.

---

*   The acquisition of Sbarro was funded out of MidOcean's third fund, MidOcean Partners III, which closed at more than $1.25 billion in 2007. Recall that MidOcean was created in a spinout from Deutsche Bank DBKGn.DE.

It was at this point that J. David Karam entered as CEO.[29] Karam was an experienced multi-unit franchisee of Wendy's (at one time owning more than 350 stores) and later tried to buy the parent company. When Wendy's board opted instead to accept a competing bid from Nelson Peltz and his Trian Partners in 2008, Karam came in as president to run the business under Trian for several years. Karam took over as CEO of Sbarro in early 2013. Karam recalls the major steps in the reboot process and the results:[30]

> From my perspective, the prior restructuring wasn't as effective as it could have been. There was still too much debt relative to EBITDA, and they didn't take the opportunity to abrogate bad lease deals. I started in March 2013 and by November we had aligned around a plan. We filed for bankruptcy again in April 2014. It was a lot to get through at the time—of course, franchisees, lenders, and vendors were alarmed about the second bankruptcy. But we explained how we planned to turn the brand around. Apollo and Guggenheim remain invested in the brand today, and I am now the majority owner along with my sons. We repositioned the brand around New York–style pizza by the slice and built out the team. It took time to heal from a decade of misdirection and the bankruptcies, but we're back on a solid path.
>
> We see a huge opportunity in front of us. Pizza is the second- or third-largest quick service restaurant category. What we provide is unique, high-quality pizza by the slice. We defined and now dominate the impulse pizza category. Our offering is differentiated by its quality. For example, we make our own dough and shred our own cheese daily in our stores. We know that if we put our locations in high-foot-traffic areas, our beautiful displays of food and our craveable offerings will get their share of that customer traffic. Five years ago, we also added third-party delivery, and it's grown to be a significant part of our business.
>
> We have tremendous momentum. Last week we opened our 700th location. We opened 103 new stores last year and should open 110 this year. There are 1,000 malls in the US, but we're only in 250. There are 150,000 convenience stores and 20,000 travel centers in the US alone. These are important new store development venues. We also target colleges, airports, casinos, and other high-traffic locations where this type

of concept will resonate. International markets are high growth for us. More than half of our development is outside the US. We've posted two years of 20 percent year-over-year same-store sales growth, and even higher overseas. EBITDA has grown significantly, and we've reduced our leverage... we should be debt-free in 36 months. We grew to $8 million EBITDA last year [2022] even with a bit of a COVID overhang remaining, and we should achieve $12.5 million EBITDA this year [2023].

Under an experienced management team with the right turnaround plan, better balance sheet, refocus on the core customer and franchisee value propositions, together with the backing of patient capital, Sbarro is now back on a growth path.

Key Elements Needed for Successful Turnarounds

Although franchise turnarounds are tough, one of the most compelling things about franchising is that lagging or failing brands *can* be reinvigorated with enough effort, patience, and skill. Franchising is incredibly resilient in that way.[31] Franchisees must believe in and underwrite the turnaround for it to take hold. There are three clear themes visible in successful franchise turnarounds:

1 **Leadership usually has significant operating experience, often as franchisees themselves.** There are interesting second or third career options for former multi-unit franchisees and corporate leaders with strong operating and also turnaround experience. It's a unique skill set.

2 **Sponsors are patient but also provide a clear mandate for change.** There is a big difference between patience and passiveness. There must be a clear mandate for change, willingness to reinvest in the business at the corporate level, and strategic support.

3 **There is a focus on re-creating the value proposition for both customers and franchisees.** It's back to the drawing board. What is differentiated and special? A complete rethink about unit-level profitability is also needed. Franchisees will be understandably skeptical, so communication and collaboration with franchisees is key.

Stall-outs that remain stuck are missing these elements. Scale brands held by "long-hold" investors are at the greatest risk. The temptation is for the sponsor to milk cash flow too long.

Continuously Building Insights and Market Expertise

What of MidOcean? It closed on Fund IV in 2015 and went on to raise $1.2 billion for Fund V in 2018 (the fund was oversubscribed).[32] MidOcean Partners VI, LP closed in April 2023 as the largest fund raised in the firm's 20-year history, with over $1.5 billion in capital commitments.[33] MidOcean has grown into a confident and prolific franchise investor, including building out large platforms:

▶ Jenny Craig (2002–2006: as previously mentioned, sold to Nestlé for $600 million, a reported 5× originally paid for the company)[34]—this predated MidOcean's 2007 Sbarro investment.

▶ Empower Brands (formerly called LYNX) combined with Outdoor Living Brands: as of this writing comprises 11 services brands—JAN-PRO (see earlier case study), Intelligent Office, FRSTeam, Archadeck Outdoor Living, Outdoor Lighting Perspectives, Conserva Irrigation, Superior Fence and Rail, Koala Insulation, Wallaby Windows, Canopy Lawn Care, and Bumble Roofing.[35]

▶ Full Speed Automotive: an aftermarket auto services platform of 700+ corporate and franchised locations, including Grease Monkey, SpeeDee, and Uncle Ed's Oil Shoppe. Additional brands include 10 Minute Oil Change, American Lube Fast, AutoLube Car Care Center, Excel Car Wash, FLP, Herbert Automotive, Ingelside Auto & Tire, Kwik Kar, Minit Man Oil Change, Mobil 1 Lube Express, and Super Lube Plus.[36] Full Speed has pursued a strategy of tuck-in acquisitions including nonfranchise businesses.

Despite difficulties experienced in MidOcean's Sbarro investment, MidOcean put its learnings to good use. This is an important point. Given the learning curve of the franchise model itself, whether an investor has franchise experience is something to consider. Tremendous capital is flowing in, and some PE firms are new to the sector.

> When considering potential capital partners, look at the firm's overall history as a sponsor of franchise businesses. What is their track record elevating brands or operating groups and helping them achieve improved scale and performance? In PE's investing history, have they tended to take an operational approach or to prioritize financial engineering tactics?

Don't automatically discount an experienced PE investor if there have been challenges in some of their portfolio companies. Instead, look for patterns. Were mistakes repeated? Have sponsors learned? Has their approach changed? If you speak to GPs, can those GPs keep it real and talk candidly about lessons learned? *Some of the best and smartest people in business are the best at what they do precisely because they have learned by doing, demonstrated by their ability to course-correct along the way.* Interview potential partners and really get to know them. Check references and franchisee validation.

If you're a founder or MUO franchisee considering bringing on a private capital partner, you need to network well ahead of time. It's difficult to understand the track record, cultures, and players during the heat of an auction process while you're also responding to numerous questions about your own business and your financials. If you're a prospective franchisee, the pace of the sale process can sometimes encourage participants to sail along on a wave of optimism, whereas digging into references, the business model, and the track record of management and PE sponsors would lead to a more informed purchase decision.

To close this part of the debt discussion, it's not just the absolute size of debt that counts; it's important to pay attention to the *accumulation* of debt compared to overall trends in the business and what PE decision-makers keep the management team focused on. If total debt accumulates faster and higher relative to company EBITDA, then the reduction in cash flow to service that debt can negatively impact investments in the future (lack of innovation), staffing (cuts to franchisee support), technology updates (impacting the customer and franchisee experience), and so on. Now not only does the brand have a high and accumulating debt load, but the business is also less competitive.

Financial disclosures in franchise FDDs are all over the place on this issue. Some do a terrific job of sharing details about debt service and also demonstrating what investments are being made in the business. Others provide sparse information. This is where engaging your independent franchisee-owner association can be very useful. Franchisees are contractually obligated to keep up with brand standards and required remodels. But there is no reciprocal obligation for the franchisor to make investments in the business to keep up with the times or to avoid overleverage. Therefore, investment in the future of the business must be an ongoing conversation that should be part of the formal agenda and dialogue between the franchisee association and management.

THE (POSITIVE) EVOLUTION OF PRIVATE EQUITY'S FRANCHISE DEBT STRATEGY

Let's turn back to our deeper discussion of the use of debt in franchises, especially at the franchisor level. Because of the well-known issues stemming from overleverage in PE-backed deals generally and highlighted in a few specific examples we have covered here, *it is important to talk about what's changed for the better.* There has been a transformation of approach that is important to understand and discuss. There are two significant, positive changes regarding PE's use of debt in franchise investments in recent years:

▶ First, both PE and the debt markets appeared to have learned from earlier franchise investing missteps. Even in the case of larger, PE-backed franchise businesses, debt levels and strategies are now relatively more conservative compared to the earliest years of PE investing, when junk bonds were often used.

▶ Second, for larger companies, and even some midsize companies, debt is now commonly backed by audited recurring revenue streams such as royalties in what are called "securitizations" (this will be discussed further shortly).

Both of these developments signal PE franchise stewards are much more cognizant of maintaining balance between equity and debt. The debt products used are also more directly tied to unit-level and overall system stability. In the case of securitizations, PE-backed brand debt levels are now similar to those of both family-held and publicly traded franchise brands. There is far more consistency of approach. PE's chosen level of debt is no longer an outlier.

> Recently, more equity is going into companies than decades ago. PE has backed off heavy leverage, and research shows that private equity firms are effective helping their portfolio companies navigate through market challenges. You can't supercharge growth without investing in the business. The research also shows that PE-backed loans perform better than comparatives.
>
> **—DREW MALONEY**, president and chief executive officer, American Investment Council[37]

Of course, the *cost* of debt (interest rates) impacts how much leverage companies can take on or are willing to take on. Periods of cheap debt fuel acquisitions and recapitalizations. We saw this as interest rates fell in response to the pandemic. Falling interest rates drove higher debt ratios, higher deal multiples, and an increase in PE dealmaking from mid-2020 through mid-2022.

But looking across the entire market, PE firms active in franchising and even publicly traded franchise systems are in line with overall market levels and are not taking out amounts of debt inconsistent with market averages.

FIGURE 3: New Leveraged Loans and Debt Multiples, by Year

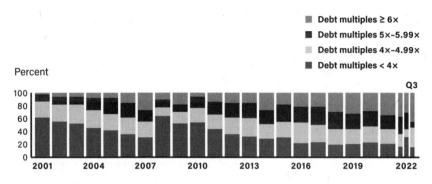

Source: Federal Reserve Stability Report, November 2022[38]

▼

As shown in the Federal Reserve figure above, nearly half of all new leveraged loans (i.e., loans to companies that already carry debt) issued in 2022 had debt multiples greater than six. It is worth watching because this will put long-term pressure on returns because higher interest rates reduce the fair value of future cash flows.[39] Certainly some readers will look at these numbers and decide the ratios are still higher than they are comfortable with, but it remains the case that especially in franchising it represents a change from more aggressive historical rates seen in many deals. In terms of middle market averages (total enterprise value lower than $100 million), average debt/EBITDA multiples were 5.5× EBITDA in 2021 and hit 5.7× EBITDA in Q2 2021, the highest level since 2005.[40] Not surprisingly, while debt was relatively cheap, middle market recapitalizations in 2021 also hit their highest level since 2018.[41]

Every PE deal team carves out its own approach based on how much leverage a portfolio company can carry, market conditions, cost of debt (interest rates), and the PE firm's own lending relationships, risk tolerance, and confidence in portfolio company future cash flows. As an illustrative example, when ServiceMaster (owned by Roark) contemplated the acquisition of Two Men and a Truck in 2021, it proposed a securitization of $400 million, of which $180 million would be used for the Two Men acquisition. The proposal represented leverage of 7.6× total debt / adjusted EBITDA or 8.0× if the company fully drew down the entire variable note. (This is one reason why Roark has been so effective at accumulating companies. With more than 108 brands under management, the cash flow of each large platform can be tapped to make acquisitions, in addition to available moneys raised within each fund.)

When the ServiceMaster rating was issued, S&P cited total leverage of peer franchise brands with similar investment grade (meaning a low risk of default) credit ratings (BBB+, BBB, or BBB-). In the table on the following pages, I have taken the peer group considered by S&P and added context based on publicly available information to fill out the entire picture.

In other words, while certainly at the higher end of the comparative set S&P considered, the ServiceMaster securitization proposed in 2021 was still roughly comparable to other franchise systems of similar size with similar investment ratings, whether those brands were publicly traded, backed by PE, or privately held.

This is a critically important development within franchising. Since overleverage is something to be avoided for all the reasons previously mentioned, a more consistent debt strategy across ownership types, tied to audited unit-level financials and system cash flow stability, represents an evolution in approach.

One reason for this shift, especially in the largest franchised systems, is thanks to certain architects within a corner of structured finance. I will keep this as nontechnical and breezy as possible, but it's important for franchise stakeholders to understand.

TABLE 3: Leverage (Total Debt/Adjusted EBITDA) for Select Brands

Leverage ratios comparatives according to s & p Global.[42]

Author's comments and additional data in italics. Ownership status listed at the time each securitization was completed. This chart is not intended to be a complete list either of all WBS issuance between 2015 and 2021 nor a complete list of all WBS transactions of the listed companies.

BRANDS	LEVERAGE (TOTAL DEBT/ADJUSTED EBITDA)
ServiceMaster Brands (2021) *(acquired for $1.553 billion by Roark in 2020)*[43] *$400 million securitization proposed in 2021*	7.6 to 8.0
Five Guys (2021) *(family held, minority PE investor)* *$250 million securitization*[44]	7.8
Wendy's (2021) *(publicly traded)* *$900 million, partly to refinance prior securitizations*[45]	6.9
Domino's (2021) *(publicly traded)* *$1.5 billion*[46] *Domino's first came to the securitization market in 2007, and returned in 2012, 2016, 2017, 2018, and 2019.*	6.4
SERVPRO (2021) *(Blackstone acquired 2019)* *$260 million*[47]	8.1
CKE Restaurants (Hardee's/Carl's Jr.) (2020) *(Roark owned)* *$400 million*[48]	6.8
ServiceMaster Brands (2020) *(Roark owned)* *$700 million securitization*[49]	7.1
Driven Brands (2020) *(Roark owned)* *$175 million securitization*[50] *The company completed its first whole business securitization in 2015 and returned again in 2021 for another $450 million securitization.*[51]	6.7
Sonic (2020) *(Roark owned)* *$400 million securitization*[52]	5.9
Wingstop (2020) *(publicly traded)* *$480 million securitization*[53]	6.5
Jersey Mike's (2019) *(privately owned)* *$500 million securitization*[54] *Raised another $500 million via WBS in 2021*[55]	6.4

BRANDS	LEVERAGE (TOTAL DEBT/ADJUSTED EBITDA)
Planet Fitness (2019) *(publicly traded)* $550 million[56] *This follows a $1.2 billion securitization in 2018.*[57]	6.5
Wendy's (2019) *(publicly traded)* $850 million new securitization to refinance[58] *This follows a $2.275 billion securitization in 2015*[59] *that itself was refinanced in 2017.*[60]	6.6
Jack in the Box (2019) *(publicly traded)* $1.3 billion *JIB had attempted to sell the company in 2018 but opted for refinancing after franchisee pushback.*[62] *In 2018, it also sold off its Qdoba business to Apollo Global Management for $305 million.*[63]	4.9
Applebee's/IHOP (2019) *(publicly traded, Dine Brands)* $1.3 billion refinancing of senior notes from 2014[64]	6.0
Dunkin' Brands (2019) *(publicly traded at the time, acquired by Roark in December 2020)* $1.85 billion[65]	6.2
Taco Bell (2018) *(publicly traded, YUM Brands)* $1.45 billion securitization[66]	5.3
Jimmy John's (2017) *(Roark acquired in 2016)* $850 million securitization[67]	5.2
Cajun Global (2017) *franchisor of* **Texas Chicken** *and* **Church's Chicken** *(owned by High Bluff Capital Partners)* $210 million securitization[68] *Cajun Global's first securitization was in 2011. It returned again in 2020 for a $250 million securitization.*[69]	5.2
Five Guys (2017) *(privately held, minority PE investor)* $440 million securitization[70]	6.7
Arby's (2015) *(Roark owned)* $650 million securitization[71]	5.3

WHOLE BUSINESS SECURITIZATION

Recently (over the last 15+ years, starting after the financial crisis of 2007–2009), the largest brands in the franchise sector have shifted to whole business securitization rather than higher cost and/or traditional bank debt.

Asset-backed securities as an area of structured finance got off the ground in the 1980s, starting with securitizing auto loans and credit card receivables. It is now a $1.9 trillion market with $242 billion in new issues forecast for 2023.[72] Asset-backed securities are split into various types. The type of asset-backed security applicable to franchising is called whole business securitization (WBS). Whole business securitization is basically debt supported by cash flows from operating assets such as franchise royalties. Back in 2012, WBS issuance represented only a tiny sliver of all asset-backed securities,[73] or around $2.4 billion. This has since grown substantially as the market has gotten comfortable with the stability of these income streams, including those of franchise businesses. By 2018, WBS new issuance exceeded $8 billion.[74] In 2021, new WBS issuance hit a record year of $14.5 billion before settling back to new issuance of $6.4 billion in 2022, with total WBS outstanding reaching $44 billion at the beginning of 2023.[75]

The appeal of securitized debt is that larger amounts can be borrowed at lower interest rates, creating a more efficient capital structure. This approach also represents a change in how PE firms acquire large, highly franchised companies. Acquisitions can be initially funded with a mix of equity and essentially bridge loans—high-yield (more expensive) debt—but then later can be refinanced via WBS into lower-yield (less expensive) debt. This allows the time necessary to secure credit ratings and set up the appropriate holding structure, a lengthy process that can take up to a year to complete. It makes little difference to the market if the franchise royalty stream is a publicly traded firm or backed by PE. If the franchise system demonstrates stability and acceptable unit-level economics such that the market believes that debt can be serviced, then that income stream can be securitized.

> The key WBS enabler is the creation of carefully constructed *bankruptcy-remote* special purpose vehicles, also called special purpose entities.[76]

Expertise creating the correct entity structure was the key breakthrough, led by market makers such as Guggenheim Securities, that empowered this recent and important shift in approach. If the parent (the franchisor, in this case) goes bankrupt, the special purpose entity is not seen as a "core asset" of the parent, and thus the special purpose vehicle is both protected and earns a higher credit rating, which makes the debt less expensive. This also means that the parent sponsor can actually have a lower credit rating than the WBS stream itself.[77] Note that the originator, the franchisor, retains no legal interest in the transferred assets. *For franchisees, this means the contract you signed and are tied to can be transferred to a new owner, including a special purpose entity.*

The basic steps are straightforward:

1 Create a special purpose entity. This is a new "bankruptcy-remote" subsidiary owned by the parent (the franchisor, in this case), which is owned by a holding company, which is owned by the private equity firm or public company sponsor.

2 Transfer key assets to the special purpose entity (e.g., intellectual property, franchise agreements, company store EBITDA, vendor rebates, rental income). Asset quality should be good enough to achieve a BBB- investment rating or better. Bonds are marketed to outside investors backed by the underlying assets.[78]

3 Service the debt using cash flows generated by the assets. Investors in the special purpose entity receive residual cash flows.

The figure at right is a useful visual aide to describe the flow.

FIGURE 4: How Securitization Works

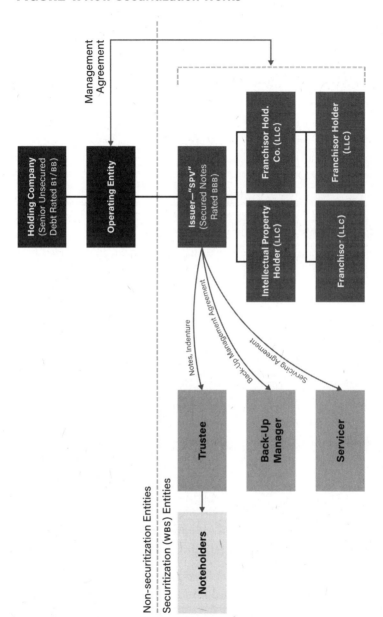

Source: Quisenberry, Jenn. (August 3, 2016) New England Asset Management. https://www.neamgroup.com/insights/whole-business-securitization-the-power-of-structure Used with permission.

▼

With a master trust, a franchised business can issue new debt in the future to monetize cash flow growth, organically through same-store sales or through the addition of new franchise agreements. The company doesn't need to reprice the existing debt or seek consent from existing note holders. Several other advantages make securitization more compelling than other debt products for franchisors. Securitization provides more prepayment flexibility and more flexibility to deploy free cash flow. You can do a revolver from within the existing securitization structure. The debt is generally portable in a change of control. And most importantly, the securitization achieves a much lower cost of funds and often a higher debt quantum. That's what really appealed to issuers, especially financial sponsors. The first large deal we did financed the Dunkin' leveraged buy-out at the end 2005, early 2006. Now, the WBS market is approaching $50 billion in outstanding debt.

—**CORY WISHENGRAD**, senior managing director and head of fixed income, Guggenheim Securities[79]

Note that this approach also works for smaller franchise businesses. For example, in 2011, Church's Chicken had modest EBITDA but was able to secure a successful $245 million securitization.[80]

Key Whole Business Securitization Takeaways

Why does this matter to you as a key franchise stakeholder? There are three main takeaways:

1 **Large franchisors have broadly adopted securitization financing since the financial crisis of 2007-2009.** Scale franchisors have largely moved away from junk bonds and more aggressive leverage vehicles and settled into a strategy backed by audited income streams of the core business.

FIGURE 5: 17-Year Franchisor Trend—Switch to Securitization Financing

	2006	
BANK DEBT / BONDS		**SECURITIZATION**
Arby's	IHOP	
Burger King	Jack in the Box	
Church's Chicken	McDonald's	
CKE Restaurants	Papa Johns	Quiznos
Domino's	Planet Fitness	
Dunkin' Brands	Sonic	
Focus Brands	Wendy's	
Hooters	YUM	

17-YEAR TRANSFORMATION

	TODAY	
BANK DEBT / BONDS		**SECURITIZATION**
	Anytime Fitness	Jersey Mike's
	Arby's	Jimmy John's
	Authority Brands	Neighborly
	Bojangles	Nothing Bundt Cakes
	Church's Chicken	Planet Fitness
McDonald's	CKE Restaurants	Self Esteem Brands
Restaurant Brands International	Domino's	ServiceMaster
Papa Johns	Driven Brands	Sonic
	Dunkin' Brands	Taco Bell
	European Wax Center	TGI Fridays
	Five Guys	Wendy's
	Focus Brands	Wingstop
	HOA Brands	Zaxby's
	Jack in the Box	

Source: Guggenheim Securities, used with permission. Please also see an important disclaimer listed in the endnotes.[82]

The fixed-rate nature of this debt has reduced the volatility in cash needed to service debt. Many issuers have commented that before securitization the most volatile uses of cash flow in their business were at the interest expense line.

—**MATT PILLA**, senior managing director, consumer and retail investment banking, Guggenheim Securities[81]

▼

Note that none of the companies listed in Figure 5 switched from securitization to bank/bond financing since the financial crisis. Some of these securitizations are massive. For example, Dunkin' Brands (acquired by Roark-owned Inspire Brands in 2020) returned to the market and raised $2.35 billion in 2021 via WBS. S&P Global Ratings noted at the time that total debt outstanding (assuming all notes were drawn) after the new issuance would amount to $4.35 billion.[83] S&P cited Dunkin's long operating history, pandemic recovery, and overall growth as considerations. As S&P Global pointed out regarding this transaction, the money was used to cover prior transaction fees, pay down prior debt, *and fund a distribution to the parent of the franchisor.* (We will return to the subject of distributions.) More than $2.2 billion in net distributions were made between 2020 and 2022, according to Dunkin's 2023 FDD.[84]

The WBS approach lowers the cost of debt while simultaneously providing an incentive to take out more. But at the same time, it helps keep franchisors and franchisees somewhat aligned to preserve system revenues and outlet count, since a key component of a successful securitization is the stability of the system and thus the recurring revenue stream.

2   **The market recently (prior to interest rate hikes) got comfortable with leverage above 5× EBITDA for large, highly franchised businesses.** Figure 6, at right, provides relevant examples.

Keep in mind, what the market will bear is constantly changing. In mid-2022 and into 2023, inflation pressure and rising interest rates changed the equation again. The ratings agencies will grade each brand's strengths and debt capability. The strongest brands have debt in the 4–6× range. Thanks to rising interest rates, anything above 7× as of this writing will be looked at very closely and could be problematic, possibly resulting in lower ratings.

3   **Although heavily franchised restaurant chains remain the largest users of WBS, total non-restaurant WBS outstanding has recently been growing faster.** Restaurant WBS outstanding grew from $21 billion to $30 billion from 2019 to mid-2023, an increase of 42 percent. But

FIGURE 6: Leverage Levels of Large, Highly Franchised Brands

The debt market has become comfortable with leverage of 5.0×+ for highly franchised companies over the last several years; it is yet to be seen if the increased rate of environment will result in lower leverage targets for some of these issuers.

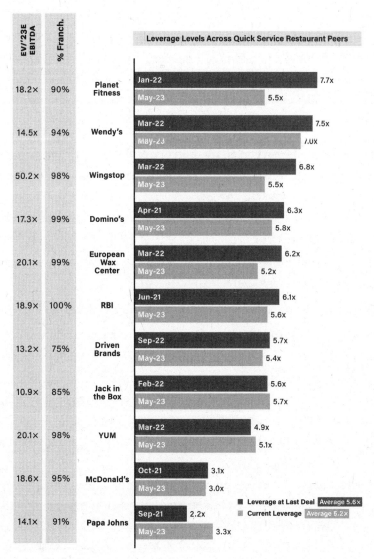

Leverage Levels Across Quick Service Restaurant Peers

EV/'23E EBITDA	% Franch.			
18.2x	90%	Planet Fitness	Jan-22: 7.7x	May-23: 5.5x
14.5x	94%	Wendy's	Mar-22: 7.5x	May-23: 7.0x
50.2x	98%	Wingstop	Mar-22: 6.8x	May-23: 5.5x
17.3x	99%	Domino's	Apr-21: 6.3x	May-23: 5.8x
20.1x	99%	European Wax Center	Mar-22: 6.2x	May-23: 5.2x
18.9x	100%	RBI	Jun-21: 6.1x	May-23: 5.6x
13.2x	75%	Driven Brands	Sep-22: 5.7x	May-23: 5.4x
10.9x	85%	Jack in the Box	Feb-22: 5.6x	May-23: 5.7x
20.1x	98%	YUM	Mar-22: 4.9x	May-23: 5.1x
18.6x	95%	McDonald's	Oct-21: 3.1x	May-23: 3.0x
14.1x	91%	Papa Johns	Sep-21: 2.2x	May-23: 3.3x

■ Leverage at Last Deal — Average 5.6x
▨ Current Leverage — Average 5.2x

Source: Guggenheim Securities, used with permission. Current leverage reflects data as of May 2023. See also important disclaimers in the endnotes.[85]

non-restaurant WBS outstanding grew from $8 billion to $14 billion, a 75 percent increase over the same period. This signals that the market and even large non-restaurant franchise systems have reached a similar appreciation for both the value of a stable franchise system as well as the WBS approach to capital planning. (See Figure 7, at right.)

▼

WHOLE BUSINESS SECURITIZATION IMPLICATIONS FOR FRANCHISEES

Franchisors must make a long-term commitment to system stability to maintain investment-grade credit ratings and tap WBS as a capital planning option. This has predictable consequences for franchisees:

Scale franchisors in particular will be very protective of their royalty streams. For franchisees, realize that your franchisor (thanks to existing or anticipated securitizations) will invest significant time and effort monitoring system financial health, including collecting information from franchisees on their own indebtedness, to model risk within the franchise system. The pandemic accelerated this effort and drove it down into even regional systems not yet engaged in WBS transactions.

Franchisors may step up requirements for transfers. Franchisees can expect franchisors to be more assertive regarding transfer approvals to protect royalty streams. For example, the franchisor may increase buyer net worth requirements, and/or require the buyer to complete remodels as a condition of the transfer. If a seller is in distress, unless the unit is in an undesirable location or market, the franchisor will fight closures and push instead for transfers. After all, the franchisor has already sold that cash flow and wants to avoid "impaired air."

As we discussed, PE buyers are actively rolling up franchise outlets in some systems. Their significant capital backing should encourage franchisors, but the franchisor may want to see more cash on the acquiring entity's balance sheet than the PE buyer of those outlets may want to fund. Franchisors will be more likely to prevent early PE exits and may

FIGURE 7: Securitization: Preferred Financing Vehicle for Franchised Restaurants and Growing Prominence in Non-restaurant Franchises

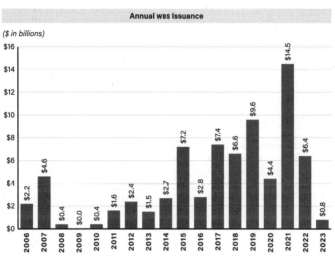

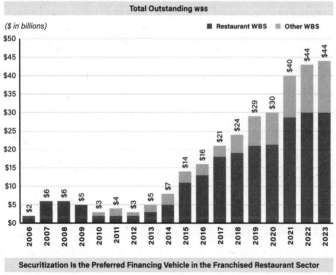

Securitization Is the Preferred Financing Vehicle in the Franchised Restaurant Sector

Source: Guggenheim Securities, used with permission. As of March 3, 2023. Note also important disclaimers in endnotes.[86]

add conditions. This is because there is a fundamental disconnect between shorter PE timelines if they are backing multi-unit franchisees and the need for the franchisor to protect the long-term (already securitized) royalty stream. This could delay or disrupt exit transactions and is something for retiring franchisees to budget into their sale timing. If franchisor-imposed transfer conditions become too onerous, this could chill PE interest, impacting resale values.

> Independent franchisee associations should monitor changes in transfer requirements to ensure they are reasonable and to preserve resale values and protect franchisee exit options.

Large franchisors are especially likely to be aggressive about enforcing development agreements for similar reasons.

Contract language should be carefully considered, especially around guarantees. Contractual language around liquidated damages and back royalties tied to personal guarantees are an important backstop to the franchisor to try to recoup potential lost royalties if a franchisee fails. Carefully read this language before purchasing any franchise. Some industry watchers have noted that more emerging brands are starting to include more sophisticated contractual language, or "over-legalese" as one put it, than has traditionally been the case. This is in acknowledgment of the reality that as brands trade up the deal ladder, those early agreements could be part of a securitization someday. Attorneys anticipate this and are baking this more stringent language into even emerging brand franchise agreements.

If your system hasn't securitized yet, once it's large enough it likely will. The larger the system, the more likely the income streams will be securitized. This means your franchise agreement could be transferred to a special purpose vehicle. If you get into a legal dispute with your franchisor, this structure adds complexity (time and cost) for your legal process.

WHOLE BUSINESS SECURITIZATION IMPLICATIONS FOR FRANCHISORS

Since the above approach works for both midsize and large companies, the biggest shift we will see ongoing is that well-advised franchisors will start to prepare themselves early. When emerging brands first get going, setting up the appropriate corporate entities and having the right franchise agreements in place are part of the tangle. Some emerging brands make errors early that must be unwound later. We are seeing more discipline pushed down to smaller brands especially via legal counsel and through audits with larger accounting firms who can see what's coming. If the brand continues to grow, the ability to tap the WBS market later is important for both capital planning and overall enterprise value. For emerging brands, the earlier you can monitor system health by collecting financial statements from franchisees and analyzing them to find areas for improvement, the better. This will boost both system performance and long-term enterprise value, provided franchisors do something with that information.

- ▶ **Prepare agreements in advance.** The franchise should be operating from standardized agreements and ensure that franchise agreements don't prohibit transfer to another entity, including a special purpose entity.

- ▶ **Prepare accounting and revenue tracking in advance.** Ideally franchisors should have a long-established point of sale system that allows the franchisor to collect system data in an efficient way. This information will be analyzed by the ratings agencies. It's also important to work with an accounting firm that has experience working with capital markets to help you prepare.

- ▶ **Connect ahead of time.** We advise firms of any size. Many are looking to prepare their business years in advance. We stayed in touch and guided them on how to successfully access the capital markets.

—**CORY WISHENGRAD**, senior managing director and head of fixed income, Guggenheim Securities[87]

WHAT TO DO NEXT? MAKE SURE YOU ARE WELL INFORMED

To wrap up the discussion about leverage, if you are a founder, franchisee, or even a corporate employee, the use of debt (both amount and strategy) in the franchise business should be on your radar. It is worth taking the time to understand the prospective investor-owner's "debt personality," franchising track record, and philosophy on the use of debt before you commit. This is true whether the franchise business is privately held, owned by a PE/FO/hybrid, part of a platform, or publicly traded. As a founder/seller, if you are rolling any equity forward, higher leverage may increase your selling price but also puts pressure on the business and thus on your future returns. So you must have confidence in the PE sponsor and the plan. Leverage is a business tool. **Make sure a prospective partner has a track record of solid exits and good franchising outcomes.**

Adopt the PE mindset itself, which is a commitment to digging until you get as full a picture as you can. Old-fashioned networking with franchisees and founders in other systems owned by any PE firm you're considering working with will give you useful information. Internet research from publicly available sources can be enlightening. Review franchise financial disclosures carefully. You can choose partners who use leverage responsibly while they continue to make investments in the future of the franchise.

▼

The market rewards long-term system stability, which in turn keeps owners and management teams, especially of large systems, focused on preserving long-term enterprise value. The use of leverage has moderated considerably in franchising. This is positive for our sector. However, there is another side to leverage that must be considered. We'll move now to the remainder of our bloopers list in the next chapter.

CHAPTER 17

More Private Equity Head-Scratchers and Flameouts in Franchising

"I have not failed 10,000 times—I've successfully found 10,000 ways that will not work."

—**THOMAS EDISON**, inventor

CONTINUING OUR DISCUSSION, as a reminder, our top concerns are the following:

> Franchise Value Destruction: Things for *All* Players, Not Just Big Money, to Avoid
>
> ▶ Overleverage
> ▶ Short-timers' syndrome
> ▶ Not protecting unit-level profitability
> ▶ Growth focus: the dark side
> ▶ Destroying franchisee trust

We looked at overleverage in some depth in the previous chapter. Number two on our hit list is "short-timers' syndrome." This can often stem from lack of available resources due to overleverage, so it is appropriate to tackle next. But it also is about willingness to invest in the future of the franchise, not just the ability to do so.

SHORT-TIMERS' SYNDROME: STARVING THE FUTURE TO PROFIT IN THE PRESENT

Private equity owners of franchise businesses that *invest for the long-term benefit of the business* (no matter what their own hold period) ultimately create brands with the greatest and most sustainable success. Revisiting the concept of "good PE lineage," it's important to recognize the good stewardship of PE firms that do make longer-term investments in their franchise portfolio companies. Those investments maintain brand momentum and relevance.

Current PE sponsors must judge every investment they make in the business against the potential return on that investment either (1) within their hold period, or (2) reflected in a higher sale price. They will be reluctant to invest otherwise.

I am reminded of a tense call I heard about between franchisees and their private capital–backed franchisor about proposed changes to the brand's marketing fund. The franchisor wanted to raise the required franchisee marketing contribution to reboot the brand image and boost national advertising efforts. Based on the unit-level economics in that system, that marketing fund increase would for some franchisees represent a material reduction in unit-level profits.

No surprise here: franchisees weren't happy with the proposal and didn't feel adequate proof was provided that the increase in fees would drive more traffic to outlets. One of them reportedly said something on that call with the PE owners that sticks with me. She said (well, it sounded from the description more like screamed into the phone), "You mean to tell me that you've been taking tens of millions in cash out of this business every year, but you want *us* to kick more into the marketing fund? *How about you guys kick something back in for a change!*"

This lively exchange raises a fair question. Just how much should current owners of a franchise brand invest in the future of that brand? How much cash flow should be reinvested in the business instead of being taken out by ownership in the form of distributions and fees (sometimes enabled by the WBS mechanism previously described)? How much reinvention cost should be borne by franchisees? This isn't just a question for PE owners of franchise businesses. But the risk of "short-timers' syndrome" is almost baked into the very model of PE investing itself unless the PE owner chooses to make investments that benefit the brand in the long term.

In their seminal book *The Blue Line Imperative: What Managing for Value Really Means*, Kevin Kaiser and S. David Young talk about the importance of enterprises building sustainable value. Companies can sometimes end up pursuing strategies and tactics that don't build value because the team doesn't know what drives the most value for the business. But PE is laser-focused on value creation. This means that operational improvements are often front-end loaded during the earliest years of PE's ownership.

Kaiser and Young assert that PE's changing priorities over the life of a portfolio company hold can make the value line pliable. Initially, PE invests in growth, and that spend is visualized as an upward-sloping line like this: /. However, in the latter years of PE's hold period, those investments are likely to decrease so much that, if you were to plot the investments out over time, the line would appear to bend into an upside-down "u" shape, like this: ∩.[1] Think back to our PE Profit Ladder and visualize it heating up under competitive pressures thanks to underinvestment. Eventually heat bends the metals, the ladder wilts, and the brand may stall out and trade down.

For those PE firms holding their investments for the typical three to eight years, PE initially (during the first one to three years) focuses on growth initiatives and on addressing near-term fixable issues such as filling staffing gaps, optimizing costs, streamlining operations, removing franchisee pain points, and investing in franchise development and brand marketing. PE also tries to show franchisees that there is new positive energy in the business. The end goal is to create an uptick in new license sales and accelerate new unit openings.

At some point, PE's attention flips to thinking more about selling the business, and so PE's focus and spending habits change. This usually happens around year three or four, depending on whether PE plans to hold the business for five years or a bit longer. From here, shorter-term payback initiatives are more likely to be undertaken. Meanwhile, the finance and operations teams may have renewed focus on boosting EBITDA (to help drive a higher sale price). Reductions or changes in spending (or "burning the furniture," as one financial leader I know dubbed it) may temporarily plump up the balance sheet. Things like expensive technology upgrades are more likely to be postponed.

So innovation and investment in the future can be starved for years while PE sponsors focus on shorter-payback investments in the business. What isn't likely to be cut, especially ahead of a sale transaction? Marketing. This spend drives an increase in same-store sales to demonstrate positive growth trends to potential buyers and ideally also create some good franchisee validation about "momentum" in the business. Smart buyers won't overpay for sales that are essentially pulled forward from future quarters into the present through aggressive marketing, specials, or discounting. So buyers will be on the lookout for this, but the marketing spend is less likely to be cut back compared to innovation spending or spending on things like technology that could take years to monetize.

If you're a franchisee in a system that was bought several years ago and that's now being positioned for resale, you may be disappointed when longer-payback investments in the future of the business, such as technology, R&D, or product innovation, slow down or seem indefinitely delayed. As one of my friends with extensive C-suite experience under PE sponsors recently quipped, "PE would never have gotten us to the moon. You need long-term R&D investments to achieve the big breakthroughs in life. PE is too short-term-focused for moon shots." Assuming the PE fund has a 10-year life span and seeks to hold investments in the fund for three to eight years, this transition from thinking about growth to thinking about positioning for exit meaningfully overlaps with franchisee license agreement commitments, which themselves average 10 years in length.

In theory, dedicated long-hold private capital investors should be well aligned with franchisees and committed to preserving the health of the brand, especially if the royalty stream has been securitized. The PE sponsor understands periodic investment will be needed. But in practical terms, this isn't always the case. It can take time for the parent to follow through and spend money.

> The tension point then becomes whether franchisees perceive that the parent is investing adequately in the long-term viability of the brand. This can become especially contentious if the parent is taking out large cash distributions if financed with debt without also making necessary and periodic investments in the future.

CASE STUDY: CKE RESTAURANTS AND ROARK CAPITAL GROUP

CKE Restaurants was purchased by Roark in late 2013 from Apollo Global Management LLC. The brand had already been through many ups and downs before Roark acquired the company. Apollo had taken the company private in 2010 and was said to be interested in taking CKE public in 2012. However, market concerns about CKE's debt load reportedly scuttled the offering and instead CKE refinanced its debt.

When acquired by Roark in 2013, the brand had 3,413 restaurants combined across both the Carl's Jr. and Hardee's brands.[2] As of May 2023, the company had 3,800 locations, so unit growth over 10 years has been modest.[3] Looking just at the Hardee's brand as an example, average unit volumes have been essentially flat in the $1.1 million range from 2011 to 2022.[4]

There has been some drama along the way. For example, when CKE's chief executive at the time, Andrew Puzder, was tapped in 2017 to be the US labor secretary, the company became a magnet for both personal and professional controversy. (Puzder later withdrew his name from consideration.)[5] For a franchisee who's just trying to run a good business and make a living, when unit revenues are flat for multiple years or if there is corporate drama that prevents the brand from moving forward within a dynamic sector like quick service restaurants, it can be frustrating. Franchisees expect active oversight by management and the PE sponsor to address challenges and opportunities in the business.

Whatever focus the CKE corporate team has or has not put on improving core business operations or franchisee profitability, they have been busy in the debt markets. Total long-term debt as of January 31, 2022, stood at $1.15 billion,[6] inclusive of a new note of $180 million issued in June 2021[7] and a $400 million note issued in 2020.[8] Total interest expense for fiscal 2022 was $63.2 million.[9] The company also paid out a total of $452 million in distributions just in fiscal 2021 and 2022.[10] Paying out large distributions to the parent while same-store sales remain flat in an environment of rising business costs for franchisees is the type of activity that can frustrate franchisees.

In May 2022, CKE announced a $500 million reimaging program along with growth incentives. According to the company's announced plans, the money will be spent by both the parent and franchisees to remodel locations, improve the guest experience, upgrade technology, and streamline the operating model. The announcement was notable for mentioning that 95 percent of units had already committed to the plan.[11] Regarding this investment in the future of the brand, one can almost hear the cheers of "finally!" from Hardee's and Carl's Jr. franchisees.

Underfunded innovation is a risk, especially in large, established brands with strong cash flow and a history of moderate but steady growth. While long-hold PE sponsors are theoretically more inclined to invest in the future, follow-through is key. The temptation is to milk a cash cow business long past its prime.

> PE sponsors and management can get into trouble when they're not in touch with the market… and not keeping pace with innovation that is happening within the category. It's great to create systems, but if you don't have the products and services that resonate with customers so your franchisees can drive volume, then franchisees can't win. You need to constantly innovate and optimize the model.
>
> —JEREMY HIRSCH, senior vice president, Houlihan Lokey[12]

As a franchisee of a PE-backed brand, consider the following questions:

- ► How long has the PE firm already held this investment?
- ► Has spending on growth initiatives and innovation been consistent?
- ► How much debt has been put on the business? How much cash is going toward debt service compared to growth and support/infrastructure?

- ► How much has been paid out in distributions compared to reinvestment in the business?
- ► What are franchisee satisfaction and profitability trends?
- ► Are existing franchisees expanding?
- ► What is the brand's innovation pipeline? What percentage of corporate revenue is reinvested in R&D? Technology? Acquiring or developing new products and services?
- ► What new marketing initiatives have been launched, and what has been the impact? What are same-store sales trends? Are marketing campaigns brand builders or too reliant on discounting?
- ► Have franchisees noticed positive changes? What are their concerns?
- ► What do franchisees believe are the greatest gaps in the model or areas where they would like to see more corporate investment?
- ► How long does this PE firm tend to hold on to their investments?
- ► Is this brand likely to trade again during my license agreement?
- ► What is the track record of the investor backing this franchise? Have their franchises grown and kept up with market trends?

Maximizing the opportunity for all stakeholders and protecting long-term brand relevance requires a longer view. As Matthew Frankel from LLCP reminds us,[13]

If you starve the business, it will show in the trends. But if you help the business grow and invest to ensure a strong brand long term, you'll get a giant multiple when you eventually bring it to market because you did all the right things.

NOT PROTECTING UNIT-LEVEL PROFITABILITY

Franchises are not evergreen cash machines. Their competitive position and brand relevance must be maintained. Product and service offerings need a periodic rethink in our fast-moving marketplace. Outlets have to be kept up and refreshed. Technology interfaces and the entire customer experience need ongoing, continuous improvement and focus. But who pays? And how is that investment shared between new franchisees and existing franchisees (who may have different franchise agreements), and between the parent and franchisees?

This is a fertile area of franchisor-franchisee disputes and litigation no matter what the ownership. But given PE's timeline, typical playbook, and pace of decision-making, the changes when PE takes over sometimes can be jarring to franchisees, even when those changes are intended to move the brand forward. And despite PE's usually rigorous due diligence process, errors of due diligence have, occasionally, been made. Errors of franchise model execution is another theme whenever stall-outs and franchisee dissatisfaction are visible.

> When PE just acquires assets and doesn't understand how to maximize the value of those assets in the franchise context, they can get into trouble. When they treat all franchisees the same rather than recognizing there are many different types of franchisees in their system, with different needs and experience and even different contract terms. PE can get excited about a brand and miss things, not really understand what's going on at the unit level.
>
> PE doesn't always do the work. They get excited about the brand but don't think about the company; they don't do enough digging into what's really happening with franchisees at the unit level. This is particularly true of PE firms new to franchising.
>
> **—MICHAEL SEID**, managing director, MSA Worldwide[14]

The danger with private equity decision-makers is they sometimes can't see beyond the financial lens. *People* are the ultimate leverage point in a franchise business. I've seen great managers resurrect troubled businesses, and I've also seen poor managers and their incompetence bring great brands to their knees. It takes a lot of energy to really optimize a franchise business. PE may struggle to identify good management for what the business needs, and then also can struggle to have the patience to support and sustain the team with a properly levered balance sheet,... to give the team enough time to drive maximum value creation.

— **J. DAVID KARAM**, chief executive officer, Sbarro[15]

Common sources of dissatisfaction for franchisees specific to unit-level profitability include the following:

New expenses or shifting expense responsibility: Problems can surface when expenses shift from the franchisor to franchisees. In some cases, the franchisor hasn't been charging enough to maintain viability (for example, underinvesting in technology), and fixing this can necessitate adding new fees. In other cases, expenses historically held at the corporate parent level are redistributed to franchisees to boost corporate profits.

Excessive use of marketing promotions (discounts) to drive same-store sales: Special promotions can drive customer traffic and attract new customers but can also train customers to wait for discounts. Since the franchisor is paid royalties from the top-line revenues, discounts that hurt unit profitability predictably create franchisee dissatisfaction.

Cuts in franchisee support and/or dismantling area developer role: Although corporate teams often aren't large, if PE intends to make personnel cuts to realign costs, PE tends to move quickly. They may over-hire in boom times and then cut personnel when the market shifts. It also can get contentious when PE comes in and forces out area developers. If the parent is collecting a 5 percent royalty and the area developers earn 2 percent, that's a tempting stream for PE to recapture. But area developers fund field support and coaching from those points paid. If PE doesn't replace that now missing layer of support, training, and assistance, it can leave franchisees feeling they "aren't getting much" for their royalties. In some systems this has led to litigation and other downstream challenges when support or area developer replacements don't have sector knowledge, leading to customer complaints and implementation errors. Corporate team turnover, especially in key leadership positions, also frustrates franchisees.

Blatant parent profiteering, especially at the expense of franchisee profitability: Everyone understands that the franchisor needs to make money to fund support and growth. But franchisees get heartburn when they perceive unreasonable profit taking by the corporate parent, especially when combined with underinvestment in the future, declining franchisee profitability, or mandated operational or purchasing changes that don't solve an existing problem or best serve customers—for example, funneling profits to the corporate entity while charging higher-than-market prices for products franchisees are obligated to purchase. Building too many profit centers on the backs of franchisees is guaranteed to make franchisees unhappy (no matter what the corporate ownership structure), especially if it's a change compared to when those franchisees joined the system.

> The best franchise leaders care very deeply about the unit-level economics of their franchisees. They constantly monitor profitability and talk a lot about it. It's their main focus, because it is what builds long-term brand success.
>
> **—KEITH MILLER**, principal, Franchisee Advocacy Consulting, and director of public affairs and engagement, American Association of Franchisees and Dealers[16]

Requiring vendors who charge above-market prices: This is especially true if the vendors are providing rebate kickbacks to the franchisor and/or the products are viewed by franchisees to be either substandard or commodity products.

Lack of transparency, especially around those pesky rebates: There may be very good reasons why the franchisor requires a particular vendor. Quality related to brand standards is one legitimate reason. And rebates aren't automatically "bad." If those rebates are used for the good of the system, such as to fund franchisee events such as national conventions, pay for additional marketing, or offset costs of new product innovation. But franchisees feel taken advantage of when required vendors charge *higher than market prices* (eroding profitability), especially for commodity products like forks and napkins, or for lower quality products, while nothing is disclosed about benefits accruing to the parent or how rebates are used.

Even long-hold PE players, who in theory should be well aligned with franchisees and willing to invest in the future (since they intend to hold the brand indefinitely), can sometimes end up with disgruntled franchisees regarding these issues. The ultimate long-hold PE franchise investor is, of course, Roark Capital Group, so let's look at another case study.

CASE STUDY: MASSAGE ENVY AND ROARK CAPITAL GROUP

Roark purchased Massage Envy in 2012 from Sentinel Capital Partners (after a two-and-a-half-year hold period), when the franchise had 800 locations.[17] Ten years later, ending in 2022, Massage Envy had 1,083 outlets. Although from 2017 to 2022, net units actually declined by 90 locations, ending each year during that period with fewer units,[18,19] the company has still created an enviable (pun intended) brand presence and significant scale. It's a franchise success story in many ways and has inspired other franchise founders to launch their own wellness concepts in the hopes of one day achieving similar scale and brand recognition. What's *not* enviable, according to at least some of its franchisees? Unit-level profitability.

In September 2021, a group of independent franchisees, calling themselves the "Envy Owners Association," brought several complaints about management to industry publication *Franchise Times*. According to this group, the number of arbitration actions by franchisees against the corporate parent was growing while unit-level profitability was eroding. They expressed concern about fee increases to the national ad fund, unit closures, higher costs for technology applications and supplies, and other issues.[20]

On October 4, the Massage Envy National Franchise Advisory Board, whose members are selected by management, sent a letter to *Franchise Times* in which it rebuked the other group's claims and essentially said that this was a splinter group of franchisees that did not speak for the majority. The next day, both sides issued joint letters saying they had settled the dispute.[21] This curious and messy public spat suggests at least some level of dissatisfaction brewing, which ultimately both sides wisely decided to resolve in a less public manner.

What do the company's own disclosures say about corporate and unit-level profitability? The following points were outlined in company franchise disclosure documents:

- A combined $385 million securitization transaction was completed in June 2019.[22]
- The "Massage Envy Securitization Entity" (which flows back to the parent, Roark) was then paid $4.3 million in a base fee plus ongoing fees for arranging the transaction.
- Massage Envy Franchising (also a wholly owned subsidiary of the parent) was paid total management fees of $33.4 million between June 2019 and the end of 2021.[23]
- Almost $170 million of member distributions were also taken out of the business between June 2019 and the end of 2021.[24]

Taken together, Massage Envy certainly appears to be an *enviable* cash flow business to own at the parent level!

What about supposed increased material costs and technology fees cited by the group of franchisees who came forward to complain to *Franchise Times*? Let's look at tech fee revenues collected by the parent, which increased significantly—262 percent—from $4.5 million in 2014 to $16.3 million in 2021, the year of the public spat. This increase wasn't due to unit growth. The number of units increased only slightly, by 5.5 percent, from 1,051 units in 2014 to 1,109 units in 2021, in part due to pandemic pressures.

Annual tech fees are often a bone of contention. Technology changes fast, and the cost to keep up can be steep. But at least from public disclosures, it appears franchisees had some basis for the concerns they voiced.

Both the franchisor and franchisees should expect to jointly invest to keep brands current for the benefit of all stakeholders. But there must be balance. In the case of a PE-backed brand, if millions of dollars in management fees, distributions, rebates, and other benefits are taken out by the parent while franchisee fees are increasing, more expensive suppliers are added, or other initiatives are implemented that negatively impact franchisee profitability, the optics aren't good. Sponsors and management shouldn't be surprised when franchisees push back. If franchisees don't feel their concerns are being heard, or if there is no mechanism to provide feedback and make adjustments based on that feedback, relationship problems are often the result. The sheer magnitude of benefits accruing at the

PE owner level is often breathtaking, especially in large systems generating significant cash flow. In the words of the franchisee of a different system mentioned earlier, "Why can't you guys kick some back in for a change?"

GROWTH FOCUS: THE DARK SIDE

For the most part, private capital sponsors' and franchisees' interests are well aligned. PE wants growth, but franchisees won't agree to expand if they're not confident about their return on investment. This dynamic keeps most private equity investors focused on true value creation activities that build and strengthen the brand, create positive validation, and most importantly make franchisees *want* to expand and keep up with periodic refreshes. But at times PE's tactics are more heavy-handed.

PE buyers can create self-inflicted pressure if they overpay or overleverage a business. The heat is on to deliver the business case! What is PE's response to this in a franchise context? This is where the dark side of growth can rear its ugly head, visible in the following tactics (some of which are carried out directly by PE sponsors and in some cases by other players in response to PE's presence):

- ▶ overly aggressive franchise sales
- ▶ selling large multi-unit agreements specifically to first-time business owners
- ▶ stuffing the development funnel with units unlikely to open
- ▶ allowing encroachment and oversaturation (a spin on not protecting unit-level profitability)
- ▶ overly aggressive moves to push out underperforming franchisees
- ▶ forced territory buybacks
- ▶ removing area developers (and associated franchisee support) from the equation
- ▶ field-stripping EBITDA
- ▶ building brands to "flip" to PE, rather than for sustainability
- ▶ bastardization of EBITDA

Many items in this list are self-explanatory, so I won't riff on all of these. But a few deserve discussion.

Is the Business Primarily Focused on Selling Franchises?

Some new brands in the "built to flip" category sell aggressively (or use an aggressive outsourced agent) to boost franchise fees and show "momentum," even when they have scant operating history of their own. It appears this also is how some young brands are getting around the "starvation by high sales commission" problem; they simply sell more territories to the same franchisees. Instead of selling one license for $50,000 and paying the broker or agent $30,000 to $40,000 in commission (keeping only $15,000 or $10,000 to train and support that new franchisee), they might sell 5 or 10 licenses to one franchisee to try to bring in more cash after paying commissions.

According to FRANdata's 2022 *Multi-Unit Franchisee Buyer's Guide*,[25] from 2010 to 2020 there was a 24.8 percent increase in multi-unit operators within the type of "entry-level" franchise concepts designed to appeal primarily to first-time business owners.

> When I started in franchising, more systems were filled with owner-operators. I get the sense that some systems encourage multi-unit because together you can make a good living when you couldn't owning only one. That's false logic to me. *Each unit* must make money. If you cobble together a bunch of units that aren't performing well, you haven't accomplished much that will drive value.
>
> **—AZIZ HASHIM**, managing director, NRD Capital[26]

Which leads us back to the concept of private equity as an important factor in quality control to block unworthy concepts and not underwrite overly aggressive selling tactics. Will PE itself remain diligent to avoid buying brands with suddenly swelling sold-not-open funnels? We will have to watch PE activity in emerging brands. If at least some investors are undeterred by large sold-not-open funnels, it will encourage some emerging franchisors and some outsourced sales agents to sell aggressively, especially multi-unit licenses.

Don't misunderstand me. I'm not saying that the growing trend toward multi-unit licenses or the use of outsourced agents to sell franchises is wrong. In fact, given how competitive the market is, small brands often turn to outsourced sales agents because they can't get any traction in the crowded and noisy marketplace. There are approximately 4,000 outside franchise sales agents across nearly 20 different groups in the US alone. But incentive structures and the current lack of transparency around compensation and lawsuits involving agents when they were representing other brands creates risk. More open disclosures about third-party agents used in the franchise sales process and commission structure disclosure would provide prospective franchisees more complete information. Franchise sales agent disclosures and possibly licensing of agents will likely be addressed at the state level. After all, real estate agents, insurance agents, and securities brokers all have professional requirements.

> How should anyone in franchising think about choosing a franchise to join, or a capital partner? I recommend asking one simple question: "How's business?" Then wait for the answer, because it will be enlightening. If the answer is, "We sold 50 units and will grow by 20 this year," that's very different than someone whose answer includes same-store sales growth, cost of goods, and unit profitability. Franchising is a group of individual businesses that all need to perform well. Anyone who answers the "How's business?" question with how many franchise agreements they've sold or are in their development funnel is signaling a potential problem because they're not focused on the right things to build a sustainable franchise business.
>
> **—MICHAEL SEID**, managing director, MSA Worldwide[27]

Field-Stripping Enterprise Value: Sold-Not-Open Arbitrage

Betting on high-cost sales channels to quickly fill the sold-not-open funnel is often a sprint against the clock.[28] The franchisor bets it can get units open and ramped up to drive royalty revenues before the business is crushed under the weight of franchisees it can't support. But the rub is that high-commission sales channels leave little left over to build infrastructure.

Some young brands hope their big sold-not-open funnel will attract a lucrative private equity deal before all those units need support. "By then," the thinking goes, "we'll be part of a platform or will have PE investment to create the infrastructure that wasn't built or planned for in the first place." These concepts tend to be geared to first-time franchisees. Experienced franchisees see through a flimsy support structure and untested business model and expect more substance in exchange for their royalties, but the uninitiated often do not.

It is unlikely all units sold this way will open. But let's assume for a minute they will. If that brand were then to sell to PE based on that large sold-not-open funnel, the founders might think they've bested PE at their own game. On the contrary, they handed PE a great arbitrage opportunity, *if the buyer believes those units will eventually open.* PE also knows you have a ticking time bomb on your hands. If you miss the window to flip the business to PE, you'll have to onboard all those franchisees with a skeleton staff because most franchise fees collected went right back out the door to pay sales agent commissions. If franchisee discontent or failed openings become an issue, the business can stall out. It's a game of chicken.

But this approach to building the franchise also essentially field-strips franchisor EBITDA. A PE firm or PE-backed platform can swoop in, pay less for the business based on a lower EBITDA number, and simply open all those units themselves. *Ka-ching!* Even if PE leans into the sold-not-open funnel and spends extra to give some "credit" for that funnel, founders usually still leave significant value on the table and basically put themselves in an employment agreement tied to a performance-based earnout based on opening all those units. The first scenario pays a lower multiple on a much smaller EBITDA. And that's only *if* PE's due diligence tells them the funnel is real; otherwise PE will pass. At that point you're damaged goods. If the buyer has concerns about aggressive sales tactics that bake litigation risk into the sold-not-open funnel, the seller may be stuck with an indemnification requirement, seller's note, or large escrow as a buyer risk backstop in order to close the deal. Demonstrating more proof of concept pays a higher multiple on what is also a higher *EBITDA*.

> PE won't pay a premium to fix a broken franchise model, but emerging brand specialists like picking up promising but undercapitalized brands cheap! If you are aggressively selling franchises through high-cost channels hoping to flip the business to PE, you are also transferring significant value to the franchise sales organization and handing built-in arbitrage to the PE buyer.

Outsourced sales teams are the right solution for many emerging brands in an expensive and noisy marketplace where it can be difficult to get attention. But don't rush. Don't oversell. Try to get a mix of organic deals and outsourced deals to collect more in franchisee fees so you can build up franchisee support while filling your development funnel. And make sure that all units sold get open and ramp to profitability. That is ultimately far more valuable than filling the development funnel with units that may never open.

> Private capital investors want to see proof points. How many units are you getting open? How fast do they ramp up? What is Year 1 performance? Year 2? Year 3? How do different cohorts compare to each other? If you want credit for the sold-not-open pipeline you've built, investors need to have conviction those units will open and perform consistent with how prior units have opened and matured.
>
> —JEREMY HIRSCH, senior vice president, Houlihan Lokey[29]

Built to Flip

Another negative of all this PE activity in franchising is that brands are launching now that seem designed to flip themselves to PE in short order. You can identify this flavor of emerging franchise in two ways. First, they talk less about culture and franchisee profitability and more about how fast they are selling franchise licenses.

> Traditionally, very few new brands break out. According to Franchise Grade, 72.3 percent of franchises in the US have 100 or fewer outlets, and after 10 years 50 percent had 50 or fewer locations.[30] FRANdata puts this estimate at 84 percent having 100 or fewer outlets.[31]

This new emerging brand model we're seeing, where so many new brands are racing to fill their development funnels specifically with multi-unit deals, signals a culture shift. This is an extension of the field-stripping of enterprise value we looked at in the last section. This phenomenon has given rise to a bigger-picture challenge in franchising. The relationships we used to find in franchising, where founders and their team built a franchise community over many years and really got to know their franchisees, is being replaced by a different breed of emerging brand. This type hopes to go from ground zero to 100 licenses sold and then on to a PE or platform buyout transaction, all in less than two or three years. Brands *designed to be flipped are formulaic.* You can feel and see it during the recruiting process. The corporate team is often thin as well because sales commissions eat up franchisee fees and not much is left over to hire staff. Frankly, they don't expect to have to build out the infrastructure and also may not care much about the quality of the franchisees or fit for the concept they are bringing in; they are betting on a buyout instead (the perfect setup for moral hazard).

The other worrying signal is if a new brand signs large multi-unit agreements with first-time business owners *before* proving out whether a prospective franchisee has what it takes to be a successful operator, and before even proving out the operating model itself.

If private equity continues to be a positive quality-control force within franchising, especially at the bottom of the deal ladder—elevating only worthy emerging brands and ignoring weak concepts—then "built to flip" won't be a viable strategy. Ultimately, brands following this approach will have to contend themselves with whatever mess they've created. PE will ignore them until they are more proven. This is exactly where Burgerim landed. That business was never built with sustainability or unit profitability in mind; it was built to sell franchises.* No PE firm would touch Burgerim. After selling 1,500 licenses, mostly to first-time business owners, it quickly imploded, and its founder fled the US.[32]

However, if PE somehow misses brewing issues during due diligence and acquires brands with a large but ultimately impaired development funnel, then we all have a problem. Rewarding that growth strategy with a buyout offer validates the approach. Other brands will surely be inspired to follow. This risks negative outcomes for franchisees and bad optics for franchising generally.

My sincere hope is that PE lives up to its reputation for buying smart and provides buyout offers only to truly worthwhile franchise businesses.

Bastardization of EBITDA (Earnings Before Interest, Tax, Depreciation, and Amortization)

There is one last thing to consider in terms of the "dark side of growth." The pressure to find deals sometimes pushes PE to lean into value, especially when markets get frothy. This means giving sellers "credit" for unopened units, as one common example, and recalculating adjusted EBITDA with the fictional benefit of those units already being open and operating at maturity levels. Founders are often reluctant to sell if they have a large sold-not-open funnel because they have not yet unlocked that upside value. To get around this objection, some buyers are willing to give sellers credit for these unopened units in order to get a deal done.

But taken to its extreme, the meaning of EBITDA (earnings before interest, taxes, depreciation, and amortization) can morph into fiction. Historically, EBITDA was pulled from the financial statements and reasonable one-time expenses were added back. Adjusted EBITDA is meant to be a proxy for cash flow. Enterprise value is then calculated as a multiple of that cash flow. It also tells acquirers how much debt the business can reasonably support if leverage is to be used.

---

* Burgerim's 2018 FDD even listed an auto loan for a Porsche Cayenne on its 2017 balance sheet. Prospective franchisees were apparently undeterred by this disclosed red flag. See 2018 FDD, p. 81.

But adjusted EBITDA in franchising can become "fake news" in a hypercompetitive acquisition market. While most PE firms are cautious not to overpay and will not participate in a sale process unmoored from fair market value, the reality is that some deals may be based on aggressive pro formas (projections) and add-back adjustments to EBITDA. For example, adjustments may assume every outlet is already operating at maturity, adjustments might be made for future increases in royalties that haven't happened yet, and so on. PE may win the deal, but then they are really under pressure to deliver on that aggressive business case to return capital to fund investors. A longer hold period may be required.

> What's funny is when you see the word "pro forma" all over a CIM [confidential information memorandum, the initial marketing document for a business for sale]. When everything in a CIM is pro forma, that makes you scared. When you start digging into what is the pro forma and you have difficulty getting data out of the bankers, it usually says to us, "run." We've looked at a couple of things where that puffery of the banker, who says, "Hey, this is a great asset. Look at all the things you can do with it. Look at all the savings." And then you peel back the onion and maybe the savings weren't actually implemented yet. So they're asking you to pay for something they haven't done yet.
>
> Those are things you run into pretty frequently on some of these mid-size deals, especially those that may have been somewhat distressed at one point and are getting better. Everyone is trying to sell their business and maximize their value. We just need to have discipline on our side to see through that and ask the appropriate and right questions to get to the bottom of it.
>
> —ERIC EASTON, chief financial officer, Ampex Brands[33]

This is another reason why you can't take cocktail party anecdotes about deal multiples as gospel. The seller may be telling a story that they got 13× EBITDA on a deal that the buyer on the same deal will say they paid 10× for. Many sellers aren't aware of the nuances that drive a higher multiple and thus have unrealistic expectations. You need to do and see many deals to see how it all fits together. Hire yourself a strong deal adviser.

As one PE partner told me off the record, "We go back several years in the financial statements. If we see big changes and adjustments, we know they were prepping for a sale and we'll back those numbers out. We may lose a deal because we're not willing to pay for that, and that's fine. We are willing to pay ahead of market for truly great companies but only because we have a growth plan we are confident will dramatically increase the *real* EBITDA number."

You may be thinking, "If PE overpays, good for the seller and it's PE's problem." After all, an aggressive business case could also result in PE investing more in operations to ensure achievement of the business case. This could be positive for franchisees. But if the business case isn't met, any seller earnout could also be at risk, and there may be pressure to cut costs or for PE to sell early and move on, which could negatively impact franchisees. The risks and downside are not isolated just to the PE sponsor and their investors.

DESTROYING FRANCHISEE TRUST

In a distributed ownership model like franchising, when franchisor-franchisee relationship problems surface, it usually comes down to a lack of a functioning mechanism to collect feedback from franchisees, incorporate it, and communicate it back out, as well as to share how that information was used to make decisions that impact franchisee profitability. Alignment around the right facts is also key. Management and franchisees can argue about "what's true," so getting everyone focused on the most meaningful business metrics and what the data reveals can help move the conversation forward. This is not to say there will never be disagreements.

Private equity's goal is to make money for their fund investors. Other stakeholder interests—such as those of franchisees—can end up in conflict with that aim. Only if ownership and management maintain *what is perceived by franchisees* to be balanced and positive brand stewardship can the brand truly thrive. The key here is that franchisee perceptions matter. When balance is maintained and franchisees as a group are satisfied, making a good return on their investment, and feel heard, then even changes to the operating model can be implemented with minimal drama. Decisions taken by management must be perceived by the majority of franchisees as being positive for the brand. But as we've seen, one of the fastest ways to tank a franchise brand is to destroy franchisee trust. It can literally take years to reboot the relationship.

There are common observed themes when the franchisor-franchisee relationship goes sideways. We already looked at some related specifically to unit-level profitability. Different expectations, miscommunication, and hard feelings can develop within this marriage. These are not PE-exclusive issues; any brand management team and their franchisees can land here if the marriage isn't nurtured. But PE's priorities, methods, and timelines are ripe triggers for conflict creation. There are natural and predictable flashpoints:

- ▶ perceived (by franchisees) benefit imbalance or ineffective sponsorship
- ▶ lack of transparency
- ▶ making changes without consulting franchisees
- ▶ ignoring franchisee feedback, poor change management function
- ▶ requiring large refresh investments or new technology, particularly if franchisees were not brought into the decision
- ▶ unit consolidation

The gradual shift to multi-unit operators (if the system traditionally has been geared to single-unit operators) changes the ownership mix. Smaller franchisees or legacy owners especially may feel their voice is no longer heard. This is compounded by messages from corporate essentially implying, "This franchisee over here is acquiring existing units or signing big development agreements and still believes, so what is your problem?" An internal tug-of-war can break out over what the facts are, what the narrative is, and which voices matter. Corporate would like to see the top operators have a larger share of voice, but that can create tension with smaller and longtime operators.

> The potential for conflict is greatest when big, expensive changes are needed—such as new equipment, new technology, and outlet remodels. It can be difficult to get lenders to give franchisees needed capital for the required remodels, especially when the return on investment business case hasn't been made clear. The association can sit down with the franchisor and work out how fast these changes can go. They can work together to put together funding options, negotiate costs down, and establish guardrails so the association can be supportive of the program. When change is dictated down from the parent without getting advance feedback from franchisees, that is rarely effective.
>
> Franchisees want active oversight and positive stewardship of the business. They want to see good listening and joint solutions, and for the independent association to be brought into big decisions. Franchisees look for evidence of fairness and balance in the relationship. This requires strong change management and communication. The market is dynamic and we have to be able to make changes, but there are productive and unproductive ways to do that in a franchise system. It's typically not productive to play this out in the press or in the court system. The feedback should be provided within a culture of trust in the boardroom and meetings.
>
> **—RON GARDNER**, founding partner, Dady & Gardner, PA[34]

▼

We've covered a lot of ground to this point! You should feel confident that you understand the landscape of players. You should be able to assess where your franchise business (or a franchise you're thinking of joining) is on the PE Profit Ladder. From there, playbooks are relatively predictable, and you also know the good and the bad to watch for.

If you believe that working with a strong PE partner can push your business further, faster, how should you engage and start the conversation? That is the subject of the next chapter.

PART FIVE

Moving Forward with Private Equity

CHAPTER 18

Engaging with Private Equity

"We were very prepared way in advance of engaging with private equity. You don't need to fix all your problems or you wouldn't be thinking about bringing in a partner. But get clear about your challenges and be transparent so you can get alignment with the partner coming in. If you do that work ensuring alignment up front, you're exponentially improving your chances of a good outcome."

—**SCOTT FRITH**, chairman and chief executive officer, Happinest Brands[1]

WE ARE NOT UN-RINGING this bell. Private capital has become the dominant, most influential force within franchising at both the franchisor and franchisee level. The arrival of private capital has been largely positive for franchising, accelerating, professionalizing, and stabilizing many brands to ensure long-term value creation for stakeholders. PE's arrival also opened important new exit paths for founders and franchisees that did not previously exist, boosting valuations for some concepts at the brand level and also boosting the value of outlets within high-quality franchise systems through increased buyer competition and access to capital. And there have been important learnings along the way when outcomes were not as positive. These create useful guardrails.

You can choose your own journey wisely, empowered with the benefit of this information. If you're a founder or franchisee and you wish to learn more about potential PE partners, how should you engage?

This chapter is *not* a comprehensive guide for selling your business to PE. That could fill a separate book! It is to help you frame out your best approach to due diligence, begin to prepare your own business information, and think through some up-front questions you should consider before you start networking and exploring your options. In my experience, this up-front work to get your objectives and thoughts organized and plan your approach is usually the missing piece. Many founders and MUOs jump right into networking and talking to PE or bankers without framing out their wants and needs or thinking through where the business could use help to get to the next level.

> **Many founders and franchisees get ahead of themselves and suddenly find themselves in the middle of a sale process when they should have taken more time to prepare.**

We will cover the following topics:

► discovering your (initial) "why"—it may change as your thinking evolves

► creating your (preliminary) list of "what" matters to you—it may also change

► successful networking and due diligence tips so you can learn "who" is out there

► how to best use your time if you decide to "wait" before taking on a PE partner

FOUNDERS AND FRANCHISEES SHOULD START WITH "WHY"

Why are you thinking about bringing in a PE partner? What are you looking to accomplish? What is your broader vision for the business? What are your personal objectives? Why now? Let's hear from several seasoned private equity investors and also founders who have been through the process of selecting a PE partner and negotiating an equity sale.

We partner with founders a lot across our firm; it's been an important part of our DNA since our inception. My advice is, first ask yourself: "What do you want out of the relationship with a PE firm?" Do you want a more passive partner who may not add a lot of value but who will help you cash out some of the illiquid chips you have invested in your business and who will otherwise mostly leave you alone? Or do you want a more engaged partner who is committed to helping and will work closely with you—maybe even push you a bit, and can bring resources and expertise to help you more effectively achieve your long-term goals? Either approach is totally valid, but each would lead to very different choices about who you would want to partner with and what you could expect from that partner once they've invested.

—PHIL LOUGHLIN, partner, Bain Capital[2]

There are lots of smart, effective, super experienced private capital teams doing great work in franchising, and many founders and franchisees have benefited from this PE activity. But it comes back to your objectives. PE isn't a bank. They hold equity. They have a seat at the table. Some founders bring in PE but then don't want feedback and they end up misaligned. You have to set expectations, communicate, ensure alignment, and understand how decisions will be made once we're working together as partners, before you make the decision.

—AZIZ HASHIM, managing partner, NRD Capital[3]

Get super clear about what you're trying to accomplish. If you plan to stay in, then you want a great strategic partner who can help you build out the infrastructure that you can't do on your own due to certain constraints. That drives a different process than if you're fully exiting. In thinking about the transition in our family business, my dad had his list and I had mine. As we evaluated the options, we kept coming back to our priorities and revisiting them. There is emotion. Keep going back to your "why" during the process. Be really deliberate.

—SCOTT FRITH, chairman and chief executive officer, Happinest Brands[4]

Here are some common reasons why franchisees seek a private equity partner:

- partial liquidity for the founder (e.g., take some chips off the table, de-risk the investment that ties up your personal net worth) or a full exit
- liquidity for other shareholders
- expansion capital
- add a strategic thought partner and assistance (e.g., help launching new consumer products, experience in a particular vertical industry)
- help accelerating franchise sales, site selection, unit openings
- pursue acquisition opportunities
- assistance to scale and mature infrastructure support, technology stack
- experience setting up affiliate/supply chain programs, lending, or other relationships
- improved ability to recruit top management positions

"WHAT" MATTERS MOST TO YOU?

Once you have your initial "why," it's time to work up your (preliminary) list of "what" matters to you—and this too will evolve as you continue to network and learn!

Here are some potential desired outcomes:

- I want a good price for the amount of equity I'm parting with at this time.
- I want marketing and growth assistance so my company becomes a household name.
- My long-term goal is to take my company public, so I want a PE partner to help me achieve that objective.
- I want to create wealth and a legacy for my family.
- I want to create a platform, launch a new product, or enter a new market but need help doing it.

► My current business partner and I aren't aligned; I want to consolidate owner-ship and find a capital partner who shares my growth vision.

► I want to take advantage of favorable market conditions and create a better exit.

What are other considerations for you? It helps to keep a running list of what your priorities are and note how they change as you speak to more people. Here are some common considerations:

► I would never sell to _____ because that company isn't aligned to our cul-ture or isn't a fit, or I don't like the team, how they do business, and so on.

► I only want to work with a PE partner that has franchise experience.

► Franchise experience is less important to me than flexible terms, experience in my sector, or other factors.

► I want some level of reasonable assurance that my company is "ready" before I even open the door to a sale process.

► I want to keep the fact that I'm exploring a sale as quiet as possible.

► I don't care who knows that I'm selling as long as I get a good price for the portion of equity I'm selling.

► I'm only looking for a minority partner right now.

  ▷ I'm only looking for a passive investor to provide expansion capital. I have a good handle on what it will take to get the business to the next level.

  ▷ I'm looking for a minority investor, but one who can also act as a consul-tant, not just a capital partner. I'm open to ideas and guidance.

► I'm looking for a lucrative second exit later and prefer to work with partners who have proven to generate strong outcomes not just in the business but also in the next trade.

► I'm looking for the right platform partner to accelerate my business.

► I don't want to join a platform; I want a partner who can help me create a platform.

► I'm concerned that even talking seriously to PE will be a distraction for me and for my team.

► I'm concerned about team attrition, especially if I can't negotiate the deal I want and end up holding off on a sale at this time.

- ▶ I want to protect my senior staff or adult child still working in the business.
- ▶ I want to work in _____ role for the next _____ years and then exit (or not), so I'm looking for a partner who will support me in that role.
- ▶ I am okay (or not) moving to another role or leaving the business if my new partner believes that another leader can take the business further than I can.
- ▶ I am most interested in an outcome that looks like _____ , and I am willing to trade or deprioritize _____ in order to achieve my primary outcome.
- ▶ I want help thinking through prep work so we can better prioritize initiatives and be better prepared to engage with PE at some point in the future.

How much money do you want to take out now versus later? What are your near-term and long-term personal financial goals? If there will be tuck-in acquisitions, remember that as the founder you will need to fund your pro rata share to avoid equity dilution. For example, if you own 40 percent of the equity of the new company and the company buys an add-on business for $5 million, you will need to fund $2 million out of your own funds to retain your 40 percent ownership. This is also where the question of leverage put on the business comes into play. If there is lower leverage and thus lower debt service, then there is more cash on the balance sheet available to fund acquisitions. Ensure the go-forward structure aligns business needs and your objectives.

Founders should consider that the largest number written on a letter of intent doesn't determine who is the best business partner. Founders should network with former portfolio companies to understand specifically what value add was, or was not, provided. Many times the number two or three bidder may actually be a better long-term partner, both in terms of total financial payout and creating a more enjoyable ride along the way. You have to think through the final outcomes you're looking for, not just that entry price.

Deal structure also matters. Some firms will make structured equity offers so that even minority capital partners can exert control. There can be complex multiple liquidation preferences and other things borrowed from the worlds of structured finance or venture capital. So the actual exit number may end up being much less than the incoming offer headline. The real deal is contained in the details.

—JEREMY HOLLAND, managing partner—origination, the Riverside Company[5]

Remember also that traditional private equity firms may not allow as much of an equity roll from founders compared to a family office investor. This could limit your ability to participate in the second exit. This is firm-specific, so think through your objectives and parameters well ahead of time so you can thoughtfully screen out potential partners. Traditional PE firms often like to see at least a 10 percent founder equity roll, but since they are trying to maximize their own capital exposure and deploy those in best-in-class assets, there may be an upward limit. They may not allow founders to roll as much as 30 to 45 percent of the total equity contribution, which limits your upside on the second transaction when the business sells again 5 to 10 years down the road. Does the PE sponsor plan to create an option pool for management to drive engagement and retention? Again, this is something you need to know before you go too far into a process with anyone to avoid a mismatch and wasting your time.

"WHO" IS IMPORTANT TO YOU?

The object of networking when you're contemplating partnering with private equity is to better understand the landscape and cultures of PE firms and advisers. Remember the ladder to stay focused on a range of firms and types that are the most likely fit for your business.

> Make time to network with other entrepreneurs who have been through the process and experienced advisers who have helped companies prepare for an acquisition transaction.

It takes time to understand the range of cultures, personalities, skills, and track records of capital partners and advisers and also to think about what you want and bounce it off advisers and entrepreneurs who have already been through a transaction process. The adviser networking conversations in particular will also help you start to gather your materials and get your house in order. For example, M&A attorneys can provide a list of things to prepare ahead of time (e.g., documentation, the best entity structure, essential business records). They can also get you thinking about deal structure and questions you want to ask during your networking. Advisers can share typical issues found during due diligence—again, providing the potential for you to scrub out problems ahead of time. For example, there are common things buyers look for in the quality of earnings due diligence that usually come early in the process. Thinking through this list in advance can help you avoid the disappointment of buyers walking away after finding something in the quality of earnings (QOE) report they didn't like. (See www.bigmoneyinfranchising.com for a basic quality of earnings checklist so you know what the auditor will look for and other helpful tools.)

> Buyers will examine the sustainability of the underlying franchised busi-
> nesses, the strength of the franchise agreements and level of negotiated
> changes, the length of the franchise term, whether or not franchisees have
> a unilateral right to terminate, oral modifications to franchise agreements,
> the size of territories granted, the number of signed but unopened units,
> regulatory compliance practices, joint-employer liability exposure, litiga-
> tion history, among other areas. Founders are sometimes shocked at the
> speed at which things come at them in a sale process. You won't have much
> time to think once the gears start turning.
>
> —LANE FISHER, partner, FisherZucker LLC[6]

Networking with Other Founders and Franchisees Who Have Worked with Private Equity

As you network and build relationships, ask pointed questions of other founders and franchisees whose companies have been acquired by PE firms so you can start to develop impressions of which firms (and firm types) you would consider working with and which firms or types you want to avoid. You will revisit these learnings when you are considering a short list of buyers during the sale process, so it helps if you have done some prework and soul-searching on this topic.

Here are some questions to ask when networking:

► What is the PE firm's working style with you as the founder?

► When there are miscommunication issues, what are common root causes?

► What is the operating and reporting cadence?

► Does the PE firm micromanage you?

► Did you end up working with a different team at the sponsor firm than you first met during the due diligence process?

► How are decisions made? When there are disagreements, what happens? As the CEO, have you ever been able to make a decision the sponsor disagrees with but they delegate that final authority to you?

► What is the most and least valuable assistance and advice your partner provides?

► Did your deal have an earnout? Did you easily hit that number? If not, what happened?

► What terms would you renegotiate now with the benefit of hindsight?

► What was important to you at the time you were looking for a partner?

► What were your "non-negotiables" at the time? Would you change those now?

► Would you recommend this capital partner to other founders?

► What would you like to change about the relationship?

► What surprised you?

► What do you wish you'd known before entering the process?

► How did you think about choosing a partner?

► Did you employ a sale adviser, and would you recommend them? Why or why not?

► Would you recommend the M&A attorney you used? Why or why not?

► How did you think about timing and your role in the business going forward?

► Would you do it again?

► What should have been better prepared ahead of time?

► If you had waited to bring on a partner, how would you have used the time, knowing what you know now?

Decide whether you will stay in the business and what type of partnership you seek. You can save yourself considerable time and energy if you can focus your networking efforts on the types of firms most likely to fit your objectives, as well as speaking to other founders and franchisees who have worked with those partners. Are you looking for passive capital or a strategic thought partner who will be active board members? What relevant experience should potential partners bring? Who do you want to have as a "boss"? While you may run the business, the private equity firm will most likely control the board and be the final decision-maker in any decision of consequence. In this sense, they may feel like the boss you haven't had in a while. Once you have a PE partner, you can't hire executives and spend money the way you were used to doing. Hopefully their strategic thought partnership, added perspective, and the opportunity for wealth creation are worth more than hanging on to your independence. But only you can decide that!

How Important Is It to You That Your Private Equity Partner Has Franchising Experience?

A PE partner should also bring intellectual resources, best-in-class service providers, and professional analysts to help understand and refine your model. If you choose to partner with private capital that doesn't have franchising experience, you shouldn't expect that same level of support and understanding of the model. New private capital is entering franchising all the time. If you do bet on a sponsor without franchising experience, at least ensure that someone on their board of advisers has franchise experience so that you're not the lone franchise voice in board meetings and thus can ensure balanced decision-making.

> Investors who can point to successful franchise investments bring more to the table in my opinion than private capital investors with no franchising experience. For example, when we partnered with Fuzzy's Taco Shop we told them that we could help them build a much larger business and position them well for a substantial second bite of the apple in another

transaction later. Our experience demonstrated that we had a solid plan to achieve that objective. We helped that founder and team over a number of years. The business was recently purchased by Dine Brands, which is publicly traded and one of the largest and best-known restaurant platforms. Who would have thought five years ago that Fuzzy's Taco Shop would attract that caliber of buyer? That's the business we're in. We told them how we would position them to be more attractive, and we delivered on that.

—**AZIZ HASHIM**, managing partner, NRD Capital[7]

It was important to us that our partner had experience in franchising, that they understood about investing in relationships with franchisees. There is a real benefit to working with a PE partner with extensive franchise experience. Personally, I wouldn't want to be the first franchise organization a PE firm ever partnered with. Bringing in institutional capital allowed us to do some things that we otherwise couldn't do.

—**SCOTT FRITH**, chairman and chief executive officer, Happiest Brands[8]

Really educate yourself. Reading this book is an excellent first step! Now you know how the players organize themselves across the PE Profit Ladder, but it's time to get to know some of the personalities and track records of various firms investing at your "rung" on the ladder. For example, don't try to network with KKR if you're an emerging brand that's been franchising for only a year with just three units open. Your time is better spent networking with emerging brand specialists, platforms, and family offices. (I actually know an emerging brand founder who ran around New York City in a quixotic quest to meet with massive PE funds like Apollo, KKR, and so on. My image of this effort reminds me of that scene in the movie *The Big Short* when initially the protagonists couldn't get past the lobby of the big investment banks.)

You don't need to feel pressure to meet *everyone*—that's not the point. This exercise is to help you suss out more details about what matters most to you and what capital partner experience, skills, and perspectives are most likely to be helpful at this stage of the business.

Talk to people who have been through it. Any good PE firm will give you an extensive list of references. Ask lots of questions about the nature of the relationship, the impact on the culture (if that is important to you), and how independently founders and multi-unit operators were able to operate post-transaction. Network with advisers as well. You need to be selective about who will represent you and how they work with you. All of this is tough to do in the heat of a sale process, especially the cultural alignment piece. It has to be started ahead of time.

> At the end of the day, you're building a relationship with someone. You want to be excited to work with them and them with you. You're going to be talking to them a lot! You need to trust and respect them. And in the case of investment bankers, they also need to be excited they can make a market for your offering.
>
> **—JEREMY HIRSCH**, senior vice president, Houlihan Lokey[9]

Conduct thorough due diligence on any potential partners. What is their franchising track record? Everyone will tell you what you want to hear during the courtship phase. You need to do reference checks on your investors just like you would on your franchisees. Does what you're hearing from others align with what they told you? If they are going to be your strategic thought partner, you need to ask them tough questions about your business. They should be able to critically think through all the elements with you. Is this a team with whom you can build trust over time? If you're planning to stay in the business, you want a capital partner who really listens to you and doesn't come with preconceived answers. They will be more helpful if they don't tell you what to do but instead help you think through what to do. They should play back what you said and help provide clarity, then help you outline a range of possible solutions. They should bring strong problem-solving skills and relevant experience. Ultimately, if you're staying in a leadership role, you are making decisions about what's best for the business with the benefit of additional perspective and assistance. So working style, decision-making authority, and governance are critically important.

Although this section is about networking and preparation ahead of bringing on a capital partner, I would argue some of these questions and considerations also apply to franchisee due diligence when joining a PE-backed brand. Are decisions dictated from on high, or is franchisee feedback gathered before changes are made? What is the level of transparency? Is the management team a close partner with franchisees, or is there tension in the relationship? What are overall trends in how the team functions, who is making final decisions, and how that impacts franchisee profitability?

"WAIT": NOT READY FOR A PRIVATE EQUITY PARTNER?

If you're a founder or franchisor determined to delay bringing on a private capital partner, make good use of that time. You may be thinking, "Why can't my leadership team and I just borrow PE's operating playbook to build my business and achieve a higher valuation when I'm ready to sell?" You can, *if* you're well enough capitalized and committed to following through. Stay focused. Don't try to accomplish the entire playbook. Pick only the most impactful two or three tactics. Once those are accomplished, work on two more improvements, and so on. For example, if you're a franchisor, improving franchisee profitability and speeding the ramp-up of new units are two initiatives with high payback value, so if you're not already putting significant effort into these two efforts, start there. If you're a franchisee, improving your unit performance to achieve above system averages is a good place to focus your efforts. But other initiatives in the PE playbook may be financially or otherwise out of reach and better left until you're ready to bring in a partner.

In working with my consulting clients, I have seen brands make significant improvements on strategic, operational, and capital planning issues to create additional value themselves, prior to coming to market. If you can make meaningful improvements yourself and demonstrate momentum, it can be worth taking the time to make focused changes because your business will be that much more attractive to outside investors. But only if you commit to following through.

At the very least, it is worth the effort to spend time cleaning up your financials, getting the top data room items ready, and having your team start to update that data on a monthly basis.

Here are the top-priority data room documents to prepare and keep updated:

- historical P&L statements (five-year look back) and current year forecast
- monthly revenue by location since inception
- opened units by month or by year (five-year look back)
- franchise licenses sold by month (five-year look back)
- projected opening pipeline (i.e., sold-not-open units and when they are projected to open)
- system sales growth by category of product/service
- prototypical franchisee P&L with payback period analysis
- multiyear franchise disclosure documents and list of major changes or updates between the versions
- Discovery Day presentation shared with prospective franchisees
- operations manual

Even putting this list together for the first time can be challenging—for example, if the corporate team hasn't been collecting P&Ls from franchisees, or if franchisees are all using a different chart of accounts, or if there are separate entities for product sales or to provide the start-up package (furniture and fixtures). Numbers may not tie between business reporting and FDD disclosures. And on it goes. All that complexity needs to be pulled together in a clean view of the business and kept updated.

The middle ground, of course, between trying to do it all yourself and partnering right now with PE is to work with advisers who can help you prepare. This isn't just about packaging, although when you get around to the sale process you need to share your story in a particular way that buyers are used to seeing. The preparation effort I'm describing uses the framework of the PE playbook to conduct a thorough diagnostic on your business (with help if needed; this is the basis of my consulting practice) to identify and implement a cogent value creation plan. This will also help you determine what you can do on your own and where a PE partner can help you.

Returning to Your Draft Value Creation Playbook

Remember the PE playbook and framework to start thinking through your value creation plan. Now is the time to revisit that plan with the benefit of your personal "why, what, and who" thinking and bring the two together. Think through what is feasible compared to your big vision for the business. Compare your personal objectives and timelines with possible initiatives to drive value in the business. This same thought process is useful whether you are a franchisor or multi-unit franchisee.

Here are some questions to ask yourself:

- ► Have we fully exploited every opportunity to build a high-quality business?
- ► What opportunities for further improvement are within reach? How soon?
- ► What needs to change about our model to improve corporate-level operating margin 5 percent, 10 percent, or more? To improve franchisee operating margins?
- ► What are the top three initiatives that will increase top-line growth and bottom-line earnings at the corporate and franchisee level? What is stopping us from implementing these improvements now?
- ► Can anything be done now to improve unit-level consistency? Is there a large gap between low and high performers in the system, or between corporate and franchised units, that can be closed?
- ► What team gaps exist? What is stopping me from making team skill upgrades now?
- ► What pain points are observed via franchisee surveys and other feedback?
- ► How are unit-level metrics trending versus competitors' metrics? (PE prioritizes a review of "comps," comparatives.)

- ▶ What technology, product, or service investments could we make now to build value and profitability for franchisees (e.g., menu innovations, customer loyalty app, back-of-house efficiencies)?
- ▶ Are there ways to add efficiencies via third-party outsourced services without making fixed commitments?
- ▶ What are customers' top pain points, and what would it take to remove them?
- ▶ What marketing opportunities can help lift same-store sales?
- ▶ Are there acquisitions we can make now that would build value?
- ▶ What are the top three levers that franchisees can pull to improve their profitability? How can the franchisor team help (e.g., training, marketing support)?
- ▶ What would it take to open every unit sold on time?
- ▶ Are we recruiting the type of operators we want? What needs to change?
- ▶ What would it take for more franchisees to want to add expansion units?
- ▶ Have we started gathering data that a PE investor would require to go through a due diligence process? (Tools, worksheets, and checklists are available as reader downloads at www.bigmoneyinfranchising.com.)
- ▶ Would I benefit from having a strategic thought partner to help me work through and prioritize these ideas?

If you delay bringing in outside capital, hold yourself accountable for making specific changes and improvements so you're not just burning daylight. Founders, management teams, and multi-unit franchisees may say they prefer to wait until they hit a specific number such as an EBITDA threshold before going to market, but they never actually change what they're doing to achieve that goal. A year or two later, the business looks the same. By that point changing market conditions and a lack of momentum may negatively impact enterprise valuation.

Several brands I know that had offers in 2021 or early 2022 decided to wait so they could grow the business more in hope of a better offer. Then the market slowed. They made no real changes to their businesses. Now, not only are their franchisees not growing and interest in opening new outlets has cooled, but so has PE interest. Worse, because those companies haven't lived up to their own pro forma, that PE interest isn't likely to return. It's one thing to invest a year or two getting the company well positioned. It's another to invest 5 to 10 more years of your life because you missed the window to bring in a great private capital and thought partner.

Candidly assess the time needed to make meaningful improvements *and the potential for that payback* versus finding the right PE partner or platform right now and working with them to accelerate your business immediately. If you're planning to stay in the business, delaying just pushes back your overall timeline. Your answer to the timing question may be very different if you're approaching 55 years old than it would be if you're 35. What other adventures are you planning once you finally exit altogether? Which path is more likely to deliver on your goals?

Following through on your objectives for the business and making operational improvements are also important if you've been through a broken sale process, a failed attempt to sell. If you try to sell the business and your offering receives negative market feedback, you need to hear that feedback and make changes. If you went through an auction process, the entire field of buyers likely knows you tried to sell and didn't (or couldn't) thanks to your banker's diligent efforts to market the business. When you next come to market, you must talk about changes and improvements you made that strengthened your company's value since the last time buyers looked at your business or heard through the grapevine that it was for sale.

But if you have exhausted opportunities to make meaningful improvements on your own, are missing out on growth opportunities, or can't recruit top talent because you are undercapitalized, it's probably time to reconsider the path ahead. Accurate self-assessment is the key. What can you do right now that will drive significant value? What are the likely results from those initiatives in one year? Two years? Many founders and MUOs spin their wheels on activities that don't lift EBITDA fast enough or high enough to be worth the extra time and effort compared to simply finding the right PE, FO, or hybrid partner (or PE-backed platform) earlier. If you're an emerging brand operating in a sector that has been largely consolidated under platforms, you face higher costs and distinct competitive disadvantages. Unaffiliated brands can burn significant cash just building basic infrastructure that doesn't, in and of itself, differentiate your brand.

> Every entrepreneur hits a ceiling; often it's access to capital and staffing. You have to find a way to accept help. You can't really build a business based on status quo. Open your mind and be honest. What's my runway on this?
>
> **—PETER ROSS**, chief executive officer and co-founder, Senior Helpers[10]

It's worth considering whether joining the right PE-backed (or other) platform or taking on the right private capital partner could take your business *further, faster.* It's also worth considering whether the right partnership can create more value on your equity roll ("second bite of the apple") versus waiting and trying too hard to "game" the first transaction.

▼

Now let's turn to the view of what changes when PE comes into a franchise business. How should you prepare? If you are a founder or on the franchisor leadership team and will work with PE for the first time, what should you expect? After months of preparation, what changes after the deal closes? For franchisee-owner associations and franchisees, when an ownership change is announced, what are the best steps forward? Up next, we'll cover what to expect when your business or franchise system is about to be acquired by private equity (or already has been).

CHAPTER 19

What to Expect When You're Expecting... to Be Acquired by Private Equity (or Already Have Been)

"I'm in favor of progress. It's change I don't like."

—MARK TWAIN, author

YOU NOW HAVE A significant amount of information under your belt about how private equity thinks, how they invest in franchise businesses, likely outcomes, and things to watch for. You understand the relative playbooks used by growth, value, and turnaround PE investors in franchising. You also know key components necessary to build a valuable franchise operating model and what value-destroying moves to avoid no matter what the ownership structure.

To review, growth investors of all sizes typically make noticeable investments in marketing, franchise development, key corporate functions, support (especially support to get units open and ramped up), product and service extensions, new market development, and technology. Value investors will focus on extending and expanding the business at scale. They want to preserve cash flow and may be more inclined to maintain status quo through efficiencies and refinements rather than making dramatic changes or large new investments in the business. Turnaround strategies are unique to the brand situation but often focus on improving unit-level economics, refreshing the customer experience, rationalizing product and service offerings, rebranding, adding marketing, supply chain improvements, investments in technology and franchisee support, and making management team changes.

> **Here are the key themes we have explored so far:**
>
> ► PE is likely to stay active in franchising so long as there are good and profitable businesses for PE to own.
> ► PE's choices and strategies for running their franchise portfolio companies and to create returns for their investors are relatively predictable.
> ► Even if you choose not to work directly with PE, anyone active in franchising needs to understand PE's impact on franchising.
> ► It's important for franchise stakeholders to get aligned with private capital.
> ► The now very active re-trading market also impacts franchise outcomes.
> ► Franchisee satisfaction and confidence in the direction of the business is most apparent when franchisees return to sign expansion agreements—that's the best form of validation.

Some readers may get to this point and say to themselves, "Okay, but my situation is different" (everyone thinks they are a unicorn) or "I'd love a checklist to help me think through all of these dynamics specifically for my franchise business." This chapter is designed to help you create your personal research to-do list, questions, and concerns (and, keeping it real, also the "what's in it for me" stuff) so you can tackle what's swirling around in your head in an empowered and organized way. It can also provide a preparation roadmap and useful thought exercises for franchisee-owner associations, founders, franchisees, and leadership to prepare for a transition or collect questions and concerns in early engagement or townhall sessions.

At the root of any healthy franchise system are satisfied and prosperous franchisees, so let's start with what all of this PE activity means for franchisees.

FOR FRANCHISEES: WHAT TO EXPECT IF PRIVATE EQUITY BUYS YOUR FRANCHISOR

This section is also applicable if you are a prospective franchisee and the brand (or platform holding company of the brand you're considering) is already owned by private equity. Yes, you have some additional due diligence to do!

Listen very carefully. Communications coming from the PE firm and management post-acquisition will include signals about what the new owner likes about the brand to begin with and what initiatives they already have in mind. They may even share early details of their plans with franchisees. PE is well aware that the changing of the guard makes franchisees uneasy and will usually try to say something helpful (or at least not *unhelpful*) about their plans.

> We spend a lot of time during due diligence getting to know franchisees as best we can. Sometimes we call them through a third party so as not to be disruptive. We ask, would they do it again? What do they love and not love about the business, what are their biggest challenges, and so on. So we know them coming in. Once they are part of HFC [Home Franchise Concepts], we are very transparent and careful about setting expectations. We're not coming in as superheroes. There's no bank truck rolling up here. Franchisees are usually most concerned about what's changing, and "what's in it for me." In our brands, it is usually their first time owning a business. We let them know their agreement is safe. We develop trust over time that allows them to see we are a servant leader organization. Our franchisees' success comes first. We want to work with their independent franchisee association. We get in front of the association and tell them that we're here to listen. We want to understand them first. We don't rush in. We invest a lot of time learning about the brand. Then we put a short-term and long-term plan together and communicate that to franchisees.
>
> **—JONATHAN THIESSEN,** chief development officer, Home Franchise Concepts[1]

Consider the new owner's track record. Conduct due diligence about the PE firm's track record in franchising. Assess where your brand falls on the PE Profit Ladder and where the brand is in its growth trajectory. This will help you understand what playbook PE is likely to follow. If you can, network with franchisees in other systems the PE firm has owned. Would they work with the sponsor again?

Is this PE sponsor an active or passive brand steward? Is the brand part of a platform? What were franchisee outcomes?

> Does the bottom line for franchisees get better, worse, or remain unchanged after a change of brand ownership? That's what franchisees want to know.

Expect personnel changes. PE firms usually won't buy a company in the first place if they don't like the management team. But once PE gets into the business, they will swiftly make changes if needed and fill gaps. If this is the management team's first time working with PE, they will find the pace and expectations are very different from what they may be used to. Many sponsors will work hard to preserve the best elements of the culture and relationships that were part of what they liked about the brand. But there may also be changes. One of the changes usually most appreciated by franchisees is filling support gaps on the team or bringing in needed expertise to reimagine marketing strategies or update technology.

If a franchise is privately owned, you need trusted advisers, counsel, and auditors. The board of directors should be chosen wisely. Too often they are friends or family of the founder and won't give you the truth. But PE is different. They are time-bound and constantly looking at broader trends and talking to people. They push management. They are always asking themselves objectively, "Do we have the right management team to take the business forward? Are they the top management team in this space? Are they passionate about this? If they are given a slight raise in salary, would they leave for another job? Are they properly incentivized and compensated?" PE doesn't mind paying up because they are going after a specific return—but the team must deliver.

—AZIZ HASHIM, managing director, NRD Capital[2]

Expect a push on development commitments. PE acquires a business based on a business case and analysis done before closing. Even if the world has changed since you signed your development agreement (e.g., new-building construction costs are up due to inflation), PE sponsors and management will still push franchisees to hit their development commitments.

Remember that things can change, no matter what the initial signals from PE sponsors are. If PE's expected return drops below their investment threshold, they will move to recover as much as possible of their position. Promised investments in marketing or technology may not happen or may be delayed. If PE discovers they've really bought a turnaround project by mistake (it happens, despite due diligence), PE may sell early or be more aggressive about recapitalizations to return investor funds. On the flip side, if the business grows much faster than expected or if another buyer comes forward with a strong offer, PE has a fiduciary duty and may sell ahead of schedule to capture that good opportunity.

Expect a renewed push on upholding system standards. Any ownership change, whether to a PE firm, strategic, family office, or hybrid, or even going public, could mean a "new day" when it comes to enforcing system standards, depending on the unique situation of that brand and the investor's business case. Often there is also a plan to co-invest in remodels, technology, and other things that will help move the system forward. If there is significant investment to be made to refresh outlets, as an example, effective PE sponsors will often have a game plan in mind to help ensure that more franchisees choose to make this commitment than will decline. For example, they may offer (via one of their financial partners) to guarantee loans needed for remodeling, or they may provide certain incentives to get the work done. Especially when PE comes into large legacy systems, often there are franchisees who have been there a long time. They may have a big voice within the company based on their tenure, and not always because they are good operators. New sponsors may feel those owners need to bring their game up. For example, older sites need to be refreshed. Service quality needs to come up. Stores need to look great and operate well. Every outlet is a "brand beacon" influencing how customers perceive the brand. It impacts everyone in the system.

Experienced multi-unit franchisees who have been with the brand through several changes in parent ownership have seen this movie. But franchisees going through their first PE ownership change are often shocked at how fast and clinical enforcement of the "new day" can be. Keep in mind that if PE owners are eyeing selling the company in a few years, they have to move quickly to improve same-store sales, as well as to increase sales of new license agreements and get units open. If the corporate team suddenly seems more aggressive about enforcement of brand standards across the system, a trade may be coming.

> It's important for the franchisor to be able to set standards. Every individual franchisee is making a living off the reputation of the entire system. Periodically, you have to force the system to refurbish and keep up. Otherwise, you have "tragedy of the commons."
>
> —JAMES GOODMAN, president, Gemini Investors[3]

Realize that, with this push on standards, underperformers will get more attention. Development timelines, area developer performance, brand standards, remodeling requirements—really anything in your contract—will be looked at with fresh eyes. Underperformers should not be surprised that they receive more intense attention from corporate after an ownership change. Somewhere in the PE business case is a pro forma section dedicated to lifting same-store performance. If franchise development doesn't already have a well-functioning resale process, new ownership will likely put one in place to facilitate exits if needed.

Be open-minded. Remember that many of the changes PE will make in the interest of promoting growth and revenue stability will be positive for the system, and thus potentially for franchisees as well. For instance, after years of franchisees begging corporate to improve marketing execution, suddenly a PE owner will come in and clear the decks in the marketing department and new life will be injected into those efforts. "Finally!" franchisees cheer. The same is true of fixing disparate technology systems, getting more support to open units, or pushing out that guy on the operations or construction team who never returns phone calls. "Finally!" franchisees say to themselves. But PE also may come in and start enforcing development agreements and system standards, may add suppliers that franchisees don't like, and, of course, may shut down exception requests. "I don't like these other changes!" is often franchisees' reaction.

Whether these changes are net positive or negative for the franchise system and for you will be unique to your system and your own situation. Understanding the typical PE growth playbook and methods used to create value for their own investors should allow you to more easily predict potential post-sale changes. Some could be extremely positive, and some may be less well received by franchisees. But either way, there shouldn't be too many surprises.

Now Is the Time to Establish an Independent Franchisee-Owner Association

Change is unavoidable in our modern business climate. Having a mechanism in place to gather franchisee feedback, test out new ideas, and manage through change will help the system deal with change in a productive way.

> **It is best to establish an independent franchisee association early and nurture it as a vehicle of positive franchisor-franchisee communications and as a forum for broad ongoing discussions about the business. This should be in place long before, and sustained through, system ownership changes.**

Used well, the independent franchisee-owner association ideally becomes the franchisor's most trusted partner and a brand builder. This means that when there are disagreements, they are handled privately at the boardroom level and C-level, but publicly the association backs management. In turn, management can expect to receive public backing from the association because management commits to really hearing association feedback and demonstrates they will make thoughtful adjustments based on that feedback. This only works if the association has a real seat at the table and the franchisor is meaningfully listening. The association can also provide continuity and value across ownership changes and share learnings when new PE owners come into the business. It can be a powerful tool to help the organization stay relevant and manage through needed changes.

> Independent franchisee associations can be very helpful creating a good relationship. Franchisees just want to be heard. Franchisees want to see new initiatives tested first before rolling things out to the system. When coupled with franchisors showing what investments they're making in the future of the business, that's when you can create momentum. The market is always changing, but if the lines of communication are open, you can always recover from the truth.

> —MATT HALLER, president and chief executive officer, International Franchise Association[4]

> The time to establish an independent franchisee association is really before you think you'll need it. Where there is a mechanism to hear franchisee feedback and for that feedback to impact decision-making at the corporate level, that is positive for the system. The system can get into the habit of hearing franchisees and sorting through differences of opinion. The association can help test concepts or changes and can help lead communication with the system. You will get stronger buy-in and can proactively iron out problems. That trust needs to be built ahead of time. But too many wait until there is an actual problem before setting up an independent association. Then everyone is coming in mad about something and it's not the best way to start out.

> —KEITH MILLER, principal, Franchisee Advocacy Consulting, and director of public affairs and engagement, American Association of Franchisees and Dealers[5]

Maintain a Sale-Ready Stance

It's always smart to keep your business operation and documentation in a "sale-ready" stance as much as possible. Usually this is so you can be ready to capture opportunities or be proactive if you find there is a buyer interested in your business. However, it is also useful in situations where you don't like changes that are happening in the business. Sometimes the right answer is to make a good exit and move on to other projects. Parent ownership transitions are a good time for you to take a gut check on how you're feeling about your business and the direction of the brand.

> Franchisees often don't come into a system with their eventual exit in mind, and that's a mistake. For many franchisees, the M&A part of the equation is difficult. They don't have the wherewithal to exit that brand. Buying and selling is stressful. But it's a necessary part of running a business and something franchisees need to actively manage. Franchisees should always be prepared to exit a brand that isn't headed in a direction they believe in. You shouldn't be underwriting ownership you don't agree with. But on the other hand, if it's positive then you should double down and expand into more stores, or at least hold neutral and see how it goes.

> —**AZIZ HASHIM**, managing partner, NRD Capital[6]

FOR FRANCHISE FOUNDERS (AND MANAGEMENT TEAMS): WHAT TO EXPECT ONCE ACQUIRED BY PRIVATE EQUITY

Post-acquisition there are of course adjustments coming for these groups as well. Again, keep PE playbooks in mind and be aware of where your company is on the growth curve to get your bearings.

Management roles will change. Many PE firms keep existing management in place, but their roles will be fundamentally different. PE typically doesn't invest in the first place if they don't like the team, and there is usually some level of built-in continuity at the team level even if the founder is retiring. However, the role of the founder and management fundamentally changes when PE has majority control of the business. If the PE sponsor is the majority shareholder, they are the final decision-maker in any decision of consequence. So management goes from *running* the business to *operating* the business. Now, this can be a hard line or a soft line, depending on the culture of the PE firm and the strength of the management team in question. Some PE firms are more hands-off and consultative with their management team, especially the CEO, than others. It depends on the talent involved, how the business is tracking, the culture of the PE firm, and how much confidence PE has in management. So, if there is a change of ownership, the key thing is to discover the PE firm's working style. Are they micromanagers, or do they give management more decision authority?

> Reporting to a PE firm is much different than working for yourself! Some of these founders answer a PE phone call and suddenly two to three months later their business is sold. Things move really fast, especially for small acquisitions. Two months ago you were an independent entrepreneur and now you find yourself "working for the man," or at least that's sometimes how it can feel. Performance agreements, representations and warranties... there are many important things in deals that need to be negotiated to give yourself the best chance of success post-closing.
>
> —LANE FISHER, partner, FisherZucker LLC[7]

Our PE sponsor [Thompson Street Capital Partners] is very partnership oriented. The dialogue is conversational and casual. After serving as CEO in PE-sponsored brands multiple times, I've learned you can't have a big ego. If you think you're the smartest person in the room, you're in trouble. I appreciate their feedback and they respect my knowledge. I'm data-driven, so we're well aligned. We're constantly looking at customer data and feedback. I have weekly one-on-one meetings with the PE managing director just as I have one-on-one meetings each week with my own direct reports. I tell Thompson Street what's working and what's not, where I need their help and where I don't. We have strong governance around quarterly board meetings and annual strategy meetings.

—CHRIS DULL, chief executive officer, Freddy's Frozen Custard & Steakburgers[8]

Given timelines and fiduciary responsibilities to fund investors, it's a safe bet to assume PE will micromanage the business, or at the very least will have frequent check-in meetings with key managers. Assume a heavy focus on reporting, metrics, and data-based decision-making. PE may even go back and reexamine prior decisions the team has already made. If the PE sponsor turns out to delegate more and is highly collaborative it will be a pleasant surprise, but you will be ready for more intensity. That said, PE sponsors may add things for the team that have never been in place before, such as putting an incentive option pool in place. This can be helpful to attract and retain great talent.

> One of the things that often needs improvement is performance metrics and compensation. You need to put in place a professionally constructed options plan that is also communicated well so the team is aligned with business objectives.
>
> Transactions are a huge time investment. But every transaction also opens a new option pool every five to seven years. These can be extraordinarily lucrative for management. If you sell to a long-hold buyer, you need to think through that scenario so options can be carved out for management, including yourself if you're rolling forward and staying in the business. You need expert help to think through the pros and cons. There are a broad range of potential partners available. For management talent, this landscape of opportunities should also be a consideration. The best PE sponsors think carefully through the talent and compensation equation to ensure alignment.
>
> —**JEREMY HOLLAND**, managing partner—origination, the Riverside Company[9]

Conversations about the business will change. Especially if this is the first PE transaction, a brand culture based on passion and purpose may gradually (or quickly) flip to a performance-focused culture revolving around metrics, reporting, and trends. *Everything that matters to PE owners will be measured and tracked.* This sometimes leads to frustration for management and founders. PE will invest money in analytics to create a deep understanding of everything potentially knowable about the business. But as seasoned operators know, not everything is "knowable." It may be unclear why unit A sells 50 more ice cream cones on a single Saturday night than unit B five miles down the road. "Experimentation" and "happy accidents," which moved the business forward in the past, now must be quantified before spending or changes are approved. PE is wired to believe that everything about the business is *precisely knowable*. Sometimes things about a business can't be readily solved for, and PE doesn't always accept that. If you're the manager trying to explain something "unquantifiable" in a board meeting, especially if trends are heading into negative territory, you better have your résumé polished and ready to go. On the other hand, there may be people in the organization who have been blocked from moving up. High performers will shine through and can accelerate their careers under PE. Performance metrics will be very clear.

> Private equity investors are very smart. If you're spitballing and don't have mastery about what you're doing, you will struggle. Many founder-led organizations have good people on their team who have been with them for years. They've grown up in the business but don't have formal training in that C-level function and don't have the benefit of outside experience in other firms. But, on the other hand, you also have people in the business who are critical to the organization and very intelligent, and they are also found out. The cream rises to the top and are found out either way.
>
> —**CHRIS DULL**, chief executive officer, Freddy's Frozen Custard & Steakburgers[10]

The franchise culture will change. PE is adept at connecting the dots. They look at the big picture and have the benefit of not being emotionally involved. They can see what parts of the culture might need to change to move the business forward. If culture has been the filter through which all decisions have previously been made, switching to a more data-driven approach can feel like swimming down through a thermocline into deeper and chilly waters for those who treasure the old ways. But sponsors can often see much more clearly where self-limitation may have set in or where different thinking about a particular issue could be beneficial. Whatever the culture changes that come along with a change of ownership, franchisees joining after the switch will be assumed to have bought in to the new culture and direction of the business. This means there can also be different opinions within the franchisee base based partly on their tenure in the business and what eras and changes that base has already been through. This is something the owners association can help navigate. In fact, since some brands trade multiple times, another reason to establish an independent franchisee-owner association is to help provide continuity, capture institutional knowledge, and manage through these transitions. Working with the independent franchisee-owner association (or setting one up if it doesn't already exist) is underutilized by PE owners, in my experience.

> When my business sold the second time from the prior PE owner to Roark, during the vetting process no one from Roark called me. No one seemed interested in my perspective on the business. It wasn't important to them whether I rolled any equity forward or not. But then I realized, they had their own plan and perspective. I had to get my head around that. The business was moving on without me. It was emotional.
>
> I knew the prior owner's plan for exit, and so two years prior to the second sale I started talking to my family. I told them that I wanted to retire. I knew that changes were coming, and I didn't think I could personally handle that. It's your business but also your baby. To watch another take over was hard. I still have my own bakeries that I own and run. But the dynamics change when a new owner comes in.
>
> —DENA TRIPP, co-founder, Nothing Bundt Cakes[11]

Founders especially may have a sense of "I wouldn't have done things that way" when new owners make different decisions, but that is part of the reality when you sell a controlling interest in your company. Sometimes new ownership opens up the company to trying new approaches that under previous ownership would never have been considered, which can be good or bad depending on your point of view and the issues involved. The point is that new franchise ownership means new eyes, new objectives, and new priorities. You will either maintain alignment or realize it's no longer a fit and it's time to create a good exit.

Your thinking and skills will evolve. Working with a private equity sponsor will forever change your outlook and perhaps even your own management style. I have watched franchise founders, franchisees, and even corporate executives who have never before worked with private equity completely evolve as businesspeople under PE sponsors. PE's thought process, pace, and metrics-based management approach are different from those of many entrepreneurs, who, as a group, tend to learn by doing and through experimentation, even if they are highly analytical and numbers-driven.

> Those who embrace working collaboratively with PE sponsors can become powerful hybrid leaders who blend the passion, hands-on experience, and drive of franchise entrepreneurs with the more data-based decision-making discipline of PE. Whether those leaders stay in the current business or move on to other adventures, their perspective is forever altered.

I believe this is another reason why we have seen a gradual maturing across franchising, as learnings from private equity sponsors seep into the thinking of those founders, franchisees, and corporate executives exposed to PE's thinking and approach to value creation. These are things you can't unlearn or unsee once you've been exposed to them. It also creates a larger divide between those leaders who have endured PE's pace, have been through a change in ownership, and have proven themselves to be effective in partnering with PE sponsors, and those who have never worked with PE. First-time business owners who have no exposure to PE, and who have never run a franchise or any other business, have the steepest knowledge hill to climb.

▼

What can we expect going forward? How will private equity's influence continue to shape franchising?

CHAPTER 20

The Future of Franchising and Private Equity

"The real trick in life is to turn hindsight into foresight that reveals insight."

—ROBIN SHARMA, author of *The Monk Who Sold His Ferrari*, speaker, and humanitarian

FRANCHISING REACHED SIGNIFICANT SCALE and many brands went public long before private equity itself got off the ground as an industry. Since PE entered, there have been learnings and growing pains along the way. Few top franchise systems have been left untouched by PE's influence in one way or another. But in the larger context, the business environment has also dramatically changed, pushing franchise businesses of all types to seek support.

> It's hard for many small businesses to get lending support, so they turn to private capital to help them grow. Smaller company investments require an operational approach. Many of these PE firms bring in former executives who have proven they can build brands. Across their investments, PE can take their learnings and help founders integrate those lessons learned. Large firms and large investments make headlines. But there are thousands of firms deploying capital into small businesses that you never read about.
>
> **—DREW MALONEY**, president and chief executive officer, American Investment Council[1]

Private capital has changed franchising. But franchising is also in greater need now of PE assistance and support given increasing economic, technology, competitive, and regulatory pressures on businesses of all types, especially small businesses, as well as pressures on the franchise model itself.

EVOLVING MARKET FORCES

These market pressures also impact what returns PE sponsors expect from franchise investments, their risk tolerance, and how PE's success playbook continues to evolve.

In a more crowded and competitive market with many more private capital players looking for franchise opportunities, PE has been forced to change tactics. No matter where they fall on the PE Profit Ladder, players have found that taking an operational approach to management of the franchise business is increasingly required, even for those inclined to pursue more financial engineering tactics. This naturally favors highly engaged PE players who are not just financiers but who understand franchising or bring a deep bench of executive advisers and operating talent to tap into. Regardless, PE has many ways to extract profits from portfolio companies. Platforms and a now fully formed secondaries market improve PE's odds of making a strong return on investment.

Market competition has forced more PE firms to work with smaller companies in order to find good investing opportunities. This mirrors overall pressures on PE both to find deal flow and to invest in businesses with the potential for tremendous growth with PE's help.

> Investments in small businesses now make up the lion's share of PE transactions in all sectors, recently reaching a high of 86 percent in North America.[2]

Many deals go unreported, especially smaller ones, so the percentage is likely higher. According to an American Investment Council 2022 study, since 2015, private equity firms have invested over $3.8 trillion in more than 30,000 American companies.[3] Moreover, 14 percent of these companies have fewer than 10 employees and 40 percent have fewer than 50 employees.[4]

**Government regulatory pressure and related costs continue to dispro-
portionately impact small businesses.** The situation is getting tougher for
small businesses, not easier. According to a study by the US Chamber of
Commerce about the burden of government regulations on small business,
"federal regulations alone are estimated to cost the American economy
$1.9 trillion a year in direct costs, lost productivity, and higher prices."[5] The
report paints a stark picture of the pressures on small businesses:

> These job creators are increasingly strangled by a growing net of complex and
> cumbersome regulation at the federal, state, and local levels. The regulatory
> cost of just the largest federal rules totals more than $40 billion, with small
> businesses shouldering a full 82 percent of the cost. State and local gov-
> ernments add to this burden with additional layers of regulation. While
> the requirements vary, state and local regulations in the areas of minimum
> wage, workers' compensation, unemployment insurance, and occupational
> licensing have an especially negative impact on small businesses.[6]

PE first came into franchising as apex capitalists who saw an opportunity to make money in one of the most vibrant sectors of our economy.
But especially since the financial crisis of 2007–2009, PE has morphed
into an important source of strategic support across franchise businesses
of all sizes. Along with inflation, regulatory pressure, and government-
inflicted costs heaped on small businesses (yes, even a 200-unit MUO is
a small business compared to the market influence and scale of firms like
Google, ExxonMobile, Pfizer, or Amazon), the pace of technology change
in particular has driven many franchise businesses to seek partners or join
platforms where strong technology knowledge, support, and tools are
part of the package. Add a market shock such as was recently experienced
during the pandemic, and it should be no surprise when entrepreneurs
turn to private capital to help their businesses survive and thrive amid
these headwinds!

PE doesn't just provide capital; PE teams are also strategists who drill
into every facet and data point of the business model to try to find areas
for improvement. To have a very well-capitalized and willing partner to

invest in infrastructure and operational support to expand, as well as to help with strategic planning and dig into the weedy details of the business looking for opportunities, is exactly what many franchise businesses need. Increasing outside pressures have done their part to drive brands and MUOS to explore working with PE, perhaps more now than at any point since PE first entered.

FRANCHISE GENERATION 4.0 (A.K.A. THE POST-PANDEMIC YEARS)

Let's return to our timeline. Market dislocations create opportunities for buyers. That is true no matter what capital structure backs the acquirer. The pandemic and related shutdowns caused greater disruption than most of us have seen in a lifetime; labor, demand, and supply chain challenges affected businesses across the globe and hurt some franchise sectors more than others. Acquisition activity across PE (whether in or out of franchising) paused from March 2020 to around July 2020. Then deal volume returned. Buyers grew more confident of the future, saw great buying opportunities, and had funds to deploy!

According to Pitchbook, deal count in 2021 jumped 55 percent over 2020, and by just midyear 2022, deal volume was tracking ahead, reaching 73 percent as many deals compared to the entire year of 2020.[7] Within franchising, more than 100 transactions were counted in just 2020 and 2021. That frenetic M&A restart was bound to cool off eventually and did just that as interest rates went up in 2022. Prospective sellers who held off in 2021 for a "better offer" were disappointed in 2022 when valuations dropped from recent frothy multiples. (EBITDA multiples in 2021 and early 2022 routinely hit the teens and into the 20s for large platforms and brands. Even transactions involving high-quality, smaller brands saw some comparatively eye-watering valuations.)

As we enter this new era of PE investing in franchising, have PE's investment priorities changed based on learnings from the pandemic? The pandemic certainly gave some franchise brands and sectors the chance to show off their recession resilience and gave some a new moniker as "necessary" services. But what PE values most in acquisition opportunities didn't change.

A survey of 200 PE firms with $1.9 trillion of assets under management conducted in 2020 by a team from Harvard Business School, the University of Chicago Booth School of Business, and Georgetown University's McDonough School of Business found the following elements (in rank order of priority) most important for PE investors. These elements and their importance ranking were consistent with pre-pandemic surveys in 2016:

1 Business model
2 Management team (in contrast, venture capitalists rank management as number one)[8]
3 Ability for the business to be cash-flow positive
4 Opportunity for PE sponsors to add value

The survey also found PE was more focused on increasing revenue than cutting costs, with PE managers placing heavy emphasis on an operational approach to value creation.[9]

Some PE investors have put added pressure on themselves thanks to paying high deal prices. Bain & Company's Global Private Equity Report notes that the average leveraged buyout multiple has nearly doubled, from 6.8× EBITDA in 2000 to 12.3× in 2021.[10] And as mentioned, quality franchisor and platform enterprise values can go higher. Not surprisingly, CEPRES Market Intelligence found that increases in the multiple paid (i.e., multiple expansion) were responsible for 56 percent of buyout value creation from 2016 through the end of 2021, much more so than increasing revenue and operating margins.[11] PE leaned in to get deals done, sometimes enabled by inexpensive debt. Higher interest rates weigh on the debt equation, operating costs, franchisees' willingness and ability to invest in remodels or expansion, and also on customer buying behavior. It's the perfect storm of pressures swirling within the PE Profit Ladder.

> To the extent that PE recently benefited from rising asset prices to increase buyout returns, there is now more pressure on PE sponsors to add value through an operational approach, not financial engineering. According to the aforementioned survey, PE appears to be well aware.

Near-Term Considerations

As we begin this new Generation 4.0 of franchise investing, the sector is already pretty well picked over by PE investors. So many deals have been done that there are few high-quality brands of any scale left untouched. There are certain predictable outcomes.

There will continue to be demand for high-quality assets at both the franchisor and franchisee level. Those few exceptional franchise businesses that are still unaffiliated will continue to be pummeled by phone calls from PE and can afford to be picky in their choice of partner when they are eventually ready to transact.

A PE "exit pileup" is looming. Many firms acquired by PE between 2015 and 2019 (prior to the pandemic) will re-trade as market conditions improve. Good exits will eventually be needed. Fortunately, other firms with capital to deploy are standing by on the PE Profit Ladder.

▶ Firms that typically prefer proprietary deals will continue to be frustrated by the lack of unaffiliated scale brands in franchising. They will be forced to participate in auction processes controlled by investment banks, dip more into emerging brands (impractical for larger funds who must write big checks), or even look outside franchising to concepts that are franchise-able in order to find deal flow. Indeed, we are already seeing exactly this type of activity.

▶ If we assume valuations for good companies will remain very competitive, this puts significant growth pressure on winning deal bidders to fulfill their business cases. In theory, this should be net positive for franchisees in those systems because PE owners will have to promote strong unit-level profitability to keep the growth engine humming. It also means there will be pressure on franchisees to fulfill their development agreements via a mix of carrot (e.g., incentives to hit targets) and stick (e.g., territory take-backs) motivation tactics. Any franchisee in the market now considering large development agreements should closely examine contract terms and also assess the brand's relative situation on the deal ladder to understand potential risks and extra pressure that may be brought to bear. PE will be hypersensitive to maintaining strong company marketability for future exits.

▸ The logjam of pending deals *could* put downward pressure on prices, but there is so much capital looking for deals right now that valuations may hold. Pitchbook estimates $360 billion of investments will be held up over the next 10 to 12 years.[12]

▸ To help relieve some of this pressure, PE may increasingly choose to trade between two different funds owned by the same PE firm (GP-led secondary), raise continuation funds, or sell minority stakes directly to LPs. This may turn some growth investors into longer hold investors by necessity.

Newly launched PE funds or those new to franchising will be aggressive in pushing portfolio company growth—for better or for worse. PE firms that raised their first funds just prior to the pandemic and then made significant franchise investments during the market peak are under pressure. They paid high prices for their first acquisitions and have no prior exit track record (because the funds are brand-new). Prior experience at other PE firms may have been cited by GPs during their first raise. Without good exits in their first fund, GPs may have to provide some concessions to raise the second fund. Especially in a high-interest-rate market, limited partners give preference to larger funds with proven successful exits. So first-time fund managers must ensure their first portfolio company exits are very strong. Meanwhile, as cited above, there is already a backlog of pending exits that need to be sorted out. I expect to see significant pressure on portfolio company management teams and talent churn especially in portfolio companies owned by newer PE firms that are investing out of their first or second fund.

A number of larger brands are waiting for market conditions to improve before going public. If that path doesn't open, they may simply trade to another PE firm (or another fund within the same firm) instead.

Existing platform portfolios will be selectively pruned. Because so many PE firms are looking for deals, we can expect some platforms to selectively monetize some of their assets and complete carve-out transactions to return capital to investors.

I predict longer PE hold times for businesses acquired between mid-2020 and mid-2022, when activity and valuations were frothy. PE firms must first "work off" any extra turns of EBITDA paid. Pressure to fulfill the acquisition business case will drive robust demand for great franchisee and management talent, as well as for franchise sales, support, and marketing services consistent with a growth agenda. Other likely bright spots will be investments in enabling technologies, real estate/construction services, and other infrastructure. Because franchisees are under significant inflationary pressure, franchisor teams will be looking for ways to decrease supply chain costs, streamline service models, and shrink fixed costs so franchisees can maintain profitability. Franchisors will also focus on getting their sold-not-open funnel producing and on refilling the development pipeline before they look to trade again. After all, the high price paid likely assumed many of those outlets were already open and performing well.

We will continue to see new franchisors launch as the next wave of entrepreneurs sets their sights on a PE buyout. This is a shift in *why* many new brands are launched in the first place. If they are purchased early in their life cycles, it also represents a shift in the trajectory of new franchise brands. This is the "built to flip" model previously discussed, where aggressive franchisee recruiting is prioritized in the hope of attracting a PE buyout. These companies are more franchise sales companies than franchise operating companies. Gone is the importance of culture and carefully proving out the operating model with corporate units and a few carefully selected franchisees before expanding further. Sales agent disclosures or licensing may be needed to avoid bad franchisee outcomes.

FRANCHISING HAS CHANGED IN FOUR CRITICAL WAYS THANKS TO PRIVATE EQUITY

In Franchise Generation 4.0, franchising and private equity are thoroughly intertwined. What has changed? How do these changes impact how franchisors, franchisees, and other stakeholders should engage with private capital? A summary is useful.

It's now unusual for new brands to achieve and maintain meaningful scale without private equity's involvement. Even legacy brands are being transformed thanks to PE investing at the franchisor or franchisee level— or both. And small brands are receiving PE sponsorship (or PE-backed platform sponsorship) much earlier in their life cycle. This is a profound change in the history of US franchising.

The traditional model of franchisors overseeing lots of "small" owner-operator franchisees has bifurcated. Half of franchise units are owned by single-unit operators. The franchise model continues to attract first-time business owners, many of whom would not be able to own a business were it not for the structure and support of the franchise model. The other half of units (and a higher percentage in certain categories) are multi-unit operators. The number of MUOS and scale of their operations is growing rapidly, especially as legacy systems continue to consolidate. Many of these franchisees run large and highly professionalized teams that rival or exceed the capabilities of many franchisors, and many larger MUOS themselves are also now backed by PE. So while contractual power still remains firmly on the side of the franchisor, the level of sophistication of many multi-unit franchisees and their private capital backers alters what effective change management and franchisee-franchisor relationships look like.

PE's successful effort to consolidate franchising around both thematic and operating platforms has completely rewired franchise competition at the brand level. As a seasoned PE investor once told me, "Without us that brand would have been nothing—just another home services brand in a crowded field struggling to get noticed. Our platform acquired them and we invested heavily in building up franchisee support and corporate infrastructure. We taught them how to build a big franchise system." In this environment, unaffiliated emerging brands in particular are at a distinct disadvantage compared to other emerging brands with PE or platform backing.

The secondary buyout market—what I call the PE Profit Ladder—is now very well established in franchising. This trading mechanism impacts brands, founders, franchisees, certainly enterprise valuation, and arguably the very culture of franchising itself. The impact is felt even by companies and individuals not themselves directly engaged with private equity.

This leads us to the final takeaway.

WHILE POWERFUL, PRIVATE CAPITAL MUST STILL RECKON WITH FUNDAMENTAL FRANCHISING TRUTHS

Large private capital firms may have millions or billions under management. But there is a mutual dependence at the core of the franchise relationship that sets up a different stakeholder dynamic compared to other business types.

▶ Widespread franchisee dissatisfaction can only burn so long. Eventually, franchise unit expansion stalls if the fundamental economic equation between the franchisor and franchisee is too unbalanced, even if most franchisees are making money, but especially if they are not. Perceptions of fairness, whether franchisees feel heard and feel their needs are considered, and a sense of balance matter in this marriage, as in any marriage.

▶ When you have more power in any negotiation—or even the perception of it—you must take special precautions to treat the other side fairly.[13] Otherwise, you practically invite calls for more regulatory oversight, negative market attention, resentment from the disadvantaged party, and suboptimal outcomes. In other words, it is possible to overplay a strong hand. Now that private capital is so influential and directly impacts so many outcomes across franchising, extra care by PE is advisable so as not to take their position of advantage too far. That is, unless PE wants more oversight and scrutiny about their franchising activities, and especially the impact of franchisor actions on franchisees.

The new era of Franchise Generation 4.0. will be influenced by

- ▸ continued private capital activity in franchising;
- ▸ ongoing franchise consolidation (at both the brand and unit level);
- ▸ continued fast pace of technological changes;
- ▸ ongoing baby boomer retirements;
- ▸ a rising group of new entrepreneurs looking for business opportunities;
- ▸ more concepts "designed to flip" from the start;
- ▸ regulatory changes or requirements that could impact the franchise model itself (e.g., joint-employer challenges, work councils); and
- ▸ increased importance for brands to have well-formed, independent franchisee-owner associations—these become even more critical partners when managing through multiple PE ownership transitions.

With the PE Profit Ladder now firmly in place, more franchise systems will reach scale thanks to PE's assistance. Emerging and fast-growth brands will provide better franchisee support and more substance than we've ever seen from this group. As PE has learned franchise best practices over time, predictability and certainty have increased as brands move up the ladder. Once brands reach scale, optimization becomes the hallmark of brands owned by longer-hold PE investors. Sponsors are being pressured into doing more to keep brands relevant in a very competitive environment for the best operator talent. Within systems with the best unit-level economics and solid franchisor-franchisee relationships, PE investors are funding more consolidation and expansion activities at the outlet level.

This is all generally positive for brands and franchisees. But once scale is achieved, new questions emerge about other important aspects that traditionally have been important to franchising but are evolving.

THE CULTURE QUESTION

How important is a brand's unique culture now that PE is so influential within franchising? Founders, and the culture they create early in a franchise business, have traditionally had a tremendous impact on what that brand will become. Decades after joining a brand, corporate employees and franchisees may still talk about the importance of the culture of the brand and tell founder stories. For many franchisees and team members, culture was a big reason why they chose to join in the first place. Those relationships are important to them. As the business scales, founders usually work very hard to preserve company values and culture and to ensure that each franchisee they bring in will be a positive addition to the brand.

When the business first steps onto the PE ladder, often the founder will choose to work with a PE team that is willing to preserve some of that culture. For that first PE transaction, it is thus often as much about fit as it is about price and deal terms. Figuring out how to navigate those waters is a primary concern for many founders, especially when they plan to stay in the business. Many have told me they knew immediately in PE interviews which firms would be a potential fit and which absolutely would not.

But the game entirely changes with the next PE transaction, and the next after that. In those later transactions, founders may no longer be active in the business. Who becomes the "culture guardian" then? Is the original culture even still important at that point, or does greater scale itself usher in a needed change in approach? Any business is a living, breathing thing that must evolve to stay relevant and competitive, and this includes evolving the company's culture. But franchising is unique in its organizational structure, with independent entrepreneurs coming together to cooperate as a system. So deft management of the intangibles, such as the franchisor-franchisee relationship, also matters as a franchise system gains scale.

Over time and especially as brands grow and trade up the PE Profit Ladder, things change. PE may take significant cash out of the business. On the surface, that's a "win" because it provides good return for fund investors. But PE will ultimately be seen as a robber baron if franchisees are unhappy or the system stalls out thanks to lack of investment in the brand and the future of the franchise, regardless of how "successful" PE is numerically at creating return on investment for themselves. The massive distributions taken at the top of the PE Profit Ladder are the biggest and most visible test of this dynamic. Protecting unit-level profitability and resale value is just tablestakes. If the relationship with franchisees is also strained and changes are badly managed, PE's brand stewardship can falter. At that point, without culture preservation, there is no cultural glue to fall back on to help manage relationship issues that come up. How do metrics-driven PE sponsors successfully manage through something that feels so... squishy?

> This is a key cultural and business focus inflection point: when founders fully exit and professional managers take over, held to task by PE ownership.

In fact, borrowing more from franchising's roots, where company culture mattered and franchisees felt they were part of something more meaningful than just a business, may be just what PE needs to be reminded of to help their portfolio companies succeed in challenging times. After all, franchising's traditional culture of scrappiness, collaboration, and succeeding together is what allowed the business model to survive and thrive across a century of incredible change.

Chief Alignment Officers, a.k.a. Independent Franchisee-Owner Associations

Independent franchisee-owner associations are even more critical to help us manage all this change as we enter Franchise Generation 4.0. When functioning well and properly respected by the franchisor and the control owner, independent associations can excel at (1) change management, (2) nurturing the franchisor-franchisee relationship, (3) driving continuity across ownership changes, and (4) protecting core brand values and culture.

Are we aligned around what we're about to do? If yes, then we can always overcome challenges. When you're aligned around the future of the business, when challenges come up, you'll find your way through the tangle together.

—TAYLOR DEHART, principal, Savory Restaurant Fund[14]

If you don't align around certain values, that's where trouble starts. We've all heard those stories. Focus on alignment. This is what I'm trying to accomplish, and this is the direction I want to take the business. If you partner with an authentic team, you should be able to point back to those core principles and refocus on that and agreed-upon top priorities. If you have selected the right PE partner, you can always go back to that common decision framework.

—SCOTT FRITH, chairman and chief executive officer, Happinest Brands[15]

Franchising has always been a symbiotic model between independent business owners (franchisees) and brands licensing their trademarks and operating systems (franchisors). Now that private equity is such an incredible force within franchising, "alignment" must exist within every conversation between management, franchisees, and PE sponsors. Smart PE sponsors will put extra effort into the care and feeding of the "alignment" question in a time when so many other things will continue to change.

> **Private capital investors creating the best overall franchise outcomes have figured out how to preserve what's special about the culture of franchising and something of the founder's unique vision, while also bringing their own perspective and efforts to transform brands—always rooted in strong unit-level economics and alignment of outcomes.**

The way we think about it, the founder, the team, the franchisees have done something amazing to get the business to this level. We are humble about that. There is a secret sauce in these businesses. You can't just come in without that understanding. You need to spend the time to learn the magic that already exists in the business. Then we bring the benefit of pattern recognition. We ask questions that may not have been explored prior.

Then we determine together what is required to scale and take the business to the next level. That joint partnership is powerful in driving change and achieving a new level of success and impact.

—KIM MCCASLIN, partner, Bain Capital[16]

PE is perhaps not well known for their softer skills, although many private capital firms are indeed quite good at building collaborative relationships with their portfolio teams and franchisees. But going forward, only PE sponsors who have these skills are likely to attract the best operators and thus create optimal enterprise value.

In my view, active and constructively managed franchisee-owner associations are the best communication, continuity, and governance bridge to ensure outcomes are positive across the board. This must be accomplished in a culture of mutual respect and partnership. The unique franchise model empowering franchisees also creates space for franchisee associations to take on this critical role across multiple PE sponsors. When the stakes are this high and sometimes exits are rapid, the association has an important consultative and protective role that used to naturally be part of a founder-led organization.

> In Franchise Generation 4.0, the independent franchisee association can provide the relationship glue, communication mechanism, and institutional memory in a franchise landscape now dominated by private equity. Independent franchisee-owner associations will need to step up their efforts.

As you seek to scale your enterprise in the era of private equity, keep in mind that what is likely to propel brands up the deal and growth ladder into more valuable businesses can't be neatly captured in a spreadsheet, no matter how hard the "quants" of this world may try. Instead, it's the feeling of being in a marriage that is a true partnership with shared goals, active mutual listening, and fairly distributed benefits. Franchisee participants say "I do" over and over again—actively choosing to stay in their marriage. Choosing to stay and continue underwriting the direction of the business is different from feeling like you can't afford to leave. I can't think of any successful marriage that is managed through a contract. It's managed around the family dinner table and in all those moments and conversations big and small that prove your prosperity, happiness, and satisfaction still matter to your partner. And I can't think of any business partnership that remains stable and successful in the long term if there is an imbalance.

Private equity has infiltrated many other sectors of our economy and bent those industries to their will sometimes with negative consequences. However, in franchising, PE has been forced to change tactics. It is true that PE has taken out rich financial rewards from franchising, even in cases where it has proven to be a weak sponsor or pursued flawed strategies. Franchise contracts have teeth and are notoriously one-sided in favor of the franchisor. PE sponsors and PE-backed management teams have sometimes used this to exert their dominance over franchisees.

But franchisees have also demonstrated over and over again the power of a business model that fundamentally requires some amount of *willing* participation from franchisees no matter what the license or development agreement says. PE sponsors can force system compliance, implement changes, and even force out low performers. But at some point, attracting and retaining the best franchisees and winning new commitments for expansion outlets requires management and PE sponsors to have a reputation for fair dealing and transparency. You can't be both bully and benefactor, someone to avoid and yet also a desired expansion partner. And the court of public opinion about private capital activities is also known to be harsh. With franchising so critically important to our economy and the individual livelihoods especially of franchisees at stake, PE can't afford to behave as if they're on the fringes (a.k.a. "Pay no attention to the man behind the curtain"). And with so many larger systems now seeing PE activity at the operator level, it sets up an interesting power dynamic and potential relationship challenges. Franchisees can ban together in any system and lobby for change, but the speed of alignment among PE-backed MUO groups and the veracity of the data generated can put corporate teams back on their heels. Adept change-management skills and attention to relationship quality become even more critical.

The franchising symbiotic model provides a unique challenge for private capital investors. The best overall results are created by following an operating approach to value creation, not purely financial engineering. When well executed, franchising also requires consideration of relationships and challenges investors to employ softer skills.

In your own climb up the PE Profit Ladder, never lose sight of what makes franchising work so well in the first place. If you can do that while holding your PE sponsor accountable for effective stewartship and maintaining balance in the relationship, you will create great outcomes for your franchise business.

Ways to Connect

THANK YOU FOR THE gift of your time. I hope you found this book helpful and thought-provoking. There are additional resources in the appendix for you to explore.

Here are ways to stay connected:

- Visit www.bigmoneyinfranchising.com to find the following resources:
  - ▷ worksheets, checklists, and additional writings about franchising and private equity
  - ▷ opportunity to provide feedback for the next edition
  - ▷ resources for researching franchise opportunities
  - ▷ resources for founders and franchisees
- Consider providing an online review on Amazon
- Connect on LinkedIn: https://www.linkedin.com/in/milleralicia/
- For consulting, board advisory, or similar engagements, please visit www.emergentgrowthadvisors.com

Appendix

RESOURCES FOR FRANCHISE DISCLOSURE DOCUMENTS

Four states have online repositories for FDDs:

California: https://docqnet.dfpi.ca.gov/

Indiana: https://securities.sos.in.gov/public-portfolio-search/

Minnesota: https://cards.web.commerce.state.mn.us/

Wisconsin: https://www.wdfi.org/apps/FranchiseSearch/MainSearch.aspx

My consulting firm has a referral arrangement with Vetted Biz (www .vettedbiz.com). Vetted Biz has FDDs for thousands of franchises (including historical FDDs), as well as analysis, news, and commentary on franchise performance. The company also provides tools that make it easy to do comparatives of different franchises across a range of metrics. At time of publishing, Vetted Biz agreed to offer a discount of 20% off their subscription offerings for Big Money readers, just use the code "Emergent20" when signing up. Note that Vetted Biz is a third party and can discontinue or change this discount program at any time, at their own discretion.

Note that some states (e.g., California) may require FDD changes specific for their state. For example, they may require the franchisor to present the earnings disclosure differently. This means that if you pull the FDD from the state of California's site but you reside in Texas, the document you are presented before you purchase a franchise may be different. So, if you are pulling the FDD from any of the free sites as part of your preliminary research, be sure to go back and closely review the document presented to you by the franchisor before you sign a franchise agreement.

Sometimes the franchise salesperson will say the franchise disclosure document is "proprietary" and thus is only shared after your application is approved. The FDD is a *public* disclosure document. If the salesperson says otherwise, either *they* don't understand franchising (red flag) or they hope *you* don't (also a red flag). Given FDDs are available on the above listed sites, asking for the FDD up front when you first start speaking to a brand is an easy test to find out what type of organization you're dealing with.

Please consult with a franchise attorney and your personal financial adviser before purchasing any franchise. Hire an experienced franchise attorney to ensure you fully understand the agreement you are signing, your obligations, the obligations of the franchisor, and what changes to the operating model are permitted under the agreement. A guide to finding counsel is included in the resources section.

RECOMMENDED READING

- Walker Deibel, *Buy Then Build: How Acquisition Entrepreneurs Outsmart the Startup Game*. Lioncrest Publishing, 2018.
- Scott Greenberg, *The Wealthy Franchisee*. Irvine, CA: Entrepreneur Press, 2020.
- Gary Prenevost, *The Unstoppable Franchisee: 7 Drivers of Next-Level Growth*. Vancouver: Figure 1, 2023.
- Robert Rosenberg, *Around the Corner to Around the World: A Dozen Lessons I Learned Running Dunkin Donuts*. New York: HarperCollins Leadership, 2020.
- Michael H. Seid and Joyce Mazero, *Franchise Management for Dummies*. Hoboken, NJ: John Wiley, 2017.
- Andrew J. Sherman, *Franchising and Licensing: Two Powerful Ways to Grow Your Business in Any Economy*. New York: AMACOM, 2023.

EDUCATIONAL RESOURCES

The subject of franchising is appearing in more business schools and entrepreneurial programs in acknowledgment of franchising's critical impact on our economy. The list of university-level programs continues to grow. The International Franchise Association has also developed a certification program focused on best practices and professional development.

► International Franchise Association—Certified Franchise Executive (CFE)
  https://www.franchise.org/certification
► Babson College—Tariq Farid Franchise Institute
  https://www.babson.edu/franchise-entrepreneurship-institute/
► Cornell University—Nolan School of Hotel Administration, SC Johnson College of Business
  https://sha.cornell.edu/about/
► Georgetown University—Certificate in Franchise Management
  https://scs.georgetown.edu/programs/382/certificate-in-franchise
  -management/
► Georgia State University—Cecil B. Day School of Hospitality Administration
  https://robinson.gsu.edu/academic-departments/hospitality/
► Palm Beach Atlantic University—Titus Center for Franchising
  https://www.pba.edu/academics/schools/centers/titus-franchising/index.html
► University of Denver—The Liniger Center on Franchising
  https://daniels.du.edu/liniger-center-on-franchising/
► University of Louisville—Certificate in Franchise Management
  https://louisville.edu/online/programs/certificate-programs
  /franchise-management/franchise-management-certificate/
► University of Nevada, Las Vegas—William F. Harrah College of Hospitality
  https://www.unlv.edu/hospitality
► University of New Hampshire—Rosenberg Franchise Center
  https://paulcollege.unh.edu/rosenberg

ONLINE RESOURCES

► American Association of Franchisees and Dealers: https://www.aafd.org/

► American Marketing Association: https://www.ama.org/

► Entrepreneur: www.entrepreneur.com/franchise

► Federal Trade Commission—Guide to Buying a Franchise: https://www
.ftc.gov/business-guidance/resources/consumers-guide-buying-franchise

► Franchise Business Review (franchisee survey ratings): www.franchisebusiness
review.com

► *Franchise Times:* www.franchisetimes.com

  ▷ In addition to extensive information about all things franchising, *Franchise
  Times* publishes a useful annual list of attorneys specializing in franchise
  law. The downloadable PDF indicates whether the attorneys have practices
  supporting franchisees, franchisors, or both: https://www.franchisetimes
  .com/franchise_resources/legal-eagles/

► FRANdata: www.frandata.com

► International Franchise Association: www.franchise.org

► Restaurants (quick service and full service) and retail food establishments
represent half of all franchise outlets in the US: 400,000 units and counting.
Even if you're not considering a food or restaurant franchise concept, several
sector publications cover information about the business of franchising and
are worth exploring:

  ▷ www.nrn.com

  ▷ www.qsr.com

  ▷ www.restaurantbusinessonline.com

► SCORE: www.score.org

► State Guides on Buying a Franchise

  ▷ These are helpful guides no matter where you reside.

  ▷ California: https://dfpi.ca.gov/wp-content/uploads/sites/337/forms
  /Securities/DFPI-SRD-QR-518.pdf

  ▷ Maryland: https://www.marylandattorneygeneral.gov/Pages/Securities
  /franchise.aspx

  ▷ Minnesota: https://mn.gov/commerce/licensing/list/securities/franchises/

▷ Check your own state's website for state-specific franchise regulations, business licensing requirements, and business start-up guides and other resources. For example, Texas provides an 87-page small business start-up guide as well as numerous links and resources to help entrepreneurs get started. It is worth exploring your own state resources and local small business development office to see what guidance and help they provide.

▷ https://gov.texas.gov/uploads/files/business/Governors_Small_Business_Handbook.pdf

► Technomic (food service and restaurant industry research): https://www.technomic.com/

► US Chamber of Commerce: Your local or state chamber of commerce also may have helpful resources. https://www.uschamber.com/co/start/strategy/franchise-agreement-guide

► US Small Business Administration: The SBA site has useful guides on business start-ups and funding but has (as of this writing) discontinued its franchise registry. https://www.sba.gov/business-guide/plan-your-business/buy-existing-business-or-franchise

Acknowledgments

FIRST, TO MY FAMILY—you have been patient and unwavering in your belief in me. I am thankful especially for Matt, DMM, Matthew, Kevin, and David. I love you and appreciate you. Like a champ, my father, David (who is also my favorite serial entrepreneur), read every single substantive draft and provided feedback. As has been the case in my life generally, his positive stamp is all over this project.

My advisory work at the intersection of franchising and private equity gave me the original idea to write this book. I could see a knowledge gap existed about the impact of PE on franchising, and I was determined to wrestle many complex threads into a cogent narrative. My efforts benefited along the way from the support, insights, and wisdom of more than 100 franchise and private equity leaders, founders, and franchisees, as well as journalists, academics, and legal, finance, and operations experts. My publishing team at Figure 1 were also a tremendous asset guiding me through the process of publishing my first book.

The following group deserves special mention and thanks:

Joseph Adler, Ernesto Anguilla, Daniel Ashenden, Nadeem Bajwa, Charlie Chase, Melissa Churchill, Nick Crouch, Taylor DeHart, Walker Deibel, Chris Dull, Eric Easton, Leo Efstathiou, Patrick Findaro, Ted Fireman, Lane Fisher, Paul Flick, Nancy Foran, Jonathan Fortman, Matthew Frankel, Scott Frith, Anand Gala, Ron Gardner, James J. Goodman, John A. Gordon, Scott Greenberg, Jamal Hagler, Matthew Haller, Aziz Hashim, Jeremy Hirsch, Jeremy Holland, David Humphrey, Glen Johnson, Kevin Kaiser, J. David Karam, Brandon Karpeles, Jeff Kropp, Chris Labonte, Peter Lagarias, Mary Jo Larsen, Steven Lee, Scott Lessne, Don Loney, Phil Loughlin, Drew Maloney, Grant Marcks, Jonathan Maze, Bill McCalpin, Kim McCaslin, Robb McCormick, Matthew McDonald, Caitlyn McTigue,

Laura Michaels, Keith R. Miller, Karen Milner, Heidi Morrissey, Holly Mueller, Paul Musser, Justin Nihiser, Gary Occhiogrosso, Cristin O'Hara, Rick Ormsby, Steffen Pauls, Joseph Perry, Matt Pilla, Gary Prevenost, Kim Ricci, Steve Ricci, Paul Rocchio, Robert M. Rosenberg, Peter Ross, Bill Rotatori, Emily Schillinger, Michael H. Seid, Robin Sharma, Andrew J. Sherman, Steve Siegel, Omar Simmons, Lara Smith, Caroline Stevens, Drew Stevens, Joe St. Geme, Jonathan Thiessen, Dena Tripp, Stephen Ullstrom, Michael Useem, Charles Watson, Glenn Weiner, Jazmin Welch, Tom Wells, Kevin Wilson, Edith Wiseman, Cory Wishengrad, Scott Zide and the Lippincott Library at the Wharton School of Business, University of Pennsylvania.

Notes

Introduction

1   While a detailed accounting of private capital activity in franchising outside the US market is beyond the scope of this book, PE engagement is visible in nearly every market where franchising has reached some level of maturity and scale. This is particularly true of PE-backed master franchisees taking brands into new markets, pairing private capital investment with in-market proven operators. Consolidation of brands into multi-brand platforms and consolidation of operating units is also happening in a number of markets.

2   This was accomplished via an initial public offering in 2004 and taking on new debt (refinancing). Bain and other investors also took out a "monster dividend" of $897 million for themselves in 2007. See Healy, Beth. (January 29, 2012) *The Boston Globe*. "Domino's Delivered for Bain Capital." https://www.bostonglobe.com/business/2012/01/29/domino-delivered -for-bain-capital/kyMAofIwPYvg2pa0UK1UfI/story.html

3   Author analysis of activity from 1920 to 2023. Sources: Pitchbook, PEHub, Buyouts, company press releases, various news media, *Franchise Times Dealmakers*.

4   Sinha, Alka, Jin Qi, and Kaylyn Matis. (2023) FRANdata. 2023 *Franchising Economic Outlook*. P.v.

5   MacArthur, Hugh, Mike McCay, and Karen Harris. (March 7, 2022) Bain & Company: *Global Private Equity Report*. "Private Equity's Inflation Challenge." https://www.bain.com/insights /inflation-global-private-equity-report-2022/

6   Flynn Group has raised millions in the private capital markets to support growth and acquisitions since its founding in 1999, including from private equity firms such as Main Post Partners, GS Capital Partners, and Weston Presidio, and from direct investments from institutions such as the Ontario Teachers' Pension Plan. See https://mainpostpartners.com/news/flynn -restaurant-group-completes-its-purchase-of-pizza-hut-and-wendys-restaurants and https://www .prnewswire.com/news-releases/flynn-restaurant-group-receives-strategic-investment-from -ontario-teachers-pension-plan-260902311.html. As of October 2023.

7   Kaissar, Nir. (July 6, 2022) *Washington Post*. "Private Equity's Goldilocks Era Is Coming to an End." https://www.washingtonpost.com/business/private-equitys-goldilocks-era-is-coming -to-an-end/2022/07/05/

8   EY. (May 2021) "Economic Contribution of the US Private Equity Sector." Prepared for the American Investment Council.

9   Thomas, Dylan. (December 21, 2022) S&P Global. "Global Private Equity Dry Powder Approaches $2 Trillion." https://www.spglobal.com/marketintelligence/en/news-insights /latest-news-headlines/global-private-equity-dry-powder-approaches-2-trillion-73570292

10 Sinha et al. (2023).

11 Prequin predicts that total PE assets under management will reach $7.6 trillion by 2027, up substantially (10.2% compound annual growth) from $4.6 trillion in 2021. Source: Prequin. (2023) "Prequin Global Report 2023." https://www.preqin.com/insights/global -reports/2023-private-equity

12 Sinha et al. (2023). Also see US Chamber of Commerce. US Chamber of Commerce Foundation. (March 2017) *The Regulatory Impact on Small Business: Complex. Cumbersome. Costly*, p. 5.

13 International Franchise Association and FRANdata. (March 28, 2023) *Franchise Business Outlook* 2023. https://www.franchise.org/franchise-information/franchise-business-outlook /2023-franchising-economic-outlook

Chapter 1: Understanding Franchising's Enduring Appeal

1 Sinha, Alka, Jin Qi and Kaylyn Matis. *2023 Franchising Economic Outlook*. FRANdata.
2 Interview with author, February 15, 2023.
3 Interview with author, March 2, 2023.
4 International Franchise Association, Franchise Action Network email, accessed July 17, 2022. https://community.franchise.org/webinar/2022-ifa-leadership-summit-franchise-action -network-fan-annual-meeting
5 Oxford Economics. (September 2021) *The Value of Franchising*. https://openforopportunity .com/wp-content/uploads/2021/09/IFA_The-Value-of-Franchising_Sep2021.pdf
6 https://www.vetfran.org/for-veterans/
7 In the US this falls under the Federal Trade Commission as well as state jurisdiction. The FTC publishes a guide to franchise investing available at https://www.ftc.gov/business-guidance /resources/consumers-guide-buying-franchise. Additional franchise information is also available at the state level. For example, *California's Franchise Buying Guide* can be found at https:// dfpi.ca.gov/wp-content/uploads/sites/337/forms/Securities/DFPI-SRD-QR-518.pdf. See also "Resources" at the end of the book for more information and guides.
8 Koch, David W., and Darrell M. Johnson (June/July 2012). "Weathering the Storm: Assessing the Resilience of the Franchise Model," *World Trademark Review*: 50.
9 Interview with author, May 5, 2023.
10 Interview with author, July 21, 2023.
11 Haarmeyer, David. (Fall 2008) *The Independent Review*. "Private Equity: Capitalism's Misunderstood Entrepreneurs and Catalysts for Value Creation." Vol. 13, No. 2, pp. 245–288.
12 Interview with author, May 30, 2023.

Chapter 2: The Private Capital Landscape—Part One: The Big Money Players

1 Alliance of Merger & Acquisition Advisors. (November 1, 2022) Webinar—Middle Market Update.
2 Post, Corinne. (November 8, 2022) *Forbes*. "Private Equity Manages $10 Trillion with Few Women Decision Makers." https://www.forbes.com/sites/corinnepost/2022/11/08/pe-manages-10 -trillion-but-is-failing-its-diversity-equation-we-should-all-be-concerned/?sh=55a3721253d2
3 Private Equity Wire. (April 22, 2021) "Private Equity Holding Period's Real All-Time High in 2020." https://www.privateequitywire.co.uk/2021/04/22/299092/private-equity-holding -periods-reach-all-time-high-2020
4 Greenburg, Andy, and Bob Dunn. (March 13, 2023) Middle Market Growth. "Investors Brace for a Bumpy Ride." https://middlemarketgrowth.org/dealmaker-gf-data-investors-bumpy-ride/
5 Corkey, Michael. (September 1, 2010) *The Wall Street Journal*. "How to Make a Killing on Burger King." https://www.wsj.com/articles/BL-DLB-26490
6 Private Equity Wire. (April 22, 2021).
7 Kelly Ford Buckley. (March 25, 2014, accessed October 29, 2023) "Edison Exits Liberty Tax Generating 14× Return. Edison Partners." https://www.edisonpartners.com/blog/edison-exits -liberty-tax-generating-o)x-return
8 These guidelines were updated in November 2022. See www.sec.gov
9 BulletPoint Network LP. (September 12, 2019) "The Rise of Direct Investing by LP's and Family Offices." https://www.bulletpoint.network/blog/bpn-blog/2019/3/19/the-power-and -pitfalls-of-using-multiples-to-value-companies-o-1
10 BulletPoint (2019).
11 Ontario Teachers' Pension Plan. (May 28, 2014) "Flynn Restaurant Group Receives Strategic Investment from Ontario Teachers' Pension Plan." https://www.otpp.com/en-ca/about -us/news-and-insights/2014/flynn-restaurant-group-receives-strategic-investment-from -ontario-teachers-pension-plan/
12 *The Daily Record*. (*September* 21, 2022) "BCI Leads Significant Minority Investment in Columbia's Authority Brands." https://thedailyrecord.com/2022/09/21/bci-leads-significant-minority -investment-in-columbias-authority-brands/#:~:text=Authority%20Brands'%20companies%20 include%2012,Heating%20and%20Air%20Conditioning%2C%20STOP

13   Falconer, Kirk. (February 7, 2022) *Buyouts*. "Franchise Investor Roark Capital Enters Last Lap with $5bn Fund IV." https://www.buyoutsinsider.com/franchise-investor-roark-capital -enters-last-lap-with-5bn-fund-vi

14   Singh, Preeti. (January 15, 2021) *The Wall Street Journal*. "Roark Capital Seeks $5 Billion for New Flagship Fund." https://www.wsj.com/articles/roark-capital-seeks-5-billion-for-new -flagship-fund-11610708400

15   LACERS provides quarterly updates on private equity performance and allocations. See Aksia LLC. (December 31, 2022) "Private Equity Performance Report as of December 31, 2022," p. 4. https://www.lacers.org

16   Ibid., pp. 17–27.

17   CalPERS 2020–2021 Annual Investment Report.

18   PGIM Global Communications. (November 15, 2022) "Private Equity's Role Grows in Volatile Times: Montana Capital Partners Annual Survey Results." https://www.pgim.com/press-release /private-equitys-role-grows-volatile-times-montana-capital-partners-annual-survey

19   Bulletproof (2019).

20   Interview with author, May 5, 2023.

21   Greenburg, Andy, and Bob Dunn. (March 13, 2023) Middle Market Growth. "Investors Brace for a Bumpy Ride." https://middlemarketgrowth.org/dealmaker-gf-data-investors-bumpy-ride/

22   Ibid.

23   Interview with author, April 21, 2023.

24   Interview with author, April 19, 2023.

25   Interview with author, February 28, 2023.

26   Restaurant News.com. (September 26, 2019) "Founding Investors of Wetzel's Pretzels and Blaze Pizza Franchise America's Next Big Fast-Casual Dining Concept." https://www.restaurantnews .com/founding-investors-of-wetzels-pretzels-and-blaze-pizza-franchise-americas-next-big-fast -casual-dining-concept-092619/

27   Coley, Ben. (January 2023) QSR. "QSR's Breakout Brand of 2022: The Sizzling Rise of Dave's Hot Chicken." https://www.qsrmagazine.com/reports/qsrs-breakout-brand-2022-sizzling-rise -daves-hot-chicken

28   Dave's Hot Chicken reportedly attracted investments from Maria Shriver and movie producer John Davis, Grammy Award–winning artist Drake, actor Samuel L. Jackson, NFL Hall of Famer Michael Strahan, and Red Sox owner Tom Werner. Coley, QSR. https://www.qsrmagazine.com /reports/qsrs-breakout-brand-2022-sizzling-rise-daves-hot-chicken)

29   Company press release. PR Newswire. (September 6, 2019) "Ace Hardware Announces Acquisition of Handyman Matters Franchise." https://www.prnewswire.com/news-releases /ace-hardware-announces-acquisition-of-handyman-matters-franchise-300913021.html

30   Dezember, Ryan. (August 4, 2014) *The Wall Street Journal*. "VCA to Acquire Camp Bow Wow Chain." https://www.wsj.com/articles/vca-to-acquire-camp-bow-wow-chain-1407175570

31   Interview with author, March 28, 2023. For more on Advocate Aurora Enterprises' acquisition of Senior Helpers, see Holly, Robert. (April 1, 2021) Home Health Care News. "'We Own the Full Health Care Continuum: Advocate Aurora Acquires Senior Helpers." https://homehealth carenews.com/2021/04/we-own-the-full-health-care-continuum-advocate-aurora-enterprises -acquires-senior-helpers/ Advocate Aurora Enterprises is a subsidiary of Advocate Aurora Health, one of the 12 largest not-for-profit, integrated health systems in the nation.

32   See https://www.pernod-ricard.com/en for updated company information.

33   NBC News and the Associated Press. (December 12, 2005) "Dunkin' Brands Sold for $2.43 Billion." https://www.nbcnews.com/id/wbna10441279

34   https://galacapitalpartners.com/portfolio/ Accessed January 15, 2023.

35   Ewen, Beth. (May 2023) *Franchise Times*. "Dealmakers." Vol. 29, No. 5, p. 33.

36   Miller, Alicia. (January 26, 2023) *Franchise Times*. "How One PE Firm Puts Its Own Capital, Operations Experience to Work." https://www.franchisetimes.com/franchise_insights/how -one-pe-firm-puts-its-own-capital-operations-experience-to-work/article_b0ee719e-974c-11ed -b076-332034155faa.html

Chapter 3: The Private Capital Landscape—Part Two: The Big Money Strategies

1 Prequin. (October 2011) "Prequin Special Report: Distressed Private Equity." https://www .preqin.com/insights/research/factsheets/preqin-special-report-distressed-private-equity

2 Interview with author, February 14, 2023.

3 MacArthur, Hugh, Rebecca Burack, Christophe De Vusser, and Kiki Yang. (March 7, 2022) Bain & Company. "The Private Equity Market in 2021: The Allure of Growth." https://www.bain .com/insights/private-equity-market-in-2021-global-private-equity-report-2022/

4 Interview with author, March 10, 2023.

5 See https://www.investopedia.com/terms/v/valueinvesting.asp

6 Sycamore also owns Belk, a regional department store that has been in and out of bankruptcy, and Ann Taylor, Loft, Lane Bryant, and Lou & Grey, which it acquired from holding company Ascena's bankruptcy. See Howland, Daphne. (November 30, 2020) Retail Dive. "Sycamore Snaps Up Ann Taylor, Other Remaining Ascena Brands for $540M." https://www.retaildive. com/news/sycamore-snaps-up-ann-taylor-other-remaining-ascena-brands-for-540m/589795/

7 In 2019, Sycamore famously financed $5.4 billion of debt on its 2017 Staples acquisition and paid itself a $1 billion dividend in the process (via $1 billion of additional debt added to the business). See Ronalds-Hannon, Eliza, and Davide Scigliuzzo. (April 11, 2019) Bloomberg. "Sycamore Gets $1 Billion in Deal That Amazed Street." https://www.bloomberg.com/news/articles/2019-04-11 /sycamore-pockets-1-billion-from-deal-that-amazed-wall-street?sref=SLBTLVKA

8 According to Goddard's public financial disclosures, Goddard had $29.5 million of operating income in 2021. See the Goddard School 2022 Franchise Disclosure Document. (Issued September 22, 2022) Financial Statements and Management Notes. So the $427 million securitization represents 14.5 times reported 2021 annual operating income. How is this possible? According to rating agency KBRA's report on the securitization, future franchise agreements and associated royalties were taken into consideration. The transaction's leverage therefore amounted to 6.0x. See KBRA Press Release. (August 8, 2022) "KBRA Assigns Ratings to Goddard Funding LLC Series 2022-1 Senior Secured Notes." https://www.businesswire.com/news/ home/20220808005682/en/KBRA-Assigns-Preliminary-Ratings-to-Goddard-Funding-LLC -Series-2022-1-Senior-Secured-Notes When contacted, the analyst who performed the evaluation confirmed that net cash flow considered in assigning this rating was $70 million (so the securitization leaned into future cash flow), and the ratio only includes the $420 million of Class A-1 and A-2 notes, not the remaining $7 million debt facility. Author email exchange with Xilun Chen, managing director ABS Commercial, KBRA. February 15, 2022.

9 Goddard 2023 Franchise Disclosure Document. (Issued April 29, 2023) Consolidated Notes to Financial Statements for the period June 30, 2022, to December 31, 2022, p. 5.

10 Interview with author, February 27, 2023.

11 Haddon, Heather. (April 20, 2023) The Wall Street Journal. "McDonald's and Franchisees Escalate Battle Over Chain Rules." https://www.wsj.com/articles/mcdonalds-and-franchisees-escalate -battle-over-chain-rules-9f7b92e4?mod=Searchresults_pos1&page=1

12 Wolf, Barney. (May 2014) QSR. "Inside Roark Capital." https://www.qsrmagazine.com/growth /inside-roark-capital

13 Brooks, Rick. (December 10, 2001) The Wall Street Journal. "Roark Capital Acquires Carvel. Plans to Expand Ice-Cream Firm." https://www.wsj.com/articles/SB1008020433544093680

14 Barnes, Jennifer. Franchises America.com. "91 Best Ice Cream Franchises in USA for 2022." https://franchisesamerica.com/franchise/ice-cream-franchises

15 Carvel 2021 Franchise Disclosure Document. (Issued March 25, 2021) Consolidated Financial Statements, Balance Sheet, p. 4, and Cash Flow Statement, p. 7.

16 Carvel 2023 Franchise Disclosure Document. (Issued March 23, 2023) Notes to Financial Statements, "Cash Distribution to Parent," p. 6, and "Guarantee," p. 12.

17 Carvel 2023 Franchise Disclosure Document. (Issued March 23, 2023) "FBLLC Consolidated Statement of Operations," p. 4.

18 Coley, Ben. (March 6, 2023) QSR. "Focus Brands' Transformation Hits Stride with Record Sales." https://www.qsrmagazine.com/exclusives/focus-brands-transformation-hits-stride -record-sales

19 See 2023 Carvel Franchise Disclosure Document. (Issued March 23, 2023), Item 20, p. 84, and 2021 Carvel Franchise Disclosure Document. (Issued March 25, 2021), Item 20, p. 78.

20   Baertlein, Lisa. (May 17, 2010) Reuters. "Arby's Problems Run Deeper Than Menu Prices." https://www.reuters.com/article/us-wendysarbys-analysis/arbys-problems-run-deeper-than -menu-prices-idUSTRE64G4MC20100517

21   Reuters. (August 12, 2010) as appeared in *The New York Times.* "Wendy's, Missing Forecast, Lowers Its Annual Outlook." https://www.nytimes.com/2010/08/13/business/13wendys.html

22   Killifer, Valerie. (July 5, 2011) Fast Casual. "Roark Capital Completes Arby's Acquisition." https://www.fastcasual.com/news/roark-capital-completes-arbys-acquisition/ A majority stake in Arby's was acquired from Wendy's in 2011 for $130 million in cash (and Roark assumed $190 million in debt). Wendy's kept a share, which it later sold in 2018.

23   Pitchbook. (August 17, 2018) "Wendy's to Sell Arby's Interest to Roark for $450M." https:// pitchbook.com/newsletter/wendys-to-sell-arbys-interest-to-roark-for-450m The Inspire Brands restaurant platform (backed by Roark) later bought out Wendy's remaining 12.3 percent stake for $450 million in 2018.

24   Franchisee Association Presentation by John A. Gordon. (September 27, 2022) Pacific Management Consulting Group. "Arby's Results." Cited with permission.

25   Company website: https://www.arbys.com/about-us/

26   Gelsi, Steve. (February 17, 2006) Marketwatch. "Private Equity Firm Wellspring Buys Checkers for $188M." https://www.marketwatch.com/story/private-equity-firm-wellspring-buys-checkers -for-188m Also see release on SEC website: https://www.sec.gov/Archives/edgar/data /879554/000119312506131282/dex991.htm

27   Beltran, Luisa, and Olivia Oran. (August 27, 2012) Reuters. "Checkers Drive-In Restaurant Chain Up for Sale—Sources." https://www.reuters.com/article/checkers-sale-idINL2E8JSDIC20120828

28   Checkers/Rally's 2019 Franchise Disclosure Document. Notes to Consolidated Financial Statements, p. 17.

29   Maze, Jonathan. (June 20, 2023) Restaurant Business Online. "Restructuring Gives Control of Checkers to Its Lenders." https://www.restaurantbusinessonline.com/financing /restructuring-gives-control-checkers-its-lenders?mkt_tok=NTYxLVpOUCo4OTcAAAGM llbzfv1uLXbHbAzSHDPnnE7xh5n9esCaV_ddTWuVIdgXPkluKgih3fWoCF8AoAQmzp9X plo2hbdFDI6DggG6GJ1Fwt96oWC3Nd8hU6rJxiL3xlIc

30   Case No. 6:20-cv-00092, US District Court of Texas, Waco, p. 4.

31   Office of Senator (Nevada) Catherine Cortez Masto. (April 2021) *Strategies to Improve the Franchise Model: Preventing Unfair and Deceptive Franchise Practices.* https://www.cortezmasto .senate.gov/imo/media/doc/Franchise%20Report%20from%20the%20Office%20of%20 Senator%20Cortez%20Masto.pdf

Chapter 4: The Parallel Tracks of Private Equity and Franchising: Where It All Began

1   Kravis, Henry as interviewed by Steffen Pauls, Founder and CEO of Moonfare. (June 20, 2023) "Deal Talk Episode 11: Henry Kravis (KKR)" https://www.linkedin.com/events /dealtalkepisode11-henrykravis-k7057677729227235328/comments/

2   Blair, Roger D., and Francine Lafontaine. *The Economics of Franchising.* Boston: Cambridge University Press, 2011, pp. 6–7.

3   For more franchising history and additional source materials, see https://www.franchise.org/blog /the-history-of-modern-franchising and https://www.franchise.org/franchise-information/

4   Note that some well-known companies are often thought of as being among the "first fran-chises" but didn't start franchising until much later. For example, Snap-On Tools was founded in 1920 but didn't start franchising until 1990. Berlitz, founded in 1878, didn't start franchising until 1996. See company websites for full history. Various franchising start dates are visible on franchise information sites. For the dates listed in this book, where there is a conflict among various online sources, dates on official company websites prevail. For example, the International Franchise Association's franchise history site lists A&W's franchising start as 1924, but the A&W's company website lists 1926, so the 1926 date is included here. In addition, there are early fran-chises that are no longer in business and so are not listed because they are not familiar to modern consumers. For example, Ben Franklin five-and-dime stores began in 1877 and began franchising in 1927. At one time they counted Samuel Walton among their franchisees (he was a 15-unit owner), before Walton founded Walmart.

5   Gordon, John Steele. (January 17, 2012) *The Wall Street Journal*. "A Short (and Sometimes Profitable) History of Private Equity." https://www.wsj.com/articles/SB10001424052970204 46800457716685022278565

6   See history at https://www.carnegie.org/interactives/foundersstory/#!/

7   See history at https://www.bessemertrust.com/what-makes-us-different/key-facts

8   See history at https://corporate.ford.com/about/history/company-timeline.html

9   National Bureau of Economic Research. *Merger Movements in American Industry, 1895–1956*. Ed. Ralph L. Nelson. "The Merger Movement from 1895 through 1920." New Jersey: Princeton University Press, 1959, p. 37. http://www.nber.org/chapters/c2526

10 See https://en.wikipedia.org/wiki/3i#:~:text=In%201983%20the%20company%20was,capital isation%20of%20%20C2%A31.5%20billion

11 MoneyWeek. (August 14, 2015) "How Jerome Kohlberg Became the Spiritual Father of Private Equity." https://moneyweek.com/404450/profile-of-jerome-kohlberg

12 Anders, George. *Merchants of Debt: KKR and the Mortgaging of American Business*. New York: Basic Books, 1992, p. 15.

13 See company website for history: https://www.dbag.com/company/history/

14 Company roots go back to 1939 and E.M. Warburg & Co., an investment banking and private investment consulting firm. See company website for full history: https://warburgpincus.com /firm/firm-history/

15 See company website for history: https://www.ta.com/about/

16 See company website for history: https://www.quilvestcapitalpartners.com/

17 See company website for history: https://www.cinven.com/who-we-are/#:~:text=Founded%20 in%201977%2C%20Cinven%20became,first%20independent%20fund%20in%201996.&text =We%20opened%20our%20first%20continental,followed%20by%20Milan%20in%202006

18 Vise, David A. (May 5, 1986) *The Washington Post and The Los Angeles Times*. "Forstmann Little: Small Firm Specializes in Major Deals." https://www.latimes.com/archives/la-xpm-1986-05 -05-fi-3441-story.html

19 See company website for history: https://www.cdr-inc.com/firm-profile#firm-profile -building-stronger-businesses-together

20 Steele 2012, and author research.

21 Mario L. Herman Law. "A Brief History of Franchising." https://www.franchise-law.com /franchise-law-overview/a-brief-history-of-franchising.shtml

22 Mario L. Herman Law.

23 FotoMat didn't survive the switch to digital photography and ceased operations in September 2009.

24 See https://www.tshaonline.org/handbook/entries/southland-corporation

25 See *Susser v. Carvel Corp.*, 206 F. Supp. 636, 640 (S.D.N.Y 1962), *aff'd*, 332 F.2d 505 (2d Cir. 1964), *cert. dismissed*, 381 U.S. 125 (1965), and also *Principe v. McDonald's Corp.*, 631 F.2d 303, 309 (4th Cir. 1980). For more background on proposed FTC Franchise Rule changes, see Patterson, Tim, and Michael Lockerby. (April 3, 2023) Foley & Gardner LLP. "'If It's Not Broken, Don't Break It.'—The FTC Targets the Franchise Business Model." https://www.jdsupra.com /legalnews/if-it-s-not-broken-don-t-fix-break-it-9751483/

26 See https://dfpi.ca.gov/about-the-franchise-investment-law/

27 For additional background and commentary, see Sanders, Laura. (November 28, 1988) *Forbes*. "How the Government Subsidizes Leveraged Takeovers." https://web.archive.org /web/20030225084830/http://www.forbes.com/forbes/1988/1128/192_print.html

28 See https://en.wikipedia.org/wiki/Employee_Retirement_Income_Security_Act_of_1974

29 Taylor, Alexander L. (August 10, 1981) *Time*. "Boom Time in Venture Capital." https://web .archive.org/web/20121022194722/http://www.time.com/time/magazine/article

30 American Investment Council. (2022) 2022 Pension Study. "Private Equity Delivers the Strongest Returns for Retirees Across America." https://www.investmentcouncil.org/wp -content/uploads/2022/07/22AIC002_2022-Report_SA-2226.pdf

31 See Boston College Center for Retirement Research. https://crr.bc.edu/

32 Gillers, Heather. (January 10, 2022) *The Wall Street Journal*. "Retirement Funds Bet Bigger on Private Equity." https://www.wsj.com/articles/retirement-funds-bet-bigger-on-private-equity -11641810604

33 Shleifer, Andrei, and Robert W. Vishny. (August 17, 1990) *Science*. "The Takeover Wave of the 1980s." Vol. 249, No. 4970, pp. 745–49. http://www.jstor.org/stable/2878074

34 Opler T., and S. Titman. (1993) *Journal of Finance*. "The Determinants of Leveraged Buyout Activity: Free Cash Flow vs. Financial Distress Costs." Vol. 48, No. 5, pp. 1985–99.

35 Hurduzeu, Gheorghe, and Maria-Floriana Popescu. (2015) *Procedia Economics and Finance*. "The History of Junk Bonds and Leveraged Buyouts." Vol. 32, pp. 1268–75.

36 See corporate website: www.mcdonalds.com

37 See company history: https://www.kumon.com/about-kumon/history

38 Uy, Sasha Lim. (July 29, 2019) Esquire Philippines. "Before Domination: The History of Jollibee in the Philippines." https://www.esquiremag.ph/long-reads/features/jollibee-history -philippines-a00204-20190729-lfrm

39 *The Globe and Mail*. (February 7, 2007) "A Brief History of Tim Hortons." https://www.the globeandmail.com/report-on-business/a-brief-history-of-tim-hortons/article20392885/

40 *The New York Times*. (1996) "The Downsizing of America." https://archive.nytimes.com/www .nytimes.com/specials/downsize/large-graphic.html#:~:text=%22During%20most%20of%20 the%201980's,nearly%20every%20kind%20of%20employee

41 See www.frandata.com

42 Fleming, Molly. (September 25, 2018) *The Journal Record*. "Arby's Parent Company to Buy Sonic." https://journalrecord.com/2018/09/25/arbys-parent-company-to-buy-sonic/

43 Robb, Gregory. (November 29, 1989) *The New York Times*. "Investcorp to Acquire 700-Shop Carvel Chain." https://www.nytimes.com/1989/11/29/business/company-news-investcorp -to-acquire-700shop-carvel-chain.html

44 See http://www.fundinguniverse.com/company-histories/yum-brands-inc-history/

45 International Franchise Association, LinkedIn, 2023 Hall of Fame background.

46 Webb, Steve. (November 1, 2000) National Real Estate Investor. "Publicly Traded USFS Accepts Offer to Go Private." https://www.nreionline.com/mag/publicly-traded-usfs-accepts -offer-go-private

47 Franchising.com. (May 29, 2006) "Private Equity Climbs on Board." Originally featured in *Multi-Unit Franchisee* magazine, No. 4, 2005. https://www.franchising.com/articles/private _equity_climbs_on_board.html

Chapter 5: Family Pizza Night Looks Like a Pile of Cash: Private Equity Discovers Franchising

1 Gladwell, Malcolm. *The Tipping Point: How Little Things Can Make a Big Difference*. New York: Little, Brown and Company, 2000.

2 St. Louis Federal Reserve. https://fred.stlouisfed.org/series/JHDUSRGDPBR (last accessed April 20, 2023).

3 Reader note: For those who remember the Motel 6 deal, KKR invested in hotel chain Motel 6 in 1985 and sold it to Accor S.A. in 1990. But Motel 6 didn't adopt the franchise model until 1994. See company website for full history: https://www.6jobs.com/working-with-us/our-history

4 Woo, Ken. (December 3, 1998) *The Los Angeles Times*. "Investor Group to Take Control of Baja Fresh." https://www.latimes.com/archives/la-xpm-1998-dec-03-fi-50100-story.html

5 See company website: https://argosycapital.com/private-equity/companies/

6 Trimaran Capital website: https://trimarancapital.com/uncategorized/trimaran-is-crazy-about -american-securities-el-pollo-loco/

7 See company website: https://www.gemini-investors.com/consumer-services

8 See https://www.nytimes.com/2002/12/14/business/company-news-consortium-to-buy -burger-king-for-1.5-billion.html

9 Beales, Richard, and Rob Cox. (September 1, 2010) *The New York Times*. "Fast-Food Redux." https://www.nytimes.com/2010/09/02/business/02views.html?_r=1

10 Healy, Beth. (January 29, 2012) *The Boston Globe*. "Domino's Delivered for Bain Capital." https://www.bostonglobe.com/business/2012/01/29/domino-delivered-for-bain-capital /kyMAofIwPYvg2paoUK1UfI/story.html. See also Domino's December 2007 10K notes to financial statements (p. 29). In 2007 net income declined due to a $75.4 million increase in interest expense due to higher debt balances. The company said in its public disclosures that it was highly leveraged as the result of recapitalizations in 1998, 2003, and 2007. As of December

30, 2007, long-term debt was $1.7 billion. The company paid a special cash dividend and anti-dilution payments together totaling $897.0 million. This is listed on p. 47. On p. 37 the company shares that it completed a $1.84 billion securitization on April 16, 2007. On p. 27 the company discloses how the new debt was partly used to fund the distribution. Historical 10K filings are available at https://ir.dominos.com/sec-filings. Interviewed at the time of the 2007 securitization, Domino's chairman and CEO David Brandon pointed out that the market was supportive because much of the proceeds from the securitization were returned to continuing shareholders (via a +$13.50/share special dividend) and because the company's strong cash flow supported total leverage was 6.9 times EBITDA. See Beales, Richard. (July 24, 2007) *Financial Times*. "Case Study: Domino's." https://www.ft.com/content/3f16afb8-36d8-11dc-9f6d-0000779fd2ac

11 Offering prospectus. Registration No. 333-131897, p. 8. https://www.sec.gov/Archives/edgar/data/1352801/000095014406005172/g00424b4e424b4.htm

12 Corkery, Michael. (September 1, 2010) *The Wall Street Journal*. "How to Make a Killing on Burger King." https://www.wsj.com/articles/BL-DLB-26490

13 Company press release: https://news.dunkindonuts.com/news/bain-capital-the-carlyle-group-and-thomas-h-lee-partners-complete-acquisition-of-dunkin-brands

14 Dunkin' Brands, Securities and Exchange Commission S1 Filing. (May 4, 2011) https://www.sec.gov/Archives/edgar/data/1357204/000119312511124980/ds1.htm

15 Lee, Lisa, Timothy Sifert, and Agnes Crane. (November 16, 2010) *The New York Times*. "Dunkin' Brands Adds to Debt." https://www.nytimes.com/2010/11/17/business/17views.html

16 Faloon, Kelly. (July 15, 2003) Plumbing & Mechanical PM (BNP Media). "Dwyer Group to Merge with Private Equity Firm." https://www.pmmag.com/articles/84965-dwyer-group-to-merge-with-private-equity-firm

17 Company website: https://www.llcp.com/levine-leichtman-capital-partners-invests-in-quiznos

18 Company press release: https://investors.dinebrands.com/news-releases/news-release-details/argonne-capital-group-acquires-existing-operations-and

19 BancBoston Capital was the PE arm of FleetBoston Financial Corp.

20 *New York Times* and Bloomberg News. (February 17, 2001) "VICORP Restaurants Has Agreed to a Buyout." https://www.nytimes.com/2001/02/17/business/company-news-vicorp-restaurants-has-agreed-to-a-buyout.html VICORP ended up being re-traded several times before declaring bankruptcy and being traded again.

21 *Biz Journals*. (November 11, 2003) "Brazos Private Equity Acquires Cheddars." https://www.bizjournals.com/dallas/stories/2003/11/10/daily17.html

22 QSR. (January 28, 2003) "Wingstop Purchased." https://www.qsrmagazine.com/news/wingstop-purchased

23 Company press release (November 3, 2003): https://www.llcp.com/levine-leichtman-capital-partners-invests-in-cicis-pizza LLCP provided $41.5 million subordinated debt. Frost Bank and GE Capital provided $50 million senior debt. LLCP received 28 percent equity in the company. Cici's was sold to ONCAP in June 2007 for $52 million: https://www.oncap.com/operating-companies/operating-investments/cicis-pizza.html Under ONCAP's ownership the company had 14 consecutive quarters of growth after bringing in a new management team in 2013. The company was then sold to Arlon Group in August 2016, generating $90 million in proceeds for ONCAP.

24 Sherrod, Pamela. (July 7, 1988) *Chicago Tribune*. "ServiceMaster Sweeps Up Housecleaning Service." https://www.chicagotribune.com/news/ct-xpm-1988-07-07-8801130439-story.html

25 Bradsher, Keith. (May 9, 1988) *Los Angeles Times*. "Lured by Pest Control Industry's Growth and Prospects for Profits, Giant Firms Are Gobbling Up Family-Owned Outfits: Getting the Bugs Out." https://www.latimes.com/archives/la-xpm-1988-05-09-fi-1724-story.html

26 At the time TruGreen was spun off, its business results were declining, losing 23 percent of its customers from 2010 to 2014. Reportedly, the parent company saw TruGreen's performance as an impediment to taking ServiceMaster public. The company had to write down some goodwill as an impairment charge, from $1.6 million in 2013 book value. Fair value of TruGreen was estimated to be $399 million at that time. After the spin-off ServiceMaster's leverage was 7.6× EBITDA. Securities and Exchange Commission company filings including management presentation. (January 8, 2014) https://www.sec.gov/Archives/edgar/data/1052045/000110465914001027/0001104659-14-001027-index.htm

27 Bowen, Chuck. (November 15, 2013) Lawn & Landscape. "ServiceMaster Details TruGreen Spin-Off." https://www.lawnandlandscape.com/news/ll-111513-trugreen-servicemaster-alone/

28 UPI. (April 24, 1989) "American Home Shield to Be Bought by ServiceMaster." https://www.upi.com/Archives/1989/04/24/American-Home-Shield-to-be-bought-by-Service Master/5113609393600/

29 $5.5 billion including the assumption of ServiceMaster's debt. Company press release: https://www.cdr-inc.com/news/press-release/servicemaster-reaches-agreement-be-acquired -clayton-dubilier-rice-15.625-share#:~:text=More%20News%3A-,ServiceMaster%20 Reaches%20Agreement%20to%20be%20Acquired%20by%20Clayton%2C%20Dubilier%20% 26%20Rice,Transaction%20Valued%20at%20%245.5%20Billion

30 Pitchbook. (June 27, 2014) "ServiceMaster Rakes in $610M in IPO." https://pitchbook.com /newsletter/servicemaster-rakes-in-610m-in-ipo

31 The businesses acquired by Roark in this transaction included ServiceMaster Restore, ServiceMaster Clean, Merry Maids, AmeriSpec, and Furniture Medic. Hemingway, Jonathan. (September 2, 2020) S&P Global Market Intelligence. "Roark Capital Secures Financing for Acquisition of ServiceMaster Brands Business." https://www.spglobal.com/marketintelligence /en/news-insights/latest-news-headlines/roark-capital-secures-financing-for-acquisition-of -servicemaster-brands-business-60191062

32 Michaels, Laura. (October 2, 2020) *Franchise Times*. "Roark Capital Acquires Service Master for $1.5 Billion." https://www.franchisetimes.com/franchise_news/roark-capital-acquires-service master-for-1-5-billion/article_de68c50a-5760-5b31-9d64-3e3b704a93bc.html

33 Company history, website: https://www.yum.com/wps/portal/yumbrands/Yumbrands /company

34 For example, 2003: The Dwyer Group was acquired by the Riverside Company; 2004: Focus Brands (Roark); 2006: Driven Brands (formed by Meineke in 2006, acquired by Harvest Partners 2011, Roark in 2015, IPO 2021); 2007: BELFOR Franchise Group (the parent company has origins in Germany, 1946, and entered the US market 1999.) In 2007, BELFOR Property Restoration acquired DUCTZ International Inc. and created BELFOR Franchise Group, which then started acquiring franchise brands (13 as of this writing) and creating a services platform. American Securities acquired the parent in 2019; 2007: DineEquity (now Dine Brands). See company history, website: http://www.drivenbrands.com.s3-website-us-east-1.amazonaws .com/about.html; Belfor. For current list of franchise brands (13 brands as of April 2023): https://belforfranchisegroup.com/. For 2019 acquisition, see https://www.american -securities.com/en/companies/belfor; https://www.dinebrands.com/en/about-us

35 Company website: https://www.sentinelpartners.com/int_news.asp?pageID=69

36 Company press release: https://www.roarkcapital.com/files/Primrose-Press_Release.pdf

37 Pitchbook. (February 25, 2010) "Franchise Investing Takes a Hit in 2009." https://pitchbook .com/newsletter/franchise-investing-takes-a-hit-in-2009

38 Baertlein, Lisa. (September 1, 2010) Reuters. "Burger King Agrees to $3.3 Billion Sale to 3G Capital." https://www.reuters.com/article/us-burgerking/burger-king-agrees-to-3-3-billion-sale -to-3g-capital-idUSTRE6801CB20100902

39 Ibid.

40 Reuters. (December 31, 2008) "Factbox—Top U.S. IPOs of 2008." https://www.reuters.com /article/ipos/factbox-top-u-s-ipos-of-2008-idUSN3138728020081231

41 Daley, Jason. (January 16, 2014) *Entrepreneur*. "Why Are All These High-Profile Franchises Suddenly Going Public?" https://www.entrepreneur.com/franchise/why-are-these-high -profile-franchises-suddenly-going-public/230313

42 Company press release (November 9, 2009): https://newsroom.hyatt.com/2009-11-05 -HYATT-HOTELS-CORPORATION-CELEBRATES-IPO-FIRST-DAY-OF-TRADING-ON -NYSE

43 Meikle, Brad. (April 11, 2011) *Buyouts*. "GNC Completes Tortured Path to IPO." https://www .buyoutsinsider.com/gnc-completes-tortured-path-to-ipo/ GNC's prior owner, Apollo, tried twice to take GNC public before selling the company to Ares Management LLC and the Ontario Teachers' Pension Plan in 2007.

44 Rooney, Ben. (July 27, 2011) CNN Money. "Wall Street Runs on Dunkin': Shares Pop in IPO." https://money.cnn.com/2011/07/27/news/companies/dunkin_donuts_ipo/index.htm

45 Reuters. (April 13, 2011) "McDonald's Latam Franchisee IPO Raises 43 Pct More." https://www.reuters.com/article/arcosdorados-ipo/mcdonalds-latam-franchisee-ipo-raises-43-pct-more-idUKWEN100520110413

46 Burger King was taken private in 2010 in a $3.26B deal by Brazilian PE firm 3G Capital Management LLC. In the 2012 reverse merger, 3G received $1.4B cash and retained 71 percent ownership. Reuters. (June 20, 2012) "Burger King Shares Rise in Return to NYSE." https://www.reuters.com/article/us-burgerking-stock/burger-king-shares-rise-in-return-to-nyse-idUSBRE85J0PW20120620

47 Hsu, Tiffany. (October 4, 2013) *Los Angeles Times.* "Potbelly IPO: Shares Up as Much as 141% in $105 Million Debut." https://www.latimes.com/business/la-fi-mo-potbelly-ipo-20131004-story.html

48 Dexheimer, Elizabeth, and Leslie Picker. (October 2, 2013) Bloomberg. "Re/Max Gains After $220 Million Prices Above Target." https://www.bloomberg.com/news/articles/2013-10-01/re-max-raises-220-million-in-ipo-pricing-shares-above-range?sref=SLBTLVKA

49 "2013: Hilton Worldwide Goes Public." (December 26, 2013) *Business Journal.* https://www.bizjournals.com/washington/news/2013/12/26/2013-hilton-worldwide-goes-public.html#:~:text=The%20offering%20was%2hailed%20as,11.

50 Pepitone, Julianne. (November 6, 2013) CNN. "Twitter Sets IPO Price at $26 per Share." https://money.cnn.com/2013/11/06/technology/social/twitter-ipo-price/

51 See https://www.bloomberg.com/news/articles/2014-09-11/blackstones-hilton-deal-best-leveraged-buyout-ever?sref=SLBTLVKA

52 Ting, Deanna. (May 18, 2018) Skift. "What Private Equity Giant Blackstone Has Meant to Hilton." https://skift.com/2018/05/18/what-private-equity-giant-blackstone-has-meant-to-hilton/

53 Eisen, David. (June 26, 2022) Hospitality Investor. "Blackstone Made a Fortune Off Hilton: Is It the Last of the Hotel Mega-Deals?" https://www.hospitalityinvestor.com/investment/how-private-equity-giant-blackstone-became-real-estate-monolith

54 Williams, Sean. (2012, updated April 7, 2017) *Motley Fool.* "This Might Be the Worst Bloomin' IPO of 2012." https://www.fool.com/investing/general/2012/08/10/this-might-be-the-worst-bloomin-ipo-of-2012.aspx. See also Cowan, Lynn. (August 8, 2012) *The Wall Street Journal.* "Bloomin' Brands Closes Up 12.8% After Cutting Price, Size of IPO." https://www.wsj.com/articles/DJFLBO0020120808e888qr9uh. See also original SEC filing (April 6, 2012): https://www.sec.gov/Archives/edgar/data/1546417/000119312512153440/d319863ds1.htm

Chapter 6: Private Equity and Multi-unit Operators: "Small" Business Consolidates

1 Deibel, Walker. *Buy Then Build: How Acquisition Entrepreneurs Outsmart the Startup Game.* N.p.: Lioncrest Publishing, 2018, p. 18. Used with permission.

2 FRANdata. 2022 *Multi-Unit Franchisee Buyer's Guide.*

3 The acquisition value of $505 million wasn't disclosed at the time but came out later when Planet Fitness's ex-CFO sued for allegedly being defrauding in the PE deal by the sellers. She was ultimately awarded $9.4 million. See https://finance.yahoo.com/news/planet-fitness-pays-9-4m-080900353.html

4 Sanders, Bob. (May 10, 2019) *New Hampshire Business Review.* "Ex-CFO Wins $5.3 Million in Suit Against Planet Fitness." https://www.nhbr.com/ex-cfo-wins-5-3-million-in-suit-against-planet-fitness/

5 FINSMES. (January 18, 2013) "Planet Fitness Receives Investment from TSG Consumer Partners." https://www.finsmes.com/2013/01/planet-fitness-receives-investment-tsg-consumer-partners.html

6 Phelps, Jon. (November 2, 2022) Yahoo Finance. "Planet Fitness Pays $9.4 Million to Former Executive Who Sued." https://finance.yahoo.com/news/planet-fitness-pays-9-4m-080900353.html

7 Company press release: https://exaltarecapital.com/exaltare-capital-partners-announces-close-of-exaltare-capital-partners-fund-i-l-p-and-recapitalization-of-planet-fitness-franchisee/

8 Vasile, Zachary. (October 25, 2021) *Hartford Business Journal.* "Orange-Based Planet Fitness Franchisee Acquired." https://www.hartfordbusiness.com/article/orange-based-planet-fitness-franchisee-acquired

9   Company press release: http://www.manavigator.com/news/towerbrook-closes-acquisition-of-us-planet-fitness-franchisee-ecp_pf-holdings

10   Dominic, Anthony. (January 7, 2020) Club Industry. "Largest Planet Fitness Franchisee Group Acquired by New York Private Equity Firm." https://www.clubindustry.com/news/largest-planet-fitness-franchisee-group-acquired-by-new-york-private-equity-firm

11   Dai, Shasha. (October 2013) *The Wall Street Journal*. "Clearlight, Riveria Buy Planet Fitness Franchisee." https://www.wsj.com/articles/DJFLBO0020131015e9afkx34z

12   Dominic, Anthony. (August 1, 2018) Club Industry. "Planet Fitness Franchisee Taymax Acquired by Private Equity Firm." https://www.clubindustry.com/news/planet-fitness-franchisee-taymax-acquired-by-private-equity-firm

13   This includes the 2023 acquisition of Saber Fitness's 27 clubs and area development right in regions of California, which will be added to the Taymax operating group. See company press release: https://www.businesswire.com/news/home/20230118005248/en/Trilantic-North-America-Backed-Taymax-Group-Holdings-LP-Acquires-Saber-Fitness

14   Interview with author, July 22, 2023.

15   Company press release (2018): https://www.wynnchurch.com/news/wynnchurch-capital-acquires-heartland-automotive. Wynnchurch is a more rare type of investor in franchising, willing to take on turnaround situations, in this case the MUO Jiffy Lube business, which had been underperforming. Because it is willing to take on projects, it believes that it is able to acquire companies at more attractive valuations. For example, in 2018, when it acquired the Jiffy Lube business, the EV/EBITDA ratio (enterprise value to earnings before interest taxes and amortization) of companies acquired during that period in the middle market was 10.6× but Wynnchurch's portfolio average paid was 6.3×. See Wynnchurch Capital. (December 11, 2019) "State of Rhode Island Meeting." http://data.treasury.ri.gov/dataset/878f82ec-74d5-46d2-bb83-bbccc6bdd197/resource/88250c1a-ac3a-4e5f-a341-99c3a3fbb163/download/Wynnchurch-Investor-Update-Rhode-Island---12.11.19.pdf

16   Ewen, Beth, and Emily Wentland. (December 13, 2022) *Franchise Times*. "*100-Unit Dunkin' Operator Sells to Exeter Capital, Plus More Bold Deals*." https://www.franchisetimes.com/franchise_mergers_and_acquisitions/100-unit-dunkin-operator-sells-to-exeter-capital-plus-more-bold-deals/article_2c237534-77f5-11ed-bbc1-0b4b479379d6.html Exeter Capital was formed in 2019, but its principals have decades of franchising experience through time at Advent International.

17   Holtz, Steve. (May 15, 2023) CSP. "bp Completes Acquisition of Travel Centers of America." https://www.cspdailynews.com/mergers-acquisitions/bp-completes-acquisition-travelcenters-america#:~:text=today%20completed%20its%20%241.3%20billion,major%20highways%20across%20United%20States

18   For list of current and realized franchise holdings, see https://www.gemini-investors.com/consumer-services

19   Interview with author, February 14, 2023.

20   Interview with author, April 21, 2023.

21   Interview with author, April 21, 2023.

22   Ewen, Beth. (April 1, 2021) *Franchise Times*. "Big Spending Begins as Flynn Crosses Finish Line with NPC." https://www.franchisetimes.com/franchise_news/big-spending-begins-as-flynn-crosses-finish-line-with-npc/article_4908f334-9306-11eb-8169-f3fdcf5d94df.html

23   Gray, Alistair. (July 1, 2020) *Financial Times*. "Largest Pizza Hut Franchisee Bankruptcy Signal YUM Brand Tensions." https://www.ft.com/content/2f37e52a-9378-42fb-aab0-43b8bca56248

24   Littman, Julie. (January 7, 2021) Restaurant Dive. "NPC International Agrees to $801M Sale of Its Wendy's, Pizza Hut Assets." https://www.restaurantdive.com/news/npc-international-agrees-to-801m-sale-of-its-wendys-pizza-hut-assets/592993/

25   Interview with author, July 19, 2023.

26   The Halifax Group press release. (December 8, 2020) PRNewswire. "The Halifax Group Invests in PJ United, a Papa Johns Franchisee." https://www.prnewswire.com/news-releases/the-halifax-group-invests-in-pj-united-a-papa-johns-pizza-franchisee-301188071.html

27   PJP already is a Papa Johns operator of more than 100 locations in the UAE, Saudi Arabia, and Jordan, and plans to expand to Iraq. NASDAQ press release. (April 4, 2023) "Papa Johns Expands Partnership with PJP Investments to Open 650 New Restaurants in India

by 2033." https://www.nasdaq.com/press-release/papa-johns-expands-partnership-with-pjp
-investments-to-open-650-new-restaurants-in

28 Company press release. *Business Wire*. (January 7, 2022) "Papa Johns Announces Historic Development Deal with FountainVest Partners to Open Over 1,350 New Stores in China." https://www.businesswire.com/news/home/20220107005204/en/Papa-Johns-Announces -Historic-Development-Deal-With-FountainVest-Partners-to-Open-Over-1350-New-Stores-in -China

Chapter 7: A Frog, More Big Money, and the Final Missing Piece

1 International Franchise Association, FRAN PAC event. Discussion with author, February 28, 2023.

2 Interview with author, January 10, 2023. Siegel was a multi-unit Dunkin' franchisee and became the first franchisee chairman of the IFA. Siegel previously held executive roles at Filene's Basement and worked as general counsel for a number of franchisors. Siegel was one of the first franchise industry experts tapped by private equity to learn about the model and identify opportunities. He has served as senior adviser to the Riverside Company for its franchising specialization since 2011 and has worked with most of Riverside's franchising investments as an adviser, board member, or both. He was inducted into the IFA Hall of Fame in 2015, which is the IFA's highest honor.

3 Rosenberg, Robert. (January 18, 2023, and April 20, 2023) Interviews and correspondence with author. Reader note: By this point Dunkin' Brands also included Baskin Robbins and Togo's.

4 Interview with author, March 31, 2023.

5 See the IFA's CFE certification page for updated courses available: https://www.franchise.org /certification

6 Interview with author, May 9, 2023.

7 This quote is commonly attributed to Vince Lombardi, an American football coach and executive in the National Football League.

8 International Franchise Association press release. (February 27, 2023) "Neal Aronson of Roark Inducted into International Franchise Association Hall of Fame." https://www .franchise.org/media-center/press-releases/neal-aronson-of-roark-inducted-into-international -franchise-association

9 Coley, Ben. (March 6, 2023) QSR. "Focus Brands Transformation Hits Stride with Record Sales." https://www.qsrmagazine.com/exclusives/focus-brands-transformation-hits-stride -record-sales?utm_campaign=20230309&utm_medium=email&utm_source=jolt Some of these new licenses include dual-branded sites (a.k.a., "splitting the box"), whereby two concepts open in the same site or an existing site is remodeled to add a second concept.

10 Reuters. (November 28, 2017) CNBC. "Arby's Owner Roark to Buy Buffalo Wild Wings for $2.4 Billion." https://www.cnbc.com/2017/11/28/roark-capital-to-buy-buffalo-wild-wings-for-2 -point-9-billion.html At the time, Buffalo Wild Wings owned an 80 percent share in R Taco. Arby's and Buffalo Wild Wings were later combined into Roark's new restaurant platform, Inspire Brands. See Thorn, Bret. (February 5, 2018) *Nation's Restaurant News*. "Arby's, Buffalo Wild Wings New Parent Inspire Brands Debuts." https://www.nrn.com/mergers-acquisitions /arby-s-buffalo-wild-wings-new-parent-inspire-brands-debuts

11 Maze, Jonathan. (December 19, 2022) *Restaurant Business*. "Inspire Brands Sells Rusty Taco to the Owner of Cici's Pizza." https://www.restaurantbusinessonline.com/financing /inspire-brands-sells-rusty-taco-owner-cicis-pizza

12 As of July 23, 2023. See company website: https://www.roarkcapital.com/about

13 See https://www.drivenbrands.com/news/driven-brands-ipo-recognized-2022-dealmaker/

14 See Maze, Jonathan. (May 14, 2021) *Restaurant Business*. "Roark Capital Buys Nothing Bundt Cakes." https://www.restaurantbusinessonline.com/financing/roark-capital-buys-nothing-bundt -cakes. See also Nothing Bundt Cakes 2023 Franchise Disclosure Document. (Issued April 30, 2023) Item 20: "Outlets and Franchisee Information," p. 70.

15 Company press release. PR Newswire. (February 17, 2016) "Orangetheory Fitness Receives Growth Equity Investment from Roark Capital Group." https://www.prnewswire.com /news-releases/orangetheory-fitness-receives-growth-equity-investment-from-roark-capital -group-300221367.html

16   Patel, Raghav. (March 15, 2022) Global Franchise. "Orangetheory Fitness Opens Milestone 1,500 Locations." https://www.prnewswire.com/news-releases/orangetheory-fitness-opens-1 -500th-studio-in-los-angeles-neighborhood-of-mar-vista-301501732.html

17   See Maze, Jonathan. (September 8, 2016) Nation's Restaurant News. "Roark Capital Acquires Majority Stake in Jimmy John's." https://www.nrn.com/mergers-acquisitions/roark-capital -acquires-majority-stake-jimmy-john-s See company website (last accessed June 18, 2023) for updated store count: https://www.jimmyjohns.com/find-a-jjs/

18   *Entrepreneur.* (October 7, 2003) "Roark Capital Group Acquires FASTSIGNS International Inc." https://www.entrepreneur.com/business-news/franchise-roark-capital-group-acquires -fastsigns/64762

19   In 2014, FASTSIGNS was acquired by Levine Leichtman Capital Partners. See company press release. (July 22, 2014) "Levine Leichtman Partners with Management to Acquire FASTSIGNS International, Inc." https://www.llcp.com/levine-leichtman-partners-with-management-to -acquire-fastsigns-international LLCP later sold FASTSIGNS in 2019.

20   Roark company press release. PR Newswire/Cision. (October 1, 2012) "Roark Capital Acquires Massage Envy. https://www.prnewswire.com/news-releases/roark-capital-acquires-massage -envy-172066941.html

21   Massage Envy, 2023 Franchise Disclosure Document. (Issued April 23, 2023) Item 20: Outlets and Franchisee Information, p. 64; 2020 Franchise Disclosure Document. (Issued May 13, 2023) Item 20, p. 67; 2017 Franchise Disclosure Document. (Issued April 20, 2017) Item 20, p. 63.

22   See https://www.qsrmagazine.com/reports/inspire-brands-and-making-restaurant-group-unlike -any-other

23   Fraidin, Stephen, and Meredith Foster. (2019) "The Evolution of Private Equity and the Change in General Partner Compensation in the 1980s." https://news.law.fordham.edu/jcfl/wp -content/uploads/sites/5/2019/09/Fraidin-Foster-Article.pdf; https://www.economist.com /briefing/2016/10/22/the-barbarian-establishment

24   Appelbaum, Eileen, and Rosemary Batt. *Private Equity at Work: When Wall Street Manages Main Street.* New York: Russell Sage Foundation, 2014, p. 2.

25   Kaissar 2022, citing American Investment Council, www.investmentcouncil.org/

26   Incline Equity Partners was founded in 2011 as a spinout of PNC Equity Management Corporation. Referenced in "Public Investment Memorandum." Pennsylvania Public School Retirement System (September 28, 2022). https://www.psers.pa.gov/About/Board /Resolutions/Documents/2022/Incline%20Equity%20Partners%20VI,%20L.P.%20-%20 Public%20IM.pdf See also https://inclineequity.com/

27   Princeton Equity Group had a predecessor called Princeton Ventures. The principals have previous franchise investing experience at other firms as well.

28   MidOcean was formed in a $1.6 billion management buyout backed by several private equity firms and acquired the private equity portfolio of Deutsche Bank.

Chapter 8: Private Equity's Playbook for Growing Franchise Businesses

1   Interview with author, March 10, 2023.

2   *Franchise Times* publishes an annual list of the top 400 brands by system revenue each year. This is the comparative list that was used to measure system revenue performance against a history of private equity activity in the brand at either the corporate or multi-unit franchisee level. As of this writing, more than 700 franchise brands have received some level of private capital support at the franchisor level, franchisee level, or both. As stated in the text, this is almost certainly an undercount since private capital activity is often not reported.

3   Interview with author, April 12, 2023.

4   Michaels, Laura. (March 8, 2021) *Franchise Times.* "Freddy's Sale to Thompson Street Capital Positions the Brand for Further Growth." https://www.franchisetimes.com/franchise_mergers _and_acquisitions/freddy-s-sale-to-thompson-street-capital-positions-burger-brand-for -growth/article_00121a0e-803f-11eb-89ba-0f9fc0a54f3c.html

5   Michaels 2021.

6   Interview with author, July 19, 2023.

7   Interview with author, July 19, 2023.

8   Company press release (February 28, 2023): https://www.prnewswire.com/news-releases
    /freddys-frozen-custard--steakburgers-set-to-open-first-mlb-ballpark-location-inside-st-louis
    -busch-stadium-301758545.html
9   Michaels 2021.
10 Interviews with author, March 7 and 10, 2023.
11 Interviews with author, March 7 and 10, 2023.

Chapter 9: Private Equity's Franchise Platform Playbook

1   Interview with author, May 12, 2023
2   Brigl, Michael, Axel Jansen, Bernhard Schwetzler, Benjamin Hammer, Heiko Hinrichs (February
    2016) Boston Consulting Group and HHL Leipzig Graduate School of Management. *The Power
    of Buy and Build: How Private Equity Firms Fuel Next-Level Value Creation.*
3   Pitchbook. (July 11, 2022) "Q2 2022 US PE Breakdown."
4   Brigl, Boston Consulting Group 2016.
5   Interview with author, April 19, 2023.
6   Interview with author, May 12, 2023.
7   Brigl 2016.
8   Interview with author, March 31, 2023.
9   For more information see https://www.bestlifebrands.com/about.html

Chapter 10: Private Equity's Emerging Brand Playbook

1   Portions of this section previously appeared in *Franchise Times*. Miller, Alicia. (March 27,
    2023) *Franchise Times*. "Here's How Emerging Brands Can Attract—or Turn Off—Private
    Equity." https://www.franchisetimes.com/franchise_insights/here-s-how-emerging-brands-can
    -attract-or-turn-off-private-equity/article_5add60a6-c98f-11ed-9f22-2793d399829f.html
    Included with permission.
2   Company website, accessed January 14, 2022: https://10pointcapital.com/growth-strategy
    #about
3   Interview with author, May 5, 2023.
4   Interview with author, July 23, 2023.
5   Portions of this section previously appeared in *Franchise Times*. Miller, Alicia. (March 27, 2023)
    Franchise Times. "Here's How Emerging Brands Can Attract—or Turn Off—Private Equity."
    https://www.franchisetimes.com/franchise_insights/here-s-how-emerging-brands-can-attract
    -or-turn-off-private-equity/article_5add60a6-c98f-11ed-9f22-2793d399829f.html. Included
    with permission.
6   Interview with author, February 14, 2023.
7   Webinar hosted by the Association for Corporate Group and GF Data (November 11, 2021)
    "State of the Middle Market."
8   Interview with author, June 2, 2023.
9   Interview with author, July 23, 2023.

Chapter 11: Private Equity Compensation: 2 and 20

1   See https://bankingprep.com/private-equity-salary-bonus/ (accessed July 15, 2023).
2   Lalley, Heather. (March 8, 2019) Restaurant Business. "El Pollo Paid $36M in Q4 to Settle
    Lawsuits." https://www.restaurantbusinessonline.com/operations/el-pollo-loco-paid-36m-q4
    -settle-lawsuits
3   See 2020 10k company website: https://investor.elpolloloco.com/financials-filings or March
    2020 10Q filing "Long Term Debt, Maturities," p. 19. Securities and Exchange Commission.
    https://www.sec.gov/Archives/edgar/data/1606366/000160636620000020/loco-10qq12020
    .htm#sC7F24D515BF959568324BA2FA1F40643. The company's public filings mention new
    borrowings as of March 2020 of $44.5 million, adding to its 2018 debt revolver. Usage was to
    bolster its cash position, account for pandemic uncertainty, and pay a legal settlement.

Chapter 12: When Everything Clicks: Positive Impacts on Franchising from Private Equity's Playbook

1   Interview with author, February 28, 2023, and follow-up, July 9, 2023.
2   Interview with author, March 29, 2023.
3   Interview with author, April 19, 2023.
4   Bernstein, Shai, Josh Lerner, and Filippo Mezzanotti. Northwestern University. "Private Equity and Financial Fragility During the Crisis." https://www.kellogg.northwestern.edu/faculty /mezzanotti/documents/PE_UK.pdf
5   Bernstein, Shai, and Albert Sheen. (December 8, 2013) Stanford University. "The Operational Consequences of Private Equity Buyouts."
6   Berstein and Sheen 2013, p. 3.
7   Interview with author, March 7, 2023.
8   Interview with author, May 5, 2023.
9   Interview with author, May 9, 2023.
10 Interview with author, March 31, 2023.
11 FRANdata. (2020) *Franchise Business Economic Outlook: 2020 Forecast*, p. 19.
12 Carey, Bill. (September 28, 2000) Nashville Scene. "Failed Fortunes." https://www.nashville scene.com/news/failed-fortunes/article_2b946400-a231-5f04-806a-2c86f11e8a17.html   and Bennett, Julie. (June 1, 2007) *Franchise Times*. "What Really Happened to Minnie Pearl Fried Chicken?"   https://www.franchisetimes.com/article_archive/what-really-happened-to-minnie -pearl-fried-chicken/article_8093c591-b894-58f7-a8fa-b63089a3d459.html
13 Lefler, Jeff. (August 2, 2019) *Franchise Grade*. "Franchise Net Growth Tells the Truth." https:// www.franchisegrade.com/blog/net-growth-matters-most
14 Interview with author, April 19, 2023.
15 Interview with author, May 12, 2023.
16 Apax Partners press release. (September 20, 2022): "BCI Leads Significant Investment in Authority Brands." https://www.apax.com/news-views/bci-leads-significant-investment-in -authority-brands/
17 PNC Riverarch Capital press release. (September 21, 2018): "PNC Riverarch Capital Successfully Exits Investment in Authority Brands." https://www.pnc.com/content/dam/pnc-com/pdf /corporateandinstitutional/riverarch/press-release/2018-LC-Authority-Brands-Exit-Press -Release.pdf
18 LinkedIn post by Jordan Wilson, chief development officer, Authority Brands. Accessed July 8, 2023.
19 Interview with author, June 2, 2023.
20 Interview with author, July 23, 2023.

Chapter 13: Accelerating Organic Growth at Each Step Up the Private Equity Profit Ladder

1   Interview: Grant Marcks, partner, the Riverside Company. December 28, 2022.
2   Interview with author, July 23, 2023.
3   As of October 2023, prior to Subway acquisition completion. See www.roarkcapital.com
4   Interview with author, March 28, 2023.
5   Interview with author, March 29, 2023.
6   Business Wire. (June 10, 2014) "Tropical Smoothie Cafe's Average Unit Volume Tops $526,000." https://www.businesswire.com/news/home/20140610006151/en/Tropical-Smoothie-Caf% C3%A9%E2%80%99s-Average-Unit-Volume-Tops-526000
7   Karkaria, Urvaksh. (August 16, 2012) Biz Journals. "BIP Gains Stake in Tropical Smoothie Cafe." https://www.bizjournals.com/atlanta/news/2012/08/16/bip-opportunities-gains-stake-in .html
8   Business Wire 2014.
9   PR Newswire. (September 8, 2020) "Levine Leichtman and Management Acquire Tropical Smoothie Cafe." https://www.prnewswire.com/news-releases/levine-leichtman-capital-partners -and-management-acquire-tropical-smoothie-cafe-301125434.html. This was the fifth invest-ment out of LLCP's sixth fund, Levine Leichtman Capital Partners VI, LP Golub Capital

provided debt financing. See https://peprofessional.com/blog/2020/09/11/llcp-buys-tropical-smoothie-bip/

10 As quoted in Littman, Julie. (September 9, 2020) Restaurant Dive. "How Tropical Smoothie's New Owners Will Accelerate Growth." https://www.restaurantdive.com/news/a-private-equity-acquisition-primes-tropical-smoothie-for-growth/584911/

11 According to the FDD, acquisition-related expenses were $13.9 million, of which $6.7 million were investment banker fees and $7.2 million were change-in-control payments. The company also paid out $64.3 million in dividends in 2021.

12 Tropical Smoothie Cafe, 2022 Franchise Disclosure Document.

13 Company press release: https://www.tropicalsmoothiefranchise.com/in-the-news/propels-franchise-momentum-q3/

14 Confirmed via email with company official. November 8, 2023.

15 Tse, Crystal, and Kiel Porter. (January 19, 2022) Bloomberg. "Tropical Smoothie Cafe Is Said to Plan to Go Public This Year." https://www.bloomberg.com/news/articles/2022-01-20/tropical-smoothie-cafe-is-said-to-plan-to-go-public-this-year

16 Company press release (April 27, 2023): PR Media. "Tropical Smoothie Café Named FRANdata's TopScore FUND Award Recipient for Third Consecutive Year." https://prnmedia.prnewswire.com/news-releases/tropical-smoothie-cafe-named-frandatas-topscore-fund-award-recipient-for-third-consecutive-year-301810279.html FRANdata fund scores are reports compiled for lenders that assess credit risk of specific franchise systems based on a number of factors, including unit-level economics. See https://www.frandata.com/fund-franchise-credit-score/ for more information. Confirmed with company official on November 8, 2023.

17 See https://franchisebusinessreview.com/top-franchises/tropical-smoothie-cafe/

18 Company press release (April 27, 2023): PR Media.

19 For more information about Dyne Hospitality, see www.dynehg.com

20 Interview with author, June 8, 2023.

21 Interview with author, June 8, 2023.

22 GF Data. (2022) "GF Data Highlights Second Quarter, 2022" and "Mid-Market PE in Q3 2022 Sees Valuations Surge in Softening Economy." www.gfdata.com

23 Surdin, Ashley. (February 1, 2007) Los Angeles Times. "Wetzel's Is Sold—to Let Even More Dough Roll In." https://www.latimes.com/archives/la-xpm-2007-feb-01-fi-wetzel1-story.html

24 Surdin 2007.

25 Company press release: https://www.llcp.com/levine-leichtman-capital-partners-acquires-wetzels-pretzels

26 Surdin 2007.

27 Surdin 2007.

28 Hofman, Mike. (November 1, 2000) Inc. "A Twist of Fate." https://www.inc.com/magazine/20001101/20909.html

29 Company press release (September 7, 2016): https://www.llcp.com/levine-leichtman-capital-partners-sells-wetzels-pretzels-llc

30 Weinburg, Rick. (Undated) California Business Journal. "California's Wetzel's Pretzels Sold to Dallas Private Equity Firm." https://calbizjournal.com/californias-wetzels-pretzels-sold-to-dallas-private-equity-firm/

31 Wetzel's Pretzels, 2016 Franchise Disclosure Document.

32 Wetzel's Pretzels, 2016 Franchise Disclosure Document.

33 Golub Capital press release (September 6, 2016): https://golubcapital.com/press/golub-capital-provides-66-5-million-one-loan-debt-facility-to-finance-centeroak-partners-acquisition-of-wetzels-pretzels-llc/

34 Wetzel's Pretzels 2018 Franchise Disclosure Document. (Issued April 25, 2018, amended October 31, 2018) Financial Disclosures.

35 Lee, Armie Margaret. (September 12, 2016) The Street. "Wetzel's Pretzels Sold After 100 Parties Express Interest." https://www.thestreet.com/markets/mergers-and-acquisitions/wetzel-s-pretzels-parent-sold-after-100-parties-submit-bids-13699695

36 Li, Shan. (September 2, 2016) Los Angeles Times and Sun Sentinel. "Wetzel's Pretzel's Sold to Dallas Private Equity Firm." https://www.sun-sentinel.com/business/la-fi-wetzel-pretzel-sale-20160902-snap-story.html

37   Wetzel's Pretel's 2018 Franchise Disclosure Document. "Refinancing with Payable-in-Kind Note," p. 20 of company 2015–2017 financial disclosure.

38   For historical interest rates, see https://www.global-rates.com/en/interest-rates/libor /american-dollar/2020.aspx

39   Wetzel's Pretzel's 2021 Franchise Disclosure Document. (May 3, 2021) Item 20, p. 71.

40   CenterOak website: https://centeroakpartners.com/investments/wetzels-pretzels/

41   Fantozzi, Joanna. (November 2, 2022) Nation's Restaurant News. "Wetzel's Pretzels to Be Sold to Famous Daves and Cold Stone Creamery Parent." https://www.nrn.com/quick-service /wetzel-s-pretzels-be-sold-famous-daves-and-cold-stone-creamery-parent-company

42   Wetzel's Pretzels 2021 Franchise Disclosure Document. (May 3, 2021)

43   Wetzel's Pretzels 2016 Franchise Disclosure Document.

44   Fantozzi 2022.

45   McNulty, John. (December 13, 2022) PE *Professional.* "CenterOak Sells Wetzel's Pretzels to MTY Food Group." Vol. 12, No. 4. https://peprofessional.com/blog/2022/12/13/centeroak -completes-sale-of-wetzels-pretzels/. See also https://montrealgazette.com/business/local -business/mty-food-group-buying-wetzels-pretzels-for-284-million-in-cash

46   See https://www.inflationtool.com/us-dollar/2006-to-present-value

47   See https://www.franchisetimes.com/top-400-2023/231-wetzels-pretzels/article_729d99fa-35ef -11ee-9629-cba67121e0af.html

48   See *Franchise Business Review:* https://franchisebusinessreview.com/top-franchises/wetzels -pretzels/

49   Company press release (March 9, 2023): "Steve Liebson of Wetzel's Pretzels Awarded 2022 Franchisee of the Year by International Franchise Association." https://www.prnewswire.com /news-releases/steve-leibsohn-of-wetzels-pretzels-awarded-2022-franchisee-of-the-year-by -international-franchise-association-301768186.html

50   Company press release (February 23, 2023): https://www.prnewswire.com/news-releases /wetzels-pretzels-makes-franchise-ownership-more-accessible-for-women-and-minorities -through-access-to-equity-program-301754723.html

51   QSR. (February 3, 2023) "Wetzel's Pretzels Rolls into 2023 Off Banner Year." https://www .qsrmagazine.com/news/wetzels-pretzels-rolls-2023-banner-year

Chapter 14: Building Enterprise Value Through the Power of Platforming and Multiple Arbitrage

1   PE Hub (December 13, 2022) "Q&A Series Interviews." https://www.pehub.com/riverside -co-ceos-have-exciting-exits-planned-for-2023-lincolnshire-bets-youre-keeping-your-old-car/

2   FMS Franchise. (December 10, 2010) "The Dwyer Group Sells for $150 Million." https://www .fmsfranchise.com/the-dwyer-group-franchise-sells-for-150-million/

3   See https://www.prnewswire.com/news-releases/the-dwyer-group-inc-to-be-acquired-by-tzp -capital-partners-i-lp-111555609.html

4   BNP Media, The News. (December 20, 2010) "Private Equity Firm Acquires Dwyer Group." https://www.achrnews.com/articles/116567-private-equity-firm-acquires-dwyer-group

5   Ewen, Beth. (May 24, 2017) *Franchise Times.* "Dwyer Launches Neighborly to Fix Sales." https://www.franchisetimes.com/article_archive/dwyer-launches-neighborly-to-fix-cross-sales /article_054eee49-8847-5f1e-95b2-a81b6e7493ad.html

6   McNulty, John. (June 4, 2018) Private Equity Professional. "Riverside Sells The Dwyer Group." https://peprofessional.com/blog/2018/06/04/riverside-sells-dwyer-group/

7   Mr. Rooter 2019 Franchise Disclosure Document. (Issued April 1, 2019) Financial Statements and Notes, p. 11.

8   Riverside company press release. (July 20, 2018) "Structured Equity Investment Made in Support of Dwyer Group Acquisition." https://www.riversidecompany.com/currents /structured-equity-investment-made-in-support-of-dwyer-group-acquisition/

9   Mr. Rooter 2022 Franchise Disclosure Document. "Neighborly AssetCo LLC and Subsidiaries Consolidated Financial Statements: No. 3 Debt Guarantee," p. 19.

10   Mr. Rooter 2022 Franchise Disclosure Document. "Neighborly Company and Subsidiaries: Notes to Consolidated Financial Statements: No. 1 Organization and Description of the Business, Acquisition of the Company," p. 11.

11 Mr. Rooter 2022 Franchise Disclosure Document. "Neighborly Company and Subsidiaries: Consolidated Statement of Cash Flows," p. 10.

12 Mr. Rooter 2022 Franchise Disclosure Document. "Neighborly Assetco LLC and Subsidiaries Consolidated Financial Statements: No. 9 Subsequent Events," p. 24.

13 KBRA press release. (January 23, 2023) Business Wire. "KBRA Assigns Preliminary Ratings to Neighborly Issuer LLC Series 2023-1 Senior Secured Notes." https://www.businesswire.com /news/home/20230123005652/en/KBRA-Assigns-Preliminary-Ratings-to-Neighborly -Issuer-LLC-Series-2023-1-Senior-Secured-Notes

14 Mr. Rooter 2016 Franchise Disclosure Document. (Issued June 1, 2016). Notes to Consolidated Financial Statements. "Acquisitions," p. 11.

15 Mr. Rooter 2016 Franchise Disclosure Document. (Issued June 1, 2016). Notes to Consolidated Financial Statements. "Acquisitions," p. 12.

16 Mr. Rooter 2016 Franchise Disclosure Document. (Issued June 1, 2016). Notes to Consolidated Financial Statements. "Acquisitions," p. 12.

17 Mosquito Joe 2018 Franchise Disclosure Document (April 30, 2018). Notes to 2017 Financial Statements. "The Acquisition of Window Genie," p. 11.

18 Real Property Management 2018 Franchise Disclosure Document. (Issued April 4, 2018) Notes to Consolidated Financial Statements. "15. Subsequent Events," p. 29.

19 Real Property Management 2017 Franchise Disclosure Document. (Issued March 24, 2017). Consolidated Notes to Financial Statements, p. 6.

20 See https://www.franchisetimes.com/franchise_news/mosquito-joes-founders-launch-new -franchise-grand-illuminations/article_a7ccc892-1f0e-11ed-9a3a-4356f888945e.html. Mosquito Joe 2015 Franchise Disclosure Document. (Issued April 15, 2015) Financial Report December 31, 2013 and 2012. "Note 7: Member Equity and Re-Issuance of Financial Statements," p. 8.

21 Mosquito Joe 2023 Franchise Disclosure Document. (Issued April 1, 2023). Item 20, Outlets and Franchisee Information, p. 74.

22 This same court case was also cited in Dr. David Weil's book *The Fissured Workplace*, which was seen by many in the franchise community as highly anti-franchising. The International Franchise Association vehemently protested (and successfully blocked) Weil's nomination to serve as administrator of the US Department of Labor's Wage and Hour Division. The International Franchise Association's stance was based on Weil's negative views and misunderstandings about franchising as outlined in his book. For more, see Oprysko, Caitlin. (March 31, 2022) *Politico*. "How IFA Brought Down Biden's Labor Nominee." https://www.politico.com/newsletters /politico-influence/2022/03/31/how-ifa-brought-down-bidens-labor-nominee-00022139

23 According to the US Bureau of Labor Statistics, in 1983, 20 percent (one in five) of workers belonged to a union; the number was higher for men (25 percent belonged to a union). By 2022, the number had dropped to only 1 in 10 workers. US Bureau of Labor Statistics. (January 24, 2023) "Union Membership Fell by 0.2 Percentage Points to 10.2 Percent in 2022." https://www .bls.gov/opub/ted/2023/union-membership-rate-fell-by-0-2-percentage-point-to-10-1-percent -in-2022.htm

24 Goldberg, Eddie. (2006) *Franchise Update Magazine*. "Jan-Pro Founder Jacques Lapointe Keeps His Hand In." https://www.franchising.com/articles/janpro_founder_jacques_lapointe _keeps_his_hand_in.html

25 Company history from J.H. Whitney website: https://www.whitney.com/

26 Starboard Capital Partners release. (September 17, 2008.) http://www.starboardcapital.net /pdf/September%2017%202008%20-%20Jan%20Pro%20Recap.pdf

27 Maid Right was a de novo brand launched by Webster and the team in place.

28 See http://www.starboardcapital.net/portfolio/StarboardExits.aspx

29 Company press release (April 1, 2021): "Susquehanna Private Capital Invests in Premium Service Brands." https://www.premiumservicebrands.com/about-us/our-blog/2021/april /susquehanna-private-capital-invests-in-premium-s/

30 Recap of transaction: https://peprofessional.com/blog/2020/06/12/incline-builds-b2b -service-brands-platform/

31 Company press release: https://www.franchising.com/news/20210120_lynx_franchising _acquired_by_midocean_partners.html?ref=rss

32　Boathouse press release: https://boathousecapital.com/boathouse-capital-completes-growth
-investment-in-largest-jan-pro-franchisee/

33　Company website: https://jan-pro.com/about/.

34　See https://empowerfranchising.com/

35　Donde, Ritwik. (November 1, 2019) FRANdata. "Old Is Gold—2019 Is the Year of Legacy
Acquisitions." https://frandata.com/old-is-gold-2019/. This article was also republished the
next year: Donde, Ritwik, and Darrell Johnson. (March 2020) *Multi-Unit Franchisee Magazine.*
No. 1. https://www.franchising.com/articles/pe_buys_into_franchising_from_unicorns_to
_warhorses_ma_is_on_the_rise.html

36　Donde, Ritwik, and Darrell Johnson. (2020) *Multi-Unit Franchisee Magazine.* "PE Buys into
Franchising: From Unicorns to Warhorses, M&A Is on the Rise." No. 1. https://www.franchising
.com/articles/pe_buys_into_franchising_from_unicorns_to_warhorses_ma_is_on_the
_rise.html

37　Donde, Ritwik, and Darrell Johnson. (2020) *Multi-Unit Franchisee Magazine.* "PE Buys into
Franchising: From Unicorns to Warhorses, M&A Is on the Rise." No. 1. https://www.franchising
.com/articles/pe_buys_into_franchising_from_unicorns_to_warhorses_ma_is_on_the
_rise.html

38　Kang, Jaewon, and Miriam Gottfried. (March 18, 2019) *The Wall Street Journal.*
"Blackstone Nears Deal to Acquire Servpro Industries." https://www.wsj.com/articles
/blackstone-nears-deal-to-acquire-servpro-industries-11552936361

39　Recall from the JAN-PRO case study that Incline Equity Partners acquired Premium Franchise
Brands (PFB) in October 2016. In February 2019, PFB then announced the add-on acquisition of
Intelligent Office. It was acquired for $13.3 million in cash consideration, plus a $2.5 million earn-
out. PFB later renamed itself LYNX in the spring of 2019. See Intelligent Office 2020 Franchise
Disclosure Document. (Issued January 31, 2020) "PFB-JP Holdings, Inc. and Subsidiaries,
Item 7 Notes to Consolidated Financial Statements. September 30, 2019, 2018, and 2017:
Note 15, Acquisition," p. 23, and Company press release. (April 9, 2019) "Premium Franchise
Brands Changes Its Name to LYNX Franchising." https://www.prnewswire.com/news-releases
/premium-franchise-brands-changes-its-name-to-lynx-franchising-300827748.html

40　Company press release. (July 1, 2019) Business Wire. "Hooters of America Acquired by
Nord Bay Capital and TriArtisan Capital Partners." https://www.businesswire.com/news
/home/20190701005887/en/Hooters-America-LLC-Acquired-Nord-Bay-Capital

41　Company press release. (July 8, 2019) Business Wire. "Automotive Leader JM Family Enterprises
Diversifies with Acquisition of Home Franchise Concepts." https://www.businesswire.com
/news/home/20190708005581/en/Automotive-Leader-JM-Family-Enterprises-Diversifies
-with-Acquisition-of-Home-Franchise-Concepts

42　Palladium company press release. (August 29, 2014) Cision PR Newswire. "Palladium Equity
Partners Completes Sale of ABRA Auto Body & Glass." https://www.prnewswire.com/news
-releases/palladium-equity-partners-completes-sale-of-abra-auto-body--glass-273229911.html

43　Leonard Green press release. (February 5, 2019) "Leonard Green Backed Caliber Collison and
ABRA Auto BodyRepair of America Merger Transaction Closes." https://www.leonardgreen
.com/leonard-green-backed-caliber-collision-and-abra-auto-body-repair-of-america-merger
-transaction-closes/

44　The company was acquired in 2013 from ONCAP, Onex Corporation's private equity platform. See After Market News. (November 22, 2013) "OMERS Private Equity Acquires
Caliber Collision Centers." https://www.aftermarketnews.com/omers-private-equity-acquires
-caliber-collision-centers/

45　Driven Brands announcement. (October 2, 2019) "Driven Brands Announces Acquisition of
ABRA Auto Body Repair of America Franchised Locations." https://www.drivenbrands.com
/news/driven-brands-announces-acquisition-abra-auto-body-repair-america-franchised-locations/

46　Romeo, Peter. (September 12, 2019) Restaurant Business Online. "Huddle House Agrees
to Buy Perkins for $51.5 Million." https://www.restaurantbusinessonline.com/financing/
huddle-house-agrees-buy-perkins-515m

47　Maze, Jonathan. (February 1, 2018) *Restaurant Business.* "Elysium Management Buys Huddle
House." https://www.restaurantbusinessonline.com/financing/elysium-management-buys
-huddle-house

48 Company press release. (April 6, 2012) "Sentinel Capital Partners Completes Acquisition of Huddle House." https://www.prweb.com/releases/huddlehouse/sentinel/prweb9374204.htm

49 Roumeliotis, Greg, Lauren Hirsch, and Mike Stone. (June 29, 2016) Reuters. "Sandwich Chain Jimmy John's to Hit the Auction Block." https://www.reuters.com/article/us -jimmyjohns-m-a-idINKCN0ZG00Q

50 Company website (accessed January 23, 2023): https://www.midoceanpartners.com/our -business/portfolio-companies/jenny-craig. The original 2002 SEC filing indicates that the founders controlled 76 percent of the shares at the time of the take-private deal and rolled $4 million forward. Value of the company was based on adjusted EBITDA for the 12 months ending June 30, 2022, of $24.4 million, amounting to a multiple of around 4.7× (EV/LTM EBITDA). A fairness opinion at the time set the range for similar companies as 3.0 to 7.8× with the mean of 5.5×. The company had 500 corporate and franchised locations in the US and 153 in Australia, New Zealand, and Canada. See https://www.sec.gov/Archives/edgar /data/878865/000095014802000849/v79143r1prer14a.htm

51 DB reportedly rolled 20 percent equity forward. Investors included the Canadian Pension Plan Investment Board (estimated $250 million), Ontario Teachers' Pension Plan Board (estimated $345 million), NIB Capital (estimated $345 million), and Paul Capital Partners (estimated $85 million). The Private Equity Analyst. (May 2003) "Man Overboard at MidOcean." Vol. 13, No. 5, pp. 50–52. https://www.wcapgroup.com/wp-content/uploads/2013/07 /PrivateEquity_5_03.pdf

52 Reuters. (June 20, 2006) The New York Times. "Jenny Craig Brings in 5 Times Its Price in '02." https://www.nytimes.com/2006/06/20/business/20diet.html#:~:text=ZURICH%2C%20 June%2019%20(Reuters),ACI%20Capital%20and%20MidOcean%20Partners

53 Geller, Martinne. (November 7, 2013) Reuters. "Nestlé Sells Most of Jenny Craig in Slimming Drive." https://www.reuters.com/article/us-nestle-jennycraig/nestle-sells-most-of-jenny-craig -in-slimming-drive-idUSBRE9A606X20131107

54 Curves Jenny Craig 2016 Franchise Disclosure Document. (Issued March 31, 2016) Notes to Consolidated Financial Statements. "Note 10—Acquisitions," p. 25.

55 Company press release (November 7, 2013): https://www.prnewswire.com/news-releases /north-castle-partners-to-acquire-jenny-craig-from-nestle-230943551.html

56 Schroeder, Eric. (April 4, 2019) Food Business News. "Private Equity Firm Buys Jenny Craig." https://www.foodbusinessnews.net/articles/13581-private-equity-firm-buys-jenny-craig

57 Jenny Craig 2021 Franchise Disclosure Document. (Issued June 22, 2021) Jenny C Acquisition Inc and Subsidiaries. Notes to Consolidated Financial Statements, pp. 19 and 24.

58 See https://www.prnewswire.com/news-releases/european-wax-center-franchisee-ewc-growth -appoints-robert-fish-as-chief-executive-officer-301644422.html

59 MKH press release. (May 18, 2021) "MKH Capital Partners Announces Platform Acquisition and Launch of Wax Centers Partner." https://www.prnewswire.com/news-releases/mkh -capital-partners-announces-platform-acquisition-and-launch-of-wax-center-partners -301293964.html#:~:text=MIAMI%2C%20May%2018%2C%202021%20%2F,of%2011%20 locations%20in%20California

60 See https://www.wsj.com/articles/DJFLBO0020130402e942jcr49

61 See company press release. (August 21, 2018) "General Atlantic and European Wax Center Announce Strategic Partnership." https://www.generalatlantic.com/media-article/general -atlantic-and-european-wax-center-announce-strategic-partnership/

62 Company press release. Business Wire. (August 9, 2021) "European Wax Center, Inc. Announces Closing of Initial Public Offering." https://www.businesswire.com/news/home /20210809005803/en/European-Wax-Center-Inc.-Announces-Closing-of-Initial-Public- Offering

63 In the PE world there are two streams of activity both commonly referred to as "secondaries." One type of secondary transaction is when a prior LP wants liquidity and a new LP wants to enter a fund. Another type of secondary transaction is when a PE firm exits a portfolio asset by selling to another PE firm. That second type is more accurately called a "secondary buyout," or SBO, and is the mechanism described by the PE Profit Ladder. But if you're doing research on "secondary transactions" you need to read the information to determine whether the information is talking about LP transactions within funds or portfolio assets trading between PE firms via SBOs.

64 Degeorge, Francois, Jens Martin, and Ludovic Phalippou. (April 2016) *Journal of Financial Economics.* "On Secondary Buyouts." Vol. 120, No. 1. https://www.sciencedirect.com/science/article/abs/pii/S0304405X15001464#:~:text=the%20selling%20fund.-,Introduction,years%20(Str%C3%B6mberg%2C%202008)

65 Ryan, Vincent. (December 21, 2022) CFO.com "Private Equity Exits Down 57% in 2022." https://www.cfo.com/news/private-equity-exits-down-57-in-2022/654767/

66 See https://www.ey.com/en_us/private-equity/pulse

67 Degeorge, Martin, Phalippou 2016, p. 128.

Chapter 15: How to Destroy Franchise Value

1   Interview with author, May 30, 2023.
2   Interview with author, February 27, 2023.

Chapter 16: Overleverage: The Burden That Keeps on Taking

1   Interview with author, March 10, 2023.
2   See Antia, Kersi D., Mani Sudha, and Kenneth H. Wathne. (2017) American Marketing Association. *Franchisor-Franchisee Bankruptcy and the Efficacy of Franchisee Governance.* Ivey Business School–Western University, Monash University and University of Stavanger Business School and BI Norwegian Business School.
3   US recessions: Q2 1979 to Q3 1980, Q2 1981 to Q3 1982 (together these were otherwise known as the "double dip" recession), Q4 1989 to Q2 1991, Q1 2001 to Q4 2001, and Q4 2007 to Q3 2009. Researchers pulled bankruptcy records inclusive of 2007 but, of course, as a result would not have picked up the full magnitude of the financial crisis from mid-2007 to early 2009. https://fred.stlouisfed.org/series/JHDUSRGDPBR
4   Bureau of Labor Statistics: https://www.bls.gov/bdm/entrepreneurship/entrepreneurship.htm
5   Company press release: https://suncappart.com/2011/03/21/how-the-sun-heated-up-bagel-chain-brueggers/
6   Primark, Dan. (March 21, 2011) Sun Capital. "How Sun Heated Up Bagel Chain Bruegger's." Sun Capital website: https://suncappart.com/2011/03/21/how-the-sun-heated-up-bagel-chain-brueggers/
7   Hausman, David. (March 18, 2011) *The Wall Street Journal.* "Sun Capital Gets 13× After Bruegger's Turnaround." https://www.wsj.com/articles/BL-PEBB-12632
8   QSR. (October 15, 2013) "Sun Capital Sells Investment in Captain D's Seafood." https://www.qsrmagazine.com/news/sun-capital-sells-investment-captain-d-s-seafood
9   Sun Capital Partners Inc. press release (December 3, 2013), via company website: "Affiliate of Sun Capital Partners Inc. Completes Sale of Captain D's Seafood Restaurant." https://suncappart.com/2013/12/03/affiliate-of-sun-capital-partners-inc-completes-sale-of-captain-ds-seafood-restaurant/
10 Al-Muslim, Aisha, and Laura Cooper. (December 3, 2020) *The Wall Street Journal.* "Friendly's Owner Hastens Exit from Restaurants with String of Sales." https://www.wsj.com/articles/friendlys-owner-hastens-exit-from-restaurants-with-string-of-sales-11606991401
11 Key, Janet. (August 9, 1988) *Chicago Tribune.* "Hershey to Sell Restaurant Unit." https://www.chicagotribune.com/news/ct-xpm-1988-08-09-8801210826-story.html
12 Feintzeig, Rachel. (December 6, 2011) *The Wall Street Journal.* "PBGC Seeks to Bar Sun Capital from Using Note in Friendly's Bid." https://www.wsj.com/articles/DJFLBO0020111206e7c6m1r6n
13 Cox, Andrew, Benjamin Johnson, and Evan Rothey. (July 2018) University of Tennessee College of Law. "Thawing Relations: The Friendly's Ice Cream Corp. Bankruptcy." https://ir.law.utk.edu/cgi/viewcontent.cgi?article=1051&context=utk_studlawbankruptcy
14 Abelson, Jenn. (December 16, 2011) *The Boston Globe.* "Settlement Arises in Friendly's Case." http://archive.boston.com/business/articles/2011/12/16/pension_agency_settles_with_friendlys/
15 Abelson, Jenn. (December 16, 2011) *The Boston Globe.* "Pension Agency Settles with Friendly's." https://www.bostonglobe.com/business/2011/12/15/pension-agency-settles-with-friendly
16 Maze, Jonathan. (November 2, 2020) Restaurant Business. "Friendly's Declares Bankruptcy and Will Be Sold to the Owner of Red Mango." https://www.restaurantbusinessonline.com/financing/friendlys-declares-bankruptcy-will-be-sold-owner-red-mango

17 Littman, Julie. (November 2, 2020) Restaurant Dive. "Friendly's Declares Bankruptcy, Agrees to $2M Sale." https://www.restaurantdive.com/news/friendlys-declares-bankruptcy -agrees-to-2m-sale/588211/

18 Smokey Bones was purchased from Darden Restaurants in 2007 for $80 million. The company had $222 million of system sales and 78 units at the time. How has the company fared under Sun? The company has refinanced its debt several times, including a $30 million new credit facility in 2015. In May 2019, Sun hired John O'Reilly, an experienced restaurant operator, to try to turn Smokey Bones around. It appears to be working on some new ideas, such as its online ordering platform BiteHall and several small offshoot concepts. At the end of 2022, Smokey Bones had 62 units. See Chediak, Mark. (December 5, 2007) The Orlando and Sun Sentinel. "Boca Firm Acquires Smokey Bones." https://www.sun-sentinel.com/news/fl-xpm-2007-12-05 -0712040506-story.html; see also Sorentrue, Jennifer. (November 15, 2015) The Palm Beach Post. "Smokey Bones Secures $30 Million to Refinance Debt, Full Expansion." https://www.palm beachpost.com/story/business/2015/11/16/smokey-bones-secures-30-million/7484024007/

19 Vaughan, Bernard. (March 24, 2011) Reuters. "MidOcean Struggles with Sbarro's Restaurant Chain." https://www.reuters.com/article/buyouts-sbarro-midocean/buyouts-midocean-struggles -with-sbarro-restaurant-chain-idUSN2411673520110324

20 Beltran, Louisa. (November 29, 2011) PEHub. "Sbarro Emerges from Chapter 11 Without MidOcean or Ares." https://www.pehub.com/sbarro-emerges-from-chapter-11-without-midocean-or-ares/

21 MidOcean press release: https://www.midoceanpartners.com/news-media/2007-01-31 -midocean-partners-announces-completion-of-sbarro-inc-acquisition-for-450-million

22 Meikle, Brad. (February 5, 2007) Buyouts Insider. "MidOcean Nears Close on Its $1 Billion Third Fund." https://www.buyoutsinsider.com/midocean-nears-close-on-its-1-billion-third-fund/

23 One of their nonfranchise firms declared bankruptcy, and losses opened up at LA Fitness. By September 30, 2010, Fund III had generated a negative 20.6 percent internal rate of return, according to the California Public Employees' Retirement System. (CalPERS had invested through Sacramento Private Equity Partners.) See Vaughan 2011.

24 Lockyer, Sarah. (August 12, 2008) Nation's Restaurant News. "Uno, Sbarro Draw Credit Downgrades, Warnings About Debt." https://www.nrn.com/archive/uno-sbarro-draw-credit -downgrades-warnings-about-debt

25 Stempel, Jonathan. (January 6, 2011) Reuters. "Pizza Chain Sbarro's Sees Default, Explores Options." https://www.reuters.com/article/sbarro/pizza-chain-sbarro-sees-default-explores -options-idINN0615165620110106

26 Bills, Steve. (May 7, 2012) Buyouts Insider. "MidOcean Tries to Get Back in the Swim." https:// www.buyoutsinsider.com/midocean-partners-tries-to-get-back-in-the-swim/

27 Beltran 2011.

28 Maze, Jonathan. (March 11, 2014) Restaurant Finance Monitor. "Sbarro's Earnings Fell Like a Brick." https://www.restfinance.com/restaurant-finance-across-america/sbarros-earnings-fell -like-a-brick/article_0bcbd60f-a8ec-5402-a40e-ebe1272e6f1f.html

29 Company press release. (March 28, 2013) PR Newswire/Cision. "J. David Karam Named CEO of Sbarro." https://www.prnewswire.com/news-releases/j-david-karam-named-ceo-of -sbarro-200464591.html

30 Interview with author, July 21, 2023.

31 A portion of this section previously appeared in Franchise Times. Reprinted with permission. Miller, Alicia. (April 29, 2023) Franchise Times. "Turnarounds Show Franchising's Resilience and Sponsor Commitment to Change." https://www.franchisetimes.com/franchise_insights /turnarounds-show-franchising-s-resilience-and-sponsor-commitment-to-change/article _ef2e7436-40f7-11ee-a8d8-7fda465c58da.html

32 Company press release/website: https://www.midoceanpartners.com/news-media/2018 -10-04-midocean-partners-raises-1-2-billion

33 MidOcean company press release (April 4, 2023): https://www.midoceanpartners.com/news -media/2023-04-04-midocean-partners-raises-over-1.5-billion-for-sixth-private-equity-fund

34 Reuters, cited by The New York Times. (June 20, 2006) "Jenny Craig Brings 5 Times Its Price in '02." https://www.nytimes.com/2006/06/20/business/20diet.html

35 See https://empowerfranchising.com/

36 See https://fullspeedautomotive.com/

37 Interview with author, May 11, 2023.

38   Federal Reserve. (November 2022) *Financial Stability Report.* https://www.federalreserve.gov /publications/files/financial-stability-report-20221104.pdf

39   Joyce, Cameron, and Angela Lai. (2022) Prequin. "Prequin Global Report—Private Equity."

40   Capstone Partners. (September 2021) "Middle Market Leveraged Finance—2021." https:// www.capstonepartners.com/wp-content/uploads/2021/09/Capstone-Partners-Leveraged -Finance-Report_September-2021.pdf

41   Capstone Partners 2021.

42   S&P Global Ratings. (July 23, 2021) ServiceMaster Funding LLC (Series 2021-1) https://www .spglobal.com/_assets/documents/ratings/research/12049848.pdf

43   ServiceMaster press release. (October 1, 2020) Business Wire. "ServiceMaster Completes Sale of Franchise Business Segment for $1.553 Billion." https://www.businesswire.com /news/home/20201001005665/en/ServiceMaster-Completes-Sale-of-Franchise-Business -Segment-for-1.553-Billion

44   Kroll Bond Rating Agency press release (June 22, 2017): https://www.businesswire.com/news /home/20210622005984/en/KBRA-Assigns-Preliminary-Ratings-to-Five-Guys-Funding -LLC-Series-2021-1-Senior-Secured-Notes

45   Wendy's company press release (June 9, 2021): https://www.irwendys.com/news/news -details/2021/The-Wendys-Company-Announces-Refinancing-Transaction/default.aspx

46   Leong, Richard. (April 5, 2021) *International Finance Review.* "Domino's Delivers ABS to Refinance Older Debt." https://www.ifre.com/story/2810968/dominos-delivers-abs-to -refinance-older-debt-dzpt3c6whd

47   KBRA press release. (January 18, 2022) Bloomberg. "KBRA Assigns a Preliminary Rating to Servpro Master Issuer, LLC 2022-1 Senior Secured Notes." https://www.bloomberg.com/press -releases/2022-01-18/kbra-assigns-a-preliminary-rating-to-servpro-master-issuer-llc-2022-1 -senior-secured-notes?sref=SLBTLVKA

48   Hintze, John. (November 17, 2020) Asset Securitization Report. "CKE Holdings Drives $400 Million ABS Deal to Successful Finish." https://asreport.americanbanker.com/news /cke-holdings-drives-400-million-abs-deal-to-successful-finish

49   King & Spalding company website. (December 31, 2020) "King & Spalding Team Closes a Variety of Esoteric Financings in Second Half 2020." https://www.kslaw.com/news-and -insights/king-spalding-team-closes-a-variety-of-esoteric-financings-in-second-half-of-2020

50   Bloomberg and Business Wire. (June 24, 2020) "KBRA Assigns a Preliminary Rating to Driven Brands Funding, LLC Series 2020–1 Secured Notes." https://www.bloomberg.com/press -releases/2020-06-24/kbra-assigns-a-preliminary-rating-to-driven-brands-funding-llc-series -2020-1-senior-secured-notes?sref=SLBTLVKA

51   Driven Brands company press release. (September 29, 2021) "Driven Brands Closes $450 Million Securitization Issuance." https://www.globenewswire.com/en/news-release/2021/09 /29/2305776/0/en/Driven-Brands-Closes-450-Million-Securitization-Issuance.html

52   Hardee's Funding LLC / Carl's Jr. Funding LLC (Series 2020-1) (November 10, 2020) S&P Global Ratings. https://www.spglobal.com/_assets/documents/ratings/research/11733014.pdf. The 2020 issuance was partly a refinancing of a 2018 securitization.

53   See Securities and Exchange 8k filing. (October 29, 2020): https://www.sec.gov/Archives/ edgar/data/1636222/000163622220000164/wing-20201029.htm. Q3 2020 EBITDA $18.4M, representing an annualized (approximate) 6.5× debt/EBITDA. Wingstop press release. (November 2, 2020) "Wingstop Inc. Reports Fiscal Third Quarter 2020 Financial Results; Completes $480 Million Recapitalization and Declares Special Dividend of $5.00 Per Share." https://www.sec .gov/Archives/edgar/data/1636222/000163622220000164/a991wingq32020earnings.htm

54   Jersey Mike's 2021 Franchise Disclosure Document. "Notes to Financial Statements, as of December 31, 2020 and 2019," p. 14.

55   Williams, Charles E., and Christopher Dereza. (November 29, 2021) Bloomberg. "Jersey Mike's Plans $500 Million with Credit Sale." https://www.bloomberg.com/news/articles/2021-11-29 /hoagie-shop-jersey-mike-s-pads-business-abs-record-with-new-sale?sref=SLBTLVKA

56   Insider and PR Newswire. (December 3, 2019) "Planet Fitness Completes Securitized Financing Transaction." https://markets.businessinsider.com/news/stocks/planet-fitness-completes -securitized-financing-transaction-1028735151

57 Planet Fitness company press release, investor relations website (July 19, 2018): https://investor.planetfitness.com/investors/press-releases/press-release-details/2018/Planet-Fitness-Prices-12-Billion-Securitized-Financing-Facility/default.aspx

58 Wendy's company press release (June 26, 2019): https://www.irwendys.com/news/news-details/2019/The-Wendys-Company-Completes-850-Million-Securitized-Refinancing-Transaction/default.aspx. See also https://www.prnewswire.com/news-releases/the-wendys-company-completes-850-million-securitized-refinancing-transaction-300875580.html

59 Wendy's company press release (June 1, 2015): https://www.irwendys.com/news/news-details/2015/The-Wendys-Company-Completes-2275-Billion-Securitized-Financing-Facility/default.aspx

60 Wendy's company press release (November 28, 2017): https://www.irwendys.com/news/news-details/2017/The-Wendys-Company-Announces-Refinancing-Transaction/default.aspx

61 Bloomberg and Business Wire. (June 24, 2019) "KBRA Assigns Preliminary Ratings to Jack in the Box Funding, LLC—Series 2019-1 Senior Secured Notes." https://www.bloomberg.com/press-releases/2019-06-24/kbra-assigns-preliminary-ratings-to-jack-in-the-box-funding-llc-series-2019-1-senior-secured-notes?sref=SLBTLVKA

62 Ruggless, Ron. (May 15, 2019) Nation's Restaurant News. "Jack in the Box Takes Company Off the Market." https://www.nrn.com/quick-service/jack-box-takes-company-market

63 Apollo Global Management company press release. (March 21, 2018) "Jack in the Box, Inc. Completes Sale of Qdoba Restaurant Corporation." https://www.apollo.com/media/press-releases/2018/03-21-2018-143515011

64 Chappatta, Brian. (June 10, 2019) Bloomberg. "Those Burgers and Tacos Are Actually Backing Bonds." https://www.bloomberg.com/view/articles/2019-06-10/those-wendy-s-burgers-and-taco-bell-nachos-are-backing-bonds?sref=SLBTLVKA

65 Dunkin' company press release. (May 1, 2019) "Dunkin' Brands Completes Securitization Financing." https://www.sec.gov/Archives/edgar/data/1357204/000135720419000019/exhibit99_1pressrelease.htm See also Securities and Exchange Commission 8-k filing (April 30, 2019): https://www.sec.gov/Archives/edgar/data/1357204/000135720419000019/closing8kfinal.htm

66 Fest, Glen. (November 8, 2018) Asset Securitization Report. "Taco Bell Serving Up Another $1.45 Billion Whole Business ABS." https://asreport.americanbanker.com/news/0-bell-serving-up-another-145b-of-whole-business-abs See also YUM Brands press release in 2021 outlining refinancing several securitizations: https://investors.yum.com/news-events/financial-releases/news-details/2021/YUM-Brands-Announces-Intention-to-Refinance-Certain-Notes-Issued-Pursuant-to-its-Existing-Securitization-Financing-Facility/default.aspx

67 Jimmy John's Franchise Disclosure Document. (Issued April 25, 2018). Notes to Financial Statements, January 2, 2018. "Securitizations," p. 10. Fest, Glen. (June 21, 2017) Asset Securitization Report. "Jimmy John's Joins in Whole-Biz Trend with $850M ABS Offering." https://asreport.americanbanker.com/news/jimmy-johns-joins-in-whole-biz-trend-with-850m-abs-offering

68 Jones Day announcement, company website. (June 2017) "Church's Chicken Completes $210 Million Private Placement of Senior Secured Notes in Whole-Business Securitization." https://www.jonesday.com/en/practices/experience/2017/06/churchs-chicken-completes-210-million-private-placement-of-senior-secured-notes-in-wholebusiness-securitization

69 Williams, Charles E., and Adam Tempkin. (October 25, 2021) Bloomberg. "Friend Chicken Chain Church's Begins Bond Sale to Refinance Debt." https://www.bloomberg.com/news/articles/2021-10-25/fried-chicken-maker-church-s-begins-bond-sale-to-refinance-debt?sref=SLBTLVKA

70 Kroll Bond Rating Agency press release (May 10, 2017): https://www.businesswire.com/news/home/20170510006288/en/Kroll-Bond-Rating-Agency-Assigns-Preliminary-Ratings-to-Five-Guys-Funding-LLC-%E2%80%93-Series-2017-1-Senior-Secured-Notes

71 Kroll Bond Rating Agency press release (October 25, 2015): https://www.businesswire.com/news/home/20151026006101/en/Kroll-Bond-Rating-Agency-Assigns-Preliminary-Ratings-to-Arby%E2%80%99s-Funding-LLC-Series-2015-1-Senior-Secured-Notes

72 KBRA research press release. (November 29, 2022) "2023 ABS Sector Outlook: Navigating an Evolving Market." https://finance.yahoo.com/news/kbra-releases-research-2023-abs-143500352.html

73 Guggenheim. (August 2013) *The ABCs of ABS: Identifying Opportunities in Asset-Backed Securities.*

74 TRexgroup.com. (April 28, 2021) "Whole Business. " https://www.trexgroup.com/insights/whole-business/

75 Guggenheim presentation "Securitization" based on Bloomberg Asset-Backed Database, data as of March 3, 2023.

76 Students of finance will recall that previous attempts at this approach, Days Inn being an often-cited example, did not work as planned because the entities were not structured correctly to protect the assets from parent bankruptcy. This has been corrected in the modern approach to securitization.

77 For example, in CKE Restaurants' April 2013 $1.15 billion WBS, the transaction included $1.05 billion of notes rated BBB- by Standard & Poor's and $100 million of variable notes. But CKE itself was rated a B- by Standard & Poors, or six notches below its own WBS vehicle. Borod, Ronald S., Andrew Srokaof, and Erin Apstein. (May 1, 2015) World Trademark Review. "The Second Coming of US Whole Business Securitization." https://www.worldtrademarkreview.com/article/the-second-coming-of-us-whole-business-securitisation

78 Guggenheim. (March 2023) "Whole Business Securitization: Highly Compelling for Franchisors." Used with permission.

79 Interview with author, May 5, 2023.

80 Lockyer, Sarah E. (March 1, 2011) National Restaurant News. "Church's Chicken Secures $245M Debt Refinancing." https://www.nrn.com/archive/church-s-chicken-closes-245m-debt-refinancing

81 Interview with author, May 5, 2023.

82 These three figures are reproduced and included by permission from Guggenheim Securities and may not themselves be reproduced, copied, or forwarded. Please note also the following disclaimer: This communication does not constitute and should not be construed as an offer or solicitation with respect to the purchase or sale of any security, loan or other financial instrument. This information is presented for informational purposes only and should not be considered a recommendation of any particular security, strategy or investment product, as investing advice of any kind, or as offering or providing any investment product or service. Guggenheim Securities, LLC and/or its affiliates ("Guggenheim") may have material relationships with the issuers of securities, loans and other financial instruments referred to herein and their affiliates. With respect to any position Guggenheim may hold, such interests may be different from or adverse to your interests. Copyright © 2023 by Guggenheim Securities, LLC, a FINRA registered broker-dealer. All rights reserved.

83 S&P Global Ratings (October 13, 2021) "Presale: DB Master Finance LLC (Series 2021-1) https://www.spglobal.com/_assets/documents/ratings/research/12144838.pdf

84 Dunkin' 2023 Franchise Disclosure Document. (Issued March 24, 2023) Consolidated Statement of Cash Flows, p. 6.

85 See above disclaimer. Used with permission of Guggenheim Securities. Note also that numbers are from a specific point in time and current information may differ from recent earnings or other guidance provided in more recent company updates and earnings call commentary. Numbers discussed in earnings calls may be net leverage as opposed to gross leverage as shown here.

86 See above disclaimer. Used with permission of Guggenheim Securities. Note also that numbers may differ from recent earnings or other guidance provided in company updates and earnings call commentary. Numbers discussed in earnings calls may be net leverage as opposed to gross leverage as shown here. As of March 2023.

87 Interview with author, May 5, 2023.

Chapter 17: More Private Equity Head-Scratchers and Flameouts in Franchising

1 Kaiser, Kevin, and S. David Young. The Blue Line Imperative: What Managing for Value Really Means. San Francisco: Jossey-Bass, 2013.

2 Company press release. (December 26, 2013) PR News Wire. "Roark Capital Closes Acquisition of CKE Restaurants, Marks 17th Restaurant Investment." https://www.prnewswire.com/news-releases/roark-capital-group-closes-acquisition-of-cke-restaurants-marks-17th-restaurant-investment-237300851.html

3 Company website: https://www.ckr.com/

4   Gordon, John A. (September 27, 2022) Pacific Management Consultants. "Presentation to Hardee's Franchisee Association." Cited with permission. See also Hardee's 2022 Franchise Disclosure Document. (Issued May 26, 2022, amended March 22, 2023) Item 19, for recent financials.

5   Merica, Dan, and Manu Raju. (February 15, 2017) CNN. "Inside Andrew Puzder's Failed Nomination." https://www.cnn.com/2017/02/15/politics/andrew-puzder-failed-nomination/index.html

6   Hardee's 2022 Franchise Disclosure Document. (Issued May 26, 2022, amended March 22, 2023.) "The CKE Securitization Entities, Notes to Combined Consolidated Financial Statements. Note 8," p. 18.

7   Hardee's 2022 Franchise Disclosure Document. (Issued May 26, 2022, amended March 22, 2023.) "The CKE Securitization Entities, Notes to Combined Consolidated Financial Statements. Note 8," p. 18.

8   Kroll press release. (November 9, 2020) Business Wire. "KBRA Assigns Preliminary Rating to Hardee's Funding LLC, Carl's Jr. Funding LLC, Series 2020-1." https://www.businesswire.com/news/home/20201109006164/en/KBRA-Assigns-Preliminary-Rating-to-Hardee%E2%80%99s-Funding-LLC-Carl%E2%80%99s-Jr.-Funding-LLC-Series-2020-1

9   Kroll press release 2020, p. 20.

10 Hardee's 2022 Franchise Disclosure Document. (Issued May 26, 2022, amended March 22, 2023.) "The CKE Securitization Entities Consolidated Statements of Cash Flows," p. 7.

11 QSR. (May 11, 2022) "Hardee's, Carl's Jr. Parent Announces $500M Reimaging Program." https://www.qsrmagazine.com/news/hardees-carls-jr-parent-announces-500m-reimaging-program

12 Interview with author, June 2, 2023.

13 Interview with author, March 7, 2023.

14 Interview with author, May 19, 2023.

15 Interview with author, July 21, 2023.

16 Interview with author, May 18, 2023.

17 Company press release. (October 1, 2012) "Roark Capital Acquires Massage Envy." https://www.prnewswire.com/news-releases/roark-capital-acquires-massage-envy-172066941.html

18 Massage Envy, 2023 Franchise Disclosure Document. (Issued April 23, 2023) Item 20: Outlets and Franchisee Information, p. 64; 2020 Franchise Disclosure Document. (Issued May 13, 2023) Item 20, p. 67; 2017 Franchise Disclosure Document. (Issued April 20, 2017) Item 20, p. 63.

19 Massage Envy, 2023 Franchise Disclosure Document. (Issued April 28, 2023) "Item 20: Outlets and Franchisee Information," p. 64.

20 Ewen, Beth. (September 28, 2021) *Franchise Times*. "Massage Envy Owners Call for New Management as Profits Cut in Half." https://www.franchisetimes.com/franchise_news/massage-envy-owners-call-for-new-management-as-profits-cut-in-half/article_9dca1828-209e-11ec-864e-43f7c8ca895d.html

21 Ewen, Beth. (October 6, 2021) *Franchise Times*. "Massage Envy Critics Agree to Settle After Rebuke from 50+ Zees." https://www.franchisetimes.com/franchise_news/massage-envy-critics-agree-to-settle-after-rebuke-from-50-zees/article_1b7e6586-26bb-11ec-9a88-2319d77af34a.html

22 Massage Envy 2022 Franchise Disclosure Document. "Note 2: Securitization," p. 12 of financial statements.

23 Massage Envy 2022 Franchise Disclosure Document. "Note 6: Related Party Transactions," p. 16 of financial statements.

24 Massage Envy 2022 Franchise Disclosure Document. "Statement of Cash Flows: Years Ended December 31, 2021, 2020 and the period ended December 31, 2019," p. 8. See also, Massage Envy 2017 FDD, submitted to the Minnesota Department of Commerce on June 21, 2017. P.4 Consolidated Statements of Income ending December 21, 2016, 2015 and 2014.

25 2022 *Multi-Unit Franchisee Buyer's Guide*.

26 Interview with author, May 30, 2023.

27 Interview with author, May 19, 2023.

28 Portions of this section previously appeared in *Franchise Times*. Miller, Alicia. (May 25, 2023) "Build a Valuable Emerging Franchise Without Field-Stripping Its EBITDA." https://www.franchisetimes.com/franchise_insights/build-a-valuable-emerging-franchise-without-field-stripping-its-ebitda/article_e511a1fc-f8b4-11ed-9a4f-83f42422322e.html

29 Interview with author, June 2, 2023.

30 Teixeria, Ed. (2022) *Franchise Grade.* "The State of Emerging Franchise Systems."

31 See https://www.franchisetimes.com/franchise_news/only-5-3-percent-of-zees-cross-100-unit-mark-says-frandata/article_6827dc51-94dc-50c1-b225-6102dc34bbab.html#:~:text=Only%20 16%20percent%20of%20U.S.,between%2025%20and%2050%20stores

32 My colleague Jonathan Maze, editor in chief of *Restaurant Business,* wrote an insightful series of articles on the Burgerim disaster. See https://www.restaurantbusinessonline.com/fall-burgerim

33 Comments from speaker at *Franchise Times.* "Dealmakers Week" webinar. April 24–27, 2023. Day 1. https://www.franchisetimes.com/franchise_mergers_and_acquisitions/dealmakers_week /day1/

34 Speaking at the International Franchise Association Legal Symposium, Washington, DC, May 9, 2023.

Chapter 18: Engaging with Private Equity

1 Interview with author, March 31, 2023.
2 Interview with author, April 12, 2023.
3 Interview with author, May 30, 2023
4 Interview with author, March 31, 2023.
5 Interview with author, July 23, 2023.
6 Interview with author, June 1, 2023.
7 Interview with author, May 30, 2023.
8 Interview with author, March 31, 2023.
9 Interview with author, June 2. 2023.
10 Interview with author, March 28, 2023.

Chapter 19: What to Expect When You're Expecting... to Be Acquired by Private Equity (or Already Have Been)

1 Interview with author, April 19, 2023.
2 Interview with author, May 30, 2023.
3 Interview with author, February 14, 2023.
4 Interview with author, May 9, 2023.
5 Interview with author, May 18, 2023.
6 Interview with author, May 30, 2023.
7 Interview with author, June 1, 2023.
8 Interview with author, July 19, 2023.
9 Interview with author, July 23, 2023.
10 Interview with author, July 19, 2023.
11 Interview with author, March 29, 2023.

Chapter 20: The Future of Franchising and Private Equity

1 Interview with author, May 11, 2023.
2 See https://www.investmentcouncil.org/investing-in-small-businesses/
3 American Investment Council. (2022) 2022 Pension Study. "Private Equity Delivers the Strongest Returns for Retirees Across America." https://www.investmentcouncil.org/wp-content/uploads/2022/07/22AIC002_2022-Report_SA-2226.pdf
4 E&Y 2023 report, prepared for the American Investment Council. (April 2023) "Economic Contribution of the US Private Equity Sector in 2022," p. 3.
5 US Chamber of Commerce Foundation. (March 2017) *The Regulatory Impact on Small Business: Complex, Cumbersome and Costly.* https://www.uschamberfoundation.org/smallbizregs/
6 US Chamber of Commerce Foundation 2017.
7 Pitchbook. (Q2 2022) Q2 2022 US PE Breakdown, p. 6.

8   Gompers, P., W. Gornall, S. Kaplan, and I. Strebulaev. (2020) *Journal of Financial Economics.* "How Do Venture Capitalists Make Decisions?" Vol. 135, pp. 169–90.

9   Gompers, Paul A., Steven N. Kaplan, and Vladimir Mukharlyamov. (September 2020) "Private Equity and COVID 19." Working paper no. 2020-140. Becker Friedman Institute for Economics, University of Chicago.

10 MacArthur, Hugh, Mike McCay, and Karen Harris. (March 7, 2022) Bain & Company. *Global Private Equity Report.* "Private Equity's Inflation Challenge." https://www.bain.com/insights /inflation-global-private-equity-report-2022/

11 MacArthur, McCay, and Harris 2022. See also https://cepres.com/insights/private-equity -value-creation

12 Choi, Jinny, and Tim Clarke. (June 30, 2023) Pitchbook. "PE Exit Timelines and the Impending Maturity Wall."

13 Harvard Law School Project on Negotiation staff. (June 20, 2023) "When Armed with Power in Negotiation, Use It Wisely." https://www.pon.harvard.edu/daily/business-negotiations /when-armed-with-negotiating-power-use-it-wisely-nb/. Also see additional resources from the Harvard Negotiation Project available online.

14 *Franchise Times.* (April 24, 2023) Dealmakers Week webinar. "Strategic Buyers and Their Appetite for Emerging Brands." https://www.franchisetimes.com/franchise_mergers_and_acquisitions /dealmakers_week/agenda/

15 Interview with author, March 31, 2023.

16 Interview with author, April 12, 2023.

Index

Figures and tables indicated by page numbers in italics

Aaron's, 43
ABRA Auto Body & Glass, 224, 225
Ace Hardware, 49
ACI Capital Corp., 226
acquisitions. *See* mergers and acquisitions;
    platforms; Profit Ladder (secondary
    buyouts)
AdvantaClean, 225
Advantica Restaurant Group, 84
Advocate Aurora Enterprises, 49
agreements (contracts), franchise, 101–2, 247,
    254, 262, 263, 338
Aire Serv, 216
Allegro Funds, 98n
Allied Domecq (formerly Allied-Lyons), 50, 108
Altares, 196
AmBath, 87
America Huts, 84
American Home Shield, 89
American Investment Council, 324
American Lube Fast, 245
American Marketing Association, 239
American Research and Development, 76
American Securities Capital Partners, 84, 97
AmeriKing, 88
Amici Partners Group, 241
analytics and data, 122–24, 263, 304, 319–20.
    See also information, access to
Anytime Fitness, 257
Apax Partners, 19, 175
Apollo Global Management, 87, 225, 242, 243,
    252, 269
Applebee's, 252
Arbour Lane Capital Management, 70
Arby's, 69, 98, 111, 113, 252, 257
Archadeck Outdoor Living, 245
Arcos Dorados, 91
area developers, 273
Ares Management, 242
Argonne Capital Group, 88, 115
Argosy Private Equity, 84, 87
Aronson, Neal, 67, 81, 86, 110, 111. *See also*
    Roark Capital Group

Arthur Murray Dance Studios, 74
Auntie Anne's, 68, 111
Aussie Pet Mobile, 165
Australia, 96n
Authority Brands, 19, 42, 175, 257
AutoLube Car Care Center, 245
Avis, 75
A&W, 74

back-office infrastructure, 136–37, 146, 207
Bain Capital: Bloomin' Brands and, 92; Burger
    King and, 41, 84–85, 90; Domino's Pizza
    and, 17, 84; Dunkin' Brands and, 50, 85, 88,
    108, 166, 168; on growth equity, 56; Profit
    Ladder and, 194
Bain & Company: Global Private Equity
    Report, 327
Baja Fresh, 84
Bajwa, Nadeem, 27–28
Baker's Square, 88
Banc Boston Capital, 88
banked process, 38
bankruptcies, franchise, 102, 239
banks, relationships with, 95, 158
Baskin-Robbins, 74, 108
Bath Tune-Up, 47, 163
Bessemer Trust, 75
Best Life Brands, 140, 148
The Big Short (movie), 301
BIP Opportunities Fund, 199, 203
Black, Leon, 225
Blackstone Group, 91–92, 251
Blaze Pizza, 48
blind pools, 40
Bloom, Jake, 205
Bloomin' Brands, 43, 92
board of directors, 40, 63, 140–41, 166, 312.
    See also management teams
Boathouse Capital, 222
Bojangles, 257
Bonefish Grill, 92
Boston College Center for Retirement
    Research, 79

Boston Consulting Group, 136
BP, 98
Brazos Private Equity Partners, 88, 228
Brightwood Capital Advisors, 97
British Columbia Investment Management
  Corporation, 42, 175
Brix Holdings, 241
Brockway Moran & Partners, 88
Brown, Paul, 69
Bruegger's Bagels, 240, 241
Budget Blinds, 224, 225
Buffalo Wild Wings, 55–56, 84, 99, 111, 222
Bumble Roofing, 222, 245
Burgerim, 282–83, 283n
Burger King, 41, 43, 75, 84–85, 85n, 88, 90, 91,
  98, 257
Butterfly Equity, 115
Buzz Franchise Brands, 219

Cajun Global, 252
Caliber Collison, 225
California, 79
CalPERS (California Public Employees'
  Retirement System), 42, 43
Camp Bow Wow, 49
Candover, 76
Canopy Lawn Care, 245
Captain D's Seafood, 240, 241
Caring Brands International, 194
Carl's Jr., 113. See also CKE Restaurants
Carlyle Group, 50, 85, 108
Carnegie Steel, 75
Carrabba's Italian Grill, 92
carried interest, 155
Carrols Restaurant Group, 43
Carvel, 67–69, 74, 78, 81, 86, 88, 111, 113
Castle Harlan, 225
Catterton Partners, 84, 92
CenterOak Partners, 115, 206–7, 208, 210
Centre Partners, 240
Century 21 Real Estate, 78
CEPRES Market Intelligence, 327
Certified Franchise Executive (CFE) program,
  109–10
CFB Group, 104
Chanticleer Holdings, 224
Charlesbank Partners, 88
Charnaux, Christian, 112
Chase, Charlie, 107
Checkers/Rally's, 70
Cheddar's, 88
Choice Hotels, 43
Church's Chicken, 252, 256, 257
Cici's Pizza, 51, 88
Cinnabon, 68, 111
Cinven, 76
CKE Restaurants, 113, 251, 257, 269–70

Claire's, 43
Clayton, Dubilier & Rice, 76, 89
Clearlight Partners, 97
club deals, 40–41
Club Pilates, 28–29
co-branding, 61
compensation: introduction, 153; financial
  incentives and decision-making,
  153–56; owner's benefit, 57; private equity
  advantages, 157–59, 236. See also finances;
  profitability
complacency, 60
complexity, 54
Concrete Craft, 225
Conserva Irrigation, 245
continuation fund, 40, 329
contracts (agreements), franchise, 101–2, 247,
  254, 262, 263, 338
Core Value Partners, 88
corporate-only business models, 149–50
Cortez Masto, Catherine, 71
Crouch, Nick, 202–3
culture, 47, 63, 77, 320–21, 334–35
Curves, 71, 227
customer service, 31, 128, 140, 151

Dairy Queen, 74, 98
Darden Restaurants, 43, 241
data and analytics, 122–24, 263, 304, 319–20.
  See also information, access to
Dave's Hot Chicken, 48
Davis, John, 205
DB Capital Partners, 226
debt. See leverage and overleverage; whole
  business securitization
DeHart, Taylor, 336
Deibel, Walker, 94
Denny's, 78
Deutsche Beteiligungsgesellschaft mbH, 76
developments: commitments push, 313;
  improving development function, 127, 131
Diageo, 41, 85n
Dillas Quesadillas, 51
Dine Brands (formerly DineEquity), 43, 252,
  301
disclosure risk, 70–71
distressed investing, 54. See also turnaround
  investing
D'Lites, 172
Domino's Pizza, 17, 27, 43, 80n, 84, 251, 257, 259
Drain Doctor, 218
Driven Brands, 43, 112, 195, 225, 251, 257, 259
due diligence, 122–24, 141, 229, 247, 264, 292,
  302–3, 311–12
Dull, Chris, 103, 126–27, 318, 320
Dunhill Personnel, 77

Dunkin' Brands (Dunkin' Donuts): 2011 IPO, 91; Bain Capital and, 50, 85, 88, 108, 166, 168; history of, 75, 78; leverage, 252, 256; multi-unit operators and, 98; securitization, 257, 258
Dunn Brothers Coffee, 51
Duraclean, 74
Dwyer Group. *See* Neighborly
Dwyer-Owens, Dina, 85–86
DYNE Hospitality Group, 202–3

Eagle Merchant Partners, 115
Easton, Eric, 284
EBITDA (earnings before interest, tax, depreciation, and amortization), 34, 283–85
Edison, Thomas, 265
Edison Partners, 41
Eldridge, 102
El Pollo Loco, 84, 157
Elysium Management, 225
emerging brands: introduction, 143; benefits from private equity, 144–46; building to flip, 20, 278–79, 281–83, 330; common challenges that private equity accepts, 147–50; common challenges that private equity does not accept, 150–52; debt and, 238; MPK Equity Partners case study, 145–46; preparing for launch, 176–78; Riverside Company and, 146–47; 10 Point Capital case study, 144–45
employee relations, 31–32
Employee Retirement Income Security Act (1974), 79
Empower Brands (formerly Premium Franchise Brands, LYNX Franchising), 43, 222, 224, 245
Encanto Restaurants, 43
entrepreneurship, 32–33, 35–36, 75
European Wax Center, 227–28, 257, 259
EWC Growth Partners, 227–28
Exaltare Capital Partners, 97–98
Excel Car Wash, 245
Exeter Capital, 98, 115
exits, 38, 103, 178–79, 328–29. *See also* Profit Ladder (secondary buyouts)
experience, 138–39, 158

fads, 152
family offices (FOS), 44–47, 100, 148, 177–78, 191, 193, 225, 238
FASTSIGNS, 88, 93, 113, 132
FAT Brands, 242
Federal Trade Commission (FTC), 78
fee recapture, 154
finances: accounting and revenue tracking, 263; financial controls, 164, 165–66; financial engineering, 61, 62, 161, 192, 195;

fundraising, 155, 190–91; shifting expense responsibility, 273. *See also* compensation; leverage and overleverage; profitability; whole business securitization
financial buyers (traditional private equity firms), 40–42
Fisher, Lane, 298, 318
Five Guys, 251, 252, 257
Five Star Franchising, 148
Five Star Painting, 218
flexibility, 35, 46
Flick, Paul, 135, 137–38, 174
flip, building to, 20, 278–79, 281–83, 330
FLP, 245
Flynn, Greg, 101
Flynn Group, 19, 42, 98
Focus Brands, 68, 111, 112, 113, 195, 257
Ford, Henry (Ford Motor), 75
Forstmann Little & Company, 76
FotoMat, 78
founders, franchise/brand, 15–16, 20, 75, 317–22
FountainVest Partners, 104
Franchise Act (1979), 78
Franchise Business Review, 202, 222
franchise disclosure documents (FDDS), 41–42, 247, 341–42
franchisee-franchisor relationship: destroying trust, 285–87; importance of, 21; lack of attention to, 60; multi-unit operators and, 101–2, 286–87; parent profiteering, 274; shifting expense responsibility and, 273; toxic relationships, 151
franchisees: expectations if acquired, 311–15; independent franchisee-owner associations, 315–16, 335–37; maintaining a sale-ready stance, 316–17; recruitment, 150; single-unit vs. multi-unit operators, 331. *See also* multi-unit operators
Franchise Grade, 172, 282
Franchise Rule, 78
Franchise Times, 208, 275
franchising: bankruptcies, 102, 239; business creation success, 29–30; business-format vs. traditional, 13; customer service, 31, 128, 140, 151; employee relations, 31–32; entrepreneurship and, 32–33, 35–36, 75; founders, 15–16, 20, 75, 317–22; Generation 1.0 (early years, 1920–1960), 74–75; Generation 2.0 (pre-PE, 1960–1990), 77–80, 80–81, 171, 171–72, 173; Generation 3.0 (post-PE, 1991–2019), 83–93, 94, 114–16, 171, 172–73; Generation 4.0 (post-pandemic), 326–28, 333, 337; history of, 73, 170–73; international expansion, 80, 80n, 104–5, 133, 194; litigation and legal challenges, 66, 71, 78, 151, 157, 221,

273; owner demographics, 30; regulations and, 78–79, 85, 176, 325; ubiquity of, 30. *See also* franchisee-franchisor relationship; franchisees

franchising, and private equity: introduction, 15–17, 23–24, 291–92, 309–10, 323; 2007–2009 financial crisis and recovery, 90–92; alignment between, 17–18, 116–17, 335–39; attractiveness for private equity, 33–34, 83–87; benefits from private equity, 34–36, 160–61, 161–62, 179–80; as both positive and negative, 21–22; building to flip, 20, 278–79, 281–83, 330; changes sparked by private equity, 331–32; commonalities between, 34–36; culture and, 47, 63, 77, 320–21, 334–35; disruptions from private equity, 20–21, 108–10; early and dominant entrants, 17–18, 87–88; evolving market forces, 324–26; expectations for franchisees, 311–15; expectations for franchise founders, 317–22; failures and missteps, 233–34, 234–35, 265; finding partners with franchising experience, 300–303; franchisor-franchisee relationship and, 21; fundamental franchising truths, 332–33; gatekeeping and quality control functions, 172–76; Generation 3.0 (post-PE, 1991–2019), 83–93, 94, 114–16, 171, 172–73; Generation 4.0 (post-pandemic), 326–28, 333, 337; vs. going public, 19, 229, 330; growing awareness of private equity, 106–8; infrastructure and, 164–65; investment approaches, 54–55; investments in brand's future, 167–68; making franchises stronger and better, 163–68; near-term considerations, 328–30; networking and, 177, 264, 292, 297–98, 298–300, 301; private equity growth, 114–16; short-timers' syndrome, 265, 266–71; "small and unproven" vs. "big growth potential," 56–58; sold-not-open funnels, 123, 149, 151–52, 185, 278, 279–81, 283, 330; stability, 166; taking franchises further, faster, 162–63; understanding what matters most for you, 294–97; understanding your why, 292–94; using time wisely, 303–5, 306–7; value-based investing model, 60–64, 309. *See also* compensation; emerging brands; finances; growth investors; leverage and overleverage; platforms; playbooks; Profit Ladder; turnarounds; whole business securitization

FRAN data: on emerging brands, 176, 282; *Multi-Unit Franchisee Buyer's Guide* (2022), 95–96, 278; *New Concept Report* (Q1 2022), 176; secondary buyouts and, 223–24; on total vs. active brands, 173, 185; on Tropical Smoothie Cafe, 202

Frankel, Matthew, 59, 121, 130–31, 168, 238–39, 271

Franklin, Benjamin, 74

Frantech, 218

Freddy's Frozen Custard & Steakburgers, 125–26, 126–28, 318

Freeman Spogli & Co., 93, 157

Friendly's, 239–40, 240–42

Frith, Scott, 108, 132, 138–39, 170, 291, 293, 301, 336

FRST eam, 222, 245

Full Speed Automotive, 19, 149, 245

fundless sponsors (independent sponsors), 48–49, 177–78, 191, 238

fundraising, 155, 190–91

fund-to-fund transfers, 191

Fuzzy's Taco Shop, 300–301

Gala, Anand, 51

Gala Capital Partners, 51, 111

Garbanzo Mediterranean Grill, 99

Gardner, Ron, 287

Garnett Station Partners, 70, 115

Gemini Investors, 55–56, 84, 88, 93, 99, 166, 221–22

gender, 30

General Atlantic, 228

general partners (GPs), 40, 157–58, 236

GF Data, 45–46, 204, 206

Gladwell, Malcolm, 83

Glass Doctor, 216

Global Franchise Group, 131

GNC Holdings, 91

Goddard School, 62–63

Golden Gate Capital, 115

Goldman Sachs Private Capital, 41, 84–85, 90

Goldner Hawn Johnson & Morrison Inc., 88

Golds Gym, 88

Golub Capital, 206

Goodman, James J., 55–56, 99, 149, 314

good PE lineage, 196, 266

goodwill, 206

GP-led secondary deals, 40, 329

Grease Monkey, 245

Greentree Capital, 221

Grounds Guys, 216

growth investors (growth focus): introduction, 55–59, 309; bright side of, 168–70; building to flip, 20, 278–79, 281–83, 330; dark side of, 277–85; EBITDA bastardization, 283–85; Levine Leichtman's approach, 130–33; near-term pressure on, 329; playbook for, 124–30; selling focus, 278–79; sold-not-open arbitrage, 279–81

Guggenheim Investments, 70, 242, 243

Guggenheim Securities, 254, 256

Halifax Group, 104
Haller, Matt, 109–10, 169, 316
Hand & Stone Massage and Facial Spa, 43
Handyman Matters, 49
Happinest Brands, 131, 139
Hardee's, 113, 172. *See also* CKE Restaurants
Harper, Martha Matilda (Harper Method hair
     salons), 27, 74
Harvest Partners, 43, 143, 193, 216–17, 218
Hashim, Aziz, 36, 233, 278, 293, 300–301,
     312, 317
health inspections, 167
Heidrick and Struggles, 154
Hellman & Friedman, 225
Herbert Automotive, 245
H.I.G. Capital, 224, 227
High Bluff Capital Partners, 252
Hilton Worldwide (Hilton Hotels), 43, 91–92
Hirsch, Jeremy, 151, 179, 270, 281, 302
HOA Brands, 257
hold periods, 45, 112, 159, 198, 267, 284
Holiday Inn, 75, 77, 80n, 225
Holland, Jeremy, 146–47, 151–52, 179, 192–93,
     296–97, 319
Home Franchise Concepts (HFC), 46, 47, 137,
     163, 164–65, 225, 311
Homevestors, 130–31, 132
Hooters, 224, 257
Howard Johnson, 74
H&R Block, 75, 77
Huddle House, 225
Hyatt Hotels, 91
hybrid investors, 50–52, 141, 148, 177–78, 191,
     193, 238

Incline Equity Partners, 43, 115, 222
independent franchisee-owner associations,
     315–16, 335–37
independent sponsors (fundless sponsors),
     48–49, 177–78, 191, 238
India, 96n
Industrial and Commercial Finance
     Corporation, 76
information, access to, 158–59. *See also* data and
     analytics
infrastructure, better, 164–65
Ingelside Auto & Tire, 245
Inspire Brands, 19, 50, 51, 111–12, 113, 195, 201,
     225, 258
institutional investors, 42. *See also* pension
     fund investments
Intelligent Office, 222, 224, 245
interest rates, 198, 248, 249, 258, 327
Interim Healthcare, 132
international expansion, 80, 80n, 104–5, 133,
     194

International Franchise Association (IFA), 29,
     30, 107, 109, 110–11, 208
International House of Pancakes (IHOP), 75,
     77, 88, 98, 252, 257
Investcorp, 81
invisible hand, 176

Jack in the Box, 252, 257, 259
Jamba, 68, 111
JAN-PRO, 220–22, 245
Jenny Craig, 224, 225, 226–27, 245
Jersey Mike's, 251, 257
J.H. Whitney & Company, 76, 221
Jiffy Lube, 98
Jimmy John's, 113, 224, 225, 252, 257
JLM Financial Partners, 97
JM Family Enterprises, 46, 164–65, 225
Johnson, Glen, 203
Jollibee, 80
junk bonds, 80, 85, 247

Kaiser, Kevin: *The Blue Line Imperative* (with
     Young), 267
Karam, J. David, 35, 243–44, 272–73
Kentucky Fried Chicken (KFC), 43, 75, 78, 80n,
     81, 98
Kitchen Tune-Up, 47, 163
KKR, 16, 19, 76, 194, 217, 219
Koala Insulation and Wallaby Windows, 222, 245
Kohl, Stewart, 212
Kolhberg, Jerome, Jr., 76
Kraft Heinz, 43
Kravis, Henry, 73, 76
KSL Capital Partners, 115
Kumon, 80
Kwik Kar, 245

labor unions, 221
Lapointe, Jacques, 221
Lawn Doctor, 131–32, 139, 194
Lee, Thomas H., 76. *See also* Thomas H. Lee
     Partners
legal challenges. *See* litigation
Leonard Green & Partners, 225
Levant Capital, 104
leverage and overleverage: introduction, 237–38;
     accumulation considerations, 246–47;
     bankruptcies and, 102, 239; debt interest,
     155; different approaches to, 238; due dili-
     gence, 247, 264; family offices and, 45–46;
     Friendly's and Sun Capital Partners case
     study, 240–42; Gala Capital Partners on,
     51; hybrid investors and, 50; interest rates
     and, 198, 248, 249, 258, 327; leveraged
     buyouts, 17, 19, 79, 327; Levine Leichtman
     Capital Partners on, 238–39; multiple
     arbitrage and, 215; multi-unit operators and,

102; new leveraged loans and debt multiples (2001–2022), 249, 249; positive evolution of, 20, 247–48; Profit Ladder and, 190; Sbarro and MidOcean Partners case study, 242–44, 245–46; successful turnarounds, 244–45; value-based investing and, 60. *See also* whole business securitization

Levine Leichtman Capital Partners (LLCP): background, 87; Cici's Pizza and, 88; FASTSIGNS and, 93; franchise acceleration playbook, 130–33, 143; on growth investing, 59; on leverage, 238–39; multi-unit operators and, 99; Nothing Bundt Cakes and, 163, 196–97; Profit Ladder and, 193, 194, 196–97; Quiznos and, 86; Senior Helpers and, 196; Tropical Smoothie Cafe and, 199, 200–201; Wetzel's Pretzels and, 205–6, 210

Liberty Tax, 41
Liebsohn, Steve, 208
LightBay Capital, 93, 115
limited partners (LPS), 40, 42
litigation, 66, 71, 78, 151, 157, 221, 273
Los Angeles City Employees' Retirement System (LACERS), 43
Loughlin, Phil, 124, 293
low-differentiation models, 152
LYNX Franchising. *See* Empower Brands

Maid Right, 222
Maid-Rite, 74
Main Post Partners, 115
Maloney, Drew, 248, 323
management teams, 31–32, 139, 151, 177–78, 312, 317–19. *See also* board of directors
Marie Calendar's, 225
marketing, 127–28, 131, 137–38, 268, 273
Marriott Hotels, 43, 77
Martinizing, 75
Massage Envy, 113, 275–76
Maze, Jonathan, 66, 234
McAlister's, 68, 111
McCaslin, Kim, 336–37
McDonald's, 43, 66–67, 69, 75, 78, 80, 80n, 91, 257, 259
McTigue, Caitlin, 28–29
Mercato Partners, 51
mergers and acquisitions (M&AS): diverse approaches to, 38; history of, 75–76, 81, 204; platforms and, 131–32, 140, 218–19; tuck-in acquisitions, 88, 135, 296. *See also* platforms; Profit Ladder (secondary buyouts)
Merrill Lynch Private Equity, 102
Merry Maids, 89
metrics. *See* data and analytics
MIDAS, 75

MidOcean Partners, 19, 115, 149, 222, 226, 240, 242–44, 245–46
Midwest Mezzanine Funds, 221
Miller, Keith, 274, 316
Minit Man Oil Change, 245
Minnie Pearl's Chicken, 172
MKH Capital Partners, 228
Mobil 1 Lube Express, 245
Moe's, 68, 111
MOIC (multiple of invested capital), 41
Molly Maid, 218
Money Mailer, 88
Montana Capital Partners, 44
Mooyah Burgers, 51
Morgan, J. P., 75
Morrissey, Heidi, 47, 163
Mosquito Joe, 218, 219
Mountain Mikes Pizza, 131
MPK Equity Partners, 115, 145–46
Mr. Appliance, 216
Mr. Electric, 216
Mr. Handyman International, 218
Mr. Rooter, 216, 217
MTY Food Group, 208
multiple arbitrage, 212–13, 215, 218–19, 220. *See also* platforms
multi-unit operators (MUOs): introduction, 94; benefits of, 95; diversity among, 98–99; family offices and, 100; focus on selling franchises and, 278–79; growth of, 95–96, 331; hybrid investors and, 50; in international markets, 96n, 104–5; power and relationship dynamics with, 101–2, 286–87; private equity and, 19, 86, 95, 97–100, 103–4; vs. single-unit operators, 331; value-based investing and, 60–61; voting with their feet, 113–14

Naf Naf Grill, 112
Nassetta, Christopher, 91–92
Nathan's Famous, 43
Neighborly (formerly Dwyer Group): about, 16, 19, 89, 216–17; building platform value, 218–19; keeping private, 85–86; pension fund investments in, 43; Riverside Company and, 88, 146, 192; securitization and, 257
Nestlé, 226–27, 245
networking, 177, 264, 292, 297–98, 298–300, 301
New Zealand, 96n
Nord Bay Capital, 224
North Castle Partners, 71, 227
Nothing Bundt Cakes, 112, 131, 163, 194, 196–97, 201, 257, 321
NPC International, 102

Oak Hill Capital Partners IV, 70
Olympus, 102
OMERS Private Equity, 225
Ontario Teachers' Pension Plan, 42
operations: immature infrastructure, 148, 150; platform advantages, 136–39; playbook for growth and operations, 124–30. *See also* unit-level operations
Orange Julius, 77
Orangetheory, 112–13
Ormsby, Rick, 46, 99–100
Outback Steakhouse, 92
Outdoor Lighting Perspectives, 245
Outdoor Living Brands, 245
overleverage. *See* leverage and overleverage
owner's benefit, 57. *See also* compensation
Oxford Economics, 30

Palladium Equity Partners, 225
Papa Johns, 27–28, 43, 104, 257, 259
Papa Murphy's, 88
Pearle Vision, 77
Peltz, Nelson, 243
pension fund investments, 42, 43, 79
people of color, 30
PepsiCo, 81, 89
Perkins, 224, 225
Pernod Ricard, 50, 108
Phelps, Bill, 205, 206
Pilla, Matt, 257
Pitchbook, 90, 205, 326, 329
Pizza Hut, 43, 77, 78, 80n, 81, 84, 90, 98, 98n, 102
PJP Investments Group, 104
PJU Holdings/PJ United, 104
Planet Fitness, 43, 97–98, 252, 257, 259
platforms: introduction, 135; acquisitions and, 131–32, 140, 218–19; benefits of, 213, 331–32; building value through, 88–90, 135–36, 212–13, 215, 220; definition, 16; due diligence, 141; EBITDA multiples by deal size (2019–2022) and, 213, 214; hybrid investors and, 50; JAN-PRO case study, 220–22; near-term pruning, 330; Neighborly (Dwyer Group) case study, 216–17, 218–19; operational advantages, 136–39; Profit Ladder and, 191, 193; Roark Capital Group and, 111; steps for creating, 139–42
playbooks: introduction, 121–22; brand/franchise-agnostic strategies, 128–29; for due diligence, 122–24; franchise growth accelerators, 126–28; Freddy's Frozen Custard & Steakburgers case study, 125–26, 126–28; Levine Leichtman Capital Partners case study, 130–33; for operations and growth, 124–30; for platforms,

139–42; value creation plans, 133–34, 305–8. *See also* emerging brands
PNC Riverarch Capital, 175
Popeyes, 43
Potbelly, 91
Premier Garage, 99, 222
Premium Franchise Brands. *See* Empower Brands
Premium Service Brands, 50, 148, 222
pre-money companies, 56
Prequin, 114
Primrose Schools, 90
Princeton Equity Group (formerly Princeton Ventures), 115, 148, 228
private, going, 85–86
private equity (PE): introduction, 15, 37, 39, 53–54, 143; buying power, 20; compensation advantages, 157–59, 236; direct investments by institutional investors, 42; diversity among, 38–39; family offices, 44–47, 100, 148, 177–78, 191, 193, 225, 238; growth and number of firms, 19–20, 114–16; history of, 75–76, 79–80; hybrid investors, 50–52, 141, 148, 177–78, 191, 193, 238; independent sponsors (fundless sponsors), 48–49, 177–78, 191, 238; investment approaches, 18, 54–55; pension fund investments, 42, 43, 79; risk aversion, 56; strategic buyers and, 49–50; traditional private equity firms (financial buyers), 40–42; wealthy individuals, 48, 75, 191, 238. *See also* franchising, and private equity
professionalism, 165–66
profitability: improving unit-level, 126–27, 131, 168–70; not protecting unit-level, 22, 60, 271–77. *See also* compensation; finances
Profit Ladder (secondary buyout (SBO)): introduction, 92–93, 183–84, 184–85, *186–87*, 188–90; academic research on, 229–30; common missteps, 229–30; establishment and impacts, 161, 178–79, 224–26, 229, 332; good PE lineage and, 196, 266; JAN-PRO case study, 220–22; Jenny Craig case study, 226–27; lack of awareness of, 223–24; lower rungs, 191–93; middle rungs, 193–94; planning your wealth creation strategy, 196–98; private equity's perspective, 203–4, 209; Roark Capital Group and, 111; seller's perspective, 210; top rungs, 194–95; trading factors, 226; trading up, down, and across, 190–91, 195–96, 197; Tropical Smoothie Cafe case study, 198–202, *200*, 202–3; Wetzel's Pretzels case study, 205–9, 210
proprietary deals, 38, 46, 328
Protect Painters, 218
public, going, 19, 229, 330

Public Company Accounting Reform and Investor Protection Act (Sarbanes-Oxley Act, 2002), 85
Puzder, Andrew, 269

Qdoba, 252
QSR, 113
Quilvest Capital Partners, 76
Quiznos, 86, 257

race, 30
Rainbow International, 216
Ravikant, Naval, 237
RBI, 259
RBJK Marketing, 222
real estate, 54, 127
Real Property Management, 218–19
rebates, vendor, 274
Re-Bath, 87, 222
recruitment, franchisee, 150
regulations, 78–79, 85, 176, 325
RE/MAX, 91
resales and transfers, 132, 260, 262. See also Profit Ladder (secondary buyout)
Restaurant Brands International, 257
risk aversion, 56
Riveria Investment Group, 97
Riverside Company: about, 87, 192–93; add-ons and, 212; Best Life Brands and, 140, 148; emerging brands and, 143, 146–47, 191; Neighborly (Dwyer Group) and, 85–86, 88, 192, 216, 217; Threshold Brands and, 50, 148
Roark Capital Group: about, 81, 86, 87, 110–13, 115, 194, 195; acquisitions success, 88, 250; Arby's and, 69; Carvel and, 67–69, 88; CKE Restaurants and, 251, 269–70; Driven Brands and, 225, 251; FASTSIGNS and, 88, 93; Inspire Brands and, 19, 50, 51; Jimmy John's and, 225, 252; leverage of brands owned by, 251, 252; Massage Envy and, 275–76; Nothing Bundt Cakes and, 201, 321; pension fund investments and, 43; Primrose Schools and, 90; ServiceMaster and, 89, 215, 249, 251; Subway and, 19; Wingstop and, 93
Roberts, George, 76
Rosenberg, Bob, 107–8
Ross, Peter, 49, 196, 308
Roto-Rooter, 77
royalties, 127, 147, 262, 273
Rusty Taco, 51, 111–12

sale-ready stance, maintaining, 159, 316–17
Sarbanes-Oxley Act (Public Company Accounting Reform and Investor Protection Act, 2002), 85

Savory Restaurant Fund, 51–52, 191
Sbarro, 239–40, 242–44
scalability, 41, 150
Schlotzsky's, 68, 111
secondary buyout. See Profit Ladder
securitization. See whole business securitization
Seid, Michael, 272, 279
Self Esteem Brands, 195, 257
Senior Helpers, 49, 131, 132, 196
Sentinel Capital Partners, 70, 90, 225, 275
Service Brands International, 218
ServiceMaster Brands, 77, 88–89, 195, 215, 249–50, 251, 257
Servpro, 224, 251
7-Eleven/Southland, 77, 78
Sharma, Robin, 323
Sheraton, 77
short-timers' syndrome, 265, 266–71
Siegel, Steve, 107
Simmons, Omar, 97–98
Singer, Albert, 74
Smith, Adam, 176
Smokey Bones, 241
sold-not-open funnels, 123, 149, 151–52, 185, 278, 279–81, 283, 330
Sonic, 81, 113, 251, 257
special purpose vehicles, 254
SpeeDee, 245
S&P Global Ratings, 251–52, 258
Spherion Staffing, 75
sponsor-to-sponsor. See Profit Ladder (secondary buyout)
stability, 166
standardization, 136
Starboard Capital Partners, 221
Stevens, Caroline, 35, 45, 145–46, 169
St. Geme, Joe, 125–26
strategic buyers, 49–50, 81, 193, 238
Subway, 19
Sun Capital Partners, 239, 240–42
Superior Fence and Rail, 245
Super Lube Plus, 245
supply chains, 132, 136–37
Susquehanna Private Capital, 50, 148, 222
Sycamore Partners, 62–63
Sylvan Learning Systems, 87
system standards, 313–14

TA Associates, 76
Taco Bell, 43, 78, 81, 98, 252, 257
Tailored Living, 225
Tastee Freeze, 77
Taymax, 97
Team Car Care, 98
tech bubble (2000–2002), 85
technology, 133, 169–70
10 Minute Oil Change, 245

10 Point Capital, 115, 143, 144–45, 191, 199
Terminix Termite and Pest Control, 75, 89
Texas Chicken, 252
Texas Pacific Group, 41, 84–85, 90
TGI Fridays, 257
Thiessen, Jonathan, 46, 137, 164–65, 173–74, 311
Thomas H. Lee Partners, 50, 76, 85, 108
Thompson Street Capital Partners, 115, 125–26, 318
3G Capital, 90
Threshold Brands, 50, 148
Tim Hortons, 80
Towerbrook Financial Partners, 97
transfers and resales, 132, 260, 262. *See also* Profit Ladder (secondary buyout)
TravelCenters of America, 98
Trian Partners, 243
TriArtisan Capital Advisors, 224
Trilantic North America, 97, 115, 225
Trimaran Partners, 157
Tripp, Dena, 163, 196–97, 321
Tropical Smoothie Cafe (TSC), 131, 194, 198–202, *200*, 202–3
TruGreen, 89
trust, 285–87
TSG Consumer Partners, 97
tuck-in acquisitions, 88, 135, 296. *See also* mergers and acquisitions; platforms
turnarounds: about, 54–55, 64–67, 71, 309–10; Arby's case study, 69; Carvel case study, 67–69; Checkers/Rally's case study, 70; disclosure risk, 70–71; failed turnaround projects, 70; key elements for success, 244–45; Roark Capital Group and, 111; Sbarro case study, 242–44; unit vs. whole-brand, 67
Twain, Mark, 309
Twitter, 91
2 and 20 fee approach, 154–55
Two Men and a Truck, 215, 249–50
TZP Group, 115, 216

Uncle Ed's Oil Shoppe, 245
undercapitalized brands, 147–48, 183, 281
underperformers, 132, 198, 314
unions, labor, 221
unit-level operations: improving refresh cadence, 168; improving unit-level profitability, 126–27, 131, 168–70; not protecting unit-level profitability, 22, 60, 271–77; optimization needed, 148; value proposition of, 97. *See also* operations
US Chamber of Commerce, 325
US Franchise Systems, 81, 86

value-based investing, 60–64, 309
value creation plans, 133–34, 305–8
VCA, 49
vendors, 274
venture capitalism, 56
veterans, 30
Vetted Biz, 173, 341
VICORP Restaurants, 88
Village Inn, 88

Wallaby Windows, 222, 245
Warburg Pincus, 76
wealthy individuals, 48, 75, 191, 238
Webster Capital Management, 221–22
Wellspring Capital Management, 70
Wendy's, 43, 69, 77, 78, 80n, 98n, 243, 251, 252, 257, 259
Weston Presidio, 225
Wetzel's Pretzels, 48, 205–9, 210
whole business securitization (WBS): adoption by large brands, 253, 256–58, 257; appeal of, 253, 256; vs. asset-backed securities, 253; bankruptcy-remote special purpose vehicles and, 254; definition, 253; franchisee implications, 260, 262; franchisor implications, 263; key takeaways, 256–58, 260; leverage levels for select brands, 251–52, 259; market comfort with, 258; process for, 254, 255; restaurant vs. non-restaurant franchises, 258, 260, 261; ServiceMaster and Two Men and a Truck case study, 249–50. *See also* leverage and overleverage
Wilson, Gary, 205
Wilson, Kevin, 219
Window Genie, 218
Wind River Holdings, 62
Wingstop, 43, 56, 88, 93, 99, 112, 166, 222, 251, 257, 259
Wishengrad, Cory, 256, 263
women, 30
Wynnchurch Capital, 98

Young, S. David: *The Blue Line Imperative* (with Kaiser), 267
Youth Enrichment Brands, 195
YUM Brands, 43, 89, 201, 252, 257, 259

Zaxby's, 257